PEANUTS
and
CRACKERJACK

PEANUTS
and
CRACKERJACK

A TREASURY OF BASEBALL LEGENDS AND LORE

DAVID CATANEO

A Harvest Book

Harcourt Brace & Company

San Diego   New York   London

To Mom, Dad, Kathryn, and Emily

Requests for permission to make copies of any part of the work should be mailed to: Permissions Department, Harcourt Brace & Company, 6277 Sea Harbor Drive, Orlando, Florida 32887-6777.

This Harvest edition is published by arrangement with Rutledge Hill Press, 211 Seventh Avenue North, Nashville, TN 37219-1823.

Library of Congress Cataloging-in-Publication Data
Cataneo, David.
Peanuts and crackerjack: a treasury of baseball legends and lore / David Cataneo.
p.   cm.
Includes bibliographical references (p.   ) and index.
ISBN 1-55853-100-9   ISBN 0-15-671568-6 (pbk.)
1. Baseball — Anecdotes. 2. Baseball — History. 3. Baseball — United States — History. I. Title.
GV873.C33   1991   91-9578
796.357′0207 — dc20

Design by Harriette Bateman
Typography by Bailey Typography, Inc., Nashville, TN

Printed in the United States of America

First Harvest edition 1994   A B C D E

CONTENTS

PREFACE

This book began one afternoon in late December 1987. I was digging through the ancient files in the Boston *Herald* library to unearth background information for a dreary baseball contract story when my fingers came across an aged and battered envelope marked, "Mrs. Babe Ruth, first wife." Soon I was snug at my desk, enraptured by the pile of crumbly newsprint, reading all about how Helen Ruth had died mysteriously in a house fire while she was married to the Babe but was keeping residence with a prominent Back Bay dentist.

Later that afternoon, as *Herald* sports editor Bob Sales was looking for the contract story, he mentioned that he was hoping for some new ideas. In particular, he wondered how to keep baseball prominent in the sports section through the long winter when hardball-hungry New Englanders mark the cold days till spring training. I mentioned the baseball tale I had just read about the first Mrs. Ruth.

"Too bad we can't find a way to put stuff like that in the paper," I said.

"Do it," Sales responded.

So an idea was hatched to start a regular column of baseball lore, observations, oddities, and anecdotes. The feature would be named "Hot Stove" in the winter and "Peanuts and Crackerjack" in the summer.

Three years in the business of baseball archaeology has reinforced the notion that lore is as much a part of baseball as spitting at the end of a sentence. The game happily stays in close touch with its past: in the summer of 1990 the Chicago White Sox played a game in which they wore replicas of their 1917 uniforms, and it was a huge success.

Baseball men easily turn back the clock. Several hours before the first pitch of a night game, the mid-afternoon dugout has the rhythm and feel of the front porch of a retirement home on a soft spring night. Stories are told, and legends are passed along to another generation of players and writers.

Baseball fans with the deepest appreciation for the game are generally schooled in its heritage. They tend to be quaint people likely to attend games in the 1990s while wearing T-shirts that say "Property of Brooklyn Dodgers." Patrons of no other sport complain about a stadium because it's too modern.

The lore on these pages was gathered by sifting through and sneezing the dust from thousands of old newspaper clippings and magazine articles, by interviewing old-timers over the telephone or when they happened to hobble into the ballpark, and by hanging around the baseball scene for four seasons on behalf of the *Herald.* A few months after the column began, a woman wrote and said that she loved the stories but, frankly, found many of them hard to believe. My response was that I sometimes found them hard to believe, too.

Truth is never a defense against lore, so I have checked all stories with a healthy skepticism to make sure that players, teams, and dates jibed. The rest is hearsay. What follows is not a definitive history of baseball. Rather, it is a collection of glimpses of the game, a chance to lounge around one hundred years worth of baseball dugouts and listen to the tales without risk of getting tobacco juice on one's shoes.

Any story about any player—Hall of Famer or bush leaguer, peanut or crackerjack—from any era was eligible to appear on these pages, but a preponderance of the tales are set before 1950. The years between the world wars were fertile for lore. The game was growing, with the attendant adolescent quirkiness, and baseball players didn't take themselves too seriously. Television had not yet swallowed up the scene, making baseball heroes a permanent presence in our homes and sapping much of the awe and mystery of the game.

Wallowing in lore tends to sentimentalize the past, but baseball stories are best when they deliver history as well as nostalgia. Given the enchanting nature of the game, a degree of dreaminess always sneaks in. Old timers like old baseball stories because they conjure names and faces from their youth. Baby boomers like old baseball stories because they conjure a simpler time when men played the game for fun and women wore frilly hats. A hard look at the archives reveals the old days were far from all good: crowds were relatively small, many players were spoiled and truculent, plenty of players were drunks, and until 1947 the major leagues operated with an unofficial but strict ban against blacks. The vulgarities of the old days, however, leave the history no less fascinating.

Covering baseball has been fun, and some of the best fun came while compiling the stories on these pages. Many deserve my gratitude. To Boston *Herald* publisher Pat Purcell and sports editor Bob Sales, my foremost appreciation. Much of the material that follows originally appeared in one form or the other in the *Herald,* and the newspaper was generous to grant full permission to author this book.

Thanks to the men and women of the *Herald* sports copy desk, whose diligent efforts over the years helped me avoid embarrassment in print. Mark Torpey, Jim Kiley, Mike Gallant, Hank Hryniewicz, Steve Solomon, Jim Matte, Mike Silverman, Steve Grabowski, George Martins, Cheryl Charles, John Vitti, Mark Cofman, Scot Petersen, and Rich McSweeney were first-rate editors. They were also magnificent good sports whenever eighty-year-old anecdotes would land on their desks ten minutes before deadline. Special thanks to Jeff Northrup, whose love and knowledge of the pastime provided valuable help, as well as useful insight into the mind of a hopeless Red Sox fan.

Thanks to *Herald* head librarian John Cronin and his staff, Tom Clark, Doug Olsen, Joe Wassong, and Roselle Kurkjian, who always made forays into the archives easier. Similar thanks to staff members of the University of New Hampshire's Dimond Library, Boston University's Mugar Library, the Boston Public Library, the Rochester, New Hampshire, Public Library, and the Hall of Fame Library at Cooperstown, New York. Thanks also to whomever invented microfilm. To the Association of Professional Baseball Players of America, thanks for helping ferret out hard-to-locate old-timers.

Estimable *Herald* baseball beat writer Joe Giuliotti graciously guided a twenty-three-year-old kid through his first baseball road trip and has never failed to point me in the direction of a good story-teller; I am forever grateful. Each paragraph I write must be accompanied by thanks to my teachers at Boston University, especially George Sullivan and the late Tim Cohane, role models whose lessons are with me each time I sit down at the keyboard.

Thanks to the baseball men who took time over the years to tell their stories, especially retired *Herald* baseball writer Jack McCarthy, Red Sox manager Joe Morgan, who could fill an entire book by himself, assistant to the general manager Johnny Pesky, and general manager Lou Gorman. Thanks go to Red Sox public relations director Dick Bresciani and his able staff, especially Josh Spofford, Jim Samia, and Mary Jane Ryan. Life around Fenway Park was always easier when Frank MacKay, Jim Gately, and Arthur Morris were on the job. Thanks to Ron Pitkin for his patience and bright ideas, and to Vi Richter for bailing out a poor typist.

To Carmine and Hortense Cataneo, thanks for being the best parents in the world and for helping me appreciate the beauty of the written word and the batted ball. Thanks to big brother Skip for passing along his baseball spikes and big sister Mary Ellen for passing along her books. None of this would have been worth the effort if not for Kathryn Boucher Cataneo, first-rate proofreader, loving wife, and devoted mommy to little Emily.

—David Cataneo
Durham, New Hampshire
February 1, 1991

PEANUTS
and
CRACKERJACK

Babe Ruth

1

THE PASTIME

On April 18, 1981, the minor-league Rochester Red Wings and Pawtucket Red Sox tangled into the wee hours and were still tied after thirty-two innings. On June 23 the teams picked up where they had left off, and Pawtucket scored a run in the bottom of the thirty-third. Professional baseball's longest game was over.

The following summer, Pawtucket owner Ben Mondor and a ballpark worker trudged to a secret location on the McCoy Stadium grounds. After digging a deep hole, they buried a time capsule stocked with artifacts from the longest game. If alien colonists unearth the cylinder five centuries hence, they undoubtedly will examine the leather mitts, white horsehide balls, and ash clubs and twiddle their antennae in bemusement. Then one of them will roll the ball around in a slimy hand, grip the red seams, and smile. He will then throw it to a companion, another will try to hit it with the bat, and a third will lay down the bases. They will choose up sides and the rest will gather to watch. Perhaps afterward, they will retire to laboratories to re-invent the ballpark weenie.

As the esteemed hardball historian Donald Honig pointed out, baseball holds a basic, simple, primitive appeal. To throw a ball, catch it, hit it with a stick, and to watch others throw, catch, and hit, are instinctive. The wide appeal of the game around the world and the deep infatuation held for it in the United States should pose no mystery. The real riddle is why baseball hasn't replaced warfare as Earth's favorite sport.

Hardball always has had a unifying effect. No one can underestimate the impact on American society of Jackie Robinson, the Brooklyn Dodger who broke the big-league ban on blacks in 1947. A friend who wore Goldwater-for-President campaign buttons at age six and who unceasingly worships William F. Buckley thinks Fidel Castro can't be all bad because the Cuban despot was once an avid baseball player.

Many who try to mask a soft heart with a hard-boiled facade repress the romantic view of baseball, but this is cruel self-denial. Baseball is commonly called "the pastime," but most often the game feels and acts like an old friend. Any devoted fan has countless pieces of personal lore that show the game as salve for the soul. Just thinking about it can make a person feel better. "I will carry with me until the day I die the feel of the ball hitting the pocket in my mitt or hitting a ball with the fat part of a bat," author Robert Parker said in April 1987 as baseball weather began to descend upon his native New England. "I know I'll end up walking around the house, whacking my hand in my mitt. I guess I'm still a little sappy about it."

Sports writer Red Smith thought baseball was a part of childhood we don't have to leave behind, which might explain why it can be as familiar and as comforting as a crib blanket amid unsettling times. One of the many salvage workers who were dispatched to Pearl Harbor within weeks of the Japanese attack in 1941 brought along a ball and mitt, and each day at dusk he played catch outside his barracks. Nearly fifty years later, he could remember how the soft Hawaiian breeze reminded him of early spring nights at home and how throwing a baseball was great solace, with the American fleet smoldering in the harbor.

Attachment to baseball, like a true friendship, grows deeper as year follows year, season follows season, gently one after the other. Satchel Paige advised never to look back, but in baseball that is impossible. More than any other sport, baseball keeps in close touch with its past. An old-time name can make a man swoon because it evokes a memory of his youth; just say "Dalton Jones" to a forty-year-old Bostonian, and he'll grin like a ten-year-old. But baseball's reverence for its legend and lore is more than nostalgia. It is history, and it deepens appreciation and joy for the present, just as reading Barbara Tuchman heightens fascination with the modern world.

Baseball's past is never really past. In the summer of 1987, when Athletics first baseman Mark McGwire hit more home runs than any other rookie in the history of the game, he was unable to go a day without hearing the name of Wally Berger, who had set the mark in 1930. Babe Ruth had been dead thirteen years in 1961, but Roger Maris carried the Bambino on his back that summer on his way to sixty-one homers. Baseball lore tends to stick to a man forever. Poor Bill Buckner, the first baseman who made a colossal error in the 1986 World Series, knows the grounder that skipped through his wickets will be mentioned in the first paragraph of his obituary, even if he perfects cold fusion tomorrow. More than most grownups, baseball people believe in demons, ghosts, and haunted houses.

"When you put that uniform on, it's something special," slugger Jack Clark said shortly before he signed with the Red Sox in December 1990. "There's a

After the Cincinnati Reds left Crosley Field, city officials used the field to store automobiles impounded for nonpayment of fines.

certain power. A spiritual thing happens. You become part of something that you really can't explain or express. Look at Fenway Park. You couldn't tear down Fenway Park. The ghosts would come out that night and have the place built back up by the next morning."

By the spring training lockout of 1990, baseball people didn't worry anymore about squashing the public's affection for the pastime. Strikes, spoiled rich players, spiraling ticket prices, and watery ballpark beer taught them something. "That's the great thing about baseball," said general manager Lou Gorman during the lockout. "No matter how hard we try to mess it up, it's still a great game." No surprise. The pastime's appeal will last forever, even after the bronze plaques in

Cooperstown turn to dust. The lure of baseball is as instinctive and as natural as romance.

"I hope both sides can get together," former big-league outfielder Harry ("The Hat") Walker offered as owners and players stood miles apart amid the silent spring of 1990. "I still think it's a great game. I hope they don't act like a couple that's been married a long time, and all they want to do is hatchet each other, no matter what. They've got to get together. Because it's still beautiful when they do."

During a trip to California in 1974, East Boston native and former Cubs shortstop Lennie Merullo decided to visit old teammate Don Johnson in Laguna Beach.

"We played in Tulsa together my first year in ball," said Merullo in 1989, when he was age seventy-one and still scouting New England for potential big leaguers. "Then we were in the same infield together for a while in Chicago. We were pretty close. We hadn't seen each other in twenty-nine years."

After dinner and reminiscing, Merullo was saying goodbye when Johnson excused himself for a moment and returned with a baseball bat. "I want you to have it," he said. Merullo looked it over and saw the inscription: George Herman Ruth. Don's father, Yankee utility infielder Ernie Johnson, had gotten the genuine Babe bat in the 1920s.

"I couldn't get over it," said Merullo. "A forty-two-ounce, thirty-six-inch piece of hickory."

A couple of months later, Merullo spoke at a Rotary Club banquet in Medford, Massachusetts, and told the story of the Ruth bat. After the dinner an elderly gentleman approached Merullo, gave him a business card, and said he wanted to get in touch with him.

Months passed before Merullo received a phone call from a woman who asked if he remembered the elderly man at the Rotary banquet. Merullo said yes and asked how he was. The woman said he had died but had left something for Merullo.

At the man's home, Merullo was given a four-page letter, in which the elderly fellow told of going to Braves' and Red Sox' games as a boy, attending Boston College and Tufts, getting a law degree, and landing as one of his first assignments the Coca-Cola account. When the Tigers were in Boston in the summer of 1923, Coke magnate and Tigers outfielder Ty Cobb dropped by the house for dinner, bringing with him a baseball bat he had used that day at Fenway Park.

"The letter said, 'This bat has got to go with your Babe Ruth bat,'" said Merullo. "Just then, the woman walked in the room with the bat and handed it to me."

Several years later, Merullo spoke at the Massachusetts Envelope baseball banquet and told the story of the Ruth and Cobb bats. Next morning at six o'clock, the doorbell rang at the Merullo home in Reading. "I thought it was the paper boy," Lennie said.

He opened the door and found Bernard Grossman, the Massachusetts Envelope owner, holding a baseball bat. Grossman and his father were at Fenway Park on July 29, 1947, when Ted Williams lined out to first, threw his bat, picked it up, jammed it in the bat rack, was nearly conked when the bat recoiled, then flung the bat into the box seats into the senior Grossman's lap.

"He told me the story," said Merullo, "then stuck the bat in my belly and said, 'You can have it.'"

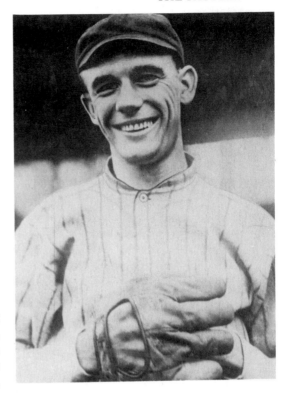

Rube Marquard

◆

On September 3, 1947, New York police conducted a routine sweep of the Bowery and hauled eighteen vagrants into night court. One by one, they appeared before the magistrate, Charles Murphy.

One of the older men—charged with disorderly conduct after he was found loitering and intoxicated—was asked to step forward and give his name.

"Richard Marquard," he answered.

Magistrate Murphy, who was an ardent baseball fan and a long-time Giants' lover, leaned forward. "Aren't you the famous Rube Marquard?" he asked, referring to the Giants' ace lefty of the pre-World War I era.

The man nodded.

"I understand you won nineteen straight games for the Giants in 1912."

The prisoner nodded again and said, "I think that record still stands." Murphy, appalled at his former hero's hard luck, asked if he had any money.

"Not a cent, Your Honor," he said.

Murphy reached into his pocket, produced a five-dollar bill, handed it to the man, and dismissed the charges.

Next day, Rube Marquard—fifty-nine-years-old, healthy, sober, happily married, and fully employed—picked up the newspaper in his Haddonfield, New Jersey, home and read that "Rube Marquard" had been arrested for vagrancy in the Bowery. He got on the phone to New York, sputtering about the impostor and how "a judge should be more careful."

Police investigated and learned the derelict had been using the name of Marquard and other notables in night courts from Albany to Manhattan. "I should have known better," said Murphy, issuing a warrant for the impostor's arrest.

That night in Hoboken, New Jersey, a man with an all-star hangover and only thirty cents in his pocket was hauled into night court. He was asked his name. "Richard Marquard," he replied.

The judge, on the lookout for the impostor, exposed the man as a fake, lambasted him for duping Judge Murphy, and asked him what had happened to the ill-gotten five dollars.

"Well, there were eighteen of us, Your Honor," the man said of the night-court crowd of the evening before. "And we had a little party."

"Well," said the judge, banging his gavel. "I can't give you five. But I can give you ten—ten days in the Hudson County jail."

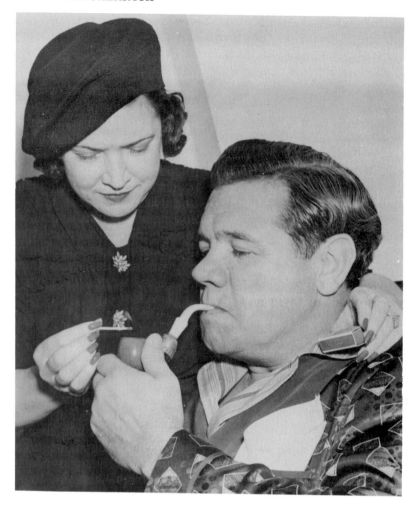

Babe Ruth and second wife, Claire

◆

When Hollywood was putting together *Pride of the Yankees*—Lou Gehrig's life story—Samuel Goldwyn telephoned Babe Ruth and asked the retired home-run king to play himself in the film. Ruth agreed and boarded a train for California.

Arriving in Los Angeles at dawn, Ruth expected to find the depot empty, except perhaps for a few porters and maintenance men. Instead, as he stepped off the train, he was greeted by a crowd that numbered in the thousands. Station agents said they hadn't seen anything like it since the heyday of Rudolf Valentino. Among the crowd was the boys' band of the House of Nazareth. As a former orphanage resident, Ruth was touched, and took the entire band to breakfast.

During his two-month stay in Hollywood, Ruth, who had been retired from baseball for six years, was similarly besieged. On the street, he was stopped every ten paces for an autograph, which he signed with a fountain pen he had specially designed for writing on baseballs. When he attended the Pacific Coast League's Hollywood Stars' baseball season opener, he was introduced to the loudest ovation of the day. He was a star in a town where Gable and Bogart could walk to the newsstand unnoticed. Ruth, veteran Tinseltowners said, was only the second man they could remember having to sign autographs for the movie stars themselves. The other was Wendell Willkie.

◆

When most folks watch scratchy, herky-jerky, black and white baseball highlight films, they gawk at the uniforms, the old-time ballparks, and the straw hats in the crowd. Batting guru Walter Hriniak studies the old-time swings.

"I see it as a teaching tool," said Hriniak in the summer of 1988, when he was the Red Sox' hitting instructor. "A laboratory."

Hriniak keeps a collection of baseball tapes at home and analyzes—in slow motion, freeze frame detail—the famous swings of hitters from Babe Ruth to Hank Aaron.

"Charlie Lau gave me a set years ago," said Hriniak. "It had a lot of the old home-run hitters. Ruth, Hank Greenberg, guys like that. Don Baylor got me a collection with the more modern guys, like Stargell and Clemente."

Of course, the Lau–Hriniak school of hitting advocates letting the top hand come off the bat in the later stages of the swing. Some think this is heresy, untraditional, and anti-American. Hriniak's rebuttal is on the tapes.

"Ernie Banks, Willie Mays, Roberto Clemente, and Willie Stargell had their hand come off the bat," said Hriniak. "Stan Musial did, too, but not every swing. Now all of a sudden, when you ask a guy to have his hand come off, they think you're trying to revolutionize the game. Guys have been taking their top hand off the bat in their follow-through for years. Now when you suggest it, people think you're a revolutionist."

Hriniak agrees the technique is not for everyone. Notable two-handed swingers included Ruth, Joe DiMaggio, Ted Williams, and Mickey Mantle.

"Ruth would cock his front leg and finish with his hands high," said Hriniak. "He wasn't just a great home-run hitter. He was a great hitter."

Anybody missing from his collection? "I don't have Ty Cobb," Hriniak said. "What amazes me about him, from the pictures I've seen, is that he held his hands far apart on the bat. Noticeably so."

Any unusual tapes? "I have Sadaharu Oh," said Hriniak. "His style was similar to Mel Ott's, in that he would lift up his front foot."

◆

When John Quinn managed a team in Columbus, Ohio, the local prison warden often invited him and his players to visit. The penitentiary baseball team was the warden's pride and joy, and input from a pastime professional such as Quinn was cherished. One of Quinn's players was also acquainted with one of the prisoners, who would introduce all of them to the various murderers, thieves, and safecrackers behind bars.

One day, Quinn and a number of his players were invited to watch a prison game, then join the warden for dinner that night. The prison team put on an awful display and was beaten soundly.

During dinner, the warden discussed his team's weaknesses and strengths. "What do you think it would take to make a rattling good club, Mr. Quinn?" the warden asked.

"Well, if you had a good shortstop, and another pitcher, they would be pretty good," Quinn answered.

For a moment, the warden sat quietly; then his face lit up with enthusiasm. "Now that fellow who killed the girl in the hotel," he said happily, "he's a shortstop and he'll get life. And this man who robbed the bank. He used to be a whirlwind pitcher for his high-school team. We'll get him, too. You wait and see—we'll have a great baseball team in here yet." The warden cheerfully resumed dinner.

◆

On April 17, 1951, motel proprietor Eugene Helton, age forty, of Chattanooga, Tennessee, was scheduled to be tried for the shooting murder of Mrs. Joy Delaney. Three weeks before the case was called, however, Judge L.D. Miller postponed the trial.

The reason was that April 17 was opening day for the Southern Association's Chattanooga Lookouts. "I've always felt it worked a hardship on lawyers and the jury as well as witnesses," explained the judge, "to try a case on opening day."

◆

Harry H. Frazee was born in Peoria, Illinois, in 1880. He worked as a bellhop at the Peoria Hotel, as a box-office man in a Peoria movie house, and as an advance man for theatrical productions, always showing great drive and ambition.

After the turn of the century, Frazee became prominent in theatre and boxing circles. He produced several successful plays, including *No, No, Nanette,* and financed and built the Cort Theatre in Chicago. In 1915 he promoted the Jess Willard–Jack Johnson heavyweight championship fight in Havana. He also managed heavyweight champion James J. Jeffries.

In 1916 he purchased the Boston Red Sox, which he owned for seven years, during which the team won two world championships. Following the 1919 season, he sold Babe Ruth and other players to New York. In 1922 his wife was granted a divorce after Frazee was found guilty of misconduct with actress Elizabeth Nelson, a star in one of his productions. In 1929, with New York Mayor Jimmy Walker at his bedside, he died of Bright's disease.

The opening paragraph of his *Boston Traveler* obituary read: "Funeral services will be held tomorrow for Harry Frazee, who sold Babe Ruth to the Yankees for $137,000."

◆

When he walks through the Hall-of-Fame gallery, Carl Yastrzemski, Sr., can find a member of the family immortalized in bronze. But there are other familiar faces on those Hall-of-Fame plaques: Roy Campanella, Josh Gibson, Satchel Paige.

"I played against them," said Carl, Sr., who for twenty-seven years farmed potatoes by day and played semipro baseball by night on Long Island. "They were with the Philadelphia Stars, and they'd barnstorm out on the island."

Also among his opponents in those days were Don Newcombe; Luis Tiant's father, who barnstormed with the Cuban All-Stars; and Eddie Popowski, who barnstormed with the House of David team and was later manager of Yaz, Jr., in Minneapolis.

"I got my share of hits against them," Yaz, Sr., said of his Hall-of-Fame opponents. "I took Satchel Paige deep. I got a triple against him, off the center-field fence. I like to tell about that one. When

UNIFORM AGREEMENT
FOR TRANSFER OF A PLAYER
TO OR BY A
Major League Club

This Agreement, made and entered into this 26th day of December 1919 by and between   Boston American League Baseball Club
(Party of the First Part)

and   American League Base Ball Club of New York
(Party of the Second Part)

Witnesseth: The party of the first part does hereby release to the party of the second part the services of Player George H. Ruth under the following conditions:

(Here recite fully and clearly every condition of deal, including date of delivery; if for a money consideration, designate time and method of payment; if an exchange of players, name each; if option to recall is retained or privilege of choosing one or more players on list of one released is reserved, specify all terms. No transfer will be held valid unless the consideration, receipt of which is acknowledged herein, passes at time of execution of Agreement.)

By herewith assigning to the party of the second part the contract of said player George H. Ruth for the seasons of 1919, 1920 and 1921, in consideration of the sum of Twenty-five Thousand ($25,000.) Dollars cash and other good and valuable considerations paid by the party of the second part, receipt whereof is hereby acknowledged.

The parties to this Agreement further covenant to abide by all provisions of the National Agreement and by all Rules of the National Commission, regulating the transfer of the services of a player, particularly those printed on the reverse side of this Agreement.

In Testimony Whereof, we have subscribed hereto, through our respective presidents or authorized agents, on the date above written :

Witness:

BOSTON AMERICAN LEAGUE BASEBALL CLUB

(Party of the First Part)

AMERICAN LEAGUE BASE BALL CLUB OF NEW YORK

Jacob Ruppert Prest
(Party of the Second Part)

Club officials are cautioned to carefully read the provisions of the National Agreement and the rules of the National Commission, printed on the back of this Agreement, for their information and guidance.

The contract under which Babe Ruth was sold to the New York Yankees.

Carl batted against Satchel in the big leagues, he only got a single against him."

◆

During World War II, fighter pilots in the South Pacific liked to wear baseball caps to keep the tropical sun out of their eyes. But early in the Pacific war, baseball hats—like Cokes, Rita Hayworth pinups, and fresh strawberries— were rare. So in the middle of the Yankees–Cardinals 1943 World Series, Marine Maj. Gregory ("Pappy") Boyington made a public offer. He and the men of his squadron were willing to shoot down a Japanese Zero in trade for each cap of the winning team.

Boyington, who a month earlier had bagged five Zeroes in a ten-minute dogfight over Bougainville, said he and his men were willing to put up the thirteen enemy planes they had shot down in the previous two weeks as collateral. They also requested the caps from the winning team only. As superstitious as ballplayers, the pilots didn't want to fly combat with badluck hats on their heads.

◆

By the late 1980s, the Jackie Robinson story had settled firmly into American history, and, like Antietam, Sam Tilden, and the Works Project Administration, the Jackie Robinson story was becoming largely forgotten. "It has been forgotten," said Rachel Robinson, Jackie's widow, in September 1989. "We see that as we go from city to city. We see schoolchildren who don't know who Jackie Robinson was. They know the name, but not who he was. I do fear he will be forgotten."

Not just by schoolchildren. Baby boomers grew up with Willie Mays model mitts, Hank Aaron baseball cards, and Bob Gib-

son asthma spray. No wonder they struggle to grasp the major leagues' longstanding color barrier and the heroic story of Jackie Robinson, the Brooklyn Dodger who broke the barrier in 1947.

Plain and simple, Robinson was a hero. He might have had more courage than anybody else in the history of the game, and he needed it. To any outsider, baseball clubhouses are forbidding places. When a stranger walks into one, he is greeted by stares, glares, and whispers. This happens to people who aren't members of the team. When he strolled into the Brooklyn clubhouse in 1947, Robinson was not a member of the race. No one could imagine his fear and the loneliness; he was the first and only black man playing America's national pastime.

Jackie Robinson (right) *is met at home plate after first professional home run.*

Only forty years later, the historical significance of Robinson's hard walk into baseball's all-white neighborhood was fading fast. "To young, black kids today, it's hard to believe any of that ever existed," said Chico Renfroe, a Robinson teammate on the Kansas City Monarchs of the Negro Leagues.

All they have to do is take a good look at baseball lore. The archives are filled with shameful relics from baseball's Jim Crow era. The October 12, 1903, edition of the Boston *Herald* included a cartoon depicting the Red Sox entraining after a World Series game in Pittsburgh. Toting their baggage were black porters, who were drawn in the cartoon to look like monkeys.

The May 27, 1912, edition of the *New York Times* tells about a New York Giants' exhibition game in Paterson, New Jersey. The Giants arrived at the game and were shocked to find the Paterson Smart Sets, a black team, waiting for them. New York righty Louis Drucke refused to play "against a colored team." He was the only pitcher the Giants had brought along. After much cajoling, Drucke agreed to pitch, but only if they didn't announce his name over the public address system. The game ended in a race riot.

The August 27, 1933, *Boston Post* included a story about the good luck charm of Boston Braves slugger Wally Berger: a black concession steward named Jim Walton. "Berger goes direct to Jim and runs his hands through Jim's kinky hair," the story related. "Wally has been hitting homers, so Jim can expect to get his wool worn thin before the pennant is won."

The 1947 Brooklyn Dodgers' yearbook lauded Robinson, then age twenty-eight, as the "first colored boy . . . in the big-time baseball arena."

Robinson waded into baseball when the uniforms were baggy and the racism was real. "He always believed he would play in the major leagues," said Renfroe. "It almost got to be a joke with Jackie. A lot of us were skeptical. But he used to tell us all the time, 'Let's hustle out there. There might be scouts in the stands.' He kept at it and kept at it. He kept at it so long, some of us actually started to believe it."

Forty years later, baby boomers can hardly understand baseball's all-white era. Blacks banned from baseball? It's a tough concept to grasp for folks brought up on Reggie Bars. But if anybody is looking for a hero, all they have to do is read about Jackie Robinson, the Dodger who changed America's pastime and America in their parents' lifetime.

"I used to visit a family in Brooklyn," Lou Gorman said. "I used to love to go see the Dodgers play. I loved to watch Jackie Robinson. My uncle owned part of a restaurant in Brooklyn. I remember looking through the door and seeing some of the Dodgers in there. Carl Furillo. Pee Wee Reese. The white players could eat there. The black players couldn't."

◆

During World War I, American troops prepared for a frontal assault on the German lines near Metz. In order to move quickly and noiselessly, the men were told to strip themselves to the bare essentials: no packs, no shovels, no canteens. Just a rifle and a bayonet.

After the battle, a chaplain came upon the body of a young soldier. He hunted for identification papers, but found none: going into battle with only the essentials, the boy had stormed the lines with nothing but his gun, his bayonet, and in his inside jacket pocket a worn baseball.

◆

◆

On August 6, 1945, the United States dropped an atomic bomb on Hiroshima and then another one on Nagasaki three days later. The world waited tensely for the Japanese surrender.

In Honolulu a false report of surrender set off wild celebrations in the streets. In the Soviet Union *Pravda* speculated the Japanese militarists wanted to prolong the war at all costs. Around the world church bells, ship whistles, and car horns were poised to signal peace.

No city was more tense than Washington, D.C. President Harry Truman waited at the White House; diplomats waited for word from Tokyo; newsmen waited for word from the government.

Then, on the afternoon of August 12, the phone rang at the United Press offices in Washington. The state department was calling. "This waiting is getting pretty monotonous," said the diplomat on the other end. "Would you give us some baseball scores?"

◆

Tom Zachary broke into the big leagues with the Athletics in 1918. In his nineteen years in the majors, the lefty hurler played for eight teams. Lifetime he won 186 and lost 191 with a 3.72 earned run average. He appeared in two World Series with the Senators, winning two games when Washington defeated the Giants in 1924.

On September 24, 1927, he surrendered a two-run home run to Babe Ruth, the Bambino's sixtieth of the season. Zachary was traded to New York the following season and that fall won another World Series game against St. Louis.

A graduate of Guilford College, "Old

Tom Zachary

Tom" was popular around his hometown of Graham, North Carolina. During the Great Depression when local farmers struggled badly, the pitcher gave them low-interest loans, with one provision: they must allow Zachary to hunt on their land.

By the spring of 1935, Zachary—then with the Brooklyn Dodgers—had seen a lot of baseball. "When Ty Cobb was in the league, it was customary to choke the bat and try to place hits instead of home runs," he observed. "It seems that a great hitter generally sets the style for the rest of the players. When Babe Ruth became the outstanding figure of baseball and the rabbit was injected into the ball, they quit choking the bat and took a full swing."

After his baseball career ended in 1936, Zachary returned to North Carolina and lived on a tobacco farm. On January 24, 1969, he suffered a stroke and died at age seventy-two. The headline on his *New York Times* obituary read:

Tom Zachary, Pitcher, Is Dead;
Served Ruth's 60th Home Run

On an opening day at Yankee Stadium in the early 1950s, the box seats were crowded with dignitaries on hand to watch New York start its season against Philadelphia. Among those seated in the VIP boxes was former president and long-time baseball fan Herbert Hoover. During a pause in play, the public address announcer spoke.

"Ladies and gentlemen, may we direct your attention to Box Sixteen and tell you that we are honored today by the presence of one of the great Americans of our time . . ."

Those seated around Hoover smiled approvingly at the ex-president.

"A man who needs no introduction to the fans of America . . . ," the announcer continued.

Hoover readied to stand and acknowledge the crowd.

"The one and only," the announcer concluded, "Connie Mack!"

John J. McGraw (left) *and Connie Mack*

In spring 1988 Charleston, West Virginia, Wheelers owner Dennis Bastien wanted to transform his club's Watt Powell Park into a 6,800-seat model of Wrigley Field, right down to the famous ivy. "I like ballparks with character," said Bastien, whose team was the Cubs' affiliate in the South Atlantic League. "Wrigley Field has so much character and we'd like to bring that here. Anybody who is a baseball fan, even if they're not a National League or Cubs fan, will tell you Wrigley Field is more than a ballpark. It's a cathedral, a sanctuary."

In September 1987, while in Chicago for an organizational meeting, Bastien pocketed a little bit of the North Side sanctuary. With permission from the Wrigley groundskeeper, he clipped twelve sprigs from the famous ivy-covered brick wall. "I wrapped them up in a paper towel," Bastien said, "and my wife kept them in her purse until we got home on the plane that night."

Bastien nurtured them over the winter in the clubhouse at Watt Powell Park and in early spring planted them near a section of his center-field fence. The ivy was supposed to grow about one foot a week and thus would cover half the center-field wall by August. "We just hope it grows," Bastien said. "If it grows like ivy does in most places, it shouldn't be a problem."

"It was struggling for a while," reported Bastien's wife, Lisa. "But we've had some rain lately, and now it seems to be doing pretty well. All sorts of people are always checking to see how it's doing. I know this is going to sound silly, but part of the outfield wall is wood and part of it is brick. The ivy is growing all right on the wood. But it really seems to be growing well on the brick. I told you it would sound silly."

◆   ◆

Reds' general manager Bob Quinn came from a baseball family. His father, John, was general manager of the Boston Braves for twenty-three years. Among his many baseball interests over the years, his grandfather J.A. Quinn at one time owned the Braves. Young Bob Quinn grew up in Newton and spent a lot of time around Braves Field, hob-nobbing with Boston's other major-league franchise.

"We were very much the other team in town," remembered Quinn, age fifty-one, in 1988, when he was in the Yankees' front office. "The Red Sox were always the team in Boston. There was that natural rivalry between us and the Red Sox."

In 1953, when he was a junior in high school, Bob Quinn packed up and accompanied his family—and the Braves—to Milwaukee. "We were the new team in town. That was very much an exciting time," he said.

But for Quinn, there were many lasting memories left behind in Boston: the pennant-winning Braves of 1948 when he was eleven; his friendship with Warren Spahn, with whom he still keeps in touch; the kitchen linoleum.

The kitchen linoleum? "In the middle of our kitchen floor, there was a great big circle with the Braves' logo," said Quinn. "My parents had it custom built into the floor. I've wondered if it's still there."

"It's not in the best of shape, but it's still here," reported Ned Canty, who occupies the old Quinn home on Commonwealth Avenue in Newton. "We're thinking about taking it up. But if we do, we'll take it up so we can save it."

"Please, if you could, send me a picture of it," said Quinn cheerfully when he received the good news. "I'd like to have a Christmas card made from it."

On August 1, 1960, the American nuclear-powered submarine *Seadragon* left Portsmouth, New Hampshire, to chart a new Northwest Passage across the top of the world to the Pacific.

In the course of the historic journey, the *Seadragon* would become the first submarine to dive under icebergs. At one juncture, while negotiating a ticklish 850-mile passage through the Canadian archipelago, Comdr. George P. Steele consulted a 140-year-old explorer's journal. Shortly before the boat reached the North Pole, the navy briefly lost radio contact with her. On the night of August 25, 1960, the *Seadragon* broke through the ice at the pole and reported all was well. The crew was fine, if in need of some exercise. Skies were clear, with temperatures in the high twenties. Baseball weather.

"We have maneuvered the ship through light ice to where we can put a life raft over to the last fifteen feet to ferry over a party to play baseball," Commander Steele radioed. "The men are wearing the warmest clothes they can get."

The 360 degrees of longitude and the International Dateline converge at the Pole. Thus the polar baseball diamond was arranged so a home run would travel "from today into tomorrow and from one side of the world to the other." A runner leaving home plate also reached first base twelve hours later. Nobody hit one into next week.

Even at the North Pole, the pastime proved to be a great equalizer: the enlisted men beat the officers, 13–10.

◆

On April 4, 1952, Connie Mack, Bill Dickey, Ernie Shore, Mrs. Babe Ruth, and other baseball dignitaries gathered in

The remnants of New York's Polo Grounds near the end of the park's destruction. The clump of grass in the center marks the location of home plate; the clubhouse is at the center background.

Fayetteville, North Carolina, for a historic event, the dedication of a Babe Ruth plaque.

This was not just another Babe Ruth plaque. It marked the spot where in the spring of 1914, young Ruth—just out of the Baltimore orphanage and playing for the Orioles—slammed his first professional home run. The inscription also noted that "in this town, George Herman Ruth acquired the nickname 'Babe.'"

The marker, brainchild of Fayetteville merchant Maurice Fleischmann, the batboy the day Ruth delivered his inaugural blast, was erected on the grounds of the state highway commission offices, former site of the Cape Fear Fairgrounds. "Babe

would have loved it," declared Mrs. Ruth at the dedication.

He'd still love it.

"Oh, it's still here, right here on the premises," drawled Ms. Melvin, who answered the phone at the state highway offices in the spring of 1988. "From time to time, people like to stop by and make a picture of it."

◆

On Friday morning, April 10, 1964, eleven men wearing steel helmets marched into the Polo Grounds and like a conquering army desecrated, destroyed, and pillaged. They were there to demolish the horseshoe-shaped ballpark, former home of the departed New York Giants, to make room for a massive housing project.

"Getting at the Polo Grounds is always something I wanted to do," said Harry Avirom, president of the Wrecking Corporation of America, and a self-confessed Dodgers fan. "This makes up for the sad day we went after Ebbets Field in 1960."

His men, cruelly outfitted in jerseys with "Giants" emblazoned across the front, trod the yellow sod wielding sledgehammers to begin their dirty work. Some seats and the Giants' dugout bench were earmarked for shipment to Cooperstown. Most of the seats would be sold to minor-league parks and to schools. The rest of the place would simply be scrapped. Among the evicted were stray dogs and cats that for years had lived in the ballpark's catacombs.

Demolition man Stephen McNair hoisted a sledgehammer and strutted to the left-field fence, near Section Thirty-three. He was another disenfranchised Brooklyn fan, and he was standing before the spot where Bobby Thomson's home run sailed out of the ballpark to crush the 1951 Dodgers. "I'm going to take that place down myself," he vowed, as he readied to smash the wall with glee.

Even conquering armies have a conscience. "No, you don't," intervened job foreman Abe Gach. "Be gentle over there. History was made there."

A few years before World War II, American banker Thomas Lamont was in Beijing to arrange loans to the Chinese government. The president of China and the cabinet invited him to a banquet, the kind of official feast that customarily began at about 6:00 P.M., ran thirty-two courses, and ended near midnight.

Three hours into the evening, a man seated near Lamont whispered that the diner seated opposite was the minister of the interior. "Why, I have an appointment with him tomorrow," said Lamont. "If only I had an interpreter, I'd go to work now."

An interpreter was summoned, and for an hour Lamont discussed loans with the minister. Then, thinking that to continue business would be impolite, Lamont dismissed the interpreter and embarked on two more hours of eating.

Finally, at around eleven o'clock, the Chinese minister of the interior leaned across the table and spoke to Lamont in perfect English. "Mister Lamont, I am sorry to disturb you," said the minister. "But I wonder if you could tell me who is pitching for Pittsburgh this season?"

SPRING

When John McNamara managed the Red Sox, reporters who covered the team generally thought of him as a grouchy guy. In the heat of the summer, Johnny Mac could be cold. Sometimes he answered reporters' questions with terse, annoyed replies; sometimes he answered questions angrily; sometimes he wrinkled his entire face in disgust, as if he had just gulped a pitcher of spoiled milk. If there was one thing McNamara hated, it was a question he judged stupid or irrelevant.

Early in spring training 1988, a reporter who had only a casual relationship with McNamara entered the manager's tiny office at the team's Winter Haven, Florida, complex just before noon on a bright, warm morning. The Red Sox had finished their light workout and were scattering to fast-food joints, golf courses, and fishing holes. The reporter knew McNamara's reputation as a hard-boiled skipper but decided not to let that reputation chill him in pursuit of a story, even a cutesy, fluffy, early spring training feature. After knocking, the reporter entered and asked if McNamara had a moment.

"What do you need?" countered the manager.

"I'm doing a kind of off-beat story," the reporter replied. "Do you remember anything at all about your first baseball glove?"

McNamara leaned way back in his ancient, squeaky swivel chair, folded his hands on his belly, and stared. *Batten down the hatches,* thought the writer. "I certainly do," said McNamara, his eyes fairly twinkling. "My uncle gave it to me when I was about six. It was his. He got a new one, and he gave his old one to me. It was a catcher's mitt. I think it was a Mickey Cochrane model. It went everywhere with me. Even to bed."

To mingle with ballplayers at spring training is like mingling with them after a long Sunday afternoon nap. They are rested and relaxed, and proceed at

Joe Morgan, manager of the Boston Red Sox

their own pace. Unlike preseason camps in football, spring training does not require paramilitary gruel. Spring training is more summer camp than boot camp. There is much stretching, spitting, shagging, sprinting, practice batting, and loitering; and many hours are spent at poolside, at pond's edge, or on the fairways.

During spring training, the weather feels great to frozen Northerners. For the first time in months, they sleep with windows open, hear birds chirp in the trees, and sweat. The romantics are right: it is a time of renewal. "I start chewing tobacco again in spring training," said Red Sox coach Johnny Pesky, happily stuffing a wad of the stringy stuff into his cheek in the spring of 1988. "I go all winter without touching the stuff. But something about being on a ball field makes you want to chew." Even when tropical rain patters on the palms and thunder rattles the windows, baseball men feel warm. They go inside, think hard about where to eat dinner that night, and tell stories about just about anything.

"I was about ten years old," said Joe Morgan, the Red Sox third-base coach in spring 1988. "There was an older kid in the neighborhood. His family had a few bucks, and he had this glove. He told me he'd give it to me. All I had to do was climb into this fifty-gallon steel drum and let him roll me down the hill in it. I didn't believe him, but he promised. I said, 'Okay, but this glove has gotta come in the drum with me when I do it.'

"So I got in the drum, and I rolled down the hill. I was bouncing around in there so much, I didn't know where I was. When I got out, I was so dizzy I fell over. I looked up, and sure enough here he comes to take his glove back. Somehow I beat him home. I didn't come out of the house for three days because I knew he'd try to take it back. That's how I got my first glove."

As opening day approaches, some players begin to snap on stern game faces; but through most of spring training, there is almost no pressure. A few players work to secure roster spots, but most just dust off their game. In the old days, players needed spring training to melt away off-season blubber, but by the 1990s that compulsion had disappeared. Wise modern players start working out and laying off chocolate doughnuts the day after Christmas.

Exhibition games are not life and death, wins and losses. They are exhibitions. Through the years, preseason and barnstorming games were forums for fun. Play a few innings, mingle with the retirement crowd on your way off the field, shower, and watch the osprey flap over the ballpark. Even tightly wrapped players find moments for fun and wistful reminiscence.

"I'll never forget it," said Red Sox pitcher Oil Can Boyd, often a bundle of jangling, nervous energy in midsummer but reflective in the early spring of 1988. "My older brother was the most valuable player at a Little League all-star game. I was the bat boy. They awarded him this glove, and he gave it to me. I remember it was a blue glove. A royal blue glove. I can still see the box it came in, I remember it so well. I had that glove my whole Little League career. All my friends would want to use it, but I wouldn't let them.

"I remember I was playing ball at the playground. I remember leaving it. Then I went back to find it. I looked everywhere, but it wasn't there. I was heartbroken."

Spring training is a spectacle. Uniforms are handed out liberally, and camps crawl with players only good enough to dream. Baseball lore is filled with tales of characters—youngsters, old men, and crazies—who wanted to be big leaguers and get their chance because they caught the game in a relaxed moment. Spring training draws teams from all over for what amounts to pickup games, and even college teams visit big-league camps. When he ended his holdout on the last day of spring training in 1987, Red Sox ace Roger Clemens pitched his one and only preseason game against Harvard. During spring training, Japanese teams visit American teams, and National League teams often visit American League teams, which can be a treat even for veteran big leaguers.

"I got to play against Willie Mays in spring training while he was with the Mets," said Red Sox right fielder Dwight Evans in the spring of 1989. "He was my favorite when I was growing up. That's why I wear number 24."

"Tom Seaver," said Red Sox relief pitcher Bob Stanley. "I went up to him in spring training when he was with Cincinnati. I told him he was my boyhood idol. He told me to go [expletive] myself. He was kidding. I think I made him feel old."

Given its class trip atmosphere, spring training was traditionally prime time for practical jokes, frat house fun being a staple of spring lore. With plenty of gullible

The ruined facade of Ebbets Field after the Dodgers moved to Los Angeles.

rookie targets on hand, many of them literally straight from the farm, and lots of time to kill in the sleepy southern towns in those days before cable television was in every room, there was ample opportunity for elaborately planned schemes. Spring hijinks have faded in the modern era. The training sites in Florida and Arizona aren't sleepy anymore, and ballplayers have better things to do than razz colleagues whether it be golf or reminiscing about their first baseball glove. Occasionally, though, they make time.

An hour after a workout ended in the spring of 1988, Red Sox manager McNamara sat on a stone wall outside the team's clubhouse chatting with a reporter in the warm sunshine. The talk was casual and meandering, from spring training in Arizona, to Joe DiMaggio as an Athletics coach, to the Boston Braves. From inside the clubhouse, Red Sox ace Clemens called out, "Hey, Mac, telephone." The manager ignored his pitcher and continued to chat with the reporter. "Hey, Mac," Clemens repeated. "Telephone." McNamara squirted a stream of tobacco juice onto the gravel path, peered through the clubhouse door, and shook his head slowly. The reporter told him to go ahead and take the phone call, that the chat wasn't important. "There's no phone call," said McNamara, calling upon decades of spring training experience. Then the hard-boiled manager grinned. "It's the shaving-cream-on-the-telephone-mouthpiece trick."

Russian immigrant Izzy Kaplan was a long-time photographer for several New York newspapers and a favorite target of ballplayer practical jokes. In spring training in New Orleans in 1922, a few Yankee players thought it would be a great gag to make Kaplan think he was a target of the powerful local Ku Klux Klan. The joke started one morning when they stuffed a note into his hotel mailbox: "Get out of town within twenty-four hours. [Signed] Ku Klux Klan."

That evening, they delivered another note: "Get out of town in twelve hours, or else. Ku Klux Klan." Later that night, another note was slipped under his door: "You now have only six hours to get out of town."

Kaplan disconnected his phone, pushed a dresser in front of his door, and sat up all night staring out the window. Next morning, the Yankee jokesters sent Kaplan a dummy telegram, purportedly from his New York office. The wire ordered him to proceed at once to Ku Klux Klan headquarters to get a picture of the imperial wizard, Dr. Hiram Evans.

A true newsman, Kaplan packed up his camera, trooped crosstown, and banged on the door of the klan convention hall. He was confronted by a masked, robed figure staring at him through eye slits. "I should like a peecture of the beeg boss," said Kaplan. "What you call him—imperial gizzard?"

"What's your name?" snapped the guard.

"Israel Solomon Kaplan," answered Kaplan, showing the telegram from New York. The guard slammed the door in Kaplan's face but soon returned and gestured for him to come in. Walking up the center aisle of an auditorium filled with hooded figures, Kaplan marched up to Evans, the imperial wizard, and handed him the Yankee-authored wire.

Happy to cooperate, Evans removed his hood. Kaplan made several flash powder pictures, which quickly filled the room with acrid smoke. As the klansmen coughed and cursed behind him, Kaplan finished the shoot.

"Do you need any more?" asked Evans helpfully, showing his profile. "Is there anything else you need?"

"Oh, yes," said Kaplan, absent-mindedly digging the threatening notes from his pocket. "I'm having a leedle trouble with some of your boys."

Evans produced a business card and wrote, "To all Klansmen: Do not bother Israel Solomon Kaplan," and presented it to the photographer.

During another spring training in Macon, Georgia, Bob Shawkey and a group of fellow Yankee pitchers went to a local carnival. Using their ball throwing skills, the boys soon walked away with the most coveted prizes under their arms: they each had at least two live ducks. Not sure what to do with them, Shawkey was hit with a brainstorm. He telephoned teammate Ping Bodie at the hotel and told him to take Izzy Kaplan away from his room for a few hours.

Bodie invited Kaplan to the movies. Thinking about the hijinks transpiring back at the hotel, Bodie found himself laughing out loud during a tragic, tear-jerking scene.

"Vot's all aboud this?" Kaplan inquired.

"I was just thinking of something funny that happened in San Francisco," Bodie managed to respond before bursting into laughter again, causing them both to be ejected from the theatre.

Back at the hotel, Kaplan said goodnight and trooped up to his room. Soon he was back in the lobby, wild-eyed and screaming. "Help! Help!" he hollered. "It's full of ghosts, my room!"

The night clerk and several Yankees investigated. Switching on the lights, they found Izzy's room packed with ducks, some in flight, some paddling happily in the full bathtub. Kaplan returned to the lobby and demanded an explanation from the rapidly gathering players.

"Were the windows open?" asked baseball writer Damon Runyon.

"Yes," said Kaplan.

"Well," said Runyon, "a flock of wild ducks probably flew in."

"Oh, yeah?" said Izzy. "Well, mebbe the ducks is turning on the water in the bathtub too, eh?"

◆

One night in the spring of 1987, Red Sox reliever Bob Stanley was having a beer at the poolside bar at the team hotel in Winter Haven, Florida. Stanley, who had

Rogers Hornsby (left) *and William Ironson, cameraman for International Newsreel.*

thrown a crucial wild pitch as Boston folded magnificently in Game Six of the previous World Series, overheard a couple of patrons perched on nearby barstools.

"That's Bob Stanley," one of them said, not realizing the pitcher was within earshot. "He lost the World Series for us. He's a bum."

Stanley whirled around and stared at the man. The man realized Stanley had heard him and tensed. As Stanley marched straight over to him, the man prepared to hop off the stool and defend himself. Stanley summoned the bartender and bought both men a drink.

◆

In the flannel era, the great snipe hunt was a favorite spring training gag. After veteran players carefully selected a rookie target, for days they let him overhear excited talk about the bountiful snipe expeditions of the previous few nights. Before long, the rookie begged to tag along on a hunt, and the grizzled veterans grudgingly agreed.

Driven by car to desolate woods, the rookie was told to take off his shoes so he could walk quietly while approaching the snipe. Upon reaching a spot which the veterans said "looked well-stocked with snipe," the older players fanned out, ostensibly to flush them out. The rookie was instructed to wait, stay still, hold the bag, and catch the critters as they scampered toward him. The older players, of course, doubled back to the car and motored home to camp, leaving the barefooted rookie stranded in the woods in the middle of the night.

Pitcher Grover Cleveland Alexander liked to tell about the time the snipe hunt trick was resurrected in Waco, Texas, in 1924. "They had a new pitcher who came from a farm in the western part of the state," Alexander said. "It seemed to the

Grover Cleveland Alexander

Waco gang that he was sent from heaven with a purpose. Right away they organized a hunt. He was very much interested, and when they suggested going after snipe he fell over himself with eagerness."

The hunting party reached an appropriately remote spot, some fifteen miles from the nearest sign of civilization. "The young pitcher asked all sorts of questions about the snipe and seemed completely sold on the importance of his job with the bag," Alexander said. "They left him and departed some distance to give the impression of rounding up the snipe."

Congratulating themselves on a joke well done, the veterans made their way back to the road. When they got there, they realized the gag had backfired. The car was gone; the rookie was gone; and the snipe bag was left spitefully in the road. "They spent all night getting back," Alexander laughed.

◆

At the Pittsburgh Pirates' camp one year, a young prospect quickly revealed a serious personal problem. He was a kleptomaniac and his weakness was pianos.

"In three separate Georgia hotels, he stole pianos by moving them out at night with the help of confederates," Pirates shortstop Honus Wagner once recalled. "Finally he was dropped from the ball club because, although he was a good player, he was incurable."

Two springs later, the Pirates played an exhibition game in Indiana. The umpire, who wore a big, black moustache, made several calls against Pittsburgh. Wagner stared at his team's tormentor and gradually realized he knew the fellow from somewhere. Another crucial call cost the Pirates the game, and Wagner sought out the umpire afterward.

"Haven't I seen you from somewhere?" he said.

"Certainly," the umpire said. "Care to buy a piano?"

◆

In the early 1920s, previously undistinguished outfielder Paul Strand began to attract attention with great seasons in the Pacific Coast League. Washington owner Clark Griffith dispatched scout Joe Engel to take a look at him. Engel reported back to the owner, "He'll never make it in the majors, Griff."

When Connie Mack purchased Strand for $100,000 in the winter of 1923–24, Griffith began to worry. Then he started to read newspaper stories that described Strand as a late bloomer destined to be another Babe Ruth or Ty Cobb, or maybe a little of both. In the spring of 1924, Strand authored a great preseason. By the time the Athletics visited Washington's camp for an exhibition game, all eyes were on Philadelphia's sensation, including the angry eyes of Clark Griffith.

Before the game, Engel rushed to the Senators' clubhouse and sought out that day's pitcher, Walter Johnson. "You gotta save my life, Walter," said Engel, dreading the fallout if Strand was able to successfully hit the great Big Train. "Please bear down on this guy Strand."

Johnson treated the game as if it meant something. Summoning his midseason fastball, he struck out Strand four times. After the game, Griffith wrapped his arm around his ace scout, Joe Engel.

◆

During a spring exhibition game in Tampa in the early 1950s, Cincinnati reliever Frank Smith was badly battered in a short, unhappy outing. "I think we were playing the Red Sox, but I'm not sure," said Joe Nuxhall, the former Reds' pitcher who told the story in the summer of 1990.

The sullen Smith preceded his teammates into the clubhouse, and when the rest of the Reds reached the locker room, they were appalled. There was Smith with a noose around his neck, mouth open, body limp, hanged from a hook in his locker.

"His arms were hanging by his side. His shirt was all pulled up near his neck. It really looked like he was gone," said Nuxhall. "We kind of yelled a little bit. For a moment there, we thought he had really done it. Then we figured it had to be some kind of gag, because he was always doing things like that."

The dead man started to giggle. Smith had worked a coat hanger under his shirt to give it a scrunched-up, stretched-neck look, tied a noose around his neck, and

Branch Rickey (left) *and Fred Haney*

alligator's head. When the creature snapped at the bait, Greenwell set the hook. "I started reeling real fast, before he had a chance to dive under, and brought him in right along the top of the water," the Florida-born Greenwell said. "Got him right up to shore."

Greenwell was eying the live and livid alligator at his feet, wondering what to do with him when he looked up and saw Red Sox manager John McNamara rounding a dog leg on the golf course. "Hey, Mac," Greenwell yelled. "Come here."

The manager approached and scowled when he saw the creature at his left fielder's feet. "How do you intend to get the hook out of that thing's mouth?" McNamara said. Then he added quickly, "I don't want to see it. All I know is you better show up at the ballpark with all ten fingers."

◆

hidden his feet behind the locker bench. He went limp and fish-eyed when he heard his teammates approach the locker room door. "It was a practical joke," said Nuxhall. "It worked."

◆

Early in spring training in 1988, Red Sox outfielder Mike Greenwell and a friend fished at a pond on a golf course in Winter Haven, Florida. The fish weren't biting, but Greenwell spotted something else to snap his boredom: an alligator lounging in the water underneath a nearby cypress tree.

"Watch this," Greenwell said to his friend. He cast an artificial worm over the

In spring training 1948, the Athletics and the Senators staged a foot race before their April 4 exhibition game in Orlando. The contestants: Philadelphia owner-manager Connie Mack, age eighty-five, and Washington owner Clark Griffith, age seventy-eight. The teams announced the pair would leg out a grueling ninety-foot course, from third base to home plate.

Just before game time the stands were filled with anxious fans. Would Griffith beat Mack? Would Mack beat Griffith? Would they complete the course before the all-star break?

An ambulance careened through the left-field gate, roared down the left-field line, and jerked to a halt at home plate. The back door was flung open, and out stepped Mack and Griffith, followed by a doctor and two nurses. Washington coach Nick Altrock, himself age seventy-one, escorted the contestants to the third-base

Walter Johnson (left) *and Clark Griffith*

starting line. With baseball commissioner Happy Chandler in place as the finish-line judge, Altrock fired his cap pistol. They were off.

Griffith stepped spryly down the base path. Mack kept pace with a long-legged gait, arms flailing at his side. They finished in a dead heat, both alive.

◆

At spring training, anecdotes are spun spontaneously. On a sunny day in the spring of 1988, Red Sox third-base coach Joe Morgan monitored the bullpen at Chain O'Lakes Park. Beyond the left-center-field wall, where a traveling carnival was pack-ing to leave town, a huge Ferris wheel stood partially dismantled.

"That reminds me of a story," said Morgan. "When I was a kid, about six years old, they were setting up a carnival at the Blessed Sacrament Church in Walpole. I was down there watching the guys put together the Ferris wheel. When they got done, the foreman says, 'OK, fellas, everybody on for a free ride.' He let me get on with them. So we go around about ten times, and everything is just fine. Then the foreman leaves. He gets in his car and goes downtown to eat his lunch. He goes off for about an hour and leaves us up there, going 'round and 'round. How many times we went around on that thing, I don't know.

I was getting so sick, I was thinking about jumping off the damn thing. When I finally got off, I couldn't walk. For three days, my head was spinning. I've never even come close to getting on one of those [expletive] things since."

◆

Late in the afternoon of March 10, 1933, in Los Angeles, the New York Giants defeated the Chicago Cubs in an exhibition game at Wrigley Field. Afterward, the Giants headed back to their rooms at the Hotel Biltmore to rest before dinner. Not long afterward, the earth rumbled and the hotel shook. Shaving kits vibrated off sink tops, and players fell out of bed. A devastating earthquake had hit Southern California, its epicenter at nearby Long Beach. "I guess it's the shock of the Giants finally winning a ball game," New York manager Bill Terry joked nervously to his roommates.

Back at Wrigley Field, Giants trainer Willie Shafer was showering in the clubhouse when the quake hit. Next thing he knew, Shafer found himself standing stark naked at second base, gazing at the new, huge crack in the grandstand clock tower. In sheer panic as the earth quivered, he had streaked from the shower room onto the field.

Reports began to reach the Biltmore of the quake's devastation. Damage was widespread, and more than one hundred were dead. There were warnings of aftershocks. Terry and his terrified ballplayers no longer joked. En masse, they marched from the hotel and plopped down in a public square across the street, where they were sure no buildings would fall on them. As evening fell, the temperature dropped, but none of the shivering Giants volunteered to leave the park. As it grew colder, someone thought it a great idea to get overcoats and blankets from the rooms.

The problem was no one wanted to re-enter the Biltmore, lest it crumble as he crossed the threshhold. Terry solved the problem: he ordered the hapless trainer Shafer to go get the blankets, an enterprise that required four harrowing trips.

◆

For dinner one night at spring training in 1988, two reporters from the Red Sox camp ventured to a roadside restaurant in Auburndale, Florida, on Highway 92, about fifteen minutes west of Winter Haven. Painted in large, white letters on the rust-colored shack was the name Cafe Turtle and Catfish. A placard in the window advised, "Warning: Guarded by Trained Attack Pit Bulls With AIDS." In the entryway just inside the creaky, wooden screen door loomed a stuffed black bear. Further inside were three clean, well-lit rooms with round tables and metal chairs. Further back was an airy hootenany hall with a bandstand. In each room, the walls, ceiling, and corners were crammed with Americana, with a strong southern accent.

Among the hundreds of items were Civil War brass knuckles; an autographed photo of Tennessee Ernie Ford; a certificate of sale for one slave, dated September 9, 1840; a Remember Pearl Harbor license plate; a ball and chain; three taxidermied tarantulas; a bear trap; a mole trap; an antique mouse trap; a life-sized wooden pig; photos of Gabby Hayes, Charles Chaplin, Gary Cooper, Laurel and Hardy, and Loretta Young; a walking stick fashioned from a bull's penis; a Texas Ranger's badge; a stuffed bobcat head; and an Abe Lincoln campaign button.

The menu included fried whole catfish, quail, frog legs, soft-shell turtle, fried rattlesnake, shark, alligator, and armadillo. A Dixie-raised diner judged the fare authentic and tasty. Missing only from a perfect evening was a touch of "the pastime." So the tattooed waitress, Anna Samarco, was asked if there were any baseball artifacts among the memorabilia. "I don't think so," she said after some thought. "But we did used to have a baseball player hang around here all the time."

Asked his name, she replied, "Ted Williams. He'd always come in and have my mother cook him up some softshell crab. He'd bring his own. Do you know if he's been sick? He's usually come in here by now, and we've been worried about him."

Diners from Boston assured her the Splinter was okay. He was just campaigning for presidential candidate George Bush and was expected the following week.

"Good," she said. "I'll tell my mother so she can stop worrying about him."

◆

On Saturday, March 19, 1927, Babe Ruth showed up at the Yankees' spring training camp in St. Petersburg decked out as follows: mauve-tinted knickers creased to a razor edge, cream colored socks with red bands, black and white shoes, a blue belt, a gray silk shirt, a baby blue tie, and a cream white sweater with a flared collar.

"What Hollywood can do to a man!" exclaimed Yankee business manager Ed Barrow as he eyed the Babe's getup.

"Huh," grunted Ruth. "You should see my Sunday clothes."

◆

During spring training in Florida one year, Braves shortstop Rabbit Maranville abducted a bellhop, locked the unfortunate lad in a room, and borrowed his uniform. Disguised in gobs of vaudeville makeup, Maranville delivered a telegram to the room of Braves manager George Stallings.

Ted Williams and Jackie Robinson

Maranville found Stallings soaking in a hot tub, handed him the wire, and lingered at the bathroom door.

"What are you standing there for?" said the manager, thoroughly duped by the disguise.

"Slip me a dime, you cheapskate," snarled Maranville.

Stallings bolted from the tub. Maranville bolted from the room and led his stark-naked manager on a long chase through the hotel's corridors.

◆

When he was in the navy, Boston general manager Lou Gorman spent time in Japan, so he knew well the Japanese respect for hospitality and proper manners. Just before the Chunichi Dragons visited Boston's spring training site at Winter Haven, Florida, in 1988, Gorman wanted to make sure he did all the right things. He telephoned the Dodgers, who headquartered the Japanese team, and asked if there were special preparations he should make. The Dodgers told him it wouldn't be a bad idea to play the Japanese national anthem before the game.

The search was on. "Looking for someone in Winter Haven, Florida, who can sing the Japanese national anthem is a major project," said Gorman. "We could only find a record. And it was just the music, without the words."

◆

In the spring of 1931, former Giants outfielder Turkey Mike Donlin dropped by his old team's Los Angeles training camp. Donlin craved attention but didn't get any. None of the young players had any idea who he was.

Soon someone from the team office came by to give Donlin a telephone message within earshot of the Giants. The message: the stickup is at two o'clock. Donlin checked his watch. "Gotta run, boys," he said with a sinister smile. The ballplayers stared in shocked silence.

What they didn't know was that Donlin was working as a bit actor in a gangster movie.

◆

On April 2, 1931, the Yankees were barnstorming north out of spring training camp when they stopped in Chattanooga, Tennessee, for an exhibition game against the Southern Association's Lookouts. Chattanooga righthander Clyde Barfoot, formerly of the Cardinals and Tigers, started against the Bombers. New York outfielder Earle Combs led off with a double, and shortstop Lyn Lary followed with a run-scoring single. Babe Ruth and Lou Gehrig were scheduled to follow.

Walter ("Rabbit") Maranville

Mike Donlin

Lookout manager Bert Niehoff strolled to the mound and signaled for a new pitcher. From the bullpen area in front of the right-field bleachers trotted a reliever: Jackie Mitchell, seventeen years old, a left-hander, and a girl.

The crowd of about four thousand cheered Mitchell as the Bambino stepped in to bat against the bambina. Ruth swung hard at the first pitch and missed. He swung harder at the second pitch and missed again. Ruth stepped out and demanded the home plate umpire examine the ball. The Babe stepped back in, watched the next pitch sail across the plate for called strike three, tossed his bat away in disgust, and stomped back to the dug-out.

Gehrig followed and missed three straight pitches. Second baseman Tony Lazzeri tried to bunt Mitchell's first pitch but missed, then took four straight balls for a walk. Done for the day, Mitchell trotted off the mound to a hearty ovation.

Later accounts claimed the girl's appearance and the strikeouts were well-orchestrated publicity stunts, but folks were still impressed. Opined the *New York Times'* editorial page two days later: "The prospect grows gloomier for misogynists."

◆

During spring training 1922, Washington coach Al Schacht accompanied Cuban-born Senators Jose Acosta and Ricardo Torres to a banquet in their honor, sponsored by Cuban community groups in Tampa. Seated next to the Spanish consul general at the head table, Schacht quickly realized he was the only dinner guest who didn't speak Spanish.

After-dinner speeches were entirely in Spanish. The only phrases Schacht could pick out were "Acosta, pitcher, Washington baseball team" and "Torres, catcher, Washington baseball team." They were followed by thunderous applause every time they were spoken.

Late in the program, Acosta leaned over and told Schacht to be ready to deliver a speech. Schacht told him he didn't speak Spanish, not even a little bit. Acosta insisted, "They'll want a speech." Fast-thinking and fun-loving, Schacht said okay, but told Acosta to introduce him as the general consul from Abyssinia.

When so introduced, Schacht stepped to the podium to polite applause and began his talk. "Eeeny, meeny, miney, brekey, coax, coax, coax," Schacht orated. He flung out his right hand and paused with great drama. "Acosta, pitcher, Washington baseball club." A loud ovation followed.

Encouraged, Schacht raised both hands to the chandelier. "Es lachelt ser see, er ledt zum bade, der knable schlief ein am grunen, Torres, catcher, Washington baseball team," he thundered. A louder ovation followed, as Schacht beamed at Torres.

"Dulce and decorum est dessipere in loco. Acosta, pitcher, Washington baseball club! Non ignara malio, Torres, catcher, Washington baseball club!" Schacht shouted, building to a crescendo. "Friends, Romans, countrymen, viva Acosta, Torres, baseball, and Erin Go Bragh!"

The crowd applauded, cheered wildly, and stood on the tables as Schacht left the podium.

◆

In January 1988 Red Sox relief pitcher Bob Stanley badly sliced his pitching hand when he fell on broken glass at his home. Two months later, he reported to spring training camp with the hand in a removable cast. He worked out but could not pitch.

Coming off the field one day at Chain O'Lakes Park, his cast in place, Stanley spied rookie catcher Tony DeFrancesco and coach Frank Malzone headed down the path toward the minor-league field, their backs turned to him. Stanley picked up a baseball and threw it left-handed at their feet. When DeFrancesco and Malzone spun around to see who the practical joker was, Stanley faked indignation. "Hey, it wasn't

Ted Williams (left) *and Al Schacht*

me," he protested, holding up his right hand enclosed in a cast. "I can't throw, remember?"

◆

During spring training in 1915, aviatrix Ruth Law flew her plane to the Brooklyn Dodgers' camp at Daytona Beach, and free rides were offered to the ballplayers. Seven years earlier, Senators catcher Gabby Street had caught a ball dropped from the Washington Monument, so the Dodgers wondered if anyone could catch a ball dropped from Law's airplane.

Brooklyn had a trainer named Kelly, a pal of Dodgers manager Uncle Wilbert Robinson, who had met him at a racetrack in Baltimore. "A trainer in those days was mostly a man who gave you rubdowns," said Casey Stengel, then a Dodgers outfielder. "And Kelly, no doubt, had experience at rubbing horses."

Dodgers pitcher Raleigh ("Redskin") Aitchison had recently been married, and

Aviatrix Ruth Law

ried the grapefruit away from the field and toward the bullpen, where Robinson was warming up a pitcher. "Look out," shouted the manager, waving all others away. "I got it."

He stuck up his glove, and the grapefruit glanced off the heel and thumped Uncle Wilbert squarely in the chest. "And he spun around and fell over, like in a Western picture where you see an Indian that's out on the hill and he goes down and turns in a circle and falls dead," said Stengel.

The Dodgers rushed to their fallen leader, then stopped and cringed. Robinson's face dripped with fleshy gore. They were certain the impact had exploded the manager's head. "The whole inside of the grapefruit had come out," said Stengel. "And parts of it were sticking to Robbie's face. When we saw it was a grapefruit, everybody commenced to laughing."

Robinson fired Kelly and harbored a lingering suspicion Stengel had something to do with the gag. "He didn't see any fun in a simpleton going up and throwing a grapefruit out," said Stengel. "Although, to tell you the truth, a baseball might have hurt him worse than a grapefruit did."

◆

his wife forbade his taking a ride in an airplane, free or not. Aitchison gave Kelly his place, with the provision that he drop a baseball from the plane as it passed over the practice field to see if anyone could catch it. In a great hurry to get to the plane and worried Uncle Wilbert would catch him away from his post, Kelly forgot to bring a baseball to the landing strip. Searching around, he snatched a grapefruit from a nearby tree and took it up with him instead.

The Dodgers were on the field when Law's plane droned overhead. As the players watched, Kelly tossed out the grapefruit. Everyone on the ground thought the black speck was a baseball. The wind car-

Uninvited dreamers often showed up at New York Giants' training camps. Often they were lousy ballplayers or a little crazy, and almost always they were as pesty as mosquitoes. Manager John McGraw knew how to sort out the fakers and dispose of them painlessly. He roomed them with pitcher Shufflin' Phil Douglas.

After one night in the same room with Douglas, the nonroster player would show up at practice eager to show his stuff. Douglas would come out to the ballpark late, with a couple of huge revolvers and a row of Bowie knives stuck in his belt.

"You're late for practice," McGraw would mutter.

John Quinn, George Kelly, and Casey Stengel (left to right)

"What the hell you got to say about it?" Douglas would growl, fingering his guns and knives. McGraw would back down.

No-talent prospects, certain they were rooming with a homicidal maniac, were forced to do some soul searching: was it worth getting murdered in their sleep for the sake of a workout with the Giants? Most fled town by nightfall.

◆

At the Phillies' camp in St. Petersburg in 1915, a scrawny, uninvited prospect arrived with a collection of odd-shaped, crooked bats. He had a line-drive bat of one shape, a sacrifice-fly bat of another shape, a spitball bat, and a curveball bat. Unsolicited, he explained the scientific theory behind each bat to his teammates.

One day manager Pat Moran dispatched the fellow to hit against Grover Cleveland Alexander in an intrasquad game. He failed to record even a foul tip. The bat man left camp that night, vowing to design a club with which to hit Old Alex, and was never heard from again.

◆

In spring 1949, former Dodgers infielder Fresco Thompson took over Brooklyn's spring training operation at Vero Beach, Florida. One day he escorted a group of baseball writers on a tour of the camp. "You may be interested to know that we're planning a big improvement," Thompson announced. "Now we have mechanical pitchers and mechanical ball retrievers. Next year we also plan to have mechanical batters." He paused. "Then," he said, "we'll be able to dispense entirely with the ballplayers."

◆

On March 21, 1930, the Yankees worked out at Crescent Lake Park in St. Petersburg, Florida. A blimp hovered, then began to slowly descend. When it landed in left field, grounds crewmen grabbed the tether ropes and guided the blimp to the pitcher's mound. The cabin door was thrown open and out stepped Yankees owner Col. Jacob Ruppert, followed by an aide carrying eight bats, which they delivered to slugger Babe Ruth.

◆

In the Red Sox clubhouse three hours before a June 1989 game, pitcher Wes Gardner ripped open a cardboard box the size of a washing machine in front of his locker. Staring from inside the box was the huge, snarling, stuffed and mounted head of a boar hog. Was this a *Godfather* remake? "I got it on an afternoon outing with the boys, in spring training," explained Gardner.

Accompanied by outfielder Mike Greenwell, pitcher Mike Boddicker, coach Al Bumbry, and outfielder Ellis Burks, Gardner was hunting on an island in Lake Kissimmee when he bagged the 245-pound beast. Cornered boar pigs are apparently a fearsome sight. "I've been hunting these things since I was a little kid," said Greenwell, who produced photographs of the expedition. "The one Wes got was one mean pig."

How mean?

"All I know," replied Greenwell, "is Al Bumbry and Ellis Burks were climbing up in a tree when Wes was shooting this thing."

Back from the taxidermist three months later, the thoroughly ugly head—the outline of a .45-caliber entrance wound still visible—was going home with Gardner after the game. Before he left, Gardner was asked what was Mrs. Gardner's reaction to this outdoorsy piece of decoration.

"I don't want to comment on that," admitted Gardner. "She don't know I have it yet. She'll find out when I carry it home."

◆

In pre-World War I days, big leaguers often dropped their bags at training camp and eagerly began to plan the spring's main event: the badger fight. Laboring like generals planning a spring offensive, they mapped out each phase meticulously. Veteran players huddled late into the night over the smallest detail. To many, the badger fight was as important as tuning up for the season.

Early in camp, huge signs appeared around town to advertise the fight. Posters were distributed. Within a week, the badger was paraded through town. The beast was even displayed in the lobby of the team hotel. Then the badger's opponent arrived: a vicious pit bull terrier, billed as the winner of nineteen straight badger battles. The badger was also adver-

tised as undefeated. Around the clubhouse, ballplayers breathlessly called it the fight of the decade.

Heavy betting began. In the saloon and around the hotel, players loudly argued the merits of the badger versus the pit bull. Excitement built to a fever pitch. On the big night, ballplayers, townspeople, and even folks from the countryside assembled at the site, usually a town hall. The arena was a large square covered with sawdust. Wagering increased. Arguments flared. Fights broke out. Then the crowd hushed as the animals were brought in.

Everything was set. The referee appeared and was loudly challenged by the crowd. More loud arguing ensued, and the referee was eventually disqualified. An objective man of integrity was needed to replace him. Someone piped up with a suggestion: how about a rookie ballplayer?

The overwhelmed rookie was pushed into the job. All he had to do, the veteran players instructed, was make sure the match was fair. He also had the honor of tugging on the rope suspended in the middle of the arena, which would ring the bell hung in the rafters to signal the start of the fight.

The rookie proudly took center stage. The crowd hushed. The rookie tugged the rope, which was actually attached to a huge bucket of water in the rafters, and was drenched by the cascade. The town hall erupted in prolonged, uproarious laughter. Afterward everybody headed to the saloon, congratulating themselves on another successful badger fight.

◆

On a warm evening at spring training in the late 1920s, four baseball men lounged on the porch of an old southern hotel. Yankees coach Charley O'Leary had his feet propped on the railing. Athletics pitcher Jack Quinn lolled deep in a saggy chair. Cubs manager Joe McCarthy rested his hand on the head of a sleeping hound dog. Senators coach Jack Onslow was perched on the railing. The southern night was still. Ice melted in a glass jug of water. An electric fan hummed.

"The pitcher's name was Gilks," O'Leary said lazily. "Bobby Gilks."

"That fellow you were just telling us about?" McCarthy asked, standing and stretching.

"Yeah," replied O'Leary. "Once he got two strikes on a man, he'd always put the third one on him. He would twitch at his blouse before he threw the one that would strike the man out. Sometimes the batter couldn't figure out just what it was that happened. Then the truth came out. Gilks had a big diamond pin he wore just inside the flap of his blouse. When he undid the top button, it was exposed. And he turned it in such a way it flashed in the batter's eyes."

The four men on the porch were silent for a moment. "What did he do when it was cloudy?" asked Onslow.

"Oh, of course, he had to have perfect conditions to put the trick over," said O'Leary. "Did it usually on the home grounds and noticed the position of the sun. That stuff wasn't exactly new with him. In the old days they had just one umpire, and naturally he couldn't watch everything. One club used to have a man on the sidelines with a little mirror. They got wise to him."

The hound dog groaned as he shifted his sleeping position, and the four baseball men were silent again. "There was Wade Killefer," McCarthy said suddenly. "It didn't take a mirror to bother him. He had a grouch against the people in the sign-boards. That was when he was playing for Joe Cantillon at Milwaukee. He was always saying the sign directly behind the pitcher got his goat, and the ball got all mixed up

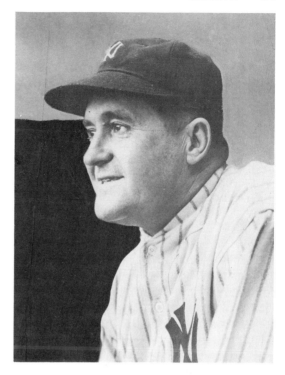

Joe McCarthy

in it. It was one of those collar ads. A boy with a marcel head and a lily face.

"Killefer got so mad at that sign, he said if he ever met a bird like that, he'd take it out on him. But the sign was paid for. And every time he came up to bat, he had to look at that sweet young thing. One night Killefer went out to the park with a flashlight and a can of paint. He found a ladder and painted that sign grass green. The sign stayed that way the rest of the season."

The four baseball men listened as Quinn told his version of how the scuffball was invented. "Bumped against a concrete wall, huh?" said Onslow. "Well, I never heard that one before. Yeah, Old Man Quinn remembers them all."

"Old Man Quinn," repeated Quinn, putting down his palm leaf fan. "I haven't been called that for fifteen years. It brings to mind that old man down in Louisville. I was pitching there in an exhibition game for the Red Sox, and for some reason the papers played me up. There was a lot of stuff about 'Old Man' Quinn. After the game, we had dressed and were coming out. An old man with a white beard stopped me. He said he had been reading in the papers about this 'Old Man' Quinn and had driven in from his place eight miles in the country, with his horse and buggy, just to see the old man pitch. He said he would like to meet him. When I told him I was Old Man Quinn, he could hardly believe me. I guess he expected to see a Civil War veteran."

McCarthy said that reminded him of a Kentucky hillbilly's first day at the Polo Grounds. "The rookie's reaction was, 'Grounds, hell! Them arn't no grounds. It's an opry house!'"

The three others chuckled. "Sounds like one of Sheriff Harris's remarks," began Onslow. "Harris had a healthy respect for umpires. Thought they were about as important as senators or judges. In Chicago, Cy Rigler was umpiring a game and he made a decision in Harris's favor that made the Sheriff think Cy was just about okay. We left the Wrigley ballpark and went downtown past the Wrigley Building. The Sheriff was thinking hard about something, and finally it came out.

"'Say, Jack,' he said. 'Doesn't it seem funny to you that a man who owns that big building and the ballpark and Lord only knows how many other pieces of property should go out there in the field and work and sweat, umpiring games every day?'"

The four baseball men laughed. The hound dog slept. The electric fan hummed. Soon, on the front porch in the still southern night during spring training, the baseball men were quiet again.

3

BETWEEN THE LINES

On an October afternoon in 1988, the telephone rang at the Pelham, New York, home of Bob Cremins. Nicknamed "Crooked Arm" in his day, Cremins pitched several seasons in the minor leagues and in 1927 appeared in four games for the Boston Red Sox. At age eighty-two, he still liked to tell anybody who was interested about the time he retired the great Babe Ruth.

"Hold on a minute," a voice said on the other end of the phone when Cremins picked up. "There's someone here who wants to talk to you."

Cremins heard the phone pass from one man to another. "This is Red Schilling," an elderly voice croaked into his ear. "Do you remember me?"

"Of course I do," Cremins shouted back. "You got a double off me in the New York–Penn League, and I still hate your guts for it."

Baseball is funny that way. A small moment in a minor-league game could rate a telephone call six decades later. A big moment in a big game could pop into a geriatric's mind a generation later, causing him to place the pillow over his head. Fans run into an ex-player in the supermarket checkout line in 1990 and vividly recall his line drive to right in an extra inning circa the Korean War. Some men will forget their names before they forget these moments.

The game issues lifetime memories without notice. In one instant a baseball game might plod along as routine, predictable, downright dull, and eminently forgettable. In the next instant, the game might jump up and slap something silly, funny, tragic, heroic, poignant, or sickening into the archives, and folks who were there will tell stories about it long, long after. Tweed-wearing observers like to think the game is a metaphor of life. Maybe an amendment is necessary: baseball games are metaphors of life on the subway.

On the field, ballplayers themselves are often unpredictable because the game rewards individual initiative and ingenuity. Baseball also leaves plenty of time for clever on-the-field conversation. Play-to-play, it is wonderfully unpredictable. The rules require players with round bats to try to hit round base-balls. The tightly sewn balls cross the plate at upwards of ninety-five miles per hour, or curving sharply at eighty-five miles per hour or knuckling softly on a puff of air. The hitter may give it direction; but, once hit, a baseball is likely to do anything its little cork heart desires. It may skip neatly along the ground and take an incredible last-minute hop; it may sail and twist in the wind; it may thump and carom crazily off an outfield wall; it may jam itself into a dometop speaker; it may stick itself into a hand-operated scoreboard; it may disappear inside somebody's uniform, as it did one otherwise routine day to Philadelphia Athletics shortstop Eddie Joost.

"Billy Goodman hit the ball," Red Sox coach Johnny Pesky recalled one afternoon in the summer of 1989. Tanned and fit at age sixty-nine, the former Boston shortstop was pulling on his red socks at his Fenway Park locker. "Joost had his shirt open, and it went right down the front." Relaxing in a clubhouse-issue plastic chair nearby, Red Sox scout Sam Mele leaned forward and squinted behind his black-rimmed eyeglasses.

"I thought it went down his sleeve," said Mele.

"No, down the front," Pesky insisted.

Mele relaxed again and began, "I remember a game when I was with Indi-anapolis and we were playing in St. Louis. They had just put all new sod in the infield. Then it rained a lot. Somebody bunted, and the pitcher came after the ball. When he stepped on the sod, a piece of it came up. The ball went in under-neath and the sod flopped back down on top of it. The pitcher couldn't find the ball. Base hit." Pesky spit tobacco juice into a paper cup, and both men laughed.

Infidels will never understand why goofy, great, or god-awful moments in a baseball game a generation ago come to mind clearer than this morning's break-fast. Even some ballplayers don't get it. On the last weekend of the 1987 season, Detroit and Toronto settled the American League East title head-to-head at Tiger Stadium. Amid the excitement, Detroit left-handed pitcher Frank Tanana said by way of perspective, "Hey, fifty years from now nobody will remember anything that happens here." Quick-thinking listeners would have taken Tanana on a bet. The prediction was wild and highly risky for any baseball game, be it amid a pennant race in Detroit or a sandlot series in Dushanbe.

Games usually assume instant distinction because of something quirky, dramatic, funny, or historic. On the morning of Tuesday, April 29, 1986, ticket holders throughout New England considered not going to Fenway Park that night. The ballpark would be cold, the lousy Seattle Mariners were in town, and the Celtics' playoff game was on television. The 13,414 who did show up watched Red Sox right-hander Roger Clemens strike out a record twenty Mariners, one of the most remarkable single-game pitching performances in hardball history.

Action at Yankee Stadium in 1946

On a hot night in the summer of 1990, Hall of Fame curator Ted Spencer motored home on the backroads of upstate New York, listening to the Red Sox–Twins game on the car radio. There was nothing special about the matchup. Minnesota was terrible, and the Red Sox were struggling. By the time he reached his house, Spencer was on the phone, arranging to get bats, balls, and gloves to commemorate the game in the Cooperstown museum. The Red Sox had grounded into two triple plays, a first in baseball history.

Cooperstown or an eighty-eight-year-old guy named Red could call at any moment. Sometimes they both call. On the night of May 23, 1963, the Kansas City Athletics engaged the Yankees in New York, and no one expected anything memorable, never mind anything immortal. With one out in the bottom of the fourth inning, switch-hitting center fielder Mickey Mantle batted left-handed against mediocre Kansas City righty Bill Fischer. On a one-ball, two-strike pitch, Mantle

Fenway Park, home of the Boston Red Sox

crushed an artillery shot into the Bronx night. The ball rode a magnificent trajectory and smacked hard against Yankee Stadium's upper deck facade, 108 feet and 1 inch above the outfield grass. It was the closest any fair ball ever came to leaving Babe Ruth's old ballpark. Mantle later called the blast "the hardest ball I ever hit." Slide rule specialists calculated the ball would have traveled 620 feet if it had not hit the roof.

A quarter century later, in the summer of 1988, the Boston Red Sox with pitching coach Bill Fischer visited the stadium to play the Yankees. A photograph of Mantle about to clobber Fischer's pitch was on the wall in New York manager Billy Martin's office. "I threw him four curveballs, then a fastball. He hit the fastball," said Fischer, smoking a cigarette in front of his locker cubicle. His rascally pitchers were always glad to recall the moment for him. For the team's 1988 yearbook, the Red Sox were asked to pick a moment in history they would like to travel back in time to witness. Some listed the birth of Christ; others, Lincoln's Gettysburg Address. Red Sox righty Jeff Sellers opted for Mantle's home run against Fischer. "I didn't put that in there," Sellers later protested. "Roger Clemens wrote that in for me."

Sellers was out on the bench, where a handful of early Boston arrivals were already in uniform. They chewed gum and tobacco, whacked fists into their mitts, and absently stared at the groundskeepers watering the infield under a brilliant blue sky. Someone let his gaze meander to right field, then follow up the mass of navy blue plastic seats to the top of the second deck, where the pre-reconstruction copper facade used to be.

"Hard to believe Mantle almost hit a ball out of here," someone said.

Shaken from his reverie, Red Sox reliever Bob Stanley popped his hand into his glove. "See that apartment building over there?" he asked, pointing to a brown brick building beyond the right-field bleachers that was barely visible behind the elevated subway tracks that run outside the ballpark. "There was a guy watching the game from the roof that day. When Mantle got up, the guy went inside to get his glove."

The Red Sox laughed about a pitch thrown when they were still in diapers. Some day when he is eighty-two years old, Fischer might get a call from Mantle, who will say, "Remember me?"

In the summer of 1896, John McGraw was playing third base for the Baltimore Orioles when he chased a foul pop near the grandstand. As the ball descended, McGraw quickly checked his proximity to the seats, and suddenly his head was covered by a blanket tossed by a fan in the front row.

Thirty-six years later at a train station in the summer of 1932, an elderly gentleman approached Giants manager McGraw. "I don't guess you remember me, Mr. McGraw," the man said with a wry smile. "You only saw me once, and that was only for a couple of seconds."

The white-haired manager eyed the fellow for a moment. "Sure I do," he said. "You're the fan who threw a blanket over my head and kept me from catching that fly ball in Pittsburgh in 1896."

Known as something of a weasel in his playing days, McGraw could certainly appreciate the tactic. Just one umpire worked each game in the 1890s, and McGraw loved to take advantage of the fact that no man could be in two places at once. For instance, when the umpire was occupied watching a play at the plate, McGraw liked to go from first to third by cutting directly across the diamond over the pitcher's mound. The opposition always protested loudly, but the umpire couldn't rule on what he hadn't seen.

While playing third base, McGraw had a trick he pulled when opposing runners tagged up and tried to score on fly balls. As the lone umpire turned his back to the infield to monitor the catch, McGraw would hook his fingers into the back of the baserunner's belt and firmly tug him backward. The lost step or two were usually enough to get the runner thrown out at the plate. When baserunners complained, McGraw was the picture of innocence.

One afternoon, Louisville outfielder Pete ("The Gladiator") Browning arrived safely at third with one out. When the next batter hit a long fly to left field, the umpire hurried out to watch the catch. Browning tagged and scored standing up. After he crossed the plate, he looked back at third base, yelped, and jubilantly called everyone's attention to the sight. McGraw stood near the bag, sheepishly holding Browning's belt in his right hand. Just before the pitch, Browning had unfastened the buckle.

Charley O'Leary, Charlie Grimm and John ("Red") Corridan (left to right)

◆

In the late afternoon of June 17, 1914, black thunderclouds plunged the ballpark in Pittsburgh into near darkness. The game went on, with the Giants and Pirates tied at 1–1 into the twenty-first inning.

In the top of the inning, New York scored twice. In the bottom of the inning, the Pirates placed two runners on base with two out, and the next batter cracked a high, twisty fly to deep right field. Although he could barely see the ball sail through the gloomy sky, Giants outfielder Red Murray angled back toward the wall. Near the fence, Murray saw the ball was going to drop just out of his reach. At the last moment, he leaped. Just then, lightning flickered and thunder cracked, the flash illuminating the entire field for an instant, and allowing all a clear, well-lit view of the ball as it smacked into Murray's outstretched glove.

As he clutched the ball and landed on his feet, Murray careened hard into the fence and brushed against a strand of wire

that had been temporarily electrified by the lightning strike. The shock knocked Murray cold. When his teammates got to him, they found the ball still tightly wedged in his glove.

◆

When he managed the Red Sox farm club in Lynchburg, Virginia, in the summer of 1988, Dick Berardino had a catcher named Paul Devlin who had appeared briefly in the hit baseball movie *Bull Durham.* In his scene, Devlin was batting, Kevin Costner was catching, and Tim Robbins was pitching in a game at Durham. To aggravate the big-headed Robbins, Costner tipped Devlin that the next pitch would be a fastball. Devlin hit a home run.

On June 10, 1988, the Lynchburg team was in Durham, North Carolina, to play the Bulls. That afternoon, Berardino took the team en masse to see *Bull Durham.* "We went to the two o'clock show, then out to the ballpark for the game," said Berardino.

On a hunch, Berardino put Devlin in the lineup that night. The first time up, Devlin stepped to the plate with the bases loaded. "He hit his first professional home run," said Berardino. "A grand slam, to the exact same spot in the ballpark he hit the home run in the movie. The same spot."

◆

During a game at Boston's South End Grounds in 1892, Hugh Duffy was playing center field for the Boston Beaneaters when Cleveland outfielder Jimmy McAleer slammed a long fly ball over his head. Just beyond center field at the South End ballpark was a neighborhood garbage dump. Duffy raced back to the edge of the garbage patch and leaped high, but the ball sailed just out of reach and clunked neatly into a rusty, upright tomato can.

As the crowd screamed at him to hurry a throw to the infield, where McAleer was rounding second, Duffy tried hard to yank, tug, and squeeze the ball out of the can. Then McAleer rounded third. With the crowd nearly hysterical, Duffy did what he had to do: he heaved the baseball-filled tomato can to relay man Billy Nash, who turned and fired to catcher Charlie Bennett, who planted the ball and the can on McAleer as he slid across the plate.

◆

Usually a second baseman, Brooklyn's Fresco Thompson was inserted at third base one afternoon against the Cardinals. Obeying instructions from Dodgers manager Uncle Wilbert Robinson, Thompson crept in on the grass when St. Louis slugger and vaunted righty pull-hitter Chick Hafey stepped to the plate. Hafey crushed a low line drive that cracked Thompson on the right shin, ricocheted, and cracked him on the left shin. By the

Fred Haney (left) *and Casey Stengel*

time Thompson stopped writhing and howling in pain, Hafey had reached second base.

The next time Hafey came to bat, Thompson retreated to the edge of the outfield grass. Hafey wisely bunted down the third-base line and easily beat out the base hit. At the end of the inning, Hafey returned to the Cardinals' dugout for a drink of water and was greeted by the Brooklyn batboy, who was holding an ice cream cone.

"Fresco Thompson says this is for the bunt, Mr. Hafey," the batboy said, handing over the treat. "What's more, he told me to tell you that from now on, every time you bunt while he's playing third, you get another one."

◆

In the summer of 1968, outfielder Howie Bedell, who was thirty-four years old, taught high school history during the day and played minor-league baseball for the Reading Phillies at night. One day when the team was in Elmira, Bedell, who hadn't played in the big league in six years, was summoned to manager Frank Lucchesi's office. Lucchesi told him the Phillies wanted him to join the big club right away in San Francisco.

"Frank told me as I was leaving that he wanted me to go out there and break Don Drysdale's streak," said Bedell. "It was just talk. Just kidding, of course."

Drysdale's streak was the talk of baseball. The Dodgers' tall right-hander had rolled through shutout after shutout and was closing in on Hall of Famer Walter Johnson's all-time record of fifty-six consecutive innings without allowing a run. On June 8, Bedell and the Phillies were at Los Angeles and Drysdale was on the mound. Opening the third inning, Philadelphia shortstop Roberto Pena grounded out and the crowd gave a standing ovation. At fifty-six and one-third consecutive

scoreless innings, Drysdale had broken Johnson's mark. The question was, when would it end?

In the fifth inning, Phillies third baseman Tony Taylor and catcher Clay Dalrymple singled. With one out, Taylor at third, and pitcher Larry Jackson due up, manager Gene Mauch told the lefty-hitting Bedell to get a bat. "I wasn't thinking about breaking Drysdale's record. I was just thinking about making contact," said Bedell.

He fouled off the first pitch, then sliced the second pitch down the left-field line. Los Angeles left fielder Len Gabrielson—Bedell's roommate in the Braves' system—gave chase. "He remembered I went that way a lot, so he was playing me toward the line," said Bedell. "He made a diving catch and fell flat on his stomach. He couldn't get up in time to make the throw and Taylor scored from third. It was my only RBI of the year."

Joe DiMaggio's hitting streak was stopped at fifty-six games by Indian pitchers Al Smith and Jim Bagby. Drysdale's scoreless streak was stopped at fifty-eight and two-thirds innings by pinch-hitting former high school teacher Howie Bedell. "When I came into the dugout, Bill White said to me, 'Howie, that's the best fly ball you'll ever hit,'" said Bedell.

◆

By the time he was twelve, Charley (later Casey) Stengel tagged along with his older brother, Grant, to play pickup games in Kansas City. When Casey pitched and Grant played shortstop, the brothers concocted a typically Stengelesque play. Before he took his position, Grant would stash a peeled, nicely rounded potato in his back pocket or in his waist above his belt. When an opposing runner reached second base and Grant took the return throw from the outfield, he would toss the potato instead of the base-

Clyde Wares, Rogers Hornsby, and Gabby Street (left to right)

from third sprinted toward the plate, Bresnahan produced the real ball and tagged him out. Williamsport, at the time a Class–AA affiliate of the Cleveland Indians, was not amused or impressed with his ingenuity, and the team gave Bresnahan his outright release. He was also fined fifty dollars.

An onslaught of national publicity followed. Virtually all sentiment was with the kid, who caught the fancy of baseball fans tired of watching the fun drain from their game. By the following May 30, Bresnahan was invited back to Williamsport, not to play but to participate in a ceremony retiring his uniform, number 59, in honor of the spud play. "He's probably the only .149 hitter in baseball to ever have his jersey retired," said Williamsport team spokesman Ken Weingartner. "Everybody knows about the guy who threw the potato in the minor leagues."

◆

ball back to Casey on the mound. When the runner stepped off second to take his lead, Grant would gleefully tag him with the ball.

"We pulled that one day in a game about twenty-five blocks from our neighborhood," Casey recalled sixty years later. "They started after us, everybody on that playground, and we had to run all the way home. So we cut the potato trick out. We didn't try that anymore on the other team's grounds."

◆

During an August 31, 1987, game against Reading, Williamsport Bills catcher Dave Bresnahan took his position with a peeled potato, about the size and shape of a baseball, stashed in his pocket. When a Reading runner reached third, Bresnahan staged a pickoff throw. He hopped to his feet and purposely heaved the potato into left field. As the runner

In Japan during the 1920s, Buddhism found itself in direct competition with Christianity. Trying hard to keep up with the racier Western ways of Christian missionaries, Buddhists adopted many of their rivals' methods, such as sermons, Sunday school, weekly prayer meetings, and athletics.

M.E. Hall, an American missionary in Kyoto, was shocked one spring day in 1921 when he received an invitation from the high priest of the Higashi Hongwanji temple. It proposed a baseball game on the temple grounds to pit the young Buddhist priests at the temple against the students and faculty of the missionary school. Hall was intrigued and immediately accepted.

On the day of the big game, Hall arrived at the temple and was slightly taken aback to see the high priest himself taking ground balls at shortstop. The rest of the Buddhist team were polite, athletic young men who wore white baseball caps on their shaved heads. "What a setting for a game it was," Hall recalled later. "Pilgrims had swarmed to the grounds to see the strange sight of a ball game at the temple, the temple bells ringing, the mumbling of prayers, and the temples themselves surrounding us. It was complete."

The Buddhists, who graciously allowed their visitors last licks, showed skill with the American game. The score was tied at 0–0 until the top of the ninth, when the Buddhists pushed across a run. In the bottom of the ninth, the missionaries placed runners at second and third with two out. A grounder was rapped to shortstop, and the ball squirted through the high priest's legs. The final score was Christians 2, Buddhists 1.

◆

A Boston Braves outfielder in the late 1800s and later a Red Sox coach, Hugh Duffy liked to tell the story of fellow Boston outfielder Tommy McCarthy and the slapstick triple play.

Playing the Braves in Boston, the Pirates put runners at first and second with none out. Pittsburgh catcher Bill Merritt lifted a fly ball to McCarthy in left field. McCarthy positioned himself under the ball, and both runners held. When McCarthy deliberately let the ball drop in front of him, chaos ensued.

When the runner at second saw the ball hit the ground, he broke for third. McCarthy gunned the ball to Boston second baseman Bobby Lowe, who tagged the Pittsburgh runner just a few steps off the bag. Meanwhile, the man at first had headed to second. Lowe wheeled, scampered to second, and tagged the runner as he slid into the base.

Having recorded two outs, Lowe stood in the baseline and held the ball in his hand. He didn't notice Merritt had run to first base after hitting the ball and—assuming McCarthy had made the routine catch—walked with his head down back to the Pittsburgh bench. McCarthy noticed. Racing in from right field, he snatched the ball from Lowe's hand and headed toward the enemy dugout. Merritt saw McCarthy closing in with a ball in his hand. Realizing he was a hunted man, he tried to escape, hopping over and around a couple of his teammates before falling over a pile of bats. McCarthy swooped in and applied the tag to complete the triple play.

◆

O n August 31, 1989, Red Sox second baseman Marty Barrett came down with a stiff neck during batting practice and was a late scratch from the starting lineup. Before the national anthem, replacement Jody Reed trotted out to take his position. Umpire John Shulock sidled over.

"What are you doing out here?" the umpire asked. "You're not supposed to be playing tonight."

Reed told him about Barrett's injury. "You know what?" Shulock said. "You're going to go four–for–four tonight and have a great night."

"Yeah, sure," said Reed.

In the first inning against the Angels, Reed dumped a single down the right field line. In the field at the start of the second inning, Reed approached Shulock. "You were kidding, weren't you?" he asked the umpire.

In the third inning, Reed doubled. In the fifth, he singled. In the seventh, he doubled and scored. In the top of the eighth, Reed checked in with swami Shulock. "If you get up a fifth time, I don't know what's going to happen to you," Shulock said. "I've never seen anyone go five–for–five." In the

Carl Hubbell (left) *and Bill Terry*

the seams. As the winning run scored, King tried to eat the baseball.

Once when he was in the Western Association, King was at the plate and behind in the count by two strikes when he stepped out of the box and pointed at the pitcher.

"I'm old John King," he announced. "Men walk around me like I was a swamp. I'm going to hit your next pitch and drive it into the next state. As I go around the bases, I'm going to undress all the infielders with my spikes. Then, if you're not already running, I'm going to chase you out of the ballpark."

King stepped back in and hefted his bat. The young pitcher gulped, shakily toed the rubber, and pitched. King swung, and missed.

◆

eighth, Reed stepped to the plate for his fifth appearance and walked.

◆

During a Southeastern League game one afternoon in the summer of 1916, Selma led Pensacola, 3–1, entering the bottom of the ninth. With two out, Pensacola loaded the bases. The count was full on the batter when he lifted a lazy, high fly ball to center field. Selma outfielder John King settled under the ball, ready to squeeze the game-ending out.

"Float on down here, little ball," King said to himself. "Old John King is waiting to catch you. Come on down."

The ball smacked into King's glove, squirted loose, and plopped onto the outfield grass. As the Pensacola baserunners hotfooted around the bases, King pounced wildly after the ball. His teammates shouted at him to throw to home plate. In frenzied anger, King ignored them, took the ball in his teeth and tore viciously at

Once when he managed Charleston, Joe Morgan watched his team botch seven consecutive rundowns. Nothing rankles a manager more than catching an opposing runner between bases, then allowing him to slip away. Morgan was rankled, sevenfold.

"So I said, 'That's enough of that,'" the Red Sox manager recalled. "We were in Syracuse and I got the field for an hour. We practiced nothing but rundowns. At all bases. In all situations."

Morgan's men devoted extra time practicing rundown plays at third. Hoping to cause balks, Syracuse runners had a habit of breaking toward the plate as the pitcher started his delivery. "So I told our pitchers if they got a guy at third, don't even bother looking in for the signs. Just put your foot on the rubber and get ready to throw over there as soon as that guy moves. Guaranteed we catch him off base," said Morgan.

That night, Syracuse placed a runner at third. As instructed, the Charleston pitcher toed the rubber and quickly fired the ball to third baseman Jose Martinez. Just as it had worked during morning practice, the Syracuse runner was caught off base and a rundown ensued.

During the back-and-forth chase between third and home, a throw hit the Syracuse baserunner in the back. As the ball rolled away, the run scored. Charleston had blown its eighth consecutive rundown. "I looked down the left-field line, and the groundskeepers were rolling around the ground in laughter," said Morgan. "They had been out there watching us practice those rundowns for an hour that morning."

◆

Hartford opened the 1931 baseball season with a game at New Haven. The visitors were ahead, 10–3, in the bottom of the ninth when New Haven erupted for an astonishing rally. New Haven scored with such rapidity that both teams lost track of the score. Finally a New Haven batter lined a hit against the outfield fence and several runners crossed the plate; both teams left the field thinking New Haven had won, 11–10.

Official scorekeepers knew better. Frantically recounting the runs as the teams clomped into the clubhouses, the statistics men confirmed their suspicion. The game was tied at 10–10.

Word was passed to the New Haven clubhouse, and the player who had been at first base hurriedly pulled on his uniform and scurried out to the field to try to score the eleventh run. Word was also passed to the Hartford clubhouse; and, when the New Haven runner reached the field, a Hartford fielder was waiting and applied the tag. But the game could not continue. No one could locate the umpires. The Hartford team showered, dressed, and started the journey home by bus.

Down the road, the team was headed off by a courier who ordered the players back

Lou Boudreau

to the ballpark. The umpires had returned, and New Haven was ready and waiting. The Hartford men changed back into their smelly uniforms and play resumed. The first Hartford pitcher walked the bases loaded before a reliever was summoned. He walked home the winning run.

◆

One afternoon circa 1950, Bob Feller and the Cleveland Indians led the Yankees by two runs late in the game when New York placed runners on first and second. After Gene Woodling stepped to the plate, Feller rang up two strikes, then unleashed a wild pitch. The runners advanced to second and third. Convention called for an intentional walk.

"But I hated to walk a guy with two strikes on him," Cleveland shortstop-manager Lou Boudreau recalled. "There was something I had been thinking about a long time but never had the guts to do."

After a conference on the mound that included Boudreau, Feller, and catcher Jim Hegan, Cleveland set up for an intentional walk. Feller threw ball two and ball three to Hegan, who stood with his mitt extended about three feet outside the strike zone.

Before the next pitch, Hegan tiptoed back behind home plate. Feller grooved a pitch, and the astonished Woodling was called out on strike three. "He chased me all the way to the dugout," said Boudreau, grinning about his masterstroke some four decades later. "I thought he was going to hit me over the head with his bat."

Bob Feller

◆

Because he was born in Chicago and still frequented Windy City taverns in the off-season, Tigers second baseman Germany Schaefer was a favorite at Comiskey Park. One afternoon in 1906, Detroit was in town, but Schaefer was out of the lineup because of an injured thumb, which he had damaged flipping the tops off beer bottles. The Chicago crowd moped.

In the top of the ninth, the Tigers trailed Chicago's Hitless Wonders, 2–1. Detroit shortstop Charley O'Leary led off with a scratch single. When Schaefer emerged from the dugout to pinch-hit for pitcher Red Donahue, the grandstand erupted with cheers and applause. Germany strode to the plate and with a sweep of his hand silenced the crowd.

"Laaaaaadies and gentlemen," he bellowed. "Permit me to present to you Herman Schaefer, the world's premier batsman, who will now give you a demonstration of his marvelous hitting powers."

The crowd liked Schaefer, but this was too much. They showered him with hisses and boos. Undaunted, he assumed his crouched stance at the plate and cracked Doc White's first pitch for a long, two-run home run. While the crowd gaped silently, Schaefer slid into first base, bounced up and announced, "At the quarter, Schaefer leads by a head!"

He slid into second base, dusted himself off, and shouted, "At the half, Schaefer leads by a length!" He slid into third and yelled, "Schaefer leads by a mile!" He dashed down the third-base line and slid hard into the plate at the feet of bewildered Chicago catcher Billy Sullivan.

Schaefer got up, carefully dusted off his uniform, and tipped his cap. "This, ladies and gentlemen, will conclude today's performance," he announced. "I thank you, one and all."

◆

On September 15, 1946, the second game of a Cubs–Dodgers double-header at Ebbets Field was stopped after five innings because of gnats. "They were all over the place," said Phil Cavarretta, who was stationed in center field for Chicago when the bugs arrived. "It was a hot, humid day. The ventilation wasn't too good. They got to be pretty thick out there."

When the swarm infested the ballpark, the Dodgers—close behind the first-place Cardinals—were leading, 2–0. The umpires gamely tried to allow the important contest to continue. Fielders flicked gloves at the bugs, and batters tried to see through them. Finally, the umpires called the game.

"They had to call it," said Cavarretta. "When you were at bat, instead of swinging at the ball you found yourself swinging at gnats."

Four decades later, Cavarretta remembered the day of the gnats well, but he didn't remember being surprised by it. "It was in Brooklyn. Anything could happen in Brooklyn," he said.

◆

When he was with the New York Giants, outfielder Heinie Mueller was notorious for having tried to break up a double play by leaping into the air between first and second bases to catch the relay throw in his mouth. When he joined the Boston Braves a few years later, Mueller showed he had maintained his famous baserunning style.

With a teammate on third base during a game in 1929, Mueller laid down a suicide squeeze bunt along the first-base line. As Mueller scurried up the line, Giants first baseman Bill Terry charged to scoop up the bunt. As Terry flashed near him, Mueller dived to the ground. Terry threw home to catch the runner trying to score from third. When the dust cleared at the plate, Mueller was still face down in the base line, covering his head as if he were a doughboy under artillery fire. The New York catcher strolled over and gently applied the tag.

Back on the bench, Braves manager Judge Emil Fuchs asked Mueller why on earth he stayed sprawled in the dust. "I didn't think they'd notice me there," Mueller answered.

◆

On June 20, 1989, Red Sox center-fielder Ellis Burks underwent arthroscopic surgery on his left shoulder. After healing, he reported to Boston's Triple–A team in Pawtucket, Rhode Island, to play himself back into shape. On the night of July 31, Burks collected one hit in five at-bats against the Mud Hens in Toledo. After the game, he received the go-ahead to report to the big club in Boston.

After only four hours' sleep, Burks was rousted from his motel bed by his 5:00 A.M. wakeup call. He hopped on a 6:15 shuttle bus to the Toledo airport and caught a 7:00 A.M. plane to Providence. When the flight arrived at 11:00 A.M., Burks found his truck in the airport parking lot and made the one-hour drive north to Boston, where the Red Sox were scheduled to play a doubleheader against the Orioles starting at 1:00 P.M.

When the bleary-eyed Burks walked into the Boston clubhouse, Red Sox manager Joe Morgan took one look and told him to stretch out and get some sleep during the first game. Morgan would use him in the nightcap. Burks dutifully hit the couch in the back office of team physician Dr.

Arthur Pappas and conked out. He slept while his mates dueled Baltimore.

Suddenly he was shaken awake by Morgan. The Orioles had a 3–2 lead in the sixth, and the manager needed someone with speed to pinch-run if slow-footed designated hitter Jim Rice reached base. Still half-asleep, Burks stumbled out of the doctor's office.

Rice doubled. Burks finished putting on his uniform jersey, stretched out, and trotted into his first big-league game in six weeks. The fans applauded as he made his way out to second base. The ovation helped to wake him up. The next batter, catcher Rick Cerone, popped a double down the left-field line, and Burks motored home with the tying run. The next inning, Burks batted with teammates at first and third and the score tied. He doubled home the winning run.

"The fans were behind me," said Burks afterward. "The best thing that could have happened was to get a hit. And I got a hit."

What more could he ask for? "Food," answered Burks. "And sleep."

◆

At a game in Chicago in the summer of 1888, a hometown batter unleashed a mighty swing but only dribbled the ball toward shortstop. In the late afternoon shadows, outfielders struggled to pick up the flight of the ball. When Giants outfielder Elmer Foster saw the big swing and the batter dash wildly for first base, he scanned the skies anxiously and spotted a dark object soaring over his head.

Using his famous speed, Foster turned and ran hard toward the fence. He heard the crowd hoot and holler as he gave chase. Near the wall, Foster produced a final spurt of speed, leaped, stuck out his glove, and made a splendid catch—of a startled English sparrow, whose immediate

goal in life had been to land on the outfield fence. The bird was set free.

Some dozen years later in Louisville, a similar avian victim of mistaken identity wasn't as lucky. St. Louis pitcher Ted Breitenstein mistook a foul tip for a line drive and speared a sparrow as it swooped innocently past the mound. Trying to double the runner off first base, Breitenstein frantically dug into his mitt to get the ball and instead produced something warm, feathery, and squashed between his fingers.

◆

On August 29, 1947, Birdie Tebbetts Night was held at Fenway Park. As part of the festivities, the Red Sox's combative catcher—acquired from the Tigers three months earlier—was honored by a contingent of fans from his hometown of Nashua, New Hampshire, before the game against the Philadelphia Athletics.

During the game, Tebbetts lined a hard shot foul into the rooftop box seats, where the ball struck Mary Driscoll, age sixty-three, in the face. The impact of the ball knocked her out of her chair. Carried to the ballpark first-aid station, she was then rushed by car to Carney Hospital, where she was treated for lacerations and contusions and held overnight.

Knowing the woman was hurt, Tebbetts was preoccupied through the rest of the game. He was still feeling sorry about the accident as he walked through Kenmore Square to his apartment across from the Hotel Kenmore.

When he got home, he found a case of whiskey sitting outside his apartment door. "It was a case of all the best stuff," Tebbetts, age seventy-eight, remembered one night at Fenway Park in 1988. "All mixed together."

Confused, he spotted a card, which read,

"From the Boston Retail Liquor Association, in Appreciation." Said Tebbetts: "I still didn't know what the hell it meant."

Next day, it all made sense. The woman Tebbetts had smacked in the face, Mary Driscoll, was chairman of the Boston Licensing Board, and she had been cracking down on local liquor establishments.

◆

On the morning of September 13, 1942, the wife of Cubs shortstop Lennie Merullo gave birth to a boy. That afternoon, Merullo took the field in Boston to play the Braves at Braves Field. He should have stayed home and passed around cigars. "I made four errors in one inning, which is the record," said Merullo. "Four errors in two balls. I booted a grounder and threw it wild. Then I booted a relay throw from the outfield and threw it over the catcher." Thus, on the first day of his life, Merullo's infant son got a nickname that stayed with him long into adulthood. "He has been known as Boots Merullo ever since," said Lennie.

◆

On May 16, 1953, the White Sox trailed the Yankees, 3–1, in the top of the ninth inning at Yankee Stadium. Chicago loaded the bases. With ex-Reds ace Ewell Blackwell on the mound, Vern Stephens was scheduled to bat. It was a proper moment for the Chicago third baseman: he had ten career grand slams.

White Sox manager Paul Richards called the startled Stephens back to the dugout and looked for a pinch hitter. Richards summoned pitcher Tommy Byrne from the bullpen.

"Have you ever hit against Blackwell?" Richards asked.

"Yeah," said Byrne. "Eleven years ago, when I was with Newark and he was with Syracuse. I had two–for–four against him."

"Good. Then why don't you go up there and hit one out of here," said Richards.

Byrne worked the count to 2–2. "I hadn't taken batting practice that day," Byrne recalled from his Wake Forest, North Carolina, home exactly thirty-six years later. "I usually did. But a couple of days before, I hit a line drive that someone caught. I got mad and said, 'I don't need batting practice.'"

When Blackwell delivered a fastball over the plate, left-hitting Byrne swatted it into the right-field porch for a home run. "Just one of those things. Richards had a hunch," said Byrne in the summer of 1989. "That win put us in first place. Not long after that, they traded me to Washington. From first place to last place."

◆

On May 15, 1894, some 3,500 spectators arrived at the South End Baseball Grounds in Boston for the National League engagement between the Boston Beaneaters, who were the forefathers of the Braves, and the Baltimore Orioles. Baltimore's stars included shortstop Hughie Jennings, third baseman John McGraw, right-fielder Wee Willie Keeler, and catcher Uncle Wilbert Robinson. Beaneater favorites were outfielder Hugh Duffy and pitcher Kid Nichols. The Boston partisans took their seats anxious to witness revenge. The previous day, the Orioles had thrashed the home team, 16–5.

The ballpark, a magnificent Victorian structure with four majestic spires atop the grandstand, was situated near the current site of Northeastern University. The right-field bleachers had been recently refurbished, and piles of scrap planks and wood chips had been left behind by the construction workers. In the third inning, youngsters playing underneath the stands set a match to a wood pile. Bleacherites

South End Baseball Grounds in Boston

soon felt their seats turn hot. A policeman discovered the fire and tried to damper it by pulling apart the burning pile of boards.

The Orioles and Beaneaters noticed the right field commotion, then saw bright yellow flames poke through the bleachers. The game stopped. Annoyed grandstand patrons shouted, "Play ball!" Those who evacuated the twenty-five-cent seat section ran onto the field. They did not leave the park, lest they not be readmitted when the game resumed. Ballplayers rushed to right field to help fight the fire, but they were driven back by the heat.

As the wooden bleachers crackled and blazed, strong winds floated embers into the grandstand and throughout the surrounding tenement neighborhood. Ballplayers scrambled to the clubhouses to retrieve their belongings, and within fifteen minutes the grandstand was consumed. Gathered in the outfield as the fire spread across Tremont Street toward Roxbury Crossing, the crowd watched the magnificent towers flame and topple. Before the night ended, twelve acres in the

South End were burned. Left standing was a forest of chimneys amid smoldering rubble. Miraculously, no one was killed. In all, the fire destroyed 164 wooden homes, 18 brick homes, and 1 wooden ballpark.

◆

After getting tagged out on the basepaths in a game circa 1942, Boston Braves outfielder Max West made his way back to the dugout. As he passed behind home plate, a wild pitch soared over the catcher's head, and a Braves runner rumbled down the third-base line trying to score. The ball rolled at West's feet. He absent-mindedly picked it up and tossed it to the catcher, who tagged out the stunned Braves runner.

Back on the bench, West's outraged teammates showered him with invective. Not saying a word, West bent over the dugout water cooler to get a drink. At bat for the Braves, Paul Waner sliced a hard foul into the dugout. The ball cracked West in the mouth.

◆

Dazzy Vance, zany Brooklyn righthander in the 1930s and 1940s, was pitching in a semipro game in Hastings, Nebraska, one day when he walked a batter. As Vance prepared to pitch to the next hitter, the runner on first took off for second. "I whirled around to throw," Vance later recalled, "but the second baseman was slow to cover the bag and I had to wait a little. Naturally when I did throw, I cut loose with everything I had."

Vance saw the second baseman stick up his glove to snare the throw just as the baserunner arrived. The ball bounced thirty feet into the air. *What's that guy wearing, a rubber glove?* Vance said to himself. After the inning ended, Vance approached his young second baseman.

"Say, kid," he said. "What kind of glove are you using? I never saw a ball bounce like that."

The young man grinned. "Hell," he said. "That ball didn't hit my glove. It bounced off my forehead."

◆

During a game in 1907, Larry MacPhail went to bat for Beloit College with two outs in the ninth, runners at second and third, and Beloit trailing Sacred Heart, 2–1. The count reached two balls and two strikes. The pitcher wound up, and MacPhail tensed at the plate. The Sacred Heart catcher, Reindeer Bill Killefer, squirted a stream of tobacco juice into MacPhail's eye.

"The stuff blinded me," MacPhail recalled. "And a fastball right down the middle of the plate went by for strike three and the ball game. Killefer ducked out before I could see straight. Lucky for him, or I would have brained him with the bat."

Thirty years later, MacPhail was president of the Brooklyn Dodgers. After thirteen years playing and nine years managing, Killefer was out of work. "Killefer was without a doubt the dirtiest ballplayer who ever lived," said MacPhail when his name came up. He hired Killefer to coach the Dodgers.

◆

In the spring of 1917, the Tigers shipped outfielder Bing Miller to the minor league team in Chattanooga, Tennessee. Before starting its season, Chattanooga played an exhibition game against the Washington Senators, who were barnstorming their way north for opening day.

In his first at-bat, Miller singled against Washington great Walter Johnson. The next inning, Miller was on the bench when a messenger boy came through calling his

Honus Wagner

◆

One Friday night in the summer of 1989, Yankees catcher Don Slaught was bowled over on two plays at the plate in the same inning. Around the batting cage the next morning, home plate collisions were the topic of conversation, and Red Sox manager Joe Morgan was asked if he had ever seen two baserunners barrel into home plate at the same time.

"Yes, I have," said Morgan. "In fact, I was involved in one." Morgan was playing for the Atlanta Crackers in a home game against Nashville. "Dick Phillips was on second base," said Morgan. "I was on first. Neither of us had any speed. Dutch Dotterer was the catcher. Joe Schultz was the third-base coach. Somebody, I can't remember who, hit a long, long fly ball to center field."

Waiting to see if the ball would be caught, Phillips held up a few feet off second base. Morgan held up a few feet behind second base. The ball dropped in, and Phillips began to run, with Morgan close on his heels.

They arrived at third base just a few feet apart. Schultz barked his instructions clearly: "Phillips, you go. Morgan, you stay." But Morgan had a different assessment. *If Phillips can make it, so can I,* Morgan thought to himself. *I'm only about a step-and-a-half behind him.*

Phillips slid into home plate, and Morgan slid in right behind him. "Phillips was tagged out one way, and I was tagged out the other," said Morgan, finishing the story at the batting cage. "And the next day in the paper, Dutch said he looked to see if anybody else was coming."

◆

name. There was a telegram for him. "I figured the news got around pretty fast that I had made a hit off Johnson and this was a telegram of best wishes and congratulations," said Miller.

Miller tore open the envelope. The message: he was drafted.

◆

Before a Giants–Pirates game in May 1935, a pair of high school players visited the Polo Grounds to take batting practice, shag flies, and possibly leave a good impression with the Pittsburgh coaches. After the workout, the sweaty boys found themselves seated in the dugout next to the former Pirates great Honus Wagner. They listened closely as the weathered old man began to spin a story.

"It was in Waynesburg, Pennsylvania," began Wagner, gazing out at the field as he spoke. "A couple of teams were playing for the county championship or something, and I was hired for the day. Well, of course, the team that had me would win easily. So I played for both sides. I pitched for both sides, in fact."

The boys were enraptured. "Well, I'm in pretty good pitchin' form," Wagner continued. "So we go thirty-six innings to a tie, 0–0, and then the visiting team gets two runs. Looks like curtains. Then the home team comes up and gets three on with one out.

"The batter hits a high one over the left-field fence. But wait. There's a railroad track there and a freight engine is coming along: choo-CHOO-choo. The ball goes down the smokestack as the engine goes choo. It blows the ball back over the fence when it goes CHOO. The left fielder is running out fast. He spears the ball with his gloved hand, but runs his hand—glove, ball, and all—through the fence and can't get it loose. So the three runners score and the home team wins, 3–2. It was a triple sacrifice fly and the longest one I ever hit in my life."

The boys were silent in thought. Finally one of them spoke. "Didn't you say you pitched for both sides, Mr. Wagner?"

"You run inside and go take a shower. And don't ask so many questions," said Wagner, picking up a fungo bat.

4

PLANES, TRAINS, AND AUTOMOBILES

Forty-four years later, New York Giants manager and legend John McGraw could remember every detail. He was still just a boy, riding in the smoker of a train that clackety-clacked across the landscape outside Truxton, New York. Two middle-aged gentlemen in the car with him puffed harder on their big, black cigars as their argument grew more spirited. It was the summer of 1888, when men enjoyed a good smoke and a lively debate.

"Don't tell me a baseball can be made to curve," said the skeptical middle-aged man. "All newspaper talk."

"I'm telling you, I saw it with my own eyes," said the other.

A third passenger piped up. "No argument there," he said. "I've seen it myself, right in Truxton where I live." He pointed to the skinny, teenaged McGraw seated nearby. "That little fellow right there can pitch a curve."

As the train rocked on the tracks, the two middle-aged men leaned forward to eye the boy. He was not quite sixteen years old and weighed just barely one hundred pounds. "Bet you ten dollars he can't," said the skeptic. "At least he can't prove it to me."

"Go ahead and bet him," said McGraw. "I'll take a dollar of it myself."

The argument continued. Finally the challenge was accepted and the money was collected. The conductor stopped in the aisle to join the wager. "Certainly it can be done," he said, handing over his cash. He put a hand on McGraw's shoulder. "Figure out a way to prove it, Johnny, and I'll hold the train."

"Wait till we get to the next town," said McGraw. "I'll stick three stakes in the ground twenty feet apart and in a straight line. Then I'll stand at one end and put the catcher at the other. I'll start the ball from the left side of the stake on my

John McGraw (left) *and Dave Bancroft*

end, make it pass to the right of the middle stake, and the catcher will catch it on the left side of the stake at his end. That would be a curve, wouldn't it?"

The skeptical middle-aged man agreed. "And I'm betting this man ten dollars you can't do it," he said.

"I've got the tools right here," answered McGraw. He slipped a glove and ball from his travel bag.

"I'll do the catching for you," volunteered a passenger.

"We'll settle it at the next stop," said the conductor, holding himself steady in the aisle.

At a dusty vacant lot near a small railroad station in upstate New York, a small crowd gathered as young McGraw hammered three stakes into the ground. "Let me know when you're ready," said the catcher.

"I'm ready," answered McGraw.

He wound up and threw. As promised, the ball snaked to the right of the middle stake and to the left of the far stake, where it thumped into the catcher's mitt. The crowd applauded.

"That proves it all right," said the skeptical middle-aged man, as the crowd trooped back to the train. "Can't beat a man at his own game." He handed ten dollars to his opponent, who handed two of the dollars to skinny young McGraw.

White-haired and thick-bodied when he told the story in 1932, McGraw laughed like a teenaged boy as he finished. "Since that day, it seems that I've been riding railroad trains all my life," he said. "I'm just as keen for the game and get just as big a kick out of it as I did forty years ago. The thing that palls on me, though, is the traveling."

From past to present, baseball men have never liked to travel. The old-time trains were hot and took forever to get from New York to Chicago. Modern-day jetliners are air conditioned, but often take forever to get from New York to Chicago. When a gate is blocked, or planes are stacked high, or the airport is fogged in, or the plane is 214th in line for takeoff, big leaguers have to wait like everyone else. Not even an autographed ball can help them. Somebody else makes their reservations and carries their luggage, but traveling forty to a party also has drawbacks. Like old-style Christmas lights, if one goes out they all go out; if one charter reservation is botched, they all wait while the traveling secretary hassles with the gate attendant.

The pace is not leisurely. They play night games, catch night flights, and watch janitors vacuum the airport while they wait for their luggage at 3:00 A.M. Long train rides were boring, but at least old-timers could walk around, stretch, look at the scenery, dine at tables covered with linen, and pull up covers in a sleeper. Jet-set ballplayers sit up with seatbelts fastened, read the same in-flight magazine twenty-one straight times, eat meals wrapped in plastic, and stare at white clouds.

Baseball men have always hated to travel, but they have always loved to tell travel stories. Anybody in the game for more than two seasons, big leagues or bush leagues, usually has a good one. Retirees tell the best. Seat a bunch of them together, and they'll try to one-better each other. When a career's worth of traveling is boiled down, tedium and monotony are forgotten and the stuff of wonderful tales—poignancy, hijinks, laughable mishaps, and stone-cold fear—lingers forever. Like aging war heroes, crinkled ballplayers even remember tales of life and death with wistfulness.

The Cincinnati Red Stockings took a western tour in the summer of 1869 and were nearly frightened out of their red stockings when their train was threatened by Indian attacks. They breathlessly told stories about it well into the next century. As he settled into a box seat to watch Cincinnati engage the White Sox in the 1919 World Series, ex-Red Stockings shortstop George Wright, age seventy-two, enraptured whippersnappers with details of the 1869 trip, such as how the ballplayers slept with pistols under their pillows.

Everyone has a favorite travel story from hell, and everyone is convinced his is the most hellish. Rankings are unofficial, but among the worst in baseball history was Phillies outfielder Eddie Delahanty's trip in 1903, when a conductor put him off the train near Niagara Falls for drunkenness. Unsteady Eddie wandered down the tracks, fell through a drawbridge, and was swept over the falls to his death. Ex-Tiger pitcher Wild Bill Donovan's train trip to the 1923 winter meetings was close: he was killed when his train crashed in upstate New York.

Over the years, nonfatal tough trips get easy to talk about. In the summer of 1990, former slugger Johnny Mize recalled hot summer Sundays in the mid 1930s when he and his Cardinal mates walked from Crosley Field to board Pullman cars that had baked all day in the train yard. Once underway, "We stripped down to our underwear, opened the window, and tried to catch a little breeze," said the Big Cat. Over the years, tough trips can get downright funny. More than forty years later, former Red Sox pitcher Boo Ferriss could chuckle about the tray of steaks, potatoes, vegetables, and desserts that cascaded over his head when the train he was riding from Boston to New York lurched and upended a waiter in the aisle.

Trauma makes the best tales, but not all the memories are of mishaps and misery. Some travel stories are random snapshots that for one reason or another stuck to a player's soul, such as the teenaged McGraw's curve-ball challenge. Lennie Merullo, Cubs shortstop in the 1940s and long-time big-league scout, relished his train rides with washed-up, but still popular, pitcher Dizzy Dean in the Texas League in 1940. "We ate well because of him," said Merullo. "We'd get on

Johnny Mize

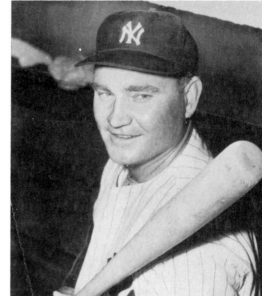

the train, and the people from town would put on bushels of chicken and watermelon. They wanted ol' Diz and his teammates to have it."

Trains were also a great place to tell stories. Not surprisingly, the subject often was travel. Aboard the Yankees' comfortable team train as it cannonballed to Chicago in the summer of 1939, manager Joe McCarthy told about trips with Louisville in the primitive 1920s. "We'd get to Chicago in the morning and hustle over to catch the train for Milwaukee," he said. "Our suits would be soggy with perspiration and filthy with dirt. What we did was hang them out the train window, clamp the window down hard, and dry them that way. Used to scare the farmers along the way half to death, those sleeves and shirttails flapping along in the wind at fifty miles per hour."

Trains seem charming in retrospect, especially as airline travel grows more impersonal and cruel. The nostalgic view makes riding the rails seem as much fun as a pajama party. Any Three Stooges aficionado knows Pullman cars can be a blast. Long rides meant plenty of camaraderie, card playing, boozing, and practical joking, such as secretly taking bites out of a teammate's straw hat.

One night soon after he was appointed manager of the Chicago Cubs, notorious rollicker Rabbit Maranville walked the aisles in the sleeper cars, pouring ice water into the berths of his snoozing players. "No sleeping under Maranville's management," he told his victims. "Especially at night."

After winning the 1928 World Series in St. Louis, the Yankees' train trip back to New York was classic whistle-stop champagning. Most men who were on the train that night remembered the trip long after their playing, partying, and even walking days were over. The twenty million other dull rail miles of their careers faded like locomotive smoke.

Former Cleveland shortstop-manager Lou Boudreau was in Boston in the spring of 1989, and he happily recalled what happened after his Indians won the World Series there against the Braves in 1948. "We had our celebration on the train to Cleveland," he said. "Bill Veeck had champagne and food for us. I remember a lot of food ended up on the ceiling." Boudreau was seventy years old when he told the story, but he was grinning like a boy with a slingshot.

When he was a teenager in Sayreville, New Jersey, in the early 1930s, Eddie Popowski worked on an ice wagon and played semipro baseball. One day the barnstorming House of David team came to town, saw his stuff, and signed him. Popowski gladly hit the road. "I was making $18 a week on the ice wagon," he said. "The House of David paid $175 a month."

Not easy money. Besides requiring players to grow full beards, the House of David demanded stamina. "We played four games a day, 256 games a year," said Popowski, later a minor-league manager and Red Sox coach. The grueling schedule called for hectic travel, always by car, often at high speeds, and customarily in the dead of night.

One summer night in 1931, Popowski and a group of teammates were crammed in a touring car as it motored through the Ohio countryside. About one o'clock, after roaring through a dark, sleeping town, they were pulled over on a quiet stretch of highway by a dozen excited, nervous state troopers.

The ballplayers immediately knew they were suspects for crimes more serious than speeding. "They made us get out of the car with our hands up," said Popowski. "They had spotlights on us. They had machine guns. Scared the hell out of us. One of our guys, a kid from Brooklyn, was so nervous he reached for a cigarette. They thought he was reaching for a gun and they almost shot him."

Certain the bearded players wore disguises, a trooper tugged and tugged at one set of whiskers, dragging the ballplayer around in the darkness until he drew blood. Other officers ordered the players at gunpoint to unpack all the baseball equipment and spread the uniforms, bats, balls, gloves, catcher's masks, and chest protectors along the highway. "After a while, they just turned off their spotlights, backed off, and drove away," said Popowski. "Just left us picking up our gear on the highway." The shaken ballplayers later found out the reason for the fuss. Popowski and his pals were traveling in a Lincoln sedan. Spotted that night in the area, also in a Lincoln sedan, were public enemy John Dillinger and his gang.

Eddie Popowski

◆

On September 16, 1935, the Dodgers dropped a game, 1–0, to the Cardinals in St. Louis. Afterward, Brooklyn manager Casey Stengel dispatched slumping and troublemaking outfielder Len Koenecke, who had batted .320 the previous season, and pitchers Les Munns and Bobby Barr back to Brooklyn. The trio boarded an American Airlines flight to New York.

Not long after departure from St. Louis, the twenty-nine-year-old Koenecke, who was well down the road to intoxication when he got on the plane, became belligerent and disorderly. During a scheduled stop in Detroit, he was refunded the balance of his ticket and banned by the airline. Koenecke decided to get home on his own. He drank some more, then chartered a small private plane to take him to Buffalo, where he hoped to catch a train to New York.

Midway through the chartered flight, the ballplayer became restless. "Koenecke was sitting up front with me," pilot William Joseph Mulqueeney said later. "For no particular reason, he started to rock toward me and nudge me with his shoulder. I told him to cut it out, that horseplay in a plane was dangerous. But he kept it up." Mulqueeney ordered Koenecke out of the cockpit. He told the ballplayer to join co-pilot Irwin Davis in the rear cabin. Koenecke complied.

Shortly thereafter, Mulqueeney heard a great commotion in the rear cabin. He looked back and saw Koenecke punching and biting Davis. The pair grappled and wrestled heavily on the floor, dangerously rocking the small plane. With one hand on the controls, Mulqueeney reached back through the cockpit door to try to get a hand on Koenecke. Davis struggled free, picked up a fire extinguisher, and heaved it at Koenecke, but the ballplayer deflected it to the cabin floor. As the plane jerked and dived out of control, Mulqueeney grabbed the fire extinguisher and swung it at Koenecke, but hit Davis instead. The pilot swung again and hit Koenecke in the head. Koenecke stayed on his feet. Mulqueeney hit him again. Koenecke still lunged toward the pilot. Mulqueeney bashed him in the head once more, knocking him out.

The pilot regained control of the plane and made a forced landing on Long Branch Racetrack in Toronto. Authorities raced to the scene and found one slightly damaged plane, two shaken aviators, a blood-splattered cabin, and one dead Brooklyn Dodger. The pilot and co-pilot were held in a Toronto jail pending manslaughter charges, but three days later a coroner ruled they had acted in self-defense and released them.

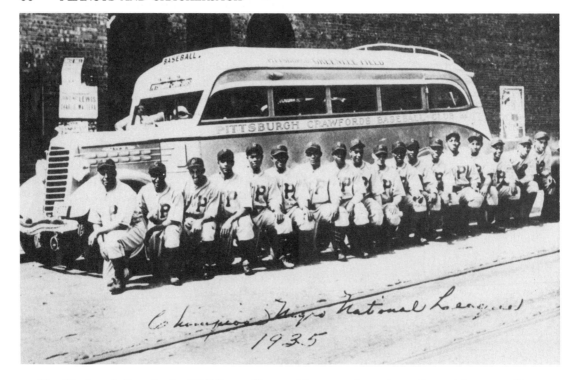

The Pittsburgh Crawfords, 1935 Negro National League champions. One of the great Negro League teams, it included five future Hall of Fame players: Oscar Charleston, Judy Johnson, Cool Papa Bell, Josh Gibson, and Satchel Paige.

◆

After sweeping the Cardinals in the 1928 World Series, the Yankees jubilantly rattled home on a train from St. Louis to New York. By the time they reached Terre Haute, Indiana, in the middle of the night, the Yankees were half-dressed and full of beer. A throng of fans gathered at the station stop, and a small rally developed.

One man climbed a baggage truck and called for cheers. "Three for Babe Ruth!" the man hollered. The crowd responded with three enthusiastic hoorays. Ruth gazed approvingly from the rear platform. Having consumed his share of brew, the

Babe lifted a mug of beer in one hand and a pig's knuckle in the other and called for silence. The presidential campaign was in its final month, and Ruth wanted to plug his candidate, New York Gov. Al Smith.

"How about giving my pal, Al Smith, the next president of the U.S.A., a big hand," shouted the Babe. "Ready, now. One, two, three . . ."

There was silence. Witnesses said they could hear the wind rustle through the apple trees. Indiana was staunch Herbert Hoover territory. Ruth stood stunned amid the quiet, beer mug and pig's knuckle still raised. "To hell with you, if that's the sort of mugs you are," he finally growled and pushed his way back into the train.

Babe and Claire Ruth

◆

Long-time National League umpire Bob Hart liked to tell the story about a colleague who worked one summer shortly after World War I in the bush leagues somewhere in the Deep South. After a particularly rough and controversial game, the umpire had to travel to the next town that night on the same train as the players. All through the journey, the umpire grew increasingly disgusted with the ballplayers' pettiness, complaining, and general insistence on preferential treatment.

When they reached their destination, the players got off the train, lined up to accept their baggage, and readied for the hike to the team hotel. The umpire stepped down off the train and was greeted by a man who spoke with a thick southern accent. "Empiah, suh?" the man said. The umpire nodded and said, "Why, yes, I am." The man took his baggage, loaded it into a car, and motioned the umpire into the back seat.

The players down this way may be unreasonable, the umpire thought to himself as he climbed into the vehicle, *but the magnates sure treat an umpire great.* As the car motored past the players hauling their luggage down the road, the umpire couldn't resist. He gave them a loud, mocking horse laugh.

After riding about three miles, and apparently journeying farther and farther from downtown, the umpire decided he should ask exactly where the driver was taking him. The umpire thought perhaps some wealthy baseball fan who lived on the outskirts of town was going to entertain him for the night. "Where are we headed?" he asked.

"This heah bus only goes but one place, suh," the driver said, "To Empiah, the next town ovah."

Luggage in hand, the umpire walked the three miles back to his hotel.

O n July 4, 1937, the Red Sox and Athletics played an afternoon game at Fenway Park. Both teams boarded late trains that night departing from South Station.

Boston infielders Eric McNair and Oscar Melillo settled down for the overnight trip south. As the train roared down the tracks, they noticed a couple of Athletics in the next compartment. They figured the Red Sox must have engineered some sort of trade with Philadelphia after the game.

Soon McNair and Melillo noticed more and more Athletics in the compartments and corridors, and it dawned on them: they were on the Athletics' train. They got off in Providence and waited on the platform for the Red Sox express to catch up with them.

♦

W hen he was in the Army Air Corps during World War II, Matt Batts— later a catcher with the Red Sox, Tigers, Reds, Browns, and White Sox—was stationed at Randolph Field, Texas. One afternoon, Batts and the rest of the squadron baseball team piled into a dilapidated B–24 to fly to their game in Enid, Oklahoma. The flight had no movie, no meal, and no stewardesses, but each man was grateful to get a parachute.

"The pilot told us if we heard that buzzer go off, we sure better get out of there because that meant he was getting out of there," said Batts. "He said that old plane was a real piece of junk."

Once airborne, the pilot decided to give his passengers in-flight entertainment. He pushed the creaky old bomber into a power dive. The ballplayers pitched and

Zack Taylor, Ned Garver, and Matt Batts
(left to right)

tumbled forward, heaping against the bomb-bay door, which creaked open a crack and threatened to dump the lot of them. One man's parachute popped open, spreading a tangle of silk and lines over the pile of ballplayers. Up front, the pilot struggled desperately to pull the crate out of the dive. "The plane was so old, he almost didn't make it," said Batts.

The wobbly-kneed ballplayers landed in Enid, played the game, then boarded the old bomber for the journey home. The return flight progressed uneventfully, to the delight of the already over-stimulated passengers. The ballplayers relaxed and dozed as the bomber droned into the summer night.

Suddenly the harsh sound of the dreaded buzzer filled the compartment. It was the signal to jump; the plane was in trouble. "The lieutenant ordered us to jump in alphabetical order," said Batts. "That meant Tex Aulds, who later caught for the Red Sox, was going first. And I was going second. But there was no way I was jumping out of that plane."

The ballplayers pulled open the underbelly hatch. Wind whistled in. Just then, the crew chief wandered back from the cockpit, saw the open hatch, and nearly took a bite out of the bulkhead. "*What* are you doing?" he hollered.

The ballplayers explained they were bailing out, as instructed by the buzzer. "Oh, my God!" sputtered the chief. "That wasn't the buzzer to jump. That was just us getting the radio beacon from the base in Randolph. Now *shut* that damn door!" The ballplayers happily complied.

"It's a good thing he came back there when he did," said Batts. "We all would have been floating around, somewhere over Waco, Texas."

Certain he had experienced enough stunt flying for a lifetime, after he was discharged from the Air Corps Batts promised himself he would never again set foot in an airplane. He kept his vow for seven years. Then Batts was with the Detroit Tigers in Washington, concluding a three-week road trip. The team gave the boys a rare treat in the train-travel era. Arrangements were made to fly them home.

Although trembling at the thought of being airborne again, Batts badly wanted to get home, so he forced himself to go to the airport. "When we got there, the worst, most violent thunder and lightning and rainstorm you ever saw rolled in," said Batts. "It was terrible. Our flight was the only one they were going to allow to fly out." His buddies on the team—Virgil Trucks, Dizzy Trout, Hal Newhouser, and Bob Swift—knew about his fear of flying and did their best to comfort him.

"The plane is going to crash and kill us all," said one.

"Matt," said another. "Don't you think this storm is God's way of telling us not to get on this plane?"

Batts bravely ignored his mates and walked across the rainswept tarmac to the airplane. "Crash and kill us all," a teammate repeated solemnly. Batts placed his foot on the bottom step of the stairway. He was going to do it. He was going to do it. He couldn't do it. He turned around and

scurried back to the safety of the terminal.

Later in the day, Batts caught a bus, rode all night and all the next day, and finally reached Detroit after a thirty-hour journey. "I looked like a tramp when I got off that bus," said Batts. How about Trucks, Trout, and the other voices of doom? "They flew," said Batts. "They were home in two hours."

◆

During the 1910 season, Giants manager John McGraw rewarded office boy Eddie Brannick by letting him accompany the team on a western road trip. Except for an occasional dip in the Hudson River, Brannick had never ventured west of 10th Avenue. As the team train rolled through the wide open land outside Chicago, Brannick looked out the window and gaped at the acres of stalks in a freshly mowed wheat field. He elbowed Giants infielder Art Fletcher.

"What are those?" he asked.

"Those?" said Fletcher. "Those are matches."

"Matches!" Brannick gasped. "Matches growing in the ground?"

"Yes sir," said Fletcher. "There you see the great match fields of Illinois. Soon they will pull them up, dust off the roots for striking, trim them to size, and ship them all over the world."

"Wow!" exclaimed Brannick, looking back out the window.

◆

A few hours past midnight early on the morning of April 2, 1933, an express train sped through Delaware bound for New York. Among those on board were the Boston Red Sox, barnstorming north from spring training in Sarasota, Florida. Suddenly the train hit an open switch, jumped the tracks, and scattered Pullman cars as if

Arthur Fletcher

men. They went pattering around in and out of the wreckage in their bare feet, as calm and efficient as though they were in train wrecks every day." Afterward, the Red Sox hiked to the nearby town of Wyoming, where they breakfasted on generous portions of ham, eggs, and coffee. In an exhibition game that afternoon in New Jersey, Red Sox pitcher Bob Kline was too shaky to throw a baseball, but Boston beat the Jersey City Skeeters, 12–0.

◆

In June 1904 first baseman Ben Houser signed his first professional contract with Louisville, just in time to catch the team train for a trip to Indianapolis. During one stop, the train took on an additional passenger car. The Louisville players, who had been riding in the smoking car, moved to the new compartment.

Soon after the trip resumed, the train was involved in a hellish head-on collision. Forty passengers were killed, most of them in the smoker that had just been vacated by the Louisville team. The ballplayers received only minor bruises and injuries. The game in Indianapolis was canceled.

The team proceeded to St. Paul, but again there was no baseball. A June snowstorm canceled the game. The ballplayers got back on their train and headed toward their next stop, Kansas City. Not long after they got underway, the train hit a section of track washed out by the overflowing Missouri River and derailed, sending one car—the one containing the Louisville team—bouncing down a gully into the river. The ballplayers again received only minor bruises and injuries.

After boarding a new train, the Louisville team reached Kansas City just before game time. Having dressed in their compartments, the team quickly detrained and boarded a waiting bus, which pulled out of

they were Lionel toys. One car, which contained the team's equipment trunks, was flung from the tracks and nearly through the wall of a nearby cold storage warehouse. In their three-car section, the Red Sox were tossed violently out of their berths.

Barefoot and in their pajamas, the shaken but generally unhurt ballplayers wandered out of the wreckage into the night. Outfielder Tom Oliver tried to extricate the engineer from the smashed locomotive but stopped when he realized the man was dead. Manager Marty McManus, coach Rudy Hulswitt, and catcher Eddie Connolly helped passengers to safety. Team trainer Doc Woods tended the injured.

"I don't know what kind of ballplayers they are," said Capt. Henry Ray of the Delaware State Police, "but they sure are real the station quickly and roared toward the ballpark. *Finally,* Houser thought to himself, *after all these mishaps, I'm going to get to play a ball game.* The bus collided with a trolley.

◆

In the late 1960s, former Dodgers backup infielder Luis Alcaraz played second base for the Kansas City Royals' Triple–A team in Omaha, Nebraska. Late one year, as the minor-league season was ending, Royals director of player development Lou Gorman visited the farm to check out the help.

Alcaraz had played well, and the Royals needed infield backup as they wrapped up their season. Gorman directed Omaha general manager Bob Quinn to ship Alcaraz immediately to the big club in Kansas City. The next night at the Omaha ballpark, Gorman was in the stands again. He peered into the dugout and saw Alcaraz on the bench. Gorman sought out Quinn and asked him why the second baseman wasn't in Kansas City, as he had ordered. Quinn said he had told Alcaraz to pack up and drive to Kansas City. He had no idea why he hadn't left. Quinn hurried to the clubhouse to get answers.

"Lou," said Quinn when he returned. "You're not going to believe this." Alcaraz had gotten on the interstate in Omaha, but, instead of driving 200 miles south to Kansas City, he had driven 130 miles east to Des Moines, Iowa. In Des Moines, he asked for directions to Kansas City, got back in his car, resumed driving, and somehow ended up back in Omaha. Next day, Gorman personally accompanied Alcaraz to Kansas City on an airplane.

◆

Lefty ace Rube Waddell disappeared from the Athletics for two weeks one season, and for once even manager Connie Mack's best detectives couldn't find him. During Waddell's hiatus, Washington played the Athletics at Philadelphia and after the game filed onto the team bus for the ride back to the hotel. Suddenly the bus rocked and heaved violently. Certain they were caught in an earthquake, the Senators scrambled out.

On the street, the ballplayers found the cause of the quake and one missing Athletics lefthander in a single glance. Wearing nothing but a T-shirt and pants, Waddell was beneath the bus, groaning and straining mightily to lift the vehicle onto his shoulders.

◆

One day in the early 1950s, fledgling New York *Journal-American* sports reporter Til Ferdenzi was summoned into the office of sports editor Max Kase. The

Rube Waddell

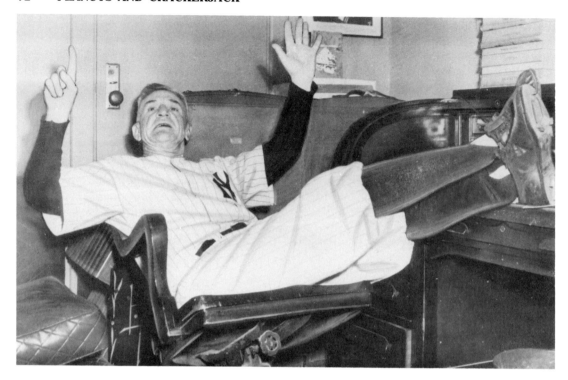

Casey Stengel relaxes in his office at Yankee Stadium.

kid was told to go home, pack a bag, and hotfoot over to Penn Station to go on a road trip with the Yankees. The regular beat writer, Hugh Bradley, was sick. Ferdenzi was giddy with excitement because, until then, he had covered only high school sports. Traveling with the Yankees had seemed a faraway, if not unreachable, goal.

Having barely caught the train, he settled into his assigned compartment and looked out the window. Suddenly he was aware of someone peeking in at him. It was Yankee manager Casey Stengel.

"You the new man with the *Journal-American*?" Stengel asked. Ferdenzi nodded. Stengel stuck out his hand and offered one of the more unnecessary introductions in baseball history.

"I'm Casey Stengel," Stengel said. "I am the manager of the New York Yankees." He paused. "You ever been to Chicago?"

"No," said Ferdenzi. "Never been there."

"You ever travel with ballplayers?"

"Never did."

"You drink?"

"Sure I drink," said Ferdenzi.

"Lemme give you a tip," said Stengel, rocking slightly as the train rolled out of Manhattan. "On the road, do all your drinking in the hotel bar. Don't go wandering around here and there looking for new places to drink. I'll tell you why.

"Now you're sitting at the bar somewhere where people don't know you. You slip and fall off the stool." In the train compartment, Stengel pantomimed a tumble from a barstool. "The next thing you know, some stranger's cleaned out your pockets and you're dead broke the next morning and with a hangover, too.

"Now you're drinking in a hotel bar where the club stays, and you fall off the stool there. The bartender leans over and sees who it is on the floor. 'Hey,' he says. 'this is one of them famous writers from New York. Take the key out of his pocket and help him to his room.'"

Ferdenzi nodded. Stengel continued. "You get lots of trouble if more than four players go out to have a drink after a game," he said. "Player number one buys a round, player number two buys a round, and so on to player number four. If you get more than five—say, six, seven, or eight or more—they each got to buy a round, and by the time that happens you might have somebody trying to do a tap dance on the bar or maybe pick a fight with a waiter."

Stengel was silent a moment. The train whizzed past junk yards and unmown back lots in New Jersey. "You work for the *Journal-American,* right?" he repeated. Ferdenzi nodded.

"You gotta get quotes," Stengel said. "You write for an afternoon paper. In the morning the people on the subway going to work back there in New York, why they're reading them morning papers. The *Times,* the *Herald Tribune,* and the rest of them. They're reading how Whitey Ford went nine and how Yogi and Mantle and Bauer and the rest of them made the runs.

"Now they're on their way home from work. They want to know more than what happened. They want to read quotes from Stengel, the ballplayers. Stuff the morning writers can't fit in. Oh, if you need a quote from Stengel and I'm not there, go right ahead, but don't make me sound like I went to Harvard."

Ferdenzi nodded. Stengel talked. The train raced into the sunset.

◆

On the morning of September 3, 1941, Reds manager Bill McKechnie—his team scheduled to play the Pirates that night at Forbes Field—stepped off the airplane from Chicago, walked through the terminal, and slid into the back seat of a cab at curbside.

"Forbes Field," he told the driver.

"Huh?" said the cabbie.

"Forbes Field," said McKechnie, trying to keep the edge out of his voice. "You know, where the Pirates play."

The driver twisted around in his seat to McKechnie. "Mister," he said. "I don't know nothing about no Forbes Field and no Pirates."

McKechnie struggled to keep his temper. *Of all the cab drivers in Pittsburgh,* he thought, *I've got to get the chump who never heard of Forbes Field.* As a parent would explain a simple task to a simple child, McKechnie tried to get across who he was and where he wanted to go.

"Look," said McKechnie, "I'm Bill McKechnie. Maybe you've heard of me. I'm manager of the Cincinnati Reds. That's a baseball team. We're going to play your Pittsburgh Pirates today at Forbes Field, and I want to go out there right away."

The taxi driver turned completely around and stared into McKechnie's eyes. The cabbie said he knew all the best routes to Briggs Stadium and he knew all the Tigers' batting averages by heart. But he didn't have a clue how to get to Forbes Field. They were sitting in a cab parked at the City Airport in Detroit.

◆

Cap Anson, legendary ballplayer and manager in the late nineteenth century, liked to tell a story about Ed ("Ned") Williamson, third baseman with the old

Forbes Field in Pittsburgh, site of the 1960 World Series.

Chicago White Sox. Williamson was with the Chicago club when Albert Spalding took it and a squad of all-stars on an around-the-world tour in 1888–1889. The team was on a steamship crossing from England to France when one of the most violent storms ever to hit the English Channel blackened the skies and churned the water. "Things got so bad," said Anson, "even the captain of the ship surrendered in despair."

Williamson grabbed two life preservers, strapped them on, closed his eyes, and offered a prayer out loud. "Oh, Lord, I will lead a different life if you will spare this ship and our lives," he howled.

The ship reached port safely, and Williamson kept his promise. He quit the team, returned to Chicago, and opened a saloon.

◆

Touring the minor leagues as a baseball clown in the 1930s, ex-Senators pitcher Al Schacht was driving on a deserted road near Tulsa, Oklahoma, when he stopped for gasoline. As Schacht pulled out of the station in first gear, two men hopped onto the car's running boards and hoisted themselves into the front seat with him. Hoping they were merely overly aggressive hitchhikers, Schacht struck up a friendly conversation about the weather and the magnificent countryside.

"Did it ever occur to you, chum," one of the men interrupted, "that this is a holdup?" Schacht did his best to appear unruffled. *Once they find out who I am,* he thought, *these guys will relent.* "You fellas interested in big-league baseball?" he answered cheerfully, hoping perhaps they'd settle for a couple of free passes.

"Yeah," said one of the bandits warily. "Why?"

Schacht sighed with relief. "Boys, that's great news," he said. "I'm Al Schacht. Yeah, Al Schacht."

One of the bandits stared at Schacht and scowled. "Never heard of you," he growled. The pair robbed him of seventy-six dollars, but obligingly left behind five dollars for gas.

◆

When Red Sox manager Joe Morgan was a young outfielder with the Wichita Braves in the late 1950s, the team assembled at the ballpark early one morning to embark on a journey to Charleston, West Virginia. The team bus left for the airport at 6:00 A.M. After a series of takeoffs, landings, delays, and cancellations, the Braves were still in the air at 6:00 P.M.

"We were flying over Watt Powell ballpark in Charleston just in time to look down and see the Charleston team take the field—for the first game of our twi-night doubleheader," said Morgan.

By the time the Braves finally reached the ballpark, dressed, gobbled sandwiches for their first meal of the day, and took the field, play got underway around 7:30. "We were nipped in the first game by something like 3–2," said Morgan. "The second game we lost, but it lasted nineteen innings and ended sometime after 3:00 A.M."

Finally scrounging up a taxi after the game, Morgan and a cab-load of teammates pulled up in front of the Daniel Boone Hotel at 4:45 A.M. During the ride over, catcher Joe Lonnett, who had recently joined the team from the Philadelphia organization, griped about Wichita's lack of speed. "No speed at all,"

Lonnett was saying as they piled out of the cab. "We would have won that first game and maybe even the second game with any sort of speed."

Morgan asked exactly who these slow players were. "Well, you're one of them," Lonnett said. "I could beat you in a race anytime."

"No way," said Morgan. They each produced ten dollars and instructed the cab driver to hold the bets. Morgan raced Lonnett in a forty-yard-dash down the street in Charleston, West Virginia, at 5:00 A.M., twenty-three hours after the team bus had left the ballpark in Wichita. "I beat him," said Morgan. "He claimed it was because he had loafers on and kept slipping."

◆

During interminable train trips, old-time big leaguers often passed the hours with practical jokes. Often their targets were fresh-faced, gullible rookies. For instance, berths in Pullman cars were equipped with small mesh slings for storing personal items. Veterans helpfully instructed many a young hurler on how to properly care for his pitching arm: sleep with it in the mesh sling. Many rookies tossed and turned for many nights, trying to get comfortable with one arm tangled in a sling. Some developed sore arms, which was just fine with the veteran pitchers.

Another training trick was the lantern gag. Veterans would take rookies aside and tell them major-league teams feared train wrecks above all. To prevent rear-end collisions, the manager would select one of his most trustworthy players for sentry duty. The chosen player would spend the night on the rear platform of the last car and would wave the lantern to warn trains that approached from behind. It was tough, important duty, the rookies were told. In fact, many big-league stars owed their success to diligent sentry work. Several wrecks had been averted, and managers figured a player alert enough to prevent a train crash was alert enough to play big-league ball.

Thus, rookie after rookie spent night after night on the rear platform, peering into the darkness, waving a red lantern, and hoping to stop a wreck to win a job. Before long, railroad companies kept their lanterns under lock and key whenever baseball teams were aboard. The joke was getting dangerous. Several rookie sentries had fallen asleep on duty and had been discovered in the morning, teetering near the edge of the platform as the train roared down the tracks.

◆

Traveling in the Class C minor leagues after World War II, catcher Matt Batts, pitcher Mel Parnell, and their teammates often felt as if they were back in the service. "We rode in one of those old Army troop carriers," said Batts, who later played for the Red Sox and Tigers, among others. "Except they took the seats out and put in a bunch of lawn chairs. You bet we bounced around back there."

On the way home from a game in West Virginia one night, the bus bumped and rocked down mountain roads. The night air grew colder and colder. "We were freezing to death," said Batts. "Mel Parnell and some of the other boys decided we better do something to stay warm." Gathering all the broken bats they could find, they piled them together and built a blazing campfire.

"The one thing we didn't count on was the smoke," said Batts. "Pretty soon the inside of that thing was pretty thick. We were all fighting each other to stick our heads out the window for some air." The bus rolled down the road, billowing smoke as ballplayers leaned out the windows gasping and coughing. Either the manager or the driver up front in the cab finally glanced into a sideview mirror, saw the smoky trail and orange glow, and hastily pulled over so the boys could extinguish the blaze.

"Mel Parnell lives about seventy miles from here," said Batts, reminiscing from his Louisiana home in the summer of 1990. "We were talking about that fire on the bus the other day. We laughed and laughed. We'd do it all over again if we had the chance."

◆

During a Yankees' road trip in the 1920s, a rookie pitcher complained about his assignment to an upper berth in the sleeper car. Team business manager Edward Barrow heard about the problem, and at the next station stop he grabbed the lad by the collar and coattails and tossed him off the train onto the platform.

After the journey resumed, another member of the Yankee party approached Barrow, who was relaxing in his compartment. The man showed the business manager a suitcase belonging to the rookie who had been booted off the train. Barrow told the man to leave the bag with him and he would take care of it. After the man left, Barrow heaved the bag out the train window into the night.

5

SUPERSTITIONS

Before a game one afternoon in the 1920s, a newspaperman approached Philadelphia Athletics pitcher Ed Rommel and struck up a conversation about superstitions. Rommel shook his head and smirked. Some baseball guys, he said, believed in a lot of purely nonsensical hoodoo.

"Urban Shocker was the worst," Rommel continued. "If you got hold of his glove between innings, he was licked. He used to lay it on the ground until the opposition coaches got the habit of picking it up in passing. After that, he carried it to a special spot on the bench."

Rommel shook his head again. "One day in St. Louis, Al Simmons grabbed Sam Gray's glove and tossed it to Sam as he was going to the box," Rommel recalled. "It was a tight game, but that very inning we got to Sam for four runs. Did Sam boil! I thought he was going to swing on Al. That's a fact. 'You leave your hand off my glove, see?' he growled."

Rommel smirked again and snorted, "That's all bunk, I guess."

There was a long pause. On the field behind him, the Athletics worked out. Balls smacked into gloves and cracked against bats. "But, by George, it's a fact that every time I see that 6777, we win," Rommel said.

The 6777? "It's a trolley car," Rommel explained impatiently. "Every time I see that 6777 before a game, we win. It's liable to come along Lehigh Avenue any time outside our ballpark. And if I don't see it, I know we're in for a tough day."

Baseball men seldom call themselves superstitious. Habitual? Perhaps. Ritualistic? Maybe. Superstitious? Not me, and don't touch my bat because it's bad luck. Ballplayers don't like to admit belief in hexes, good-luck charms, or curses, but they should. Like fighter pilots and riverboat gamblers, they work in a profession twisted by fate. Games are lost, careers are ruined, and hearts are broken by demons, gremlins, and plain, dumb bad luck. Softly smacked bloopers fall between outfielders. Wickedly hit line drives wail directly to infielders. Baserunners fall rounding third. A sun-blinded fielder thrusts out his glove, and the ball plops into the webbing.

On a larger scale, the game poses unsolvable mysteries. Pitchers have to wonder: *why was I granted a fastball that flies at one hundred miles per hour?* Hitters have to wonder: *where did I get the hand-eye coordination to connect with a baseball thrown one hundred miles per hour?* They all have to wonder: *how did I land a job where people pay ten dollars for my autograph?* Each of them fears the sharp pain behind the shoulder or the snap, crackle, and pop in the knee that could turn him into an aluminum siding salesman in an instant.

Face-to-face with murky parts of the game that can't be manipulated through weight training, extra batting practice, jogging, or a terrific agent, ballplayers (ancient or modern) turn to voodoo. However, a few old-time beliefs are defunct: in the 1920s and 1930s, a cart of hay meant good luck, while a cart of empty barrels meant bad luck. Carts loaded with either are uncommon around ballparks in the 1990s. But, all in all, the better-educated modern millionaire is as superstitious as his rough-edged forefather. A study of superstitious lore shows that most common odd practices have lasted throughout the century: when doing well, ballplayers wear the same underclothing, unlaundered, until luck runs out or the health board intervenes; they never step on the baseline exiting or entering the diamond; they don't let anyone touch game bats or gloves.

History proves that hardball superstitions can work. The tiniest Little Leaguer knows baseball is a game of failure: the best hitters bat .300, which means they flop seven times out of ten. When long streaks of failure befall a player, he is tempted to tinker with his technique. Batters ponder a change in stance, and pitchers mull an alteration in delivery. However, substantive changes often lead to prolonged failure and, occasionally, a trip back to the bushes. Players are better off changing deodorant, growing a beard, shaving a moustache, or eating hats for breakfast until the ball eludes infielders again.

The tiniest Little Leaguer knows baseball is a mental game. If eating a lemon pie before each start fills a pitcher with confidence as well as gas pains, bake him one. If a dozen lucky gold chains calm a batter before he hits, let him jangle as he walks to the plate. Superstition is the opiate of the ballplayer. Anything will do. New York Giants third baseman Heinie Zimmerman liked to carry teammate Art Fletcher's bat along with his own to the plate, then toss Fletcher's into the mud for luck as he stepped to bat, which worked fine until Fletcher began hiding his bats.

History proves hardball superstitions occasionally backfire. If a player believes in good luck charms, he must also believe in demons. If a player truly believes he is hexed, he might as well be hexed. Existing problems merely worsen. Legendary minor league outfielder John King struggled to hit left-

Bobo ("Buck") Newsom

handers. Before long, King believed lefties had a curse on him, thereby guaranteeing he would never hit them, except perhaps with a right cross. Sometimes an entire franchise is crippled by hoodoo. Many around the Red Sox think the team has been haunted since it sold Babe Ruth to the Yankees, a nice bit of self-defeatism that should last till Ruth returns to Boston.

Lore is loaded with stories of men impaled on their own superstitions. When opposing players or mischievous teammates knew a fellow's phobia, they used it as a weapon. Pitcher Bobo Newsom hated scraps of paper near the mound; so when he pitched, the other team busily shredded scorecards and littered the infield grass. Boston Braves manager George Stallings obsessively kept the dugout free of pigeons, peanut shells, gum wrappers, and bits of paper. Opposing players threw peanuts toward the Braves' dugout to attract pigeons, doubly cursing the Boston manager with a single toss.

Superstition occasionally hurts innocent bystanders as well. Stallings assigned infielder Oscar Dugey to shoo away the birds, and Dugey claimed his career was shortened by a sore arm caused by heaving pebbles at pigeons. Stallings probably didn't think he was superstitious. He was merely certain pigeons and paper around the dugout doomed his team.

Before Game Two of the 1932 World Series, Cubs righty Lon ("The Arkansas Hummingbird") Warneke was mobbed by photographers who asked him to pose with his Yankee counterpart, Lefty Gomez. Warneke refused. "I never pose for photographs on the day I pitch," he said.

"What's the matter, Lon?" prodded one cameraman. "You superstitious?"

"Superstitious, hell!" Warneke snapped. "I just think it's unlucky."

On July 16, 1988, a fan sent Red Sox left fielder Mike Greenwell a birthday present: a tiny, plastic, windup, toy frog. The Red Sox embarked on an amazing winning streak, and Greenwell adopted the frog as a good-luck charm.

His Red Sox teammates decided to torture him for it. Before a Sunday afternoon game against the White Sox at Fenway Park, Greenwell sat in the clubhouse winding up the frog and watching it clatter across a table. Shortstop Spike Owen sneaked up with a bat and hacked at the plastic critter, who avoided a crunching demise by half a hop.

"You missed it," Greenwell said, spiriting the frog to the safety of his locker.

"I'll get it," Owen vowed.

Greenwell went to the trainer's room for a moment. When he returned, his green and yellow charm was gone. The frognappers had left behind a hastily scrawled note. "Your frog will be fried today."

"I want my frog," howled Greenwell.

"The hostage has been killed," third baseman Wade Boggs chortled from a nearby locker.

"It's my lucky frog, man," Greenwell said. "I can't believe they're messing with my lucky frog."

Below the frognapper's note, Greenwell posted a note of his own: "$1,000 reward: A reward has been offered for any information leading to the arrest of anybody holding in their possession a green and yellow frog." By game time, no witnesses had stepped forward.

After the Red Sox dispatched the White Sox, Greenwell, who tripled and doubled in four at-bats, hurried into the clubhouse, returned to his locker, and saw his frog hanged from the ceiling. A piece of medical tape was wrapped around its tiny, plastic feet, and the tape was on fire.

Greenwell sprang into action, ripped away the blazing tape, and rescued the frog. "I saved him," said Greenwell. "He's got some hot feet, but I think he's okay. I don't know who did it, but if I find out, I'm going to have to get even."

"I don't know anything about it," said Owen, the prime suspect.

Greenwell wound up the frog, its feet slightly blackened, put it down, and watched it hop across his chair. "He's okay," he sighed. The Red Sox had just won their eleventh straight game, and the frog had been present for nine of them. "He's coming on the road with us," Greenwell insisted.

Heilmann hopped out of the car to help his teammate find whatever he had dropped. "What did you lose?" Heilmann asked.

Crawford stood, smiled, and cried, "Got it!" Traffic whizzed by and horns blared louder as he showed Heilmann what he had found: a woman's hairpin. "That means a two-base hit," Crawford explained, happily examining his treasure in the midst of traffic. "Don't you know that? A lady's hairpin means a two-base hit."

◆

In 1943, Detroit Tigers pitcher Art Houtteman, who wore uniform number 15, started the year with eight consecutive losses. Houtteman pitched well, but was doomed by rotten luck. He lost several decisions, 1–0 and 2–1. Hoping to jolt fate, Houtteman made a deal to trade his uni-

Vernon ("Lefty") Gomez

◆

Sam Crawford, a Detroit Tiger outfielder in the Ty Cobb era, believed strongly in trinkets and omens and their effect upon hitting baseballs. Crossed bats in front of the dugout made him cringe, like Dracula confronted with a crucifix.

One afternoon in downtown Detroit, Crawford rode in a car with Tiger outfielder Harry Heilmann. Just as a signal light turned from red to green and traffic began to surge forward, Crawford leaped from the car and began to scour the pavement. A car in the next lane of traffic nearly ran over him, and horns bleated from the line of cars behind them.

Sam ("Wahoo Sam") Crawford

form for that of third baseman George Kell, who had number 21.

Shortly after Kell got Houtteman's old number, a line drive shattered Kell's wrist. When he recovered, a bad-hop grounder broke his jaw. Kell was through with number 15.

The following spring, Houtteman didn't want his old number back either. The team promised to issue him number 10 once the season started, but asked him to keep number 15 just until opening day. Houtteman agreed. Three weeks into spring training, he suffered a fractured skull when his convertible collided with a fruit truck near the Tigers' ballpark in Lakeland, Florida.

◆

A legend in the southern bush leagues around World War I, Texan John King was vexed by left-handed pitching. Before long, King was sure he was cursed by lefties. He developed hatred and fear of left-iness in all walks of life.

"All I know is, I've studied those birds and there's something funny about 'em," he said. "I don't like wrong-handers."

Once during a train trip, King's manager found him on the rear platform with a six-gun and a box of cartridges, shooting at the telegraph poles as they whizzed by. After each shot King yelled "There goes another southpaw!"

Whenever a left-handed pitcher entered a game, King was lifted for a pinch hitter. He smoldered on the bench and rooted for his replacement to strike out. Once in Okmulgee, Oklahoma, Cy Williams came in to pitch and Everitt Booe batted for King. Booe hit a line drive back to Williams, and King exploded on the bench. He jumped, screamed, "Booe hitting for King!" ripped open his shirt, and flung a water jug onto the field.

At a restaurant, a famished King once ordered a steak, saw the waitress deliver it left-handed, and walked out. Strolling down the street on another occasion, King came across a blind fiddler sitting on the curb. "Poor cuss," he said, and tossed a quarter into the man's cup. When he noticed the fellow fiddled left-handed, he retrieved his quarter. During World War I, King scanned casualty lists, even though he had no friends or family overseas. After the war, King read a story about the baseball men killed in France.

"Too bad, ain't it," said a teammate.

"Yeah," said King sadly. "But it's fate. There wasn't one left-handed pitcher killed in the war."

One day in the Texas League, a small boy tried to sneak into the ballpark over the outfield fence and whistled for help. King obligingly hoisted the boy in. As the youth walked happily toward the grandstand, he picked up a pebble and tossed it left-handed. King pounced on the lad and heaved him back over the fence. "What do you mean trying to sneak into this ball game?" he hollered after the fleeing youngster.

In 1931 oil was discovered on King's West Texas ranch, and he retired from baseball. When his only son was born, King was scared speechless when the baby began to reach for objects with his left hand. King desperately laced the tiny south paw in a tobacco pouch and kept it there until he was certain the boy was adequately indoctrinated to rightness.

◆

During an eastern swing in the mid 1930s, St. Louis Cardinal outfielder Pepper Martin was stuck in a dreadful slump. During the series in Philadelphia, kindly St. Louis baseball writer Ray Gillespie decided to give Martin a boost.

The Polo Grounds during the opening game of the 1936 World Series.

Gillespie slipped a generous tip to the maid at the Bellevue-Stratford and asked her to round up every stray hairpin in the hotel. She obligingly delivered a handful, of various shapes and sizes. At the time, finding a hairpin was considered great luck to a ballplayer.

At the ballpark that afternoon, Gillespie loitered in the Cardinal dugout. When Martin trotted in from the outfield during batting practice and approached the steps, Gillespie scattered the hairpins on the floor, right where Martin would see them.

Suddenly Martin spotted a pal in the stands and wandered over for a chat. Right behind him from the outfield came Joe ("Ducky") Medwick, who trotted in unhesitantly, clattered down the steps, and

stopped in his tracks when he spotted the hairpins. Medwick's eyes grew large. He dropped to his knees to gather his treasures.

"No, no, Joe," Gillespie protested in hushed tones. "Those are for Pepper, you know, to get him out of his slump."

"To hell with Martin and his slump," hissed Medwick, gleefully scooping up the hairpins. "Let Martin find his own base hits."

◆

When he was a young ballplayer at Walpole High School in Massachusetts, Red Sox manager Joe Morgan was given a bat by a minor-league catcher and Walpole native named Walter Novick.

"He caught Hal Newhouser and the likes, but he was basically a Triple–A fellow," said Morgan. "One spring he came home for some reason, and he gave me a Louisville bat. A real professional model. It was a K–48. A Red Kress model."

The bat quickly became a favorite of the Morgan boys. "My brother and I were the only ones allowed to use it," said Morgan. "We used it all spring. Got a ton of hits out of it. Then came Fenway Park."

Walpole High School was at Fenway for a playoff game against Newton North High. "A pitcher broke the bat during batting practice," said Morgan. "We didn't know he was using it. I cried. I went zero–for–five and we got beat, 9–5, by North."

In the minor leagues years later, Morgan experimented with a number of different bats: the L–5 (Buddy Lewis model), the S–1, and the M–110.

Finally he came across one that felt just right. "I got smart and found another K–48," Morgan recalled. "And I started hitting again."

◆

A member of the 1910 Athletics once ate pineapple for lunch and smashed a home run that afternoon, giving birth to a teamwide theory that the fruit was good for hitting. Word got around. In Chicago for the World Series, the Athletics were eating breakfast at the LaSalle Hotel when a prosperous Philadelphia businessman marched in, followed by workers hauling crates of pineapples. "That'll make you hit, boys," he smiled. The fruit was prepared in the hotel kitchen and consumed by the ball club. That afternoon the Athletics battered the Cubs, 12–5.

◆

The Giants were scheduled to play a Saturday afternoon doubleheader against the Phillies at the old Polo Grounds. The mighty starting pitchers for New York were Christy Mathewson and Rube Marquard.

Long before the game, Phillies third baseman Eddie Grant and teammates walked across the field from the visitors' clubhouse. A group of newspapermen and spectators were lounging in the wooden stands. Suddenly, Grant spotted something in the grass and picked it up: a domino, with seven white dots.

"See it?" said Grant, proudly. "Seven marks. That means seven hits for me this afternoon."

The onlookers laughed. Grant was a .249 lifetime hitter. Seven hits against Mathewson and Marquard? They laughed some more.

In the first game against Marquard, Grant got four hits. In the second game against Mathewson, he got three.

◆

In 1953, Fred Haney, manager of the Pittsburgh Pirates, who were in last place, was relaxing in his New York hotel room one night when the telephone rang. The operator told him to hold for a long-distance call from Cincinnati.

"This is Dr. Teeney," said the voice on the line. "I am the world's most famous gypsy fortune teller, astrologer, and seer. I have discovered a magic formula that guarantees a pennant for the Pirates this year."

"You may be just the man I'm looking for," Haney snorted, rubbing his eyes.

"I certainly am," said Teeney firmly. "Order your players to spit on their left palms as they go to bat tomorrow and you'll beat the Giants. Be sure they spit like

Christy Mathewson

this." Haney heard a sound like the pop of a champagne cork. No longer in the mood for a crackpot, the manager hung up.

Next day, the Pirates did not spit on their palms but beat the Giants anyway. Dr. Teeney called again that night, long distance.

"I told you so," he said triumphantly. "Use my formula again tomorrow, and you'll beat them, 4–2."

Next day, the Pirates did not spit on their left hands and won, 4–3. Dr. Teeney phoned that night to gloat. "What's the idea of crossing me up?" said Haney, feeling playful amid a two-game winning streak against the defending pennant winners. "You said we'd win, 4–2. The score was 4–3."

"One of your lads didn't spit right," said Teeney. "If you really want to clinch the pennant, you'd better have me travel with the club. By the way, what's the highest salary on your payroll?"

"A hundred thousand," said Haney.

"Then my fee will be one hundred grand, Haney," Teeney said. "And I'll be worth every cent. When do I report? Tomorrow?" Haney hung up.

On a whim, Haney told his players to spit in their left palms before going to bat the next day. The Pirates lost, 15–1. A few weeks later, the telephone company called Haney to ask about a Dr. Teeney of Cincinnati, who had stiffed them for a number of long-distance calls to New York.

◆

On April Fools' Day 1990, Red Sox pitcher Mike Boddicker's wife concocted a great practical joke to spring on her father. She had Mike telephone to say he had been traded to the Milwaukee Brewers. Boddicker pulled it off beautifully, not chuckling at all when he told his father-in-law about the deal that was sending him to Milwaukee in exchange for outfielder

Rob Deer and pitcher Bill Wegman.

Boddicker hung up, had a nice laugh with his wife, then redialed his father-in-law to let him in on the gag. The line was busy. "He was calling around to everybody to let them know about the trade," said Boddicker.

Boddicker was unable to get through for several hours. By then a good portion of the hilarity had worn off. "It wasn't very funny after four hours of phone calls," said Boddicker.

Like a guy who had just plopped onto a whoopee cushion, Boddicker's father-in-law immediately vowed revenge. "He put a hex on me," said Boddicker.

The Milwaukee hex hit hard. One week in April, the Brewers crushed Boddicker at Fenway Park, 18–0. Four days later in Milwaukee, they stuck him with a bitter 5–0 loss. In July in Milwaukee, he couldn't get out of the third inning en route to a 13–0 disaster. His three-start total against the Brewers was 0–3, with an 11.38 earned run average. The Red Sox scored no runs during the three starts.

"It was a curse," said Boddicker. "I'm telling you, my father-in-law put a curse on me."

On September 12 in the middle of the pennant race, Boddicker was scheduled to start a crucial game at Fenway Park against the Brewers. That morning, he telephoned his father-in-law and requested he lift the curse. "I begged him to take it off," said Boddicker. "And he did."

When he arrived at the ballpark, Boddicker cheerfully told his teammates to stop worrying. The curse was off. He shut down Milwaukee, 7–1. "I'm not going to mess with my father-in-law anymore," Boddicker said afterward.

Getting ready for the 1941 minor-league playoffs, Columbus outfielder

Harry ("The Hat") Walker traveled to Louisville to secure a selection of new bats from Hillerich and Bradsby. When Walker got there, Mr. Hillerich himself said he was sorry, but they didn't have Harry's model in stock. Disappointed, Walker thanked Hillerich and started to leave.

"Wait a minute, Harry," said Hillerich. "I just remembered. I was mixing some stain out back with one of your bats. I'll let you have that one if you want." Hillerich produced the bat, stained brown from the barrel to just above the trademark.

In his first postseason at bat, Walker used the two-tone model to slam a home run. He hit three home runs in three days. In the deciding game of the Little World Series against Montreal, Walker was at the plate with a full count, two outs, his team down by two runs, and two men on. He fouled off thirteen consecutive curve balls. On the fourteenth he slammed a game-winning home run.

For the rest of his career, including eleven years in the big leagues, mostly with the Cardinals, Walker never used anything but a two-tone bat. "They call the two-tone bat the 'Walker finish,'" he said in the summer of 1990. "I still have that first one here in my house."

◆

Don Wetherston was born into a seafaring family in Liverpool, England, in 1890. In 1906 he secured a job as smoking room bartender aboard the new Cunard Line passenger steamer *Lusitania.*

In the spring of 1915, Weatherston took ill while ashore in New York. When the ship embarked for the return voyage to England, Weatherston was too sick to be on board and the *Lusitania* sailed without him for the first time.

The *Lusitania* was torpedoed and sank off the Irish coast. Wetherston's replacement behind the smoking room bar was among the 1,198 lost. Understandably convinced he was blessed with good luck, Weatherston stayed in New York, became a Giants fan, and appointed himself the team's good luck charm. From 1918 through 1940, he attended every game at the Polo Grounds while carrying three wishbones in his left pocket.

◆

In the summer of 1926, sixteen-year-old outfielder Paul Fisher traveled with a team through Missouri, Oklahoma, and Arkansas. The barnstormers challenged local nines, the winner getting 60 percent of the receipts and all side bets.

In Watts, Oklahoma, a big gate and $750 in wagers were at stake. As the barnstormers finished warmups, three brand new hearses, two black, one pearl gray, rolled to a stop. Out piled two dozen Indians, who were fabulously wealthy men, the locals said, because oil had been discovered on their land. In their entourage were Bearpaw, Dryshell, and Wildflower, who immediately began warming up in tandem, all left-handed. "I'd swear they were quadruplets," muttered barnstorming outfielder Cornbread Jones.

The lefty Indians threw devastating curveballs. The barnstormer lineup included seven lefty hitters. The barnstormers scored just one run in the series, lost all three games, and left town with empty pockets.

Next day, Fisher was induced to join another team in Joplin. Upon arrival, he was warming up in the outfield when he called for a fly ball. Suddenly he felt himself lifted off the ground from behind. It was John King, the legendary bush league outfielder who hated lefties.

"Junior, are you a natural left-hander? Or were you sent here just to devil Old John?" King drawled.

Manager Fred Haney faced severe fan resentment at Pittsburgh.

"Natural," squeaked Fisher.

"Junior, you want to know the rules when you play the outfield alongside me?" said King, dangling the youngster.

"Yes, sir," said Fisher.

"Never say, 'I got it,'" said King. "I'll tell you when to get it. Come here with me. We'll draw a little line. One side will be your pasture, and the other side will be mine. You stay in your pasture, and you won't get hurt. I don't like wrong arms, Junior. You're a wrong arm. And that means you're no good in my book."

"I don't like lefties, either," Fisher blurted. "But I'll bet you've never been plagued by three lefty Indians who lived in hearses and threw nothing but hooks." King stared at the boy, dumbfounded.

In the second game of a doubleheader

against Fort Smith, which started two lefty pitchers, King joined Fisher on the trot to the dugout.

"Them left-handers in the hearse," King muttered quietly. "You ever run across left-handers out in the deep sticks?"

"I did," said Fisher.

"Curveballs?"

"Nearly every pitch."

Now they were in the dugout. King assumed a fatherly tone. "Junior," he said, "you a football player?"

"Fair," said Fisher.

"Fair will get you some schooling," said King. "Why don't you skip all this? If I was you, Junior, I'd go to school." The boy nodded.

Fisher searched out King that night, found him still in the clubhouse, and approached him. "I've decided to take your advice," said Fisher, suitcase in hand. "I told the old man this was my last day."

"Okay, son," said King. "Good luck. Stay away from them left-handed Indians."

Touched by the gruff man's gentle treatment, Fisher stuck out his hand. King didn't move.

"One thing I told you," King said, staring at the boy's extended hand. "I still don't like wrong arms."

◆

Brooding over another loss by his last-place Pirates in the summer of 1953, manager Fred Haney sat by himself in the lobby of a New York hotel. Suddenly he felt a hard slap on his left shoulder.

"It's there," boomed a man standing behind Haney's chair. "Never take it off. It's Bridget, the leprechaun. Keep her perched beside you, Haney, and the Pirates will nevermore lose a game." Haney had a friendly chat with the fellow, mumbled thanks, winked, and said, "Have Bridget report to the Polo Grounds tomorrow."

Next day at the ballpark, the Giants were

Al Simmons (left) *and Babe Ruth*

beating Pittsburgh, 5–0, when Haney, standing in the third-base coach's box, heard a voice holler from the stands.

"Talk to Bridget, Haney!" the man bellowed. "Ask her what to do!"

Haney bent his head and pretended to whisper to the invisible leprechaun. On the bench, the Pirates, who had heard the leprechaun story from Haney, chuckled heartily. The next Pirate doubled. Then came two walks, an error, and a home run. Pittsburgh went on to win, 7–6.

◆

When Philadelphia Athletics slugger Al Simmons sank into a slump, he often sank deeper into a haze. One day after a horrible game at the plate, Simmons emerged from the shower stark naked, stood dripping wet in front of his locker, and absent-mindedly put on his hat. Amused by the sight of Simmons wet and naked except for his fedora, the other Athletics teased him hard. Simmons got dressed and stomped out.

Next day, Simmons cracked four hits. Thereafter, he emerged from the shower after every game and stood in front of his locker, dripping wet and wearing nothing but his hat. The A's kept laughing at silly old Simmons. Silly old Simmons kept hitting. Before long, Philadelphia's postgame clubhouse was filled with players standing in front of their lockers, dripping wet, and naked except for hats.

6

REAL FANS

Born and raised a few miles from Yankee Stadium, the kid packed off to Boston in the mid 1970s to attend college. The rivalry between the Red Sox and Yankees was in its golden era, but the kid was smart enough to cloak his loyalties when behind enemy lines. He avoided discussions of religion, politics, those funny New England accents, and baseball.

One evening in a smoky bar packed with student bodies, the kid sipped bottled beer and shouted over the jukebox to carry on a conversation with a new woman friend. The dialogue rambled through the usual ice-breaking topics: majors, dormitory life, and professors. Then the woman friend said, "So where are you from?"

"New York," said the kid.

The woman lowered the green bottle from her lips and grimaced, as if her appendix had just burst. "You're not a Yankee fan, are you?" she asked, nearly choking on the words.

"I can't help it," muttered the kid, staring at the floor. "That's the way I was brought up."

Even in the name of romance, the kid couldn't change. Real fans acquire their baseball tastes in childhood and carry them the rest of their lives, wherever they may wander. Father and uncle screamed and hollered about the Phillies; junior screams and hollers about the Phillies, even when he is forty years old and living in Milwaukee. Unlike spouses and religious affiliations, baseball fealty is not something real fans cast aside lightly. St. Louisans transplanted to New York still wear Cardinals hats. Los Angelenos residing in Atlanta wear Dodgers hats. Real fans never trust anyone who switches.

"Are you from around here?" the real fan asks a stranger at a cocktail party in Seattle.

Babe Ruth autographed baseballs that later were auctioned off to support Disabled American Veterans.

"No, I was born and raised in Detroit," says the stranger.

"How about those Tigers?" the real fan says.

"Well, I was a Tigers fan when I was a kid," says the stranger. "But since we moved here, I figured I'd start rooting for the Mariners."

"Think I'll go into the kitchen and help mix the punch," says the real fan.

Real fans get goofy over their team and aren't ashamed about it. They know real passion requires forays into silliness. Real fans snuggle into sleeping bags and camp on the sidewalk overnight to be first in line for playoff tickets. They run onto the field after the pennant is clinched to take home a hunk of turf. Real fans listen to the games on the radio and watch them on television. Real fans throw the radio and kick the television. In their youth, real fans chased players for autographs and were stoic when their heroes told them to get lost.

Real fans never outgrow their childhood affliction. They hear mature men say the game is really a business and the game is only a game, as if these were astounding revelations. The real fan says hogwash. Business? Few truck drivers cry over the ups and downs of ITT. Game? No one stays depressed for months over a disastrous checkers match. Real fans feel sorry for people who just don't get it. First Santa Claus, then the Tooth Fairy. People who lose belief in baseball magic must have nothing left.

When they are old and gray, real fans still root. Maybe they don't worship individual players, but they still love the old team. Real fans know life is cold and barren without something to stand up for, such as the Chicago Cubs. Real fans don't blindly admire impartiality; straight lines on a heart monitor are impartial. Real fans know taking sides is fun. They wouldn't wager a nickel at the race track but will bet cases of beer on the World Series to show their obnoxious pals they are willing to put their money where their heart is.

Real fans know happiness is a pair of tickets in the coat pocket. They know a quick fix for the blues is a spontaneous pop over to the ballpark. Real fans don't complain about high prices, crummy parking, drafty stadia, and tiny seats as long as they can see, hear, and smell the game.

Real fans can't walk past a stickball game without watching an inning or two. When they see a baseball, real fans always pick it up and roll it around in their hands. They pound fists into their dried out mitts in the springtime and pitch wadded up paper into the wastebasket at work, as if throwing a full-count fastball with the bases loaded.

Sometimes a boyish eye for baseball is a window to a man's soul. In September 1988 the Red Sox clinched the American League East title in Cleveland. Early the next morning, a reporter ventured into the Red Sox clubhouse to look for manager Joe Morgan. The visiting manager's office at Municipal Stadium is around a sharp corner near the locker room showers. Folks customarily listen around the corner before entering the office to determine if the manager is meeting with a player or talking on the phone. The reporter listened and heard a strange, rhythmic noise: *Thwack-slap. Thwack-slap. Thwack-slap. Thwack-slap.* The reporter gingerly peeked around the corner. The fifty-seven-year-old Morgan was by himself, bouncing a baseball against the cinder block wall and catching it in his mitt, just the way seven-year-old kids do in their bedrooms.

Real fans never grow completely old, no matter how much responsibility and hair loss they've known in their lifetime. "When I was a boy growing up in Kansas, a friend of mine and I went fishing, and, as we sat there in the warmth of a summer afternoon on a river bank, we talked about what we wanted to do when we grew up," recalled Dwight Eisenhower. "I told him I wanted to be a real major league baseball player, a genuine professional like Honus Wagner. My friend said that he'd like to be president of the United States. Neither of us got our wish." Real fans read the quote and remember why they liked Ike.

In his day, retired schoolteacher Dutch Doyle was a renowned Philadelphia Athletics fan. "I went to my first game in 1929 when I was eight years old," Doyle, age sixty-seven, said in the fall of 1988 from his Philadelphia home. "I saw Al Simmons hit two home runs versus Earl White-hill that day. So from then on, Al Simmons was my favorite player. I can remember it like it was yesterday."

He grew up in Philly, at 17th and Lehigh, just a few blocks from both Baker Bowl, the home of the Phillies, and Shibe Park, the home of the A's. "I'd say between the two of them, I attended twenty-five hundred games," said Doyle. "But the A's were my favorites. Mr. Twer, the neighborhood tailor, used to press the suits for the visiting ball clubs. The games would start at 3:15, just when we were getting out of school.

Honus Wagner (left) *and Mel Ott*

He used to go to the ballpark with the suits at around the second inning. I used to carry a couple of suits for him and go with him. I'd follow him right into the visitors' clubhouse. Then he'd go back to his tailor shop, and I'd stay in the grandstand to watch the game."

Over the years, Doyle got work at Shibe Park. "I started selling seat cushions," he said. "I sold scorecards, worked behind the refreshment stands." He was working for the Reading Railroad full-time—and still at Shibe Park part-time—when the Athletics left Philadelphia for Kansas City after the 1954 season.

"To know you went through all the tough times with a team . . . it was a crushing thing," said Doyle. "It was a sad thing for me. I was crushed."

Even in 1988, he had a chair from demolished Shibe Park in his home and still felt a twinge when he passed where the old ballpark used to stand. "It's still an empty lot," Doyle said. "It's a hard thing to explain how you feel."

Two cities and thirty-four years after they departed Philly, the Athletics were in the World Series against the Dodgers. Did the heart of an old Philadelphia A's lover beat faster with the Oakland A's in the series?

"No. I don't feel anything for them," said Doyle. "I still lean toward the American League, but I don't have any feeling for them. They could be any team. I'll be rooting for them because they're the American League. But it's not anything like it would be if they were the Philadelphia A's. For one thing, I won't feel as bad if they lose."

George V. Brown, father of Boston Celtics and Boston Bruins executive Walter Brown, was a big fan of Red Sox second baseman Jack Barry. When the team released Barry in 1919, the elder Brown stopped attending games at Fenway Park and stopped rooting for the Red Sox altogether.

"All he would talk about was what a great player Barry had been," Walter Brown once recalled, "and how baseball had slumped since the day he left the Red Sox."

In the summer of 1938, Walter finally convinced his father to return to Fenway for an important doubleheader against the Yankees. "Everything was going along nicely," Walter said, "until one of the Yankees hit a short fly to left field."

Boston outfielder Buster Mills misjudged the ball, which bounced squarely off his head. George Brown got up and started to walk out of the ballpark.

"That proves what I've been telling you all," he said as he left. "These modern ballplayers aren't any good. The game hasn't been the same around here since they let Jack Barry go."

◆

Larry Doyle

On April 21, 1941, a Brooklyn native was executed at the Massachusetts state prison in Charlestown for the murder of a Milton policeman. Just before the switch was thrown on the electric chair, the condemned man was asked if he had any last words, requests, or statements.

"Yeah," he said. "Tell me, did the Dodgers beat the Giants today?"

Told that Brooklyn had won, he smiled broadly.

◆

On the morning of July 5, 1950, Red Sox fan Joe Capillo of Gloucester arrived in Kenmore Square, accompanied by some twenty friends and one mackerel. In the spring, the twenty-one-year-old Capillo had bet his pals—many of them Braves fans—that if the Red Sox weren't in first place on the Fourth of July, he'd push the

Braves Field, site of 1948 World Series

fish down Commonwealth Avenue with his nose.

On July 4 the Red Sox were in fourth place, and the next morning, Capillo slapped the mackerel onto the Kenmore pavement, donned a rubber noseguard and yellow oilskins, and nudged the fish along the sidewalk for about ten feet. His friends protested; they insisted the bet mandated he push the fish the ten or so blocks to the Public Gardens.

◆

On opening day 1946 fans flocked to America's ballparks to welcome back postwar baseball. At Braves Field in Boston, a crowd of 19,483, the largest opening day gathering at the Common-

wealth Avenue ballyard in years, showed up to watch the Braves engage Brooklyn. The afternoon left many fans with a lasting impression, on their clothing.

Sometime during the game, several patrons in the refurbished grandstand noticed their clothes were smeared with green paint. Much of the park had been re-painted over the winter; some seats were touched up as late as three days before the opener.

After the game, about three hundred fans lined up outside the Braves' offices to complain about the paint smears. General manager John Quinn announced the club would pay all cleaning expenses. The next day in the Boston newspapers, the Braves' management issued an "Apology to Braves Fans," which promised to "reimburse any of its patrons for any expense to which they may be put for necessary cleansing of clothing as a result of paint damage."

Some thirteen thousand claims poured in, some from as far away as Florida and California. About five thousand were paid. The average claim was $1.50, the highest was $50. Until the paint dried, Sox owner Tom Yawkey offered the Braves the use of Fenway Park.

◆

As the moment faded deeper into lore, folks sitting around Fenway Park forty years later eyed the red seat in the otherwise blue right-field bleachers with skepticism. The seat was painted red because a ball hit by Ted Williams purportedly landed there during a game in 1946. Even Red Sox manager Joe Morgan, who was listening to the game on the radio when Williams hit it, began to wonder out loud about the clout.

"I wasn't there, but I know who was," William J. McGuire of Quincy, Massachusetts, wrote the Boston *Herald* in 1990. "My grandfather, Joseph A. Boucher, was in that seat, and as you can see from the picture the ball did a job on his straw hat."

McGuire's enclosed newspaper clipping and photograph told the story of the historic hit, smacked in the first inning of the second game of a doubleheader on June 9, 1946. Boucher, age fifty-six, sat in his bleacher seat in the thirty-third row when Williams's blast conked him squarely on top of the head, punching a hole in his straw hat. "I didn't even get the ball," Boucher said afterward. "They say it bounced a dozen rows higher, but after it hit my head I was no longer interested."

Boucher died in 1954. Thirty years later, his grandson McGuire secured Williams's autograph: "To the great and grandchildren of Joseph Boucher, I'm glad it didn't hurt him. Best to all, Ted Williams."

◆

In early July 1969, the Mets were charging after the first-place Cubs. On July 8 Chicago visited Shea Stadium for an important afternoon game.

In his Queens apartment, Frank Graddock, age sixty-six, watched his Mets on television. Late in the afternoon, however, his wife, Margaret, announced she wanted to watch the popular daytime soap opera "Dark Shadows" on another channel.

Graddock insisted on watching the game. The couple argued loudly, and Graddock was alleged to have severely beaten his wife around the head and body. She went off to bed, and he finished watching the game, which the Mets won with three runs in the bottom of the ninth.

Cheerful over his team's big victory, Graddock went to his wife's bed, perhaps to make amends. She was dead. He was charged with homicide.

◆

When Red Sox general manager Lou Gorman went through his mail one afternoon in the summer of 1990, he came across the following hand-printed letter (name changed to protect the young and innocent):

Dear Mr. Gorman,
I read in the newspaper you needed another pitcher for the Red Sox. My name is John Smith. I live in Stoughton, Mass. I am nine years old and play for the Pirates in the Stoughton Little League. I am a pitcher, and I am looking for a summer job with the Red Sox. Maybe we could help each other.
   Please let me know.
   Your friend,
   John Smith.

◆

Thirty-eight years later, someone who was there remembered:

On April 30, 1952, the Red Sox held Ted Williams Day at Fenway Park to say goodbye to their left fielder, who was shipping out to fly jets in the Korean War. Standing on the mound and surrounded by dignitaries and photographers, Williams stepped to the microphone to deliver a short speech. The crowd cheered. Just behind him, Eddie Costello, sports editor of the Boston *Herald,* whispered, "Tip your hat."

Everyone knew Ted Williams never tipped his hat. The crowd kept cheering. Costello whispered again, "Tip your hat."

Williams tipped his cap to the right-field grandstand. The crowd went wild. Williams tipped his cap to the seats behind home plate. The crowd went wilder. Williams tipped his hat to the left-field grandstand. The crowd was in a frenzy. It was a touching moment: Williams and the Fenway fans in a warm, possibly final, embrace.

"Center field," whispered Costello. "Don't forget center field."

"Not those [expletives], too!" whined Williams.

◆

On October 9, 1908, the Cubs visited the Giants for a season-ending, pennant-deciding engagement at the Polo Grounds. A good portion of New York wanted a ticket, and at daybreak fans were already poised to storm the gates of the horseshoe-shaped ballyard. By 10:00 A.M., two thousand were in line. By 10:30 there were five thousand. Soon the streets crawled with men, women, and children on their way to the game. More trainloads arrived by the minute. By 12:45, with forty

Ted Williams served as a fighter pilot with the U.S. Marines during the Korean Conflict.

thousand squeezed into the ballpark, every seat was occupied and every inch of standing room was crammed.

Meanwhile, thousands more were outside, straining to get in. Some scaled the fifteen-foot-high, barbed-wire fence behind the grandstand. Others shimmied to the top of the grandstand to perch precariously on the pitched roof. More crowds gathered at the 155th Street viaduct. Others sat high on Coogan's Bluff.

Mounted police, trying desperately to contain the throng, were brushed aside like toy soldiers. Soon the rusty elevated train tracks that overlooked the ballpark were dangerously crowded. Some onlookers clambered to the tops of trains but were quickly discouraged when cars began to pull out of the neighborhood, taking with them screaming fans clinging to the roofs. The only fatality of the day was one spectator who fell to his death from the elevated track. His vacated spot was quickly filled.

◆

When Dennis and Julia Gavin purchased their colonial farmhouse in Sudbury, Massachusetts, in 1984, they were moderate baseball fans. "But we've become bigger fans since we moved here," said Julia. They reside, after all, in a baseball landmark. In the 1920s their home was owned and occupied by Babe Ruth. "People will drive up, and one will get out and hold a bat while the other takes his picture," said Julia.

All kinds of fans have dropped by. In 1988, for instance, the Gavins were visited by the Babe's daughter, Dorothy Pirone, who helped point out some historical features of the house. "One floor had a lot of burn marks on it," said Julia. "His daughter said that's where his old leather chair stood. He used to drop his cigars on the floor."

There were not many other remnants of the Ruth era. Research shows Ruth once blew up a fireplace in the house when he stoked the flames with gasoline. He was conked on the head by a flying fireplace iron. Ruth was once sued when one of his many dogs strayed away from the farm and killed a neighbor's cow.

Living in the Sultan's old kingdom has a way of transforming moderate baseball fans. "We now have a Babe Ruth memorabilia room," said Julia Gavin.

◆

On July 27, 1938, despondent John Warde, age twenty-five, perched on the seventeenth floor of the Gotham Hotel in Manhattan and threatened to jump. For eleven hours Warde kept thousands of onlookers and a live radio audience in sus-

pense. His sister arrived to try to talk Warde off the ledge, but Warde ignored her. A friend, Patrick Valentine, arrived on the seventeenth floor and also tried to help.

"Come on in, and let's go over to the ball game," said Valentine. "The Dodgers are at Ebbets Field this afternoon."

"I'd rather jump than watch those Dodgers," Warde said gloomily. He jumped.

◆

John Keiley of Boston grew up in Somerville, Massachusetts, next door to Frank ("Shanty") Hogan, catcher for the Braves and Giants in the 1920s and 1930s. In 1988, Keiley remembered: "I have a true story Frank told me one winter. Besides overeating, Frank had another failing. He imbibed too much. Only beer, but at times a little too much.

"One afternoon at the Polo Grounds, Frank was hung over. John McGraw noticed this in Frank's first turn at bat, so he told him to take a shower and told Andy Cohen to bat for him.

"The public address system in those days was a man with a megaphone. He stood in front of the first-base stands and announced, 'Cohen now batting for Hogan.' At the third-base stands, the same, 'Cohen now batting for Hogan.'

"A big Irishman stood up in the seventh row and in a very loud voice bellowed, 'Moriarty now leaving the ballpark!' A true story."

◆

On the morning of October 15, 1929, Dallas, Texas, residents Forrest F. Cole and Ernest Luttrell embarked on a trip to Philadelphia, planning to get there around February 1. Their mode of transportation: a bat and a handful of baseballs.

Because the Athletics had beaten the

Cubs in the World Series, Cole was required to knock fly balls from Dallas to Shibe Park in Philadelphia. Luttrell—his betting opponent, and apparently a good sport—accompanied him and supplied the fungo bat and the baseballs.

◆

On a cold autumn afternoon in late October, 1934, a baseball game was played at the Clarkestown Country Club in Nyack, New York. Preceded by a twenty-piece band and three elephants, the participants paraded onto the field before five hundred shivering onlookers. One team, which called itself the 21–Hangovers, wore red jerseys, red stockings, and gray golf knickers. Their lineup included Bill Corum, Francis T. Hunter, Woolworth Donohue (the dimestore heir), William Corrigan, Jr., Ernest Truex, Humphrey Bogart, Tom Shevlin, Erskine Gwynn, and Prince Mike Romanoff.

The other team, the Nyack Eagles, wore navy uniforms, ranging in rank from swabbies to admirals. Their lineup included prizefighter Bugs Baer, columnist and future television host Ed Sullivan, Robert L. Ripley (of "Believe-It-or-Not"), Billy Rose (nightclub owner and Fanny Brice's husband), Jimmy and Sal Savo, Bert Lahr (the Cowardly Lion in *The Wizard of Oz*), Robert Sherwood (author of *The Best Years of Our Lives*), Paul Gallico (author of *The Poseidon Adventure*), Dan Parker, newspaper columnist and radio star Walter Winchell, and dramatists Ben Hecht and Charles McArthur (who wrote *The Front Page*).

The game was played with an oversized "baseball" designed for indoor use. The longest hit of the charity game was Gallico's triple; Baer stole a base. At the end of three innings, the public address an-

Satchel Paige was furnished with a rocking chair at ground level because the dugout was "too cold for his old bones."

nouncer declared the umpires ahead, 5–3. Spectators shivered. At the end of five innings, with the Eagles ahead, 7–4, the game was called because of cold. Presumably, some participants proceeded to imbibe a measure of antifreeze.

◆

Harry Ruby was a successful Hollywood songwriter in the late 1930s, but, since his boyhood days in New York, he was more interested in another field of dreams: baseball.

He never made a team in his life, but even while pulling in $1,500 a week at RKO, Ruby dropped everything to work out with the Cubs, White Sox, and Pirates at their California spring training camps. In 1930 manager Walter Johnson invited him to the Senators' camp in Biloxi, Mississippi. Ruby bolted RKO and labored hard with the Washington ballplayers. Johnson never got a chance to grant Ruby's greatest wish: to play in an exhibition game.

In the winter of 1931, Ruby joined a Hollywood semipro team owned by comedian Joe E. Brown, a notorious jokester who was well aware of Ruby's obsession. Brown played Ruby's position, second base, and keeping Harry out of the lineup was a season-long prank.

On the last day of the season, Ruby still hadn't played. Then Brown faked a finger injury, returned to the dugout, and looked up and down the bench, pretending not to see the eager Ruby.

"What a mess!" said Brown. "No one to put in."

"Me! Me!" said Ruby, jumping up and grabbing Brown's jersey. "What do you mean, nobody? Me! Me!"

"OK," Brown said with a sign. "Go on in."

Ruby gleefully ran to second base. The first batter whistled a sharp grounder between first and second, a clean single Charlie Gehringer couldn't have knocked down. Brown stormed out of the dugout in a mock rage and removed Ruby from the game. "Get off the field, you bum," he hollered. Burning with anger, Ruby refused to leave. Brown had him ejected by the police.

In the spring of 1932, Ruby received a telegram from Washington manager Johnson telling him if he would report immediately to Baltimore, he could play in an exhibition game. *Wait till Joe E. Brown hears about this,* Ruby thought. Not good enough for Brown's crummy semipro team, but good enough for the Senators! Ruby caught the next train to Baltimore.

When Ruby replaced Buddy Myer at second base in the seventh inning, eight thousand fans were in the stands. Ruby dreamily pictured himself making a diving stop or a leaping catch. When the first batter reached base, Ruby fantasized about turning a double play. A double play for the Washington Senators—what would Joe E. Brown make of that?

The crack of the bat didn't shake Ruby from his daydream. Ossie Bluege fielded the ball at third. Drawn to his right by the grounder, shortstop Joe Cronin shouted for Ruby to cover second. Ruby didn't budge. Bluege double-pumped, then held the ball. Both runners were safe.

Heartbroken, Ruby returned to Hollywood, having traveled six thousand miles for two innings, and one muffed chance. When he got home, a friend relayed worse news: Joe E. Brown already knew all about his blunder.

On the last day of the 1935 season, the Hollywood team let Ruby play one inning against the San Francisco Seals. Dizzied by the opportunity, Ruby trotted out to replace Bobby Doerr and didn't notice the new guest umpire at first: Joe E. Brown.

Lefty O'Doul hit a routine grounder to Ruby, whose throw to first baseman Ray Jacobs beat the runner by six feet.

"Safe!" shouted Brown.

Ruby barreled across the infield and lunged for Brown's throat. Jacobs stepped between them. "Take it easy, Harry," said Jacobs, who couldn't resist joining the torture. "I think Lefty really beat your throw."

Enraged by his teammate's teasing, Ruby slugged Jacobs and was thrown out of the game. A headline in the next day's trade paper read "Ruby Misses Easy Play."

◆

As far as landmark sports cases go, *People* v. *Porto* was almost as far-reaching as the Andy Messersmith decision. On June 24, 1930, at Wrigley Field in Chicago, Cubs slugger Hack Wilson fouled a pitch into the grandstand. Spectator

Arthur Porto, age seventeen, retrieved it. The boy was quickly set upon by a ballpark usher who demanded Porto surrender the ball, claiming the Cubs could not "afford to let the customers walk off with their baseballs."

Porto and his two pals resisted, a fight ensued, and the three youths were arrested for disorderly conduct. The next day, a judge listened gravely to the details of the case, held that a ball hit into the stands belongs "to the boy who grabs it," and dismissed the charges.

Here's a farmer story passed down over the years:

Around Ripley Mills, Maine, in the early 1920s, there were four farmers who had been longtime cronies. One summer, one of them bought a radio. Thereafter, at 6:00 P.M. each night, the farmer would stop whatever he was doing to listen to the baseball summaries and take notes on a piece of wrapping paper.

Before long, an old Ford would clatter down the road and stop in front of the house. The farmer with the radio would come out onto the porch, and the farmer in the car would call out, "Lo, Bill. Git any t'day?"

"Yup. Got one."

Soon the other two cronies would come to the house, and similar conversations took place. What they all wanted to know was whether Babe Ruth—the Yankee outfielder who captivated the country with his slugging—had hit any more home runs. Sometimes there wouldn't be any. Sometimes there'd be more than one. Whenever Ruth had a big day, the four farmers would retire to the harness room and discuss details over a jug of cider.

Legend has it that when Ruth hit three home runs in Game Four of the 1926 World

Andy Cohen

Series, the four farmers didn't know their own names for a week.

♦

When Andy Cohen supplanted Rogers Hornsby at second base for the Giants for the 1928 season, some Rajah lovers wouldn't give the new kid a break. On their way north in the spring, the Giants stopped in Charlotte, North Carolina, for an exhibition game. In the stands was a man called the Georgia Boy, famous throughout the Sally League for his bull-horn voice and steady stream of abuse.

"Back to Buffalo for you, Cohen!" Georgia Boy howled when Cohen struck out in his first at-bat. "You won't see the big show long! Hornsby wouldn't have struck out like that! Know how many double plays he hit into last year? None. Better get Hornsby back!"

Georgia Boy jumped on Cohen's every move, in the field or at the plate. In the seventh inning, with the score tied and a runner at first, Cohen smacked a long fly to deep left. The ball hit an inch or two from the top of the fence.

Cohen rounded third as the ball was relayed to the infield and made a dash for the plate. The throw from shortstop was perfect, but Cohen slid around the tag for an inside-the-park home run. As he brushed the dirt from his uniform, Cohen walked straight over to the stands and pointed straight at Georgia Boy. "I suppose Hornsby would have done better than that!" Cohen hollered.

"You're right, he would of!" Georgia Boy erupted. "Yes, sir! He wouldn't have had to slide like that. He would have hit it over the fence. Back to the minors with you, boy!"

◆

In the summer of 1990, fan C. Allyn Russell of Concord, Massachusetts, remembered: "As a teenager in upstate New York in the 1930s, I hitchhiked one day from Oneonta to Albany to see the New York Yankees play the Albany Senators in an exhibition game at Hawkins Stadium.

"The overflow crowd was so large that some of the fans were permitted to stand in foul territory along the left- and right-field lines. A foul ball was hit into the crowd along the right-field line. After a frantic struggle for the souvenir, the ball finally wound up in the hands of an overjoyed little boy. A bully overpowered the boy and ripped the ball away from him.

"The crowd in the grandstand booed, whereupon Babe Ruth, observing the action, tore into the crowd, wrested the ball away from the bully, and then lifted the lad high in the crook of his arm. With ten thousand sets of eyes riveted upon him, the Babe presented the baseball to the star-struck kid. The crowd roared."

◆

Steve Buckley, who covered the Yankees for *The National* in 1990, bears a striking resemblance to Yankee reliever Greg Cadaret. During a trip to Minneapolis, a pack of autograph-hunting kids noticed the resemblance, too, and followed Buckley from the Radisson Plaza Hotel, where the team was staying, hounding him for several blocks.

No matter how many times he told them he wasn't Cadaret, the kids persisted. After all, he looked just like the guy on the baseball cards they were trying to get autographed. Finally Buckley showed them his Baseball Writers Association of America membership card as proof, and the kids went away.

On his way into the Metrodome the next day, Buckley ran into the same group of kids. This time, they wouldn't take no for an answer. "You must be Greg Cadaret," they protested, "otherwise why would you be here?"

Buckley again tried to explain but finally surrendered to the inevitable. For ten minutes, he autographed cards, balls, and photos.

After Buckley signed and went inside, the real Cadaret came by. The dumbstruck kids couldn't believe their eyes.

"Who are you?" they asked.

"I'm Greg Cadaret," he said.

"But Greg Cadaret just signed these for us," they said. "A guy who looked just like you."

Cadaret looked at the autographs. "I think I know who you mean," he said.

In the clubhouse, Cadaret sought out Buckley. "I don't have any problem with this," the ballplayer told the writer. "But work on the signature a little bit."

◆

During early batting practice at Fenway Park late in the summer of 1990, a strapping fellow wearing Red Sox uniform number 10 limbered up for a turn in the cage. He looked familiar. Hadn't we seen him somewhere in a Hawaiian shirt? Or was it with two other guys and a baby? He looked a lot like Tom Selleck, without a mustache.

He was Tom Selleck, without a mustache.

"Hey, look at this front-runner," razzed Red Sox utilityman Randy Kutcher. "If Detroit was in first place, he'd be wearing a Detroit hat."

While touring the country to promote his Western, *Quigley Down Under,* Selleck was also preparing for his next movie, tentatively titled *Tokyo Diamond,* a film about a veteran big leaguer who goes to Japan to play ball.

"When I do the movie, I want to be able to fool people," said Selleck, a guest on the Boston bench (with the required permission from the Brewers) during that night's game. "I don't think actors always do that when they make sports movies."

So Selleck, age forty-five, worked on his swing and soaked up some major-league atmosphere as he toured. When he was in New York, he worked out with the Yankees and hit a batting-practice home run. When he was at Fenway, he hit left-handed against lefty batting practice pitcher Bill

Moloney. No Anthony Perkins at the plate, Selleck displayed a fairly nice swing for an actor.

"Don't show us up, now," said Red Sox outfielder Danny Heep.

"What if he goes yard [deep]," worried Red Sox rookie outfielder Phil Plantier, "and I don't?"

Selleck slashed a few line drives to right, but didn't reach the seats. "I was a good hitter," said Selleck, who played junior college baseball and whose brother, Bill, pitched in the Dodgers' system. "But as demonstrated, I'm not crazy about the high, inside fastball. Not crazy about curveballs from lefties, either."

He promised to swing better than William Bendix did in the horribly laughable *The Babe Ruth Story.*

"I did see Bill Bendix play Babe Ruth," said Selleck with a smile. "No comment."

◆

On May 25, 1935, thousands of Greater Boston youngsters clutching coupons clipped from that morning's *Herald* made their way to Fenway Park for Herald Baseball School Day. The coupon not only got them into the ballpark, but also onto the field before the afternoon engagement between the Red Sox and the Tigers.

On the hallowed diamond, the awed youngsters gathered for instruction on the finer points of the game offered by manager Joe Cronin, catcher Moe Berg, and outfielder Mel Almada of the Red Sox and catcher Mickey Cochrane, outfielder Jo-Jo White, and pitcher Schoolboy Rowe of the Tigers.

The luckier boys received individual tutoring, and the luckiest got a chance to catch Schoolboy Rowe. "It will be a long time before they forget their delightful experience," noted the *Herald* the next day.

"I still remember so much about that

Thousands of fans said farewell to Babe Ruth's open casket as he lay in state in the rotunda of Yankee Stadium in August 1948.

day," said Eddie Barry in 1988, age sixty-five, of Quincy, who, as a twelve-year-old, was one of those who caught the Schoolboy that day. "I brought my catcher's mitt, and my friend and I bummed a ride to the ballpark. We hitchhiked. Meeting Mickey Cochrane was such a wonderful thrill. He was a local boy, which made it much more exciting. He instructed me in respect to catching. It was wonderful."

Among the many events in Barry's life since then were serving on an aircraft carrier during World War II and being with the Quincy Fire Department for five decades, including thirteen years as fire chief. But that May afternoon at Fenway never faded.

"At the time it meant so much," said Barry. "I still have fond memories of it, even though it was more than fifty years ago. That particular kind of thing, you never forget."

◆

Frank Guido of Chelsea, Massachusetts, and his nephew were at a Red Sox–Tigers game at Fenway Park late in 1974 when Al Kaline cracked a long home run—the 399th of his career—over the left-field wall.

Walking along Lansdowne Street after leaving the ballpark, Guido noticed a crowd of kids milling around the rooftop parking garage. "I figure out they're looking for that Kaline ball," said Guido. "So we go over there with them. I must have the greatest eyesight in the world, because I spot the ball on the railroad tracks."

Guido quietly elbowed his nephew, pointed out the ball, and told him to come along. "I tried to move nonchalantly," he said. "I wanted to get down the alley to where there was a hole in the fence, before anyone noticed. They saw what was going on just as I got to the break in the fence. Like an idiot, I ran across the railroad

tracks and got the ball. I could have gotten killed, for crying out loud. In fact, a few days later a kid going after a ball did get run over by a train there."

Guido had Kaline autograph the ball, which turned out to be the last homer of his career, then donated it to the Hall of Fame, where it is currently on display.

"I tell people I'm in the Hall of Fame," Guido said. "I get a lot of mileage out of it."

◆

In February 1988 in Winter Haven, Florida, the Sox Exchange fantasy camp of Montpelier, Vermont, finally rang up the Big Daydream: the campers took a game from the ex-Sox.

In one of the three-inning games at the end of camp that pitted civilians against old pros, Neil Kennedy of Chelsea, Vermont, shut out the former Sox, 1–0. The forty-five-year-old insurance executive surrendered only three hits, harmless singles to Gerry Moses, Darrell Brandon, and Rico Petrocelli. Meanwhile, Ed Schafer, a fifty-seven-year-old banker from Little Falls, New Jersey, batted home the winning run with a single against Gary Bell. On the turf at Chain O'Lakes Park, the campers had struck one for Walter Mittys everywhere.

"Everybody said beforehand, 'Don't even think about winning,'" said Kennedy. "But I never played that way. As the game went on and we made all the plays, we started to believe we could do it. Everybody was throwing gloves in the air, jumping around, carrying people off. It was like the real thing. Like we had won the World Series or something."

There were other highlights: Dave Greenblatt, age forty-two, a doctor from Newton, Massachusetts, struck out Bill Lee. In a civilians v. civilians game earlier in the week, the oldest camper—Ed Near-

Judge Kenesaw Mountain Landis, Christy Mathewson, and Judge Emil Fuchs (left to right)

ing, age sixty-five, of Morris, Connecticut—batted home the winning run, earning him immediate congratulations from spectator Ted Williams. As he accepted backslaps from the Splinter, Nearing's wife, Jane, shouted from the stands, "Now you can die happy."

◆

During a Giants game in Pittsburgh, the crowd was so large some spectators were seated on barrels in fair ground in the outfield. The New York outfielders greatly resented the overflow fans intruding on fair territory. At one point, the Giants' right fielder was chasing after a ball when a little girl seated on a barrel was in the way. The outfielder kicked over the barrel, sending the little girl sprawling on the ground, and retrieved the ball. He then threw out a Pirate runner at home plate.

New York pitcher Christy Mathewson called time, marched to right field, picked up the little girl, found her a seat in the first row of box seats, and apologized to her on behalf of the Giants.

◆

If there were a Hall of Fame for irritating fans, Patsy O'Toole would be in it. A Detroit ballpark regular in the 1920s and 1930s, the leather-lunged O'Toole was well known for his girder-shaking volume and ceaseless repetition.

"Boy, oh boy, oh boy," O'Toole would holler. "Keep cool with O'Toole. Keep cool with O'Toole."

His repertoire included just one insult: "You're a faker! You're a faker!"

And just one compliment: "You're a great guy! You're a great guy!"

O'Toole's career peaked during Game

Jimmie Foxx was offered whiskey by an inebriated fan, who had to be restrained.

Three of the 1933 World Series between the Senators and Giants. From his seat in the Washington ballpark, O'Toole started his deafening, repetitious routine: "Boy, oh boy, oh boy. Keep cool with O'Toole. Keep cool with O'Toole." He repeated himself every few minutes.

A few rows ahead of him, President Franklin D. Roosevelt crooked his finger to a Secret Service man and whispered something in his ear. In a few moments, the agent was crouched near O'Toole.

"O'Toole, I know you're a great guy and wouldn't mind doing a favor for the president," the agent said. "He wants you to move to the other side of the field. Mr. Griffith has made the arrangements."

O'Toole moved, having reached the top of the ballpark quack's pyramid: he had annoyed the president of the United States.

In the summer of 1920, Cincinnati Judge Edward T. Dixon prepared to go on vacation. A neighbor asked how long the judge planned to be away. "Dunno," he said. "Depends on Babe Ruth."

The neighbor then asked where he was going. "Dunno that either," the judge replied. "Also depends on Babe Ruth."

Judge Dixon then explained that his young son was enthralled by Ruth, the Yankees' new home-run-hitting sensation, and he had promised to take the boy to see a Ruthian blast that summer. Sunday morning, they would leave for Cleveland, where the Yankees were to play the Indians. "If Babe makes a home run the first day out, then we will be home that day," said Dixon. "We will remain with the Yankees, go where they go, and stay where they stay until Babe makes a home run. The missus knows we will be home the morning after Babe Ruth makes his next home run. Then we will go to the country."

The odds favored an early return. Ruth had slammed a home run in every 8.48 at-bats that summer. Dixon and his son figured to be home in a couple of days.

On Monday in Cleveland, Ruth walked thrice, with no homers.

On Tuesday, the game was rained out.

On Wednesday, Ruth twisted his knee in the outfield, had to be carried off the field, and wondered if he'd be sidelined for days.

On Thursday, Ruth played, but went hitless, his throbbing knee bothering him at the plate. The Yankees—and the Dixons—boarded the train for Philadelphia.

On Friday afternoon Ruth cracked his forty-second home run. On Saturday the Dixons went to the country.

◆

Just after World War I, Peahead Walker played third base for a semipro team in West Virginia where local fans had an irritating hobby. They toted rifles to the hills near the ballpark and picked off pop flies in the infield.

Baseball target practice was not unheard of in bush-league circles. As late as 1955, Elmira center fielder Bill Joffe put up his glove to catch a fly ball and a .22-

Joe ("Duckie") Medwick

caliber slug passed through his mitt. Back in Walker's wilder days, ballplayers just put up with it.

Then one morning, Peahead stormed into his manager's office, slapped his glove on the desk, and announced he was quitting.

"Why?" asked the manager.

"I don't mind those folks shooting at pop flies," said Walker. "But last night I heard them talking about starting to shoot at grounders."

◆

Late in the 1937 season, the Cardinals were on a road trip, and outfielder Ducky Medwick was in a dreadful slump. During a night game in Cincinnati, a teen-aged boy named Fred Martin was the guest of honor. Young Martin was a big Cardinals fan and had adopted the nickname "Pepper" Martin in honor of his favorite St. Louis outfielder. The boy was also a superb schoolboy player and had been invited to the ballpark for a pregame display of his storied fly-catching talents.

After the exhibition, young Martin got the offer of a lifetime. He was invited to wear a Cardinals uniform and sit in the Cardinals dugout during the game.

Late in the game, Medwick returned to the Cardinals' dugout after his third hitless trip to the plate. Ducky fixed his gaze on that smiling, admiring teenage boy.

"I thought there was a jinx around somewhere!" Medwick hollered. "It's a wonder they don't keep those [expletive] jinxes off our [expletive] bench so a [expletive] fellow can get a [expletive] hit every once in a [expletive] while!"

Minutes later, the tearful boy removed his uniform in the St. Louis clubhouse and left the ballpark with his father.

"You don't know these ballplayers," Cardinals manager Frankie Frisch said later. "For a couple of base hits, they'd throw their grandmothers out the window."

◆

Settling into his box seat to watch the Cardinals engage the Athletics in the 1931 World Series, Babe Ruth was quickly surrounded by autograph seekers. "Listen," said Ruth, as he signed and passed back scorecards, notebooks, and baseballs, "I'm going to stop when play starts. You know, I want to see some of this ball-game myself."

An hour later, Ruth had autographed an estimated five hundred items when the first batter of the game stepped to the plate. "No, that's all," Ruth said firmly to the latest signature hound. "No more until tomorrow."

"Can't you sign this baseball, Mr. Ruth,"

a weak voice said behind him.

"No, no. I turned down all the others," Ruth said over his shoulder. "Got to see the ball game."

"I'm sorry," said the voice, now dejected. "I had to come up on crutches and just got here."

"What's that? Crutches?" said Ruth. "Well, that's different." He reached back and took the ball. "Sorry you had so much trouble." Then out of the corner of his mouth, Ruth muttered, "That'll get me in trouble for sure."

"Won't you please sign this scorecard?" a woman's voice said from behind him. "My father owns a baseball team out West."

Ruth sighed, took the ball, signed his named and scribbled an added message: "Good luck to the Indians."

◆

On the night of September 18, 1956, Mickey Mantle blasted an eleventh inning home run in Chicago to clinch the American League pennant for the Yankees.

Meanwhile, in Lodi, New Jersey, David Sassano was making a purchase in Sam Graceffo's liquor store. A television set behind the cash register was tuned to the Yankee game, and, as Mantle rounded the bases after his homer, Sassano excitedly pounded his fists on the countertop. The vibrations caused a .32-caliber revolver on a shelf under the counter to fire, striking Sassano. The following January, Sassano sued Graceffo for $50,000 in damages.

◆

The Dodgers had dropped ten straight games to the hated uptown Giants when on July 12, 1938, Brooklyn exacted a measure of revenge by crushing New York, 13–5.

That night, postal clerk Robert Joyce,

Babe Ruth was mobbed by fans wherever he went.

age thirty-three, retired to a Brooklyn tavern to celebrate the big victory. In the course of the evening, Joyce entered a baseball discussion with two other patrons, Frank Krug and William Diamond. Joyce bubbled about the Dodgers' great day, but Krug and Diamond were not Dodgers fans and attributed the Brooklyn victory to dumb luck.

Several drinks later, Joyce left the bar. He returned later with a revolver in each hand and shot Krug in the chest and Diamond in the abdomen, killing them both.

◆

In the spring of 1915, a ten-year-old nephew of Philadelphia multimillionaire George Elkins suffered a long illness. For a while, the boy's family feared for his life, and, during one visit, Elkins promised his nephew if he was a good boy and took all his medication regularly, the lad could have anything in the world he wanted once he got well.

When the boy finally recovered, Elkins reminded him of the promise and urged him to ask for anything, anything in the world, he wanted. Elkins was confident he could afford whatever the boy's young mind could dream up—ponies, automobiles, airplanes.

The boy thought it over for a few days, then summoned his uncle. He had decided on his gift of a lifetime.

"Uncle George," he said. "I want to

shake hands with Grover Alexander, the Phillies pitcher."

In 1988 lifelong Boston baseball fan John F. Hardy recalled the summer of 1932, when he was fifteen years old and hitchhiked from Dorchester to Braves Field to collect ballplayer autographs.

"The meanest ballplayer I never forgave or forgot was Grover Cleveland Alexander," Hardy remembered. "After a day game as a Knotholer at Braves Field, my chum and I waited outside the Braves' dressing room to get a few autographs to add to my collection, when out came Rabbit Maranville and with him the great Grover Cleveland Alexander.

"He had pitched his last major-league game with the Phillies in 1930 and was barnstorming with the bearded House of David team. We already had the Rabbit's autograph; although we had never seen Alex pitch, we knew he was one of the all-time greats and his signature in our book was a must. We asked him for his John Hancock, but he gave us a gruff no and a mean look.

"He and Maranville and their wives walked all the way from Braves Field to the Hotel Minerva on Huntington Avenue, at least a two-mile hike. We tagged quietly and politely behind them all the way, hoping old Alex would break down and sign our books. His cold heart would not melt.

"We finally gave up at the entrance to the Minerva and started our sad trip home to Dorchester, walking six miles all the way. It was too dark for hitchhiking. It was cold beans for supper that night. It is not surprising that 1932 was the last year in my autograph-collecting career."

In the summer of 1990, Red Sox fan Dick Pillotte treasured his autographed baseball, signed by the entire Red Sox team. He took the precious ball to work at Omni Resources Corporation in Millbury, Massachusetts, where he is vice president for operations, and proudly displayed it on his desk.

Omni Resources has a branch in India and commonly imports Indian workers to its Massachusetts office for training sessions. The day after he placed his treasure on his desk, Pillotte was admiring the ball when he sat up straight in his chair. Inserted next to Mike Greenwell's autograph was a nonroster signature: Devinder.

Devinder was one of the Indian trainees, and Pillotte quickly summoned him to his office for an explanation. Devinder said he had entered Pillotte's office when he wasn't there, saw the baseball, and assumed it was some sort of logbook that everyone was supposed to sign. So he signed it. Devinder was subsequently dismissed from the company. Pillotte claimed the firing was a mere coincidence.

STRANGERS IN STRANGE LANDS

Folks who imagine life on the road is chocked with excitement and glamour probably never travel. Circus clowns, rock stars, and ballplayers know the truth. To visit new places, hear different accents, and lodge at nifty hotels with mints on the pillow is fun for a short while, just as driving a car is fun to sixteen-year-olds with fresh licenses. However, hotel life, like driving, fast becomes a chore. Journeys to strange lands leave a man walking disinfected corridors, bathing with miniature soaps, dialing an outside line to talk to the kids, dining on a tray set before the television, and flirting with chambermaids. Five cities in two weeks can empty any soul. Willy Loman was a salesman, but he could have been a second baseman.

Baseball men are required to perform exactly one-half their work on the road, so they make the best of it. After five, ten, fifteen, or twenty years rotating through the same cities, ballplayers turn each stop into a temporary residence, if not a home. Regularly visited hotels become as familiar as old apartments. Head waiters at favorite restaurants know their names and reserve the best tables for them, summer after summer. Friendships and loves develop, renewable when the schedule dictates: "Goodbye, see you next May 11–13." With a little saxophone music in the background, road life might assume a murky romanticism. Old ballplayers can't forget the lady in the white summer dress in New York, the cafe across from the park in Boston, the dry-as-dust martinis the hotel bartender mixed in Los Angeles, and the time they climbed the fire escape past the manager's room in Kansas City. Saxophone music or not, most ballplayers can't forget hours and hours staring at ferns in the lobby.

Some road lore giggles on about hayseeds plucked from the backwoods to play ball in big cities, where they stared at the tall buildings as well as the lobby ferns. Before their first baseball road trip, many ancients had never ridden in an elevator. Most had never dined in a restaurant, never mind signing a meal to the room. Some thought old Washboard Falls was a big city, and suddenly they were strolling Times Square.

Few modern ballplayers hit the big leagues with such naiveté; at least they have seen tall buildings on the evening news and watched *Kojak* order restaurant meals. But there are exceptions. After he joined the Phillies' outfield in 1983, Jeff Stone, a native of Kennett, Missouri, was offered a shrimp cocktail. He replied, "No, thanks. I don't drink."

Much road lore centers on fun and hijinks, the traditional ways to negate staring at lobby ferns. In the early years, first-class hotels rated ballplayers no better than vagabonds in short pants. They were banished to seedy boarding houses on the ramshackle side of town. Many players belonged there. When teams were finally quartered in first-class hotels, the ruffians often roamed the premises like the Marx Brothers at the ambassador's reception. This left night managers with the vapors and the baseball archives with some magnificently zany stories.

Ballplayers became more refined over the years, but there are elements of rascally road behavior throughout hardball history. Unlike business travelers, baseball travelers seldom felt compelled to behave. Untethered under any circumstance, baseball life drifts further from reality on the road. Model citizens at home sometimes become hell-raising wildmen on the road. Some engaged in real wickedness, such as drinking, gambling, and debauching till dawn. Some stuck to sophomoric fun, such as throwing food in the dining room, or dropping water balloons out windows.

Some engaged in a little of both. Braves shortstop Rabbit Maranville habitually stole bellhop uniforms and twiddled evenings away running the hotel elevator to wrong floors, insulting guests, and delivering bogus telegrams. After a night of spirited drinking, he also executed a legendary dive into a St. Louis hotel fountain, bobbed up with a fish in his mouth, and chomped; but in later years he denied biting the fish.

The modern player is generally more restrained. When old-timers felt like throwing something out the window, they threw. Ballplayers of the 1990s usually eschew childish pranks. They are millionaires with reputations to protect, and hotel rooms in glass-box skyscrapers usually don't have windows that open.

When night games began after World War II, baseball life on the road was totally rearranged. The ancients played ball in the afternoon, then played around town all night. Modern players while away the day waiting for the night shift to start. The game is on their minds like an unfinished homework assignment. Few

Manager Lou Boudreau had words for the umpire crew.

want to go to the movies, shop, or stroll through a museum. A routine weekday on the road follows this pattern: get up at nine, eat breakfast, read the newspaper in the lobby, return to the room, stare at the ceiling tiles, go out to buy razor blades, return to the room to watch tape-delayed wrestling on cable, go to the ballpark incredibly early, hang around and wait for the game, finish the game around 10:30 P.M., eat a greasy postgame meal in the clubhouse, catch perhaps one round of drinks in the hotel bar, go to bed. Were it not for weekend day games, twenty-first-century baseball archaeologists might not find any good road lore from the 1990s.

Day games or night games, fun, hijinks, and friends aside, the road usually wins a war of attrition. A baseball writer, born and raised in the East with all the attendant snobberies, once described the best and worst about the baseball tour: "Every city is worth visiting once. If not for covering baseball, I would never have seen Cleveland. If not for covering baseball, I would never have seen Cleveland twelve times." When he retired from the Red Sox after the 1989 season, pitcher Bob Stanley said he might have hung on a few more years but for the road, not an uncommon refrain.

Some men lose the war early. In the spring of 1933, slugger George Washington of the Shreveport team in the Texas League was sold to the Chicago White Sox. Washington had barely ventured outside of Cass County, Texas, where he was born and raised and where he happily worked a farm, hunted, and fished. Before his ballplayer left for the big city, Shreveport business manager Walter Morris tutored him on the rudiments of life in strange lands, such as how to order dinner in a restaurant, find a men's room in a public building, and hail a taxi on a busy street. Morris then issued Washington a train ticket to Chicago and wished him well.

Instead of reporting to the White Sox, Washington disappeared into the backwoods of Cass County. Angry telegrams from Chicago piled up on Morris's desk.

"Have you sold us the original George Washington?" said one.

"You don't happen to have an outfielder named Abraham Lincoln who is also for sale, do you, Walter?" asked another.

Morris hunted down his man. Bribing a local boy to pinpoint the ballplayer's favorite fishing hole, he hiked through forests, crossed streams, and squeezed through thick bushes until he finally came across Washington, who was lounging on a bank with a fishing pole in his hand.

"Morning, Mister Walter," Washington said.

"Morning, George," Morris answered, mopping his brow as he plopped down on the grass beside him. "Why didn't you report to the White Sox?"

"I'm sorry," said Washington. "But I just don't want to play ball none for them Chicago fellows. Too far to go to play ball."

With the Pittsburgh Pirates in the early 1920s, shortstop Rabbit Maranville roomed on the road with mop-up relief pitcher Chief Yellow Horse. Maranville had a reputation for hell-raising, and Yellow Horse had a reputation for eccentricity. The chief preferred to be paid in silver dollars, slept fully clothed with a straw hat pulled over his face, and took long walks to nowhere.

Not completely trusting the odd couple, Pittsburgh manager Bill McKechnie always quartered the pair on the same floor as himself. During a trip to New York, the Pirates struggled badly, and McKechnie was in no mood for Gotham hijinks of any kind.

After dinner at the Hotel Ansonia, he approached Maranville and Yellow Horse and asked about their plans for the evening. The chief said he was going out for a walk, and Rabbit said he would have friends up to the room. "Well," said McKechnie, "I expect to find you both in your room by ten o'clock."

After Maranville's visitors left and the chief returned from his aimless stroll, the two ballplayers decided to go to bed early. However, both found it impossible to sleep. Outside their open twelfth-floor window, a family of pigeons cooed and fluttered loudly. Suddenly Yellow Horse shot out of bed.

Joe McCarthy (left) *and Connie Mack*

Horse stepped in through the window, three hysterical pigeons flapping in his hand.

"For God's sake, what have you got there?" said McKechnie. "And where is Maranville?"

"He's out on the roof catching the rest of them," the chief answered calmly. "He'll be right in."

McKechnie rushed to the window and to his horror saw his shortstop clinging to the narrow ledge with one hand and tearing out pigeon nests with the other. Finished with his search and destroy mission, Maranville inched back along the ledge and caught sight of his manager.

"Hello, Bill," he remarked cheerfully. "We weren't in our room, but we weren't very far away, were we?" Thereafter, McKechnie quartered Maranville and Yellow Horse on ground floors.

◆

"Where are you going, Chief?" Maranville asked.

"I'm going to get rid of those damned pigeons," Yellow Horse shouted. "I've been laying here for fifteen minutes but haven't been able to close my eyes on account of the noise they're making."

Maranville, who during his Braves' days had walked the ledge of a St. Louis hotel while teammate Johnny Evers screamed at him to climb back in, decided to join the chief. The two ballplayers shuffled along the ledge in the night, twelve stories above Broadway. Finding the pigeon nest over a bathroom window, Yellow Horse climbed on Maranville's back to reach it.

Meanwhile, the clock struck ten, and McKechnie came to check on Maranville and Yellow Horse. Knocking on the door and getting no response, the manager walked in. Seeing the beds empty, he called out their names. Suddenly Yellow

Shoeless Joe Jackson first broke into the big leagues with Connie Mack's 1908 Athletics. Fresh from the backwoods of Greenville, South Carolina, Jackson was pure bumpkin. On the morning of a game, Mack once wandered by Jackson's dining-room table at the team hotel. Jackson was digging into a plate heaped high with fried eggs.

"How do you expect to play baseball after eating a meal like that?" Mack asked.

"I didn't order them, Mr. Mack," Jackson pleaded. "I just asked for two eggs. Honest."

Mack requested details. Jackson explained. The hotel dining room had guests write down their orders. Jackson wanted two fried eggs. "I didn't know how to make a two," Jackson confessed, "so I put down two ones." The waiter took the order form and served eleven eggs.

◆

Throughout his career, catcher Shanty Hogan fought a never-ending battle with excess weight. When he played for the Giants in the late 1920s and early 1930s, Hogan's waistline was closely watched by New York manager John McGraw. In one break between morning and afternoon practices, McGraw couldn't find Hogan. Noticing the rest of the players eating light sandwiches, McGraw figured Hogan had taken off to find heartier fare.

McGraw found him in the hotel dining room, halfway through a large steak. McGraw grasped Hogan by the arm and led him out of the restaurant. "Aw, have a heart," Hogan protested. "The first steak was just a little one."

McGraw eventually resorted to screening everything Hogan consumed. The manager ordered every meal check signed by Hogan to be delivered to his room for inspection. Incredibly, McGraw discovered that at nearly every meal Hogan was eating three portions of spinach, carrots, and peas. The vegetarian diet aside, Hogan still packed on pounds. When McGraw investigated, he discovered that Hogan had worked out a code with the waiters. Spinach meant steak, carrots meant potatoes, and peas meant pie.

◆

Johnny Allen pitched for five teams in thirteen big-league seasons, at each stop cementing his reputation as one of the most ornery men in baseball. "He was just plain mean," said Lou Boudreau, who played shortstop behind Allen for two seasons in Cleveland. "He wanted to hit the batter every time he had the ball in his hands. I remember the time he beaned a kid in spring training. Ended his career, if I remember right. I just never went near him. You never wanted to go near him anytime anything went wrong."

On the last day of the 1937 season, Allen was 15–0 and defending his perfect record against the Tigers in Detroit. He lost a duel with Detroit lefty Jake Wade, 1–0, on an error by second baseman Odell ("Bad News") Hale. That night, Allen attempted to throw Hale out of a sixteenth-story window at the Book-Cadillac Hotel.

◆

On April 4, 1933, the Red Sox exhibition game against the minor-league Newark Bears in Newark was rained out. The boys had an afternoon to kill in Gotham. Pitcher Henry Johnson, a native of Bradenton, Florida, decided to hole up in his hotel room. "Broadway never held any attraction for me," he said. "I'm just a small-town fellow. And while you birds may think Bradenton is a one-hoss town, it's good enough for me."

Outfielder Tom Oliver of Montgomery, Alabama, went off to the movies. "I just have to go to Broadway once in a while," he said. Outfielder Suitcase Bob Seeds of Ringgold, Texas, wandered off to Times Square. When he returned to the hotel, he was scratching himself furiously.

"What's the matter, Suitcase?" someone asked.

"I don't really know," he said. "But I just came from the trained flea circus on 42nd Street, and I really believe one of those fellows became attached to me."

◆

On Providence Street in Boston's Back Bay, site of the Brunswick Hotel, Babe Ruth and Yankee hurler Red Ruffing were relaxing on the afternoon of July 31, 1931, when the Babe smelled smoke. Ruth sniffed around the room, then looked out the window. Two floors below, a window

Babe Ruth signs autographs at the Polo Grounds before a game with the Giants.

♦

Winding down their barnstorming trip north before opening the 1934 season in Boston, the Red Sox found themselves rained out in Baltimore with nothing to do. Manager Bucky Harris gave his charges the day off and headed to Washington to visit his family. Next day, Harris returned to find his first baseman, Eddie Morgan, with both eyes swollen, nose broken, and face scratched.

Morgan's story: Deciding to sample Baltimore's speciality, he hailed a cab and asked the driver to take him somewhere to get soft-shell crab. The driver dropped off Morgan and picked him up after dinner. On their way back to the Lord Baltimore, Morgan told the driver he thought the seafood in Baltimore stunk. Arriving at the hotel, the cabdriver punched Morgan repeatedly.

awning was in flames. Using the pitcher from his room, Ruth poured water out the window to douse the fire.

♦

Because he was the scheduled starting pitcher for Game Five of the 1988 National League playoffs, Dodgers right-hander Tim Belcher was dispatched to the team hotel the previous night to get some sleep while his teammates stayed out late, playing Game Four with the Mets at Shea Stadium. However, one item in his room caused a problem: his television set.

"I left the ballpark and went back to the hotel around the third inning," said Belcher. "But I'll tell you, it was such an exciting game, I felt like I was there, even though I was watching it in my hotel room. I was making so much noise, hotel security came up and knocked on my door. I had waked up somebody in the next room."

♦

When the turn-of-the-century Philadelphia Athletics were finally allowed into first-rate hotels in spring training, the hotel's management quickly realized it had made a deluxe mistake. The A's were loud and abusive throughout the establishment, but particularly in the dining room, where they threw food and pinched waitresses.

Pitcher Rube Waddell was particularly demonstrative when he disapproved of a meal. One evening Waddell judged the steak he was served as far too tough, and he sent an errand boy out to fetch a hammer and nails. He then nailed the offending meat onto the dining room wall.

Waddell was once out on the town with Athletics catcher Ossee Schreckengost when, after a typically lively evening and early morning, the pair returned to the team hotel and proceeded directly to the room of manager Connie Mack. Waddell walked in without knocking, shook Mack awake, tossed a limburger and onion sandwich onto the bed, and suggested the manager hadn't been looking well for a couple days and the sandwich might help revive him. Waddell and Schreckengost walked out, and Mack sat up and stared at the sandwich.

◆

The Red Sox were in Washington with a day off on a Sunday. Young Boston lefty Babe Ruth asked manager Bill Carrigan for permission to visit his parents up in Baltimore. "I kind of hanker to drop in on the old folks," Ruth told his manager. "I ain't seen them for some time."

"Run along, Babe," said Carrigan.

On Monday, Ruth was back at the ballpark. Unknown to the Babe, Carrigan had arranged to have Ruth's father sit in a front-row box directly behind the Red Sox dugout. Carrigan also had arranged to be nearby when Ruth first emerged from the clubhouse tunnel and clattered up the dugout steps.

"Fine son you are, George," Ruth's father called out. "You never came to see your maw and dad."

Ruth peeked at his father, peeked at his manager, and skulked away.

◆

Cardinals manager Frankie Frisch was standing in front of the Hotel Kenmore in Boston one evening when something exploded at his feet, drenching his shoes, socks, pants legs, and several passersby. "It was a paper bag full of water that had been tossed from an upper window," Frisch later recalled. "If it had scored a direct hit, we could have dried off by jumping into the Charles River. It must have been a laundry bag."

Frankie Frisch (left) *and owner Sam Breadon*

Frisch stomped into the hotel in search of the culprit. When he found third baseman Pepper Martin in his room and saw the grin and gleaming eyes, he knew he had his man.

"Frank, that was a slip," said Martin, backing away from the steaming manager. "Honest it was. Now if you'll just forgive me this once, I'll go out and hit a home run for you tomorrow and win a ball game." Frisch relented. Next day, Martin hit a home run to beat the Braves.

Back in Boston later that summer, Martin looked out his Hotel Kenmore window and saw Frisch loitering on the sidewalk again. He couldn't resist. Martin giddily ran into the bathroom to fill a pitcher with water. In his hurry, he shattered the pitcher and badly cut his throwing hand. Not anxious to tell anyone about the injury, Martin fashioned a makeshift bandage from the medicine cabinet and hoped nobody, especially Frisch, would notice. Next day on his first play from the field, Martin picked up a grounder and threw the ball to first. His makeshift bandage spiraled across the infield behind the ball.

◆

When he was with Buffalo in 1958, former Red Sox outfielder Sam Mele accompanied the Bisons on an exhibition trip to Cuba to play the Havana Sugar Kings. "They moved the game to one of the outlying districts," said Mele. "We flew from Miami to some little grass airstrip up in the hills where we could hear shooting in the distance as we landed."

They also saw their escorts: bearded men dressed in army fatigues and carrying machetes and submachine guns. Mele wasn't sure which side of the revolution the fellows were on, but "they dressed like Castro."

Transported to their hotel by bus, the Bisons quickly discovered the worst part of the trip. "The food was terrible," said Mele. "There was nothing we could eat. The chicken still had hairs on it. The only thing that was good was the daiquiris. We ate cereal and drank daiquiris after the game."

Weary of the fare, after three days the Bisons happily bused back to the grass airstrip for the flight home. When they reached the plane, they wondered if they could ever go home again. Heavy rains had soaked the field, turning it into mud and deep puddles.

The pilot ordered the baggage loaded, but instructed the passengers to stay off the plane. "He told us he was going to go up on a trial run to see if he could get it off the ground," said Mele. "Then he said, 'What the heck. Everybody just get on. We'll give it a try.' It seemed like we were rolling along forever, with water splashing everywhere."

After the plane landed in Miami, nobody headed to the airport bar for a daiquiri. "Everybody scattered," said Mele. "We all went to find the biggest steak we could get our hands on."

◆

On a summer morning in Boston in 1926, Tigers player-manager Ty Cobb, Detroit coach Nig Clarke, and a reporter visited a Boston restaurant for breakfast. A young waiter delivered menu cards, then stood in nervous silence over the famous ballplayer. Cobb finally lowered his menu just a touch and slightly raised his left eyebrow. The waiter swallowed hard and leaned over solicitously, pencil poised above his order pad. "You may bring me some sliced peaches," began Cobb, who proceeded to recite a meticulously detailed order.

After the others ordered, the waiter hurried away. Cobb gently unfolded his napkin, sipped his glass of water, and gazed around the room. Soon the waiter arrived with Cobb's eggs, which he had ordered "fried in butter." When the plate was placed before him, Cobb removed the cover and held it aloft. The waiter missed his cue. Cobb raised his left eyebrow and held the cover higher. The waiter quickly plucked the cover from the ballplayer's hand.

In ominous silence, Cobb inspected the eggs from various angles. Finally he prodded one scornfully with his fork, looked at Clarke, then looked at the waiter. "I hate to look at these eggs askance," Cobb said gravely, "but I asked for two eggs fried in butter. And this—"

"Yes, sir," interrupted the waiter. "They are fried in butter, sir. I saw the cook—"

"Possibly, possibly," said Cobb. "But the main point is, how long were they fried? They were on the fire too long. And I know what I'm talking about when I speak of

Ty Cobb, Babe Ruth, and Tris Speaker (left to right)

eggs. I've cooked 'em for twenty years. When I go out on a hunting trip, sometimes we all take turns at cooking. And I have a picture in my mind's eye of what two eggs fried in butter ought to look like. Now, my boy, will you take these eggs away and bring me back some scrambled eggs? And don't cook them too long."

Soon the waiter was back with scrambled eggs. He plucked off the cover, placed the plate in front of Cobb, and scurried away from the table before Cobb could say a word. But there was no escape. Clarke's water glass was empty, and the waiter was obligated to return to the table to fill it.

"Now about these eggs," said Cobb, left eyebrow raised. "Did the cook break two fresh eggs into the pan, or did he dip some yolks out of a big bowl after the pastry cook had skimmed off the whites?"

The waiter said he was sure the eggs were prepared properly. "Well, you can see for yourself there isn't much white in that," said Cobb. "It seems to contain the yolks of about four eggs with no whites. Now you know for yourself the owner of this place would never let you use four eggs for one order. That being the case, the question is, what became of the whites?"

The waiter looked around the room, as if searching for help. "Did you ever hear of Chinese eggs?" Cobb continued. The waiter said he hadn't. "These are not Chinese eggs," Cobb continued. "But I'm going to tell you about them, so when I get through with you, you'll know something about eggs and why it is so hard for travelers to get good ones.

"In China, you know, they are very fond of chicken and have large flocks of poultry. But they don't eat eggs. They consider them waste. But enterprising foreigners buy them up in large quantities. The whites and yolks are separated and then dried and packed in bulk and shipped to this country and others, where they are used in making pastry, custard, and so forth. The scrambled eggs we used to get in the service were made of them. So when I speak of eggs, I'm not talking through my hat. I know them."

Cobb dismissed the waiter and ate his eggs. "Maybe you think I'm a crank about my food," Cobb said to the reporter. "I know for a fact that several waiters think so."

◆

By the winter of 1988, the eight-story building in Boston's Kenmore Square, on the corner of Kenmore Street and Commonwealth Avenue, housed a bank, offices, and apartments for the elderly. In an earlier incarnation, 490 Commonwealth Avenue was the Hotel Kenmore, the hub of Boston baseball.

Opened in spring 1926, the elegantly appointed hostelry eventually became headquarters for all fourteen teams that came to town to visit the Red Sox and Braves. It became known as the "Baseball Hotel" and catered to the special needs of the boys of summer. "Baseball players are wonderful guests," assistant manager Everett Kerr said in the summer of 1952. "But they can be superstitious. And they're moody."

Hired help was required to know the game thoroughly. Front-desk clerks had to be able to recognize and accommodate, say, Connie Mack if he showed up without a reservation. Bellhops and coffee-shop waitresses had to know who was in a slump in order to tiptoe around them. The staff was encouraged to listen to ball games over the radio as they worked.

After night games, the kitchen stayed open until 2:00 A.M. so the boys could grab a bite to eat before bed. Extra-long beds were supplied to taller players, such as Hank Greenberg and Ralph Kiner. Bathrooms were equipped with showerheads just like the ones in the ballpark clubhouses.

The place was rich with baseball lore. In the grille, Giants manager Leo Durocher had a lucky booth, the one he occupied while listening to the Dodgers lose a crucial game en route to the 1951 one-game playoff. When the Indians beat the Red Sox in the 1948 playoff, Cleveland owner Bill Veeck threw a party at the Kenmore that legend says lasted two days. Brooklyn shortstop Pee Wee Reese spent hours on Commonwealth Avenue feeding sugar cubes to the mounted policeman's horse. At one sitting in the dining room, Cardinals slugger Stan Musial consumed six lobsters.

Joe McCarthy quit as Yankees manager, Bill Dickey was fired as Yankees manager, and shortstop Rabbit Maranville retired from the Braves at the Kenmore. In the lobby in the spring of 1947, Detroit catcher Birdie Tebbetts was traded to the Red Sox for catcher Hal Wagner. House detectives were routinely stationed outside the room of a player known to fall asleep while smoking cigars. In the spring of 1943, Casey Stengel walked out of the Kenmore at 2:00 A.M. and was hit by a cab.

When the Braves left Boston for Milwaukee before the 1953 season, the Kenmore's baseball business was halved. In the spring of 1965, the hotel was closed and the building was sold. From the rooftop boxes at Fenway Park in 1991, fans can look up from the ball game, see the old hotel's mansard roof and dormer windows, and wonder about the old ballplayers who used to throw them open in the morning, breathe in deep, and look forward to a coffee-shop breakfast and a ball game.

◆

Hank Greenberg (left) *and Babe Ruth in 1945*

◆

Catcher Matt Batts played four seasons with the first-class, if not first-place, Red Sox before he was traded to the low-rent St. Louis Browns in the spring of 1951.

"When I was with the Red Sox, we always stayed at the Shoreham Hotel when we were in Washington," said Batts. "I always used to cash my checks there. When I was traded to the Browns, we stayed at the Shoreham, too. I went to cash my check, and the girl said, 'I'm sorry, sir, but I can't cash a check for you.' She said I'd have to talk to the manager. The manager came over, and I told him they used to cash my checks for me all the time when I was with the Red Sox.

"He said, 'Yes, sir. But you're with the Browns now.'"

◆

One night when the Boston Braves were in New York, pitcher Jack Scott challenged shortstop Rabbit Maranville to a footrace down Broadway. Scott allowed the Rabbit to open a good-sized lead, then shouted "Stop, thief!" Several passersby chased Maranville for several blocks.

◆

◆

When the Red Sox visited Yankee Stadium, Mississippi-born first baseman George Scott was customarily the houseguest of native New Yorker Joe Foy at the Foy residence in the Bronx, some half-dozen blocks from the ballpark.

One night, Scott and Foy were strolling home along the mean streets when they came across a couple sitting on a curbstone. The man and woman were engaged in close physical contact, clearly on their way toward intercourse. "Not in a car," said Scott later. "Right there on the curbstone!"

Scott gaped at them, and Foy tugged at his arm. "C'mon," said Foy. "You're liable to see that five or six times before you get to my house."

James ("Dusty") Rhodes (left) *and Leo Durocher*

◆

Not long after he joined the White Sox in 1935, rookie pitcher Silent John Whitehead pitched five consecutive complete games. In the ninth inning of his next start, on a Sunday afternoon at Fenway Park, Whitehead suddenly suffered control problems. Manager Jimmy Dykes yanked him from the game before he could waste Chicago's commanding lead.

Dykes later launched an investigation. What was wrong with Whitehead? Some White Sox told him the pitcher had been ailing throughout the game with a leg problem, which caught up with him in the ninth. Others confided that Whitehead had hurt his leg while out on the town in Boston the night before. Dykes dug further before he discovered what Whitehead, a twenty-six-year-old native of Coleman, Texas, had been up to on Saturday night.

"I never bowled before," said Whitehead sheepishly, when Dykes confronted him with the evidence. "Well, the next morning my left leg was about as limber as a telegraph pole. Sure, I knew I was going to pitch. But I didn't know what bowling could do to a stranger."

◆

When he was a second baseman with the Boston Braves in 1947, Danny Murtaugh and his roommates left the team's roadside motel one night for a poker game. The game lasted into the next morning, and the boys went straight from playing cards to the ballpark.

Unshaven and disheveled, Murtaugh and his roommate walked smack into Boston manager Billy Southworth.

"Did you sleep well last night?" Southworth asked sweetly.

"Like babies," the players said in unison.

Joe Foy

"That's good," said Southworth. "I was afraid you might have been disturbed by the truck that crashed through your room in the middle of the night."

◆

The Cardinals had just arrived in Boston from Philadelphia, and Mr. and Mrs. Dizzy Dean shared a cab to the hotel with St. Louis baseball reporter J. Roy Stockton and his wife.

"I didn't see you at the ballpark in Philadelphia, Mrs. S.," Patricia Dean said as the cab rolled along. "Whatever did you do with yourself?"

"Oh, I took in all the historical sites," Mrs. Stockton replied. "The home of Betsy Ross. Independence Hall."

Mrs. Dean turned to Dizzy and sighed. "You know, Diz, that's a wonderful idea," she said. "That's what we ought to do while we're in Boston."

Dean grunted. "What in hell is historic about Boston?" he muttered.

◆

As the game against the White Sox was about to begin at Comiskey Park one night in 1969, the press box telephone rang in front of Red Sox traveling secretary Jack Rogers. Boston manager Dick Williams was on the line with a problem regarding pitcher Vicente Romo.

"Romo's missing," said Williams. "Find him."

Like Broderick Crawford tracking an escapee, for three days Rogers combed Chicago's jails, police stations, hospitals, and morgues. No sign of Romo. "The last we heard of him he was in a Mexican restaurant," said Rogers. "Finally, on the day we were leaving for Milwaukee, I got a call in the hotel. They told me 'Romo's back.' A couple of Chicago cops came up to check him out, to make sure he wasn't hurt or anything. He didn't have a scratch on him. Just a little stubble of a beard.

"He slept all the way on the bus to Milwaukee. Then Williams had him pitch that night. Then we got to Kansas City, and Williams had him starting on a hot, hot day. He went eight innings, led off the ninth by beating out a single, and collapsed."

◆

On a far-Eastern tour one season, Yankees pitcher Lefty Gomez and his ex-dancer wife, June O'Dea, checked into their Manila hotel after an exhausting twenty-day voyage. The hotel was magnificent, with wide windows overlooking a busy boulevard. As he and his wife prepared to get some sleep, Gomez noticed a net draped over a crossbar above the bed. He called the front desk to ask what it was for. "Mosquitoes, sir," the clerk replied politely.

Lefty and June pulled the netting over

the bed and snuggled under the covers. A few minutes later, they heard something drop onto the net. They listened. Something chirped. June cringed and grabbed Lefty's arm. There was a purple and yellow lizard slithering across the net near her head. Lefty jumped out of bed, gingerly picked up the critter by the tail, and hurled it out the window.

June shrieked and gestured toward the ceiling. At least two dozen lizards were clinging to the panels. Gomez fetched a window pole, one by one poked the lizards onto the floor, picked them up, and tossed them out the window.

The telephone rang. It was the front desk. "Passersby are complaining, sir," the clerk said. "What are you throwing out the window?"

"Lizards!" said Gomez. "The place is full of them."

"I'm sorry, sir. But they are very useful, sir," the clerk said. "They eat mosquitoes. The management puts them in each room for the guests' convenience."

◆

On the morning of July 8, 1945, Boston Braves pitcher Mort Cooper breakfasted at the Commodore Hotel in New York and returned to his room to read the newspaper. Cooper wanted a cigarette, but his lighter wouldn't ignite. He took it over to the window sill, where the light was better, and began repairs.

When Cooper heard the drone of a passing aircraft, he glanced at the sky and saw a twin-tailed B-25 bomber. Cooper watched the plane roar past the RCA building. He thought the plane seemed a little low, in fact, very low.

Leaning out to get a better look, Cooper bumped his head on the window. The plane disappeared behind a tall building and emerged on the other side. Cooper followed the bomber as it flew straight into the seventy-ninth floor of the Empire State Building and exploded. As Cooper staggered back into his room, Braves pitcher Big Bill Lee ambled in. "Hey, Mort," he said, "you're shaking like a leaf!"

◆

In June 1929 White Sox first baseman Art ("What a Man") Shires, whose batting average never matched his monstrous ego, was with the team in New York when he ventured out to see a Broadway show. As he walked down the aisle to his seat before the start of the third act, he heard an outburst of applause from the orchestra section. Shires appreciated the recognition, although he wasn't surprised by it. First bowing to the left and then to the right, he then turned to bow to the seats behind him and found himself face-to-face in the aisle

Jimmy Dykes

with Douglas Fairbanks and Mary Pickford, for whom the applause was intended.

◆

When flamboyant outfielder and first baseman Ken Harrelson came to the big leagues with the Kansas City Athletics in the summer of 1963, his first roommate was pitcher Bill Fischer. The roomies quickly had a major point of contention: Harrelson's transistor radio.

"He would always play the damn thing," said Fischer. "He'd fall asleep with the radio on. He couldn't sleep with the radio off, and I couldn't sleep with the radio on. He'd be asleep, and I'd get up and turn it off. He'd wake up and turn it back on."

One night at the New Yorker Hotel, Fischer settled it. He got up, grabbed the radio, and threw it out the window. Their room was on the sixty-first floor.

◆

The Red Sox took their first plane ride as a team in spring 1946 when they flew from Sarasota, Florida, to Havana for a weekend exhibition series against the Yankees. The flight went without incident, although the hotel had turbulence. The first night at their Havana quarters, roommates Boo Ferriss and Bobby Doerr were snoozing peacefully in their beds when they were awakened by the crack of gunfire. Ferriss and Doerr bolted straight up and listened. Then they heard shouting and running footsteps in the corridor outside their room.

"We didn't know what was going on," said Ferriss. "We were scared half to death. We didn't know if the hotel was burning down, or if someone was attacking the hotel, or what." Finally, the boys screwed up enough courage to open the door and peek into the hallway. "We opened it a crack," said Ferriss. "And I do mean a

crack." They hailed an official-looking passerby, who explained that two rooms down, a Cuban staying at the hotel had been murdered by gangsters.

Ferriss and Doerr bolted the door, propped a chair against it, and sat up all night worrying. "I don't remember how we

Dizzy Dean

made out in that series or anything else about that trip," said Ferriss. "All I remember is that night with the pistol shots."

◆

New York Giants manager John McGraw required his players to eat all meals at the team hotel, signing their checks to the Giants' account. This enabled McGraw, a firm believer in good diet for ballplayers, to inspect meal tickets and monitor what his men ate. For instance, on a hot day in Cincinnati, a Giants pitcher collapsed on the mound after working just two innings. "After this," McGraw told the revived hurler, "you ought to know enough to stay away from that roast pork and two slices of watermelon at lunch."

When he joined the Giants in 1909, free-spirited Bugs Raymond was slow to grasp the McGraw diet plan. In one city, the Giants were limited to three dollars a day to eat at the team's fashionable hotel. Bugs knew McGraw kept track of meals, but he wasn't sure how. As usual, Raymond wandered the city, visiting pals in various taverns, and consuming solid food only at soup kitchens and free-lunch counters. On the night of the third day in town, the team trainer sought out Raymond in his room and warned him McGraw would inspect the meal tickets and know he hadn't eaten a single meal at the hotel. Next morning, Raymond ate at the team hotel and in his mind squared matters with McGraw's system. He had a nine-dollar breakfast.

◆

George Digby, who scouted the Southeast for the Red Sox from 1944 through 1990, figured he drove 1.5 million miles scouring six states for baseball talent over the years. Thus he often found himself a stranger in strange places.

Art ("What a Man") Shires

"I was in Louisiana in the 1940s, in a little place that looked like an old Western town," Digby began. "A livery stable and everything. I checked into the hotel just in time to get to the game. At the ballpark, I met a priest from Boston who invited me to his place to talk baseball. By the time I got back to the hotel, it was 1:00 A.M., and the door was locked. I kept banging on it, but nobody would come down to let me in.

"All of a sudden I felt a gun in my back. It was the constable, who thought I was trying to break in. He told me to sleep in the car. I tried, but the mosquitoes were too bad. I found my way back to the priest's place, which wasn't easy because there

Mort Cooper

were no lights, and stayed with him. I'll never forget that gun in my back.

"I went back to the hotel the next morning to give them hell about being locked out. I walked in and the lady at the desk said, real pleasant, 'Good morning, Mr. Digby. Nice to see you up so early this morning.' I didn't have the heart to say anything. I just packed my bag and went on to the next town."

◆

One afternoon in 1922, former Giants shortstop John Montgomery Ward and former Giants manager Jim ("Truthful Jim") Mutrie swapped stories about the old days when baseball players were as welcome in America's hotels as cockroaches.

Ward's favorite story concerned the Giants' arrival in St. Louis for an October series to find the city crammed with conventioneers. The team's usual hotel was full. "The best they could do was one big room, with cots in it," Ward said. "We tried it one night but couldn't sleep. So, by unanimous consent, we sidetracked the cots and gathered around a big table and played poker for five nights. When a poker player got so tired that sleep was an absolute necessity, he staggered into the hall and lay down on the floor, where people going to and from the dining room had to step over him."

Mutrie's favorite story was about crisscrossing New England with an amateur team in the 1860s. Seldom was there more than one hotel in a given town, so the opposing teams often bunked at the same place. Rivalries ran high. "It was common for two players to start a pillow fight. I have seen pillow fighters surging all over a hotel and the air so thick with feathers one could hardly breathe," said Mutrie. One bitter pillow battle was raging at a Lynn, Massachusetts, hotel when the baseball manager was confronted by the night manager. Feathers swirled around them, as if they had met in a snowstorm.

"I guess I better get my men out of the hotel, hadn't I?" Mutrie asked.

"I guess you will," said the hotel manager, picking feathers from his mouth. "Either your players will have to get out of here, or I will. Somebody has got to leave this hotel."

MANAGERS

asey Stengel, Ty Cobb, and Ted Turner each held the job, which proves baseball managing is strange duty. Only odd fellows could love it. Managing requires a man to wedge himself between owners with hard heads, fans with soft hearts, and players with delicate egos. Managers are usually hated by all three. Presidents of the United States do tougher work, but at least they get four-year contracts. Both occupations beg the question: why would anyone want the cursed job, anyhow?

"Hanged if I know," answered catcher Mickey Cochrane in 1938, his fourth year as Detroit manager. When he was a player with the Athletics and the Tigers, Cochrane was a renowned fun lover, always cheerful and occasionally strumming a ukulele in the clubhouse. Managing turned Black Mike's mood dark.

"Listen," he said. "When I was a player, I didn't have to worry about anybody but myself. Good money and easy work. Now what? I have to worry about everybody on the club. I have to see that they're in shape and keep them in shape. If one of them eats something that makes them sick, it makes me sick, too. If one of 'em breaks a finger, I'm hurt, too. They get paid for playing, but I get paid for keeping the club in the race. They're through when the game is over, but I'm working and worrying day and night. What a job!"

Stress and intensity build character, and characters; the archives present plenty of managers as colorful as a box of Crayolas. The job has taken all kinds. Managers can be cranks or clowns, gentlemen or goons, drunks or teetotalers. Sometimes managers mellow as the seasons pile up; sometimes they yellow around the edges. Jimmy Dykes, who managed the White Sox in the 1930s and 1940s, was a famous cutup. In 1960 he was sixty-three years old and managing the Indians, his sixth team in twenty years. "By then he just kind of sat at the end of the bench, scratching his back on the dugout wall," recalled Red Sox manager Joe Morgan, an Indian briefly that season.

Gordon ("Mickey") Cochrane   *Jimmy Dykes* (left) *and Connie Mack*

Soldiers love to talk about their old sergeants. Students love to recall their former teachers. Baseball men love to spin tales about their old skippers, so the archives overflow with lore about managers. Whether they adored or hated him, ballplayers never forget a man they played for. Some recall old managers with just a look in their mirror. Teams often assume the personality of the manager. So do individual players.

"You put New York Giants on the front of their shirts, and they think they're wonderful," Giants manager John McGraw ranted after his charges dropped an exhibition game to the Phillies in the spring of 1921. "I have never seen a team play so badly as the Giants played today. They loafed on the bases. They missed signals. World champions? Don't make me laugh. I got a good mind to fire the bunch of them. Ballplayers? They're jokes."

McGraw was reminded that the game was only an exhibition. "No, it didn't mean a thing!" McGraw howled. "Why, every time we meet the Phillies this season they'll remember the licking they gave us today."

Fourteen springs later, one of McGraw's players from the 1921 team managed the St. Louis Cardinals. "World's champions, and they put an exhibition on like that!" Frankie Frisch ranted after his charges dropped an exhibition game to the Giants. "They think they're good. They think other teams are going to play dead. How are we ever going to win the pennant this year with stuff like that? Why, a high school team could have beaten us the way we played today. The boys were loafing on the bases."

Frisch was reminded the game was only an exhibition. "Letting the Giants win today gives them confidence!" Frisch howled. "Every time we play them this season they'll remember today's game!"

McGraw and Frisch searched for ways to kick their men in the seats of their flannel pants. Into the 1990s, motivation remained a manager's top charge. They write out lineup cards, signal baserunners to stay or steal, and sweep dust onto umpires. None of their strategic decisions works if the boys won't sweat, dive, and charge on the basepaths for them. Tommy Lasorda's chief task with the 1990 Dodgers was the same as Uncle Wilbert Robinson's with the 1920 Dodgers: incite the troops.

The job becomes trickier as the players get richer and more sensitive. Oakland manager Tony La Russa tells a story about when he managed the White Sox and verbally whipped a sluggish Carlton Fisk. The veteran catcher didn't respond and told La Russa why: "Everybody needs a kick in the butt now and then, but nobody ever needs a knife in the heart." Lore offers tales of various motivational tools, from throwing tantrums to throwing dirty looks to throwing food.

John ("Red") Corriden, Bill Veeck, Sr., Charlie Grimm, Jack Doyle, and John Schultze (left to right)

A man who loves managing probably enjoys challenges, wearing a baseball uniform every day, and thankless effort. Whatever obstacles he leaps in a single bound, he almost never gets credit. Even legends needed to clap their ears to loud critics. There was no Sultan of Skippers. McGraw? Too hard on his players. Stengel? A bozo. Connie Mack? Too soft on his players. Few managers leave the job with a gold watch and a warm handshake. Most die in office or get fired.

"No, thanks," said Art Fletcher, Yankee coach and former Phillies' manager, when asked if he'd like to take over the New York team. "I had four years of it with the Phils. I promised my wife and myself I would never go through that again. And I never will."

Other thousands of distinguished baseball men have dropped to their knees to beg for the job, including Babe Ruth whose prayer was never answered. Managers may be odd fellows, or just men who don't mind cruel work as long as it involves the sweet game. When he managed the Braves, one-time dental student Stengel lit a cigarette and said, "Baseball is a lot more pleasanter than pulling teeth."

The longtime baseball writer for the Boston *Globe*, Cliff Keane, covered the Boston Braves in 1948 as they outwrestled the richly talented Brooklyn Dodgers for the National League pennant. One night while the first-place Braves were in New York, Braves manager Billy Southworth asked Keane if he had ever eaten frogs' legs. Keane said no. "Come on," said Southworth. "Let's go get some."

After consuming generous helpings of unfortunate Kermit limbs—and after Southworth had consumed several mugs of beer—the two men sat happy and bloated at the restaurant table, winding up the meal. Southworth had a question for Keane.

"Who would you say," the manager asked, "was the man most responsible for our success this season?"

Keane knew exactly the answer Southworth wanted: Southworth. He wasn't about to give it to him.

"Johnny Sain?" said Keane innocently.

Southworth stared. "Bob Elliott?" said Keane.

"Alvin Dark?"

Southworth kept staring.

"Warren Spahn?"

Southworth lifted the dining table and dumped it into Keane's lap, splattering the writer with ketchup, coffee, and bits of frogs' legs.

"Frogs' legs," said Keane, relating the story in the summer of 1989. "Haven't had 'em since."

◆

Baseball managers know a good way to discipline men is to play with their food. Sometimes they kick it around the clubhouse.

"Gene Mauch was a great food-table thrower-over," said Red Sox manager Joe Morgan, who added that, as a manager, he never resorted to heaving the post game spread. "I played for him in Philadelphia.

We didn't have a very good team that year. He was usually the first one in after a brutal game, and we'd get in there and find the food all over the place. Spaghetti or chicken or whatever. It definitely kills the old appetite, seeing your food all over the floor.

"Joe Schultz, when I played for him in Atlanta in Triple–A, was another. Joe turned over a few tables. But never when they had kielbasa. He loved that stuff."

Sometimes they dangled food in front of the starving troops. "I remember hearing about managers who, after a tough ball game, would forbid anyone to touch the postgame food until they said so," said Morgan. "They'd make them sit there for a half-hour. Then you didn't feel like eating anymore."

Sometimes they supplied food to the enemy. "Harry Walker told me this story once," began Morgan. "He was always talking about guys eating too much and getting logy before a ball game. He didn't think anyone should eat after one or two in the afternoon when there was a night game. He told about one time they had a semipro game in Leeds, Alabama. In order to ensure a win by the locals, his father would put on the biggest dinner for the visiting team at about four o'clock in the afternoon.

"But Harry also heard another guy say they knew exactly what his father was doing. But they said they had a great time anyway. They came to have a good feed, not to win a ball game."

◆

After he sent midget Eddie Gaedel to pinch-hit against the Tigers in 1951, St. Louis Browns owner Bill Veeck concocted another innovation to enhance interest in his pitiful team. He enlisted 1,115 fans to manage.

For the August 24 night game against the Philadelphia Athletics at Sportsman's Park, Veeck relegated regular manager Zack Taylor to a box seat near the dugout, where for much of the evening Taylor reclined in a rocking chair and sipped a cool drink. The Browns, meanwhile, were skippered by a selected section of grandstand spectators.

Before the game, the manager-fans chose the Browns' starting lineup by ballot. Each manager-fan was then issued two placards, one printed with a large *Yes,* the other with a large *No.*

During the course of the game, when a managerial decision was in order, large signs suggesting possible moves were held up in front of them. The 1,115 managers voted with their *Yes* and *No* placards. Circuit Judge James E. McLaughlin tabulated the votes and relayed the decisions to the field. "It's our great experiment," Veeck said. "People like to do things like this."

The committee of skippers immediately placed themselves in contention for Managers of the Year. Their starting lineup included two previously benched Browns: catcher Sherm Lollar and first baseman Hank Arft. Lollar homered, doubled, and singled, with two runs batted in. Arft also drove in a pair of runs.

In the first inning, Pete Suder came to bat with Athletics on first and third and one out. The grandstand committee voted to play the infield at double-play depth. Suder grounded into a double play.

In the Browns' first, with a three-and-two count on Cliff Mapes, Lollar at first, and one out, the grandstand consensus deigned to hold the runner. Mapes struck out. Had he been running, slow-footed Lollar would have been out, and the inning would have been over. St. Louis instead proceeded to score three runs.

All in all, the box-seat braintrust piloted the Brownies to a 5–3 victory. But the experiment wasn't a complete success; not including the managers, paid attendance was only 3,925.

◆

Former Giants outfielder Dusty Rhodes was thinking about Leo Durocher on July 27, 1990, the Lip's eighty-fifth birthday.

"To me, he was one of the best managers there ever was," Rhodes said from his Staten Island, New York, home. "I'm surprised he's not in the Hall of Fame. He was tough, but he couldn't manage today. Not with these players making all this money. They'd throw a bat at him."

Rhodes remembered the time Durocher ordered a Giant pitcher—"I won't say who, because he's still around"—to hit an opposing batter in the kneecap. "If you don't hit him in the kneecap," Durocher said, "I'm going to fine you five hundred dollars."

The first pitch sailed at the hitter's head; he ducked out of the way. The second pitch sailed behind the hitter's head; he again avoided getting hit. The third pitch rode in on the hitter's ankles; he skipped out of the way.

On 3–0, the hitter expected a pitch down the heart of the plate. The pitcher cracked him squarely in the kneecap.

"I got him! I got him!" the pitcher squealed, jumping for joy on the mound.

◆

Athletics manager Connie Mack long struggled to keep watch over pitcher Rube Waddell, a hard-drinker with a wide streak of wanderlust. Mack figured the best way to keep Waddell from trouble was to keep Waddell broke, so he dispensed the lefty wildman's pay fifty cents at a time and instructed the players not to lend Waddell a cent, under any circumstances.

One day, Waddell visited Mack's office.

Bobby Veach

"Connie, I have lost that gold watch charm that the Philadelphia fans gave me last year, and a fellow down in Hogan's Saloon has found it and refuses to give it to me unless I give him a reward of five dollars," he reported.

Always on guard about matters involving Waddell and taverns, Mack refused to give Waddell the money but agreed to accompany him to Hogan's to confront the man.

At the bar, Mack met a scruffy, burly fellow who indeed had the watch charm and indeed refused to turn it over unless properly compensated. In disgust, Mack threw five dollars to the man, who gave the watch charm to Waddell. Waddell was absolutely delighted.

"Well, Connie," he said as they neared the manager's office. "I'll be leaving you now, and I'll see you just before the game."

Recalled Mack years later: "Needless to

say, he didn't show up for that game or several games afterward. He and his precious friend divided my five dollars two ways. And you could buy an awful lot of the stuff for five dollars then."

◆

In San Antonio in 1931, the New York Giants played their first night game. Besides a dimly lit outfield and odd shadows, a big problem was apparent: great swarms of bugs drawn to the illuminated diamond.

During the game, as a rookie New York outfielder chased a fly ball, a large insect zoomed down his throat. The outfielder was consumed by a coughing fit that would not stop and had to be removed from the game.

Afterward, manager John McGraw gathered his men and offered the first bit of night strategy of his career. "One thing to

remember," he instructed. "You must keep your mouth shut when you play these night games."

◆

Worn and weary after managing in the big leagues for thirteen years, including a magnificent run to the world championship with the 1914 Miracle Braves, high-strung George Stallings kicked back to the more relaxed atmosphere of the minors.

Shortly after he took over the Rochester club, one of Stalling's outfielders badly misplayed a fly ball. After the game, Stallings ordered the man brought before him. When a coach produced the outfielder, he asked, "What do you want me to do with him?"

"Pour gasoline over him," Stallings ordered, "and burn the uniform off him."

◆

Lou Boudreau (left) *and Hank Fras*

In the spring of 1942, when he was twenty-four years old, shortstop Lou Boudreau was named player-manager of the Cleveland Indians. Boudreau was young, and he was a college guy. Those were not great managerial credentials to some of the crusty cutthroats who played big-league ball in the 1940s.

"I remember my first day on the job in spring training," said Boudreau during a visit to Boston in 1989. "I was sitting behind my desk in the office. One by one, three guys came in: Gerry Walker, Ben Chapman, and Hal Trosky. They each said, 'I put in for this job, and I know I could do a helluva lot better at it than you can.' And then they walked out. That was my first day."

Some of Boudreau's troops were less than impressed with his raccoon-coat background. "When I'd come over to the mound to talk to them, they'd say, 'Hey, college kid. Go back and play shortstop. I'll do the pitching,'" he said. "If I booted a ball, they'd yell at me to go back to college and learn how to field grounders. And I'm the manager."

Boudreau, who had coached several freshman sports at Illinois, also made the mistake of posting collegiate-style inspirational slogans in the Cleveland clubhouse.

"Things like Have a Will to Win, and Have a Passion to Score Runs," he said. "It didn't take me long to figure out they didn't go for that college stuff. Those signs lasted one day. They tore them down and spit tobacco juice on them."

◆

New York Giants manager John McGraw thought hard about how to keep pitcher Bugs Raymond sober on game day. Once McGraw hired a private detective named Fuller to tail Raymond from the moment he got up in the morning until he reported to the ballpark in the afternoon. Raymond quickly noticed he was being followed and invited Fuller to join him on the town. The pair showed up at the ballpark, both drunk.

"I'm full," Raymond chuckled. "But he's Fuller." Raymond then staggered out onto the field and shut out the Phillies.

Another time, McGraw posted two security men outside Raymond's hotel room, which had been searched and cleared of all booze, and ordered them to keep the pitcher inside until it was time to leave for the game. No one left or entered the room.

When the security men fetched Raymond to go to the ballpark, they found him thoroughly inebriated. Raymond had lowered a bucket at the end of a rope out the window to a companion, who filled and refilled and refilled the container with beer.

◆

As manager of the 1921 Tigers, Ty Cobb thought outfielder Bobby Veach was a little too easy-going for his own good. The Georgia Peach schemed hard to light a fire under him.

Cobb finally came up with an idea. He enlisted right fielder Harry Heilmann to goad Veach from the on-deck circle. Insult him, Cobb said. Call him every nasty name you know. Get him so angry he'll rip the cover off the ball.

Heilmann protested. He didn't want to lose Veach's friendship. Cobb assured him he'd explain the plan to Veach at the season's end.

Veach batted .338 and developed a deep, burning hatred for Heilmann. When the season ended, Cobb took off with his hunt-

Connie Mack, Jr., Connie Mack, and Earl Mack (left to right)

Kid Gleason (left) *and Ty Cobb*

ing dogs without a word. Heilmann himself desperately tried to explain to Veach, who told him to "not come sucking around me with that phony line." Heilmann and Veach remained enemies for life.

◆

Pawtucket was playing at Richmond, and two were out in the bottom of the first. Richmond outfielder Eddie Miller— later with the Rangers and Braves—was at third base. "There wasn't a sound in the ballpark," recalled Red Sox manager Joe Morgan, PawSox manager at the time. "Nothing. It was dead."

The visitors' dugout was about thirty feet from third base. "Very close," said Morgan. So Morgan struck up a conversation with Miller.

"Hey, Eddie, why don't you steal home?" he suggested. "Wake this crowd up a little bit."

"C'mon, Eddie. It's awfully dead in here. Steal home so we'll have a little noise," Morgan implored.

"Go head, Eddie. You can make it. Why

don't you go on the next pitch?" Morgan goaded.

Next pitch, Miller broke for the plate. "We had him out by about ten feet," said Morgan.

The inning over, Miller ran past the Pawtucket dugout on his way to the outfield. "Mr. Morgan," he yelled, "that's the last time I ever take your advice."

◆

In the summer of 1967, Red Sox third baseman Joe Foy and first baseman George Scott roomed together in Boston at the Somerset Hotel in Kenmore Square. Foy enjoyed Boston's nightlife, sometimes into the next morning.

One time when Foy was out, Boston manager Dick Williams came around after curfew to check on his young ballplayers. When Williams rapped on the door, Scott hopped out of bed, stuffed pillows under the covers in Foy's bed, and opened the door.

"So Dick Williams comes in, throws back the covers, and finds pillows instead of Joe Foy," Scott recalled in the autumn of 1989. "Dick Williams fined me $500 for covering for him."

◆

Late in the 1941 season, Red Sox farmhand Eddie Popowski got hurt, decided to cut his season short, and prepared to head home for the winter.

"Herb Pennock was the farm director then," began Popowski, telling the story in the summer of 1989 when he was age seventy-five and instructing in the Gulf Coast League. "He had just fired the manager in Centerville, Maryland, in the Eastern Shore League. He convinced me to go down there and manage instead of going home."

A veteran barnstormer going back to his House of David days, Popowski was no stranger to backwoods baseball. But he wasn't quite sure just how backwoodsy Centerville would be.

"I drove down there and couldn't find the place," said Popowski. "I stopped at a gas station and asked the guy where Centerville was. He said, 'You just went through it.' Centerville was one eight-room hotel, a hardware store, and a drug store. The owner of the hardware store owned the team."

One day, Popowski and his Centerville team, which included teenaged pitcher Mel Parnell who was later with the Red Sox, embarked on a road trip to Salisbury, Maryland. "We drove to our road games, with the team riding in three cars," said Popowski. "They kept the cars at the ballpark. They gave me the key to the gate. I was supposed to unlock the gate, go on the trip, come back, and relock the gates when the cars were back inside the ballpark."

After the Salisbury game, Popowski's car was the first to return to the ballpark. He opened the gate, parked the car, and sat in the stands until the other two carloads of players arrived. After they pulled in, Popowski locked up and returned to his quarters at the eight-room hotel.

Early the next morning, his phone rang. "You let the horse out," the voice said. Popowski hung up.

The phone rang again. This time Popowski recognized the voice of the team owner. "You let the horse out," he said.

"What horse?" said Popowski.

"The one we keep at the ballpark," said the owner, "to cut the grass."

◆

When he took over managing the Cubs for the 1926 season, Joe McCarthy inherited a last-place team and one huge

Johnny Evers (left) *and George Stallings*

discipline problem: Grover Cleveland Alexander. The once-great hurler was still good, but he was also more ornery than ever. He also was a drunk.

The Cubs finished their exhibition season that spring in Kansas City and prepared for their opener in Cincinnati. When McCarthy called a team meeting in his suite at the Muehlebach Hotel, to no one's surprise, Alexander wasn't present. McCarthy proceeded without him.

The manager was on the subject of signals when the door pushed open and Alexander teetered into the room. "Now suppose we get a man on second base—"

"Don't have to worry about that, McCarthy," interrupted Alexander, using a shaky hand to place a cigarette between his lips. "This team will never get a man that far." Before long, Alexander was sound asleep and snoring loudly.

A few weeks later, McCarthy sold Alexander to the Cardinals. That day, the rookie manager received a telegram from Chicago owner William Wrigley: "Congratulations. For years I've wanted a manager with the nerve to do that."

◆

Boston Braves manager George Stallings customarily berated his players, usually with a shower of unflattering nicknames. One day during the ninth inning of a game, it became obvious the Braves might need a pinch hitter. The count was three balls and no strikes to catcher Hank Gowdy.

"If he gets on base," Stallings said out loud in the Boston dugout, "I guess I'll let Old Bonehead take a crack at the ball."

"Ball four," shouted the umpire.

Before Stallings could summon his pinch hitter, five Braves carrying bats were already out of the dugout on their way to home plate.

◆

Once when Pirates manager Frankie Frisch was thrown out of a game at the Polo Grounds, he sneaked into a groundskeeper's shed under the left-field stands and led the troops from exile.

"From that vantage point, I wigwagged directions to my team," Frisch recalled, "until fans in the right-field stands discovered me and yelled demands that I be ejected bodily."

Frisch sneaked into a bin of sand just before umpires burst into the shed to start searching for him. "I finally crawled under the grandstand and emerged on New York's 8th Avenue, uniform stained and spiked, shoes clattering on the pavement," Frisch recalled. "Small boys asked me for my autograph and I banged on the clubhouse door, demanding admittance. It was undignified, it was nonsensical, but it was fun."

◆

In the middle of the 1944 season, Athletics coach Al Simmons took aside grandfatherly manager Connie Mack to offer some not-so-gentle advice.

"The team's loafing, Mr. Mack," Simmons said. "They'll finish in the first division if they half try. They'll listen to you. Crack down on 'em. Use tough language."

Next morning, with Simmons at his side for moral support, Mack addressed the troops. In a quiet tone, the manager asked his players for more cooperation. "Get tougher," Simmons whispered.

Mack took a deep breath and raised his voice. "I won't stand for any more nonsense," he said. "Why, damn it, you're better than . . ."

His voice trailed off, and Mack hurried from the clubhouse. Simmons went after him.

"What's the matter, Mr. Mack?" Simmons asked.

"Darn it," Mack said sadly. "I can't talk that way to my boys."

◆

One day in the mid 1970s, Red Sox manager Joe Morgan managed Pawtucket in a game against Richmond at McCoy Stadium. Morgan's young son was next to him on the bench. A Richmond player was on first. Jim Breazeale, a slow-footed first baseman who had briefly cracked the big leagues with the Braves, was at bat.

Breazeale lifted a soft pop-up behind second base. PawSox second baseman Buddy Hunter let the ball drop, picked it up, and forced the runner at second, leaving Breazeale at first on a fielder's choice.

On the bench, Morgan's son looked up to his father and asked, "Why did he let the ball drop?" Morgan turned to answer just as the next batter cracked a long drive that caromed off the wall in deep center.

Breazeale labored around second as the PawSox center fielder chased down the ball. Breazeale chugged around third as the throw came into the infield. He was barely down the line when shortstop Ramon Aviles turned and fired the relay home. Breazeale was out at the plate by at least twenty feet. Morgan looked down at his son. "That's why," he explained.

Next day, Morgan arrived at the ballpark and found a half-dozen of his players grouped in center field, staring up and pointing. Strung at the top of the flagpole was a baseball mitt.

An investigation determined that Breazeale had arrived at the field early, slipped into the PawSox clubhouse, kidnapped Hunter's glove, and lynched it in center field.

Lee Fohl

◆

For a while during his big-league managing career, Lee Fohl was known as the "Doctor of Hopeless Teams." He took over Cleveland during the 1915 season, and the Indians jumped from seventh to sixth in 1916, to third in 1917, and to second in 1918.

One afternoon at Fenway Park in 1919, the Indians and Red Sox went into extra innings. With bases loaded, Fohl summoned lefty Fritz Coumbe to face Babe Ruth. The Babe blasted a grand slam, and Fohl was dismissed that night. Next season Cleveland won the World Series.

After Fohl was hired by the St. Louis Browns in 1921, he led them to third place. Next season, St. Louis missed the pennant by just a half-game. Late in the 1923 season, Fohl was fired.

Soon thereafter, Fohl was hired to revive the last-place Red Sox. He finished seventh in 1924, eighth in 1925, and eighth again in 1926. Again he was fired.

In 1927 Fohl managed minor-league Toronto, then dropped out of baseball. "I couldn't get another baseball job," he said. "The majors didn't want me. And the minors, they'd say, 'He's a major leaguer and he'd want too much money.'"

Two years later, Fohl lost his modest savings in the stock market crash. "I lost everything but my hat," he said.

By 1939, sixty-seven-year-old Fohl was pumping gas at a downtown Cleveland filling station. "I never thought I'd be doing this," he said. "You can have the filling station. I'll still take baseball. The hours are shorter."

◆

After they won the 1914 World Series, the Boston Braves used their winning shares to purchase automobiles. When the teams started poorly the following spring, manager George Stallings referred to each man according to the car he had bought, with some embellishment.

"You Pierce-Arrow [expletive]," Stallings would mumble as he shuddered with anger in the dugout. "Why do I keep you on the club? You Buick [expletive]. Why don't I turn you loose?"

One player had purchased a cheap car produced by an obscure manufacturer. Stallings could never remember the car's make, so he improvised. "You motorcycle [expletive]," he muttered.

◆

A fter Brooklyn lost to the Cubs on a home run in the late innings, Dodgers manager Uncle Wilbert Robinson asked young catcher Al Lopez what pitch he had called for. "A curve," Lopez answered, knowing he would be blasted regardless of his answer.

"My God!" Robinson sputtered. "Any fool would know you should have called for a fastball."

The manager thought for a moment. "Lopez," he said. "Tomorrow I'm going to call all the pitches from the dugout. I want you to take your signs from me. I'll show you how to run a ballclub."

The plan worked flawlessly through the first five innings the next day. Robinson signaled to Lopez, who signaled to Dodger pitcher Van Lingle Mungo, who confounded the Chicago hitters. With the score tied, 0–0, in the sixth, Mungo walked the leadoff batter. The next man reached on a bunt. The next man was safe when Mungo fell trying to pick up a slow roller.

As the next Cub batter stepped to the plate with the bases loaded, Lopez peered into the dugout to get the sign.

With his back to the field, Robinson was drinking from the dugout water fountain.

Wilbert Robinson

Lopez whistled at him. Robinson didn't turn around. Lopez hollered. No response.

Someone tapped the manager on the shoulder. "Hey, Robbie," he said. "Lopez wants you."

"What does he want?" Robinson said.

"He wants you to tell him what pitch to call for."

Robinson stood on the top step of the

Larry Doby, Walt Dropo, Bill Fischer, and Al Lopez (left to right)

dugout and glared toward home plate. "What's the matter, Lopez?" he shouted. "Didn't you ever catch before?"

◆

Not scheduled to start that afternoon, aging Brooklyn hurler Dazzy Vance shagged flies for an hour, changed into a dry shirt, and plopped onto the bench to watch the game. Then Dodgers coach Otto Miller hollered at him. Manager Casey Stengel wanted Vance to go to the bullpen.

"Bullpen?" said Vance. "I've been chasing fungoes for an hour."

"All I know is, Casey said you're supposed to be in the bullpen," Miller answered.

When starter Less ("Nemo") Munns was knocked out in the first inning, Vance was called to pitch. When the score was tied in the ninth, Vance was still hurling. After the inning, he told Stengel he was "all in."

"All in?" said Stengel. "That's just the trouble with you pitchers. Never in shape. Well, try one more inning, and I'll have a pinch hitter ready for you."

Brooklyn lost in the tenth when nobody covered third base on a bunt. "My arm was never worth a plugged nickel after that," Vance recalled nearly twenty years later in the summer of 1953. "This is the same Stengel who will pull a pitcher out in the fifth or sixth inning because he's right-handed and a left-hander is coming to bat. Two years ago in the World Series, he pulled Whitey Ford, a twenty-four-year-old buck, in the eighth with a 3–1 lead and no trouble. Now they call him a genius."

◆

In the summer of 1943, Phillies manager Bucky Harris was in New York for a series against the Dodgers. He decided to drop by the office of William Cox, owner of the Phillies.

When Harris walked in, Cox's secretary was on the telephone asking the person on the other end for the latest odds on that afternoon's Phillies–Dodgers game.

"What are the odds?" Harris asked when she hung up.

"Twelve-to-five on the Dodgers," she answered.

"That doesn't surprise me," said Harris. "But why do you go to the bother to find out what the price is on any game?"

"Why, that's Mr. Cox's orders," she replied.

Harris thought it strange for an owner to request betting odds on his own team but said nothing to the secretary or to Cox that afternoon.

A month or two later, Philadelphia was in seventh place. In St. Louis, Harris received word that he was fired as manager, to be replaced by Freddie Fitzsimmons. The newspaper fellows naturally petitioned the deposed manager for comment.

Harris said the firing had come as a shock, but he didn't feel too badly about it. Why? "I wasn't particularly keen," he said, "about working for an owner who sought information about the betting odds on ball games."

Shrapnel from that bombshell landed in the office of Commissioner Kenesaw Mountain Landis, who summoned Harris for more information. After an investigation, Landis suspended Cox from baseball for life.

Casey Stengel in a quiet moment.

◆

At the height of the Miller Huggins–Babe Ruth feud in the early 1920s, Ruth arrived late for a game in Chicago. The Yankee manager was livid when pregame practice ended and there was still no sign of the Babe. "This is the payoff," Huggins told a group of New York writers. "This time I'll fix the big baboon's clock."

Huggins was delivering the lineup card to the umpires when Ruth sneaked out of the clubhouse tunnel, grabbed a bat, and quietly walked to the on-deck circle. *Okay,* Huggins thought to himself. *I'll get you later.*

First time up, Ruth slammed a monstrous home run. *All right,* Huggins mulled, leaving Ruth alone as he returned to the bench. *Wait till he whiffs.* In the fifth, Ruth cracked another long home run, this one into the center-field bleachers. The two blasts beat the White Sox, 5–3.

After the game, Huggins sat in the visitors' clubhouse, scratching his stomach. "Aren't you going to tell him off?" a writer asked Huggins.

"Damn tootin' I am," the manager said. Huggins turned toward where the Babe toweled off and hollered, "Nice work, big fella."

◆

With most of their star players sold off by the late 1930s, the once-proud Philadelphia Athletics were chronically stuck near the bottom of the American League. By then in his seventies, Connie Mack found managing far less fun than when he could write Jimmie Foxx, Al Simmons, and Lefty Grove on his lineup card.

One day, with Philadelphia anchored in last place, Mr. Mack prepared to depart with his charges on what would certainly be another disastrous road trip.

Hurrying to North Philadelphia Station in a taxi cab, Mack was lost in deep thought. Upon arrival, he absent-mindedly paid the driver only the sum showing on the meter, picked up his luggage, and began to walk away.

"Hey, pop," growled the driver. "What about a tip?"

Mack stopped, still lost in his own thought.

"A tip?" he repeated politely.

"Yeah, pop, a tip," snapped the driver. "How about one?"

"Certainly," the detached Mr. Mack said. "Don't bet on the A's."

◆

As he pulled on his socks in the McCoy Stadium visitors' clubhouse before an exhibition game against the Triple–A Pawtucket Red Sox, Boston manager Joe Morgan eyed the booty neatly lined up before him: five bottles, each a different size of Chivas Regal, courtesy of PawSox owner Ben Mondor.

"There's a story behind these," said Morgan.

When he managed the PawSox, Morgan always returned from road trips to find a bottle of Chivas waiting for him on his office desk. The size of the bottle was determined by the success of the road trip, like receiving eighty-six-proof gold stars. Good road trips rated a quart. Pretty good road trips rated a fifth. Mediocre road trips rated a pint.

"One time we had a great road trip," said Morgan. "We went something like 9–1. When I came back there was a gallon bottle of Chivas waiting for me."

The spirits weren't always good. On another road trip, the PawSox were simply awful. "I think it was an eleven-game trip," said Morgan. "We won one of them." A bottle of Chivas was waiting on the manager's desk when the team returned. Size: a one-and-one-half ounce nip.

◆

One day, with the meddlesome team owner watching from the stands, the minor-league Montreal Royals executed a triple play. The owner summoned manager Fresco Thompson to his office that afternoon.

"Fresco, that was a good play today," he said. "I want you to use it more often."

After grabbing the American Association pennant in 1928, Casey Stengel's Toledo Mud Hens finished dead last in 1929. Many of Stengel's troops were well-paid former big leaguers, which caused a serious motivational problem. The well-heeled players devoted more energy to the booming stock market than to baseball. "They always turned to the financial pages before the sports pages," said Stengel, riled by the idea years later.

After one extraordinarily shameful defeat, Stengel moped into the clubhouse and found his freshly defeated ballplayers engrossed in the latest stock returns.

"Say," Casey announced with fake friendliness, "I've got a tip on the market for you fellows." The players dropped their newspapers and eagerly gathered around their manager.

"Buy Pennsylvania Railroad," Stengel said with authority. "Because by tomorrow night about a dozen of you bums will be on it, riding in all directions."

◆

Burleigh Grimes

As a youngster in Hudson, Massachusetts, Uncle Wilbert Robinson worked in the produce business but honed his hardball skills on the job by hurling various baseball-shaped fruits around the premises. After his playing days, in the winter of 1914 Uncle Robbie was hired to manage Brooklyn.

Before he departed to take over the Dodgers, the Hudson Elks threw a party in his honor. Robinson addressed the crowd of old friends.

"I want to thank Hudson's best people on earth for giving me this chance to come back to the old hometown," he began. "May I ask for a show of hands from anyone in this audience I didn't hit in the back with a lemon in my younger days?" Not a hand was raised.

◆

A first baseman with the Hiroshima Carp in the summers of 1987 and 1988, Rick Lancellotti played for a manager who made no attempt to hide his distaste for American players.

"His name was Anan," Lancellotti recalled in 1988 when he returned to the United States to play for the Triple–A Pawtucket Red Sox. "That's what was on the back of his uniform, anyway. I don't know his first name. We never talked. He didn't speak to us. Not for two years. He did say something to us at the beginning of each year. But that's because he had to. Otherwise, that was it. He didn't like Americans.

"Finally at the end of the second year, I asked our interpreter, 'What is it with that guy, anyway? Why doesn't he like Americans?'

"He said, 'Oh, his father was killed in the war. He's got a thing about it.'"

◆

In the winter of 1989, Columbus Clippers manager Stump Merrill led an Eastern

League contingent on a baseball tour of the Soviet Union, where the locals were trying to pick up the rudiments of *beisbol.* Merrill is the kind of leader you want on a foreign expedition. For one thing, he made fast friends with Viktor, the vodka-loving, bushy-eyebrowed ex-army colonel who escorted the Americans. "Everything seemed to go very smoothly after that," said New Britain Red Sox pitching coach Rich Gale, who was in the Eastern League party.

However, by the time the trip hit Moscow, life in the U.S.S.R. had started to drag. The homesick ballplayers were pulling on their uniforms in the locker room when Stump and a sidekick made a vaudevillian entrance.

Merrill was wearing boxer shorts, mismatched socks (one high, one low), a hideous shirt, a hockey goalie's glove (borrowed from an Estonian lad), and an athletic supporter on his head. "He looked hilarious," said Gale. "But with his body, Stump could look hilarious in a lot of things."

Playing Costello to his sidekick's Abbott, Merrill romped through a kind of "Who's on First?" routine adapted for the Soviet trip: "What is first?" and so on.

The locker room shook with laughter. The Americans weren't so glum anymore. "We gave him a rousing ovation," said Gale.

◆

In the summer of 1968, outfielder Gene Clines was a young farm hand in the Pirates' organization, playing under Joe Morgan on the York, Pennsylvania, club. In the big leagues that summer, Astros pitcher Wade Blasingame had been badly injured by a line drive back to the mound when the ball hit him in the groin. Shortly thereafter, a memo was circulated through the Pirates' system directing all players to wear protective cups on the playing field.

"But Gene said no way was he wearing a cup," Morgan remembered. "He said he couldn't play right with one. He also said there was no way he was going to get hit there anyway, playing in the outfield. I said, 'I don't know, Gene. There are some pretty tough outfields out there.'"

During a game one day, Clines attempted to steal second base. "He was sliding, and all of a sudden he was rolling around on the ground in great pain," said Morgan. "I ran out there because I thought he'd broken his leg or something."

Morgan arrived and asked what happened. Clines could barely speak. The opposing second baseman filled in Morgan: Clines had been struck squarely in the groin by the catcher's throw.

"I leaned over and said, 'Gene, are you wearing your cup?'" said Morgan. "He said no. I ran back to the dugout laughing my butt off."

During a Mariners' visit to Fenway Park in the summer of 1989, Seattle batting coach Gene Clines was told that Red Sox manager Joe Morgan had spun an anecdote about him.

"I bet I know the story," said Clines, walking off the field after early batting practice. "He told you about the time I wouldn't wear a cup, right?"

Clines played under Morgan in Raleigh, North Carolina, in 1967 and in York, Pennsylvania, in 1968 and 1969. So what did he remember about manager Joe?

"The sign for the squeeze play was always the same," said Clines. "Joe would say, 'How's your old tomatoes?' That was the sign for the squeeze play. 'How's your old tomatoes?' It's the best, because you never forget it. I mean, how many other guys can remember what the squeeze sign was twenty years ago in the minor leagues?"

◆

◆

In the spring of 1969 during Washington's home opener, Red Sox legend Ted Williams made his managerial debut. Richard Nixon threw out the first ball. RFK Stadium was jammed, and Ted's Senators lost to the Yankees.

After finishing ten games over .500 in fourth place that year, Williams endured two more seasons in Washington, then moved with them to Texas. In 1972 the Rangers won 54 and lost 100. Their .351 winning percentage was only slightly higher than the Splinter's lifetime batting average. He retired to go fishing and make bread commercials.

They say manager Ted didn't like pitchers.

"He really didn't," Casey Cox, who hurled four seasons for Williams, recalled in the spring of 1989. "He never came out to the mound, or he came out very, very seldom. He thought sometimes pitchers weren't athletes. But I thought he was a great guy and a helluva manager. I liked him. I really did. Some didn't. I know Denny McLain didn't."

What could a pitcher learn from one of the greatest hitters who ever lived? "Personally, I learned from listening to him tell us what he couldn't hit," said Cox, then age forty-seven and in the insurance business in Tampa. "He didn't like sliders in on his hands. So I started using that pitch that year."

Cox offered two manager Ted stories:

"When we were in Texas, he had a rule that you couldn't play golf on the day of the game," said Cox. "You could sit in a boat and fish all day if you wanted. But no golf.

"My locker was right outside his office. One day, I noticed a bandage on his calf. I asked the trainer, 'What happened to Skip?' He said, 'Oh, he was out playing golf, got

Sparky Anderson relaxes while Ty Cobb looks on.

ticked off, broke the club over his knee, and cut his leg open. Took four stitches.' How do you like that?"

And there was a touching moment from Williams's first sentimental return to Fenway Park as Washington manager:

"Ted had a fifteen-minute waiting period after the game before he let the press in," said Cox. "First time he comes to Boston, after the game Dick Young is pounding on the clubhouse door telling him to open up, and Ted is yelling at him to go [expletive] himself."

◆

Red Sox general manager Lou Gorman recalled his days with the Royals and the time they employed a full-time psychiatrist to travel with the team. "Bob Lemon was the manager then," Gorman said. "He was an old-school type of baseball guy who thought the game was played strictly between the white lines. He had no use for our psychiatrist."

After a game at Comiskey Park one night, the Royals emerged from the players' entrance and walked through a mob of autograph seekers to get to the team bus. Before long, every player was aboard, but the bus didn't move. Lemon asked the driver what was causing the delay. The driver pointed outside. Lemon squinted out the bus window and could barely believe his grizzled eyes. The team psychiatrist had stopped to sign autographs.

"[Expletive], let's leave without him," growled Lemon.

Remembered Gorman: "And they pulled away and left him there. The psychiatrist had to get a cab back to the hotel."

◆

In January 1932 the Binghamton club of the New York–Penn League decided it was time for a change, which almost always means bagging the manager. Former Reds and Giants third baseman Heinie Groh was fired as the team's president and field manager, and John W. Jardine was hired as the new president.

Shortly thereafter, Jardine visited Binghamton town officials to inquire about getting another lease on the team's home field. Jardine was told the field—the only ballpark in town—had just recently been leased for the summer by someone else: Heinie Groh.

◆

Former Braves second baseman Sibby Sisti appeared in the delightful 1984 baseball film *The Natural*. In the climactic game sequence, he portrayed the opposing manager who lifted his pitcher in favor of a fastball-throwing left-hander, who promptly surrendered the mammoth, elec-trifying home run to lefty-hitting Roy Hobbs (Robert Redford).

"My movie career lasted about three weeks," said Sisti. "I had fun, but I made a bad decision by taking my pitcher out. And I keep making the same mistake every time the movie is on. Every time I watch it, I say, 'Don't take him out!' But I just keep making the same mistake."

◆

With his Dodgers in another dreadful slump in the summer of 1925, manager Uncle Wilbert Robinson retreated to the grandstand one afternoon to get a fan's eye view of his increasingly messy Bums. In Flatbush tradition, spectators offered a few peanuts and much advice. A cab driver suggested Robinson shake up the lineup.

"How would you do it?" Robinson asked. "Tell me. I want to know."

The cab driver huddled with a collection of cronies and returned with a verdict. "We'd like to bench Fournier, lead off with Andy High, and pitch Dazzy Vance tomorrow," the cabbie said.

Next day, Jacques Fournier was benched, High led off, and Vance pitched. Brooklyn won by a shutout.

◆

On November 29, 1952, former major league third baseman Arlie ("The Freshest Man on Earth") Latham died at age ninety-two years, eight months, and two weeks.

In Philadelphia, retired Athletics' manager Connie Mack, age eighty-nine, heard of his friend's death.

"I beat [John] McGraw at his best, and Fielder Jones, Charlie Comiskey, and Clark Griffith," said Mack. "Beat a lot of them for pennants and in the series. Now I want to beat Arlie Latham. I can't beat anybody

Casey Stengel (left) *and Sebastian ("Sibby") Sisti*

anymore in baseball. I'm finished. But I want to live longer than Arlie did."

On February 8, 1956, Mack died at age ninety-three years, one month, and two weeks.

◆

The big-league hidden-ball trick isn't quite as extinct as the flannel uniform, but it's close. "You could pull that once a game if you wanted to," said Red Sox manager Joe Morgan in the summer of 1990. "Whenever there's traffic on the bases and the ball is hit to the outfield, nobody knows where that ball ends up. Nobody."

Playing first base in the minors, Morgan liked to nab runners the simple way: cut off the ball from the outfield and stash it in his glove. "I got Ron Swoboda once," said Morgan. "He was a nineteen-year-old kid. I put the tag on him and he had no idea what happened. He went ape. I got out of there in a hurry."

One season in Pawtucket, Morgan managed a crafty gang of infielders—Glenn Hoffman, Marty Barrett, Dave Stapleton, Buddy Hunter, and Dave Koza—who also loved sneakiness afield.

"We pulled it a million times that year against Toledo," said Morgan. "Finally the Toledo manager, Cal Ermer, called a team meeting and said, 'If any of you guys get caught by that hidden-ball trick, it will cost you two hundred dollars.'"

A few hours later, Hoffman pulled the hidden-ball trick to nail a Mud Hen at third base. Also thoroughly tricked, however, was the third-base coach: Cal Ermer.

Briefed on the Toledo team meeting, the PawSox bench chorused for Ermer: "Take two hundred dollars from him. But take a grand from yourself!"

"We kept that up for several innings," said Morgan.

◆

One day in the late 1930s, player-manager Jimmy Dykes had seen enough errant baserunning from his White Sox that he legislated an automatic fine for anyone picked off second base. "On first base or third base when you're trying to take a lead, there might be some excuse," he said. "But not when you're out in the middle with all the action right in front of you. Anybody gets picked off there, it costs him money."

During a close game the next day, Dykes reached second base. He took a few steps off the bag and ran through his managerial checklist: Should he pinch-hit for the pitcher? Whom should he warm up in the bullpen?

Suddenly Dykes looked to his left. The second baseman stood on the bag with a baseball in his hand. Dykes tried desperately to elude the tag with a rundown and finally careened into center field. When umpire Bill McGowan called him out for leaving the basepaths, Dykes scampered to second, claiming, "He never touched me!"

Dragging himself back to the bench, Dykes stopped at the top step of the dugout and faced his men. "All right, go ahead," he said. "Say it. Come on. I've got it coming." No one said a word, or even looked him in the eye.

"That was nice of the guys," Dykes said later to his shortstop, Luke Appling. "I had it coming, but they didn't say a word."

"They couldn't," said Appling. "They said it all before you got back."

9

AFFAIRS OF THE HEART

Ballplayers have always worn little caps and short pants. They spend a great deal of time in a locker room called a "clubhouse," and their work has always been play. Old-time philosophy toward women and romance naturally fell somewhere between Dennis the Menace and Spanky's He-man Women Hater's Club. Girls? Yeech. If sappy old pulp Westerns had the cowboy kissing his horse, crusty old baseball yarns had the player kissing horsehide.

To a real baseball man, dames meant trouble, and they had the stories to prove it. The female villains were usually floosies, but even wives were considered potential turbulence. Spouses were commonly banned from spring training and all road trips. Hard-boiled managers even hated to see players' wives seated together in the stands. Between squirts of tobacco juice, any of them could have explained: one wife blurts something nasty about another's husband, arguments ensue, and the next thing you know you've got a pair of feuding ballplayers on your hands.

"It's funny what a woman can do to a ball club," Brooklyn coach Joe Kelly offered in 1926. "You can start off the season with the cockiest bunch of players in the league. You can sail through the early season games in a whirlwind of victory, so that all the wise guys have you spotted for the pennant. And then disaster breaks loose, and your team is turned into an armed camp."

The archives are stacked high with stories about wrong-headed managers convinced their club was ruined by romance. On a summer night in 1919, Boston Braves manager George Stallings and ten of his charges lounged on the porch of their St. Louis hotel. The Braves weren't without talent, but they were stumbling toward a sixth-place season. Stallings mulled his good ball club gone bad.

"I can't understand why we're not winning," he said to no one in particular. "We haven't got a great ball club. But we've got good pitching and good defensive players. It's a smart ball club, too. And we're hitting the ball. Why can't we win? What's the matter?"

The rhetorical question lingered in the air. The Braves shifted in their seats. A bellhop stepped onto the porch. "A call for Mr. Maranville," the boy said. "Calling Mr. Maranville." Shortstop Rabbit Maranville excused himself and went inside.

Stallings and his nine Braves sat in uneasy silence. The bellhop returned. "Calling Mr. Smith," he said. "Calling Mr. Smith." Third baseman Red Smith picked himself up and followed the bellhop into the lobby.

Before Stallings could resume his harangue, the bellhop was back. "A call for Mr. Wilson," the boy said. "Calling Mr. Wilson." Catcher Art Wilson rolled out of his seat and hurried away.

Before long, all ten players were summoned for telephone calls. None returned, leaving Stallings on the porch with only coach Jack Slattery. The pair stared into the summer night.

"There's the answer," Stallings said suddenly. He spit out the word: "Women."

Given the ancient attitude toward affairs of the heart, baseball lore strongly features the stuff of daytime television or the evening news: tortured relationships, public scandal, mayhem, and even murder. However, through the ages, baseball has seen its share of lovely love stories. The romance of Eleanor and Lou Gehrig is a sweet tale, even beyond the Hollywood version. Edna stayed with Casey Stengel from Toledo to Brooklyn through the Mets. Thousands of ballplayers thrived on the security of strong marriages. But lore is dominated by romance tales of pure woe or pure pleasure. There are spicy legends, such as the one about the time Phillies first baseman Eddie Waitkus was shot by a crazed female admirer in a Chicago hotel room or the one about the night Babe Ruth had intercourse with all eighteen women in a St. Louis brothel, then breakfasted on an eighteen-egg omelet the next morning.

In any case, baseball offers precious little oral history on romance. Tender or terrible, affairs of the heart are almost never bantered around the bullpen. Except for a brief time during the allegedly liberated 1960s, not many philandering ballplayers were anxious to publicize their adventures. Many tales died with the men and women who lived them or the hotel clerks who saw them sneak up the back stairs. Old-time codes of privacy—newspapers protected athletes the way they used to protect politicians—also kept most affairs of the heart out of the archives.

Most of the surviving record, therefore, is of private affairs that burst into public record. Newspapers winked at ballplayers' indiscretions, but when marriages hit divorce court, the juicy details were splashed inkily in the next editions. Boy-beats-girl stories were always well publicized if the incident reached a police blotter. Thus a distorted image emerges. Ballplayers as a group probably haven't cheated on their wives, impaled themselves on romantic triangles, or committed murder in love-struck rages more frequently than the general population.

Generally undereducated, overpaid, famous young men who spend plenty of time on the road, with plenty of time on their hands and with plenty of temptation at the end of the bar, ballplayers have had more than their share of opportunity to get themselves into trouble. As long as ballplayers have congregated in groups, they have been pursued by groupies. Before World War I, the "Two Little Girls in Blue" followed the New York Giants almost everywhere. One year a Giants wise guy suggested the loyal pair be voted a World Series share. Eight decades later, the species still buzzed around baseball teams.

After a night game in the summer of 1990, a newspaper writer dashed out of the Red Sox locker room and headed to the press box to meet deadline. In the empty corridor, two giggly young women who somehow had eluded security flagged down the writer and pointed to the clubhouse door.

"Are the players in there?" one asked.

"Yes," said the writer.

"Are they wearing any clothes?" asked the other.

Despite occasional evidence to the contrary, modern times have nudged the game away from the Beaver Cleaver view of romance. Most players today are better educated and more mature than their older counterparts. The abundance of temptation aside, most ballplayers know the high price of scandal. If they didn't know it before, they knew it after Red Sox third baseman Wade Boggs was pilloried for two years over his extramarital affair, which turned sour, then went incredibly public. At the height of the lurid episode, a handful of Red Sox scrapped in a Cleveland hotel lobby when the scandal threatened to drag in other members of the team. Some thought the hoodoo might ruin the ball club, and somewhere in hardball heaven George Stallings nodded knowingly. Most placed the blame where it belonged: on the ballplayer.

Not that baseball men have evolved from belly-scratching tobacco chewers to cardigan-wearing sensitive males. Most still share their most sensational pieces of mail, including unsolicited candid snapshots, with teammates. Some still like to scan the stands on hot days for glimpses of flesh, just as their forefathers drilled holes in the rear walls of dugouts for flashes of Victorian ankle.

But baseball isn't the men-only club it used to be, and that changes everything. When Calvin Coolidge's wife kept a scorecard after the president threw out the first ball, it was considered a novelty. Fifty years later, many of the most rabid, serious fans were women. By 1990, the Red Sox had an assistant general manager named Elaine. Women reporters work the baseball beat with distinction. A woman playing big league ball may be a generation away, although White Sox general manager Roland Hemond briefly considered signing his daughter, a track star at San Diego State, as a pinch runner in 1983. More likely, sometime not far into the next century, there will be a woman umpire telling the boys in the little caps and short pants to play ball. Managers will legitimately gripe about a woman ruining their ball club.

On Friday night, July 15, 1921, in New York, Arthur Irwin boarded the steamship *Calvin Austin* bound for Boston. Raised in the Hub, Irwin had been a first-rate shortstop in the late 1800s, playing in the big leagues for thirteen years, including seasons in Boston, Worcester, and Providence. Irwin also managed for eight years.

Now Irwin was sixty-three years old and ailing. Appendicitis had forced him to resign as manager of the Eastern League's Hartford team the previous month. The attack was followed by a severe abdominal illness. As the *Calvin Austin* steamed out to sea, Irwin confided to another passenger that he was "going home to die."

As the ship approached Boston the next morning at seven o'clock, a steward rapped on Irwin's stateroom door. There was no answer. The steward entered and found the cabin empty, except for Irwin's belongings. On deck, propped against the railing, was the stool from Irwin's stateroom. Ship authorities surmised he had jumped or fallen overboard during the night. His body was never recovered.

The following week, Irwin's son, Arthur, traveled from Boston to Hartford to attend to his father's affairs. He found one affair he didn't expect. Investigating a stray bill of sale, Arthur discovered his father had led a double life for thirty years. Arthur Ir-win had a wife, a son, and two daughters in Boston. He also had a wife and a son in New York.

"I never suspected my husband," said Mrs. Elizabeth Irwin, the Boston wife since 1883.

"How could we have any suspicion that he had another family?" said a flabbergasted Harold Irwin, the New York son whose mother had married Irwin in 1891.

Her spirit shattered, Mrs. Irwin of Boston died six months later. Mrs. Irwin of New York stayed in brokenhearted seclusion the rest of her life.

Two years after Irwin disappeared off the steamship, in the summer of 1923, Arthur Irwin was reportedly sighted managing a baseball team in the backwoods of Georgia. Sighed his sister, Mrs. E.E. Warren of South Boston, when told of the never-confirmed report, "You can't ever tell."

◆

Late in the 1908 season, the Giants, Cubs, and Pirates dueled closely for the National League pennant. New York took a severe blow when Philadelphia's twenty-two-year-old rookie left-hander Harry Coveleski beat the Giants three times in five days. Coveleski was promptly nicknamed the "Giant Killer." Giants man-

Babe Ruth with his first wife, Helen, and daughter Dorothy

ager John McGraw promised to get even with the kid.

During the winter, McGraw dispatched a scout to Coveleski's hometown, Shamokin, Pennsylvania. Before long, McGraw's henchman snooped out the young pitcher's weakness. His girlfriend had recently dumped him to run off with a trombone player in a traveling band.

The following season, each time Coveleski faced the Giants, McGraw directed one of his players in the dugout to strike up a trombone. The shaken Coveleski was 6–10 in 1909 before getting demoted to the minors. He didn't resurface again in the big leagues until 1911.

◆

During spring training in 1923, the Yankees' camp was hit hard by a messy sex scandal that threatened team unity, wobbled public faith in ballplaying heroes, and kept a bunch of lawyers busy. A love-scorned woman was suing married New York slugger Babe Ruth.

The woman, nineteen-year-old New York shop clerk Dolores Dixon, alleged she and Ruth had engaged in a four-month affair the previous summer. She also claimed to be pregnant with the Bambino's bambino, and now Ruth would not return her telephone calls. She sued for $50,000.

"Just a bunch of blackmail," the Babe said in his room at the Grunewald Hotel in New Orleans, his wife, Helen, and his three-year-old daughter, Dorothy, at his side. "I've been hounded by confidence men and crooked, scheming women ever since I made the home run record."

Mrs. Ruth stood by her man. "I'm with my husband clear to the finish of this," she vowed. "I haven't the least idea who this Dixon girl is. And when my husband says he doesn't know her, I believe him." She leaned over and patted the Babe's shoulder. "Don't you worry," she told him. "When you're right, nobody can lick you."

The Dixon camp was going to try. "Babe Ruth denies knowing Miss Dixon, does he?" asked George Feinberg, attorney for Dolores Dixon. "Then ask Mr. Ruth for me—ask him right away—what little girl he called 'My Little Watch Charm' and 'My Little Golf Girl.' Those were his pet names for Miss Dixon."

Ruth grew angrier with each allegation. During a meeting with his lawyer, Hyman Bushel, the Babe roared, "When I get a hold of that lawyer Bushel, I'll kill him. I'll kill him." Bushel reminded Ruth the other side's attorney was named Feinberg. The five-foot, ten-inch, 154-pound Feinberg said he was unconcerned about threats from the six-foot, two-inch, 200-pound Ruth. "If he came to my office with such a threat, I'd punch him in the face and throw him out," the lawyer said.

Newspapermen discovered Dixon had recently resided in the Riverside Drive apartment of Gustave and Barbara Escoe, who were Dixon's legal guardians. News hounds scoured the neighborhood for angles, and Gustave hinted the lawsuit might drag in several Yankees to corroborate Dixon's romance with Ruth, a widening of the scandal that would not play well in the New York clubhouse. "Ruth is not the only ballplayer who is going to be brought into this

Claire Ruth

case. She was a frequent visitor to the Polo Grounds when the Yankees were playing," Gustave Escoe stated. Dixon herself was sequestered somewhere in the suburbs. Feinberg asked why his client was incommunicado. "I'm sorry," he said. "She wants to avoid publicity."

Free publicity, anyhow. Dixon sold her exclusive story to the Cosmopolitan News Service. In a first-person account, she remembered every detail of her whirlwind romance with the great Ruth. The day they met through mutual friends, she had worn a periwinkle blue dress, black maline hat, and black pumps. They dated all through the summer. He drove her around town in his large, blue Packard. They dined and danced all around New York. They kissed in public. On August 29 they had their last date. She curled her hair while Ruth ironed her dress before they left for Newport, where they breakfasted at a roadside diner, blissfully spent the day on a boat, and warmly said goodbye that night.

At the end of September, she discovered she was pregnant. Four days before the start of the World Series, she hand-delivered a note to Ruth's Ansonia Hotel residence, then anxiously awaited a call from the Babe. Finally the phone rang. It was Mrs. Ruth. "Why, I know all about you, you dirty little sneak," Dixon quoted Mrs. Ruth as saying. "If you start anything, you'll get in a whole lot of trouble." Dixon wrote she was hurt by the Babe's denials but loved him anyway. She claimed she still slept with his handkerchiefs, presumably laundered, under her pillow.

On April 27, the day *Dixon* v. *Ruth* went to court, Dolores Dixon's lawyers suddenly withdrew the case. They had learned Ruth's lawyers were prepared to produce Robert McChesney, current occupant of the Tombs prison in New York and former occupant of the Escoe-Dixon residence on Riverside Drive. McChesney was ready to testify the whole Dixon affair was a scam designed to milk a cash settlement out of Ruth. Dixon signed a notarized statement declaring Ruth was not the father of her child, and he had not seduced her.

"I am vindicated," said the Babe, pulling on his uniform before a game against the Red Sox at Fenway Park. "Of course, I always knew that I was innocent. But I am glad that the public now knows it as well as I do."

◆

In the summer of 1930, Jake Powell was a twenty-two-year-old outfielder for New Haven in the Eastern League. Powell was introduced to Elizabeth Sanquinet of Dallas, sister of New Haven outfielder Bob Sanquinet. In an apparent outburst of love

at first sight, Jake and Elizabeth were secretly married two weeks later.

When the brother of the bride was clued in on the secret, he got emotional. The emotion was deep anger. Sanquinet didn't mind playing with the rascally Powell in the same outfield, but he didn't want him in the same family. Sanquinet whisked his sister out of town and escorted her back to Dallas. "Married or not, you're coming home with me," he told her. On his way out, he left a message for Powell: "Never set foot in Texas."

Eighteen years later, including eleven years with the Yankees, Senators, and Phillies, Powell was forty years old and still not having much luck with women. On November 4, 1948, Powell and girlfriend Mrs. Josephine Amber, age thirty-five, were hauled into a Washington, D.C., po-

Ty Cobb with his wife and son

lice station and questioned about a bouncing twenty-five-dollar check he had written at a local hotel.

During the interrogation, Powell asked if he could speak to Mrs. Amber privately in an adjoining room. When they were alone, Powell promised to make good on that bad check and other bad-check charges pending against him in Florida if she would agree to marry him.

"I'm ashamed of you," she said. "You've lied to me and everybody else. You've reached the end of your rope, and you might as well face the music. I'm going home."

Powell gave her four dollars for carfare and shouted after her, "To hell with it. I'm going to end it all." He produced a .25 caliber automatic, shot himself once in the chest, then killed himself with a shot to the right temple.

◆

One night during spring training in 1927, a handful of Washington Senators lolled on the front porch of their rented house. Among them were outfielder Tris Speaker, coach Jack Onslow, catcher Bennie Tate, and a rookie whom they would identify later only as "Bill." Tate casually asked young Bill if he knew anyone in Tampa. Bill said he didn't and wouldn't mind meeting someone, especially an attractive young lady. Tate suggested it might be nice to walk over some night and visit his friend Mary, "a fine, sensible girl, and very pretty" who lived in a quiet, residential part of town. Tate told Bill if he wanted to meet her, he would escort him over to introduce them on the first visit.

On the evening of the big date, Bill came downstairs from his room decked out in his best suit and tie. A number of Senators happened to be in the parlor, and many of them complimented Bill on his spiffy ap-

pearance. Tate came down from his room, and soon they were off to see Mary.

On the way, Tate told Bill about Mary's younger brothers and sisters and suggested they stop and buy some fruit or something to give to the kids. Bill agreed and purchased an armload of tangerines.

As Tate and Bill walked up the steps of Mary's home, the inside door was open. Through the screen door they could see an attractive woman talking on the telephone. Bill straightened his tie while Tate rang the doorbell.

Suddenly a burly man appeared at the door. Glaring at the two spruced-up callers, his eyes grew wide with rage. "So you're the man trying to break up my home!" he yelled at Tate. "I'll show you." The man produced a gun and pointed it at the catcher. Tate backed away from the door, threw up his hands, and pleaded, "Don't shoot! Don't shoot!" The man fired three times through the screen door. Tate clutched his gut and collapsed with a thump onto the porch floor.

Stricken with panic, Bill stumbled away on the porch, careened down the stairs, and ran down the block, dropping tangerines as he fled. A block away, he ran smack into a policeman. Babbling and gasping, Bill told the policeman about poor Bennie and how he got shot over at Mary's house. The officer nodded as he listened, then arrested Bill. He dragged the ballplayer down to the station and tossed him in the lockup.

Before long, Speaker, Onslow, and a completely healthy Tate appeared at the station. They tried hard to speak through convulsions of laughter. It was a grand joke, with all the actors—from Mary to the cop—playing their roles with authenticity. Even the gun filled with blanks had sounded great. Once every spring, the Senators liked to take a lonely rookie "to see Mary."

◆

On June 21, 1987, at McCoy Stadium in Pawtucket, Rhode Island, the Triple–A Pawtucket Red Sox lost to the Toledo Mud Hens, 6–3. Later on that Sunday afternoon, the PawSox threw their annual team get-together, where the players and their families partied and got to know one another.

Barbara Reed had come to the ballpark to watch her son, Jody, play shortstop for Pawtucket. Lee Stange had come to the ballpark to watch the PawSox pitchers, part of his duties as the Red Sox minor-league pitching coach. At the steak and barbecue dinner under the party tent near the left-field bullpen, Jody introduced his mom to the pitching coach. Apparently they hit it off. Five months later, Barbara Reed and Lee Stange were married.

◆

Philadelphia Athletics pitcher Rube Waddell's stormy marriage to May Wynne was chronicled blow by blow in the newspapers for years. The most explosive incident came on February 9, 1905, when Waddell got into an argument with his father-in-law, Edward Ross, at the Ross home in Peabody, Massachusetts. Waddell attacked Ross with a flatiron and knocked out six of his father-in-law's teeth. When Mrs. Ross tried to intervene, Waddell clobbered her with a chair. Waddell fled when he was attacked by the family bulldogs. Seeking first aid later at several North Shore drugstores, Waddell held up his mangled pitching hand and lamented, "There's that four-thousand-dollar-paw gone to hell."

Warrants for his arrest on charges of assault and battery were issued in Peabody, Lynn, and Boston. Waddell fled to Philadelphia, and later sent for a steamer trunk of his belongings. Separated during the next three years, Waddell and his wife often clashed in court. She accused him of desertion and had him hauled before a Philadelphia magistrate in 1906. He accused her of siccing the bulldogs on him and associating with people he didn't like. She sued him for divorce in the spring of 1907, serving him with a warrant at American League Park in Philadelphia.

"Well, this beats me," Waddell said. "If that isn't just like a woman. Just as I was going West with the team. I would have gone away today." In late 1908 and early 1909, Waddell—by then with the Browns—did not accompany the team to Boston lest he be arrested for nonsupport.

In March 1910 Rube and May Waddell's divorce was final. In April Rube married Madge McGuire of New Orleans. "She's a little wisp of a girl, and that's what took me right at the start," he said. "I've got a little queen for a wife, and I'm the happiest man on the diamond."

At 2:00 A.M. on June 22, Mrs. Waddell's screams awoke most of the other residents in their St. Louis apartment building. The landlady rushed to the Waddell flat and discovered the petite Mrs. Waddell on the floor. Rube held her by the ankle and was running in a circle, twisting her leg. The landlady ran back to her apartment, returned with a revolver, placed it to Waddell's head, and ordered him to stop. Waddell spent the night in jail.

Next day, his battered wife appeared at the police station to press charges. His defense was, "She's my wife and I can do what I please with her." Her complaint was, "He's crazy. He says he can't live without excitement. And I'm tired of providing the excitement." In December, Mrs. Waddell sued for divorce, charging Rube was "intoxicated the greater part" of their married life.

◆

In the winter of 1938, Yankees pitcher Lefty Gomez and his wife, former dancer June O'Dea, were embroiled in marital difficulties that eventually landed them in divorce court. At one juncture Mrs. Gomez testified about the time Lefty awoke her in the middle of the night to announce he had concocted the perfect crime: her murder.

"He could do it, he said, because everyone thought he loved me," June told the court. "He said he would wear gloves and choke me to death and leave. He would come back later, he said, and discover me and tell everybody his wife had been killed. I was very much worried and could not sleep." They later reconciled.

◆

Vernon ("Lefty") Gomez and June O'Dea

One-time White Sox pitcher and Boston University coach Chippy Gaw loved to tell the story of Pauline. With the Buffalo club in the minor leagues, Gaw was a teammate of Joe Engel. "Whenever he saw a fellow who seemed to take himself too seriously, Joe was deeply concerned," began Gaw. "He didn't rest easy until something was done about it."

One day, Buffalo selected a new captain. "You know how much a captain amounts to on a ball club. Not much," said Gaw. "But this fellow began to swell up right away. It was a crime how officious that fellow got."

Engel finally could take no more. With eager input from the other Buffalo players, he retired to the hotel writing room to compose a masterful love letter to the egomaniacal captain, purportedly from a worshipful female fan. The letter detailed her palpitating admiration and asked the captain to meet her that night at the corner of Main Street and Gennesee. The letter ended, "Oh, you home run kid, I can hardly wait until tonight!" and was signed, "Pauline B." One of the players enlisted a girlfriend to copy it over in purple ink and douse it with sweet perfume.

That night the Buffalo players gathered around to watch the cheery captain put on his best suit, stick a flower in his lapel, and strut over to the corner of Main and Gennesee. The players beat him to the rendezvous site, hid in doorways, and tried not to giggle as they watched their teammate nervously check his watch and anxiously eye every woman who strolled past. After a while, from a doorway a player cooed, "Paul-line!" and was soon joined by a catcall chorus of "Paul-line!" from the rest of the practical jokers. "That name," said Gaw, "stuck to him from then on."

◆

On August 7, 1934, Boston Braves catcher Al Spohrer was in a Philadelphia courtroom to charge his wife, Elizabeth, with "cruel and barbarous treatment and indignities." Spohrer alleged that while he was on the road playing for the Braves, she was at home playing around with 112-pound married saxophone player Eddie Fagan.

"I walked by the Spohrer house in Bywood [Pennsylvania] on July 20," Willis B. Wright testified before the magistrate. "I saw them [Fagan and Mrs. Spohrer] come out the back door and fool around just a little bit. They went out and did some shopping and came home again. Fagan stayed in the house. The shades were pulled down and the lights went out. He didn't leave until two o'clock in the morning."

Elizabeth Spohrer and Eddie Fagan

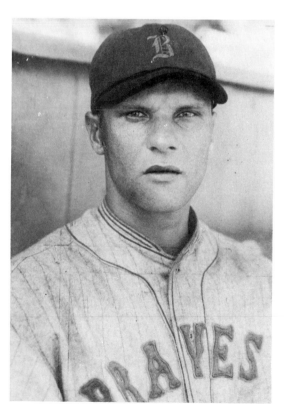

Al Spohrer

Spohrer testified he knew about his wife's indiscretion as far back as October 30, 1930, when he came home that night and found his eleven-year-old daughter serving as a lookout. "Here he comes!" she shouted as Spohrer climbed the stairs and caught Fagan hastily throwing on his coat as he left Mrs. Spohrer's bedroom. Mrs. Spohrer emerged, putting on a kimono over her pajamas. Spohrer said he took no action against his wife for the sake of the children. "But even they knew all about it," he testified. "They called Fagan 'Uncle Eddie.'"

In her defense, Mrs. Spohrer claimed "the whole thing is a frame-up. Al is trying to get out of paying a support order for me and my children." And what about the two trips she took with Fagan to Atlantic City? "They come under the heading of wholesome entertainment," she said.

The judge split the difference. He ordered Mrs. Spohrer to stay away from her "present company," and ordered Al Spohrer to come up with $27.50 a week in support payments.

◆

Casey Stengel and his long-distance sweetheart, Edna Lawson of Glendale, California, planned to be married at the conclusion of the 1923 World Series. Miss Lawson's parents had never met their daughter's ballplaying beau, so they scoured news reports from the series, hopeful for any scrap of information about outfielder Stengel of the Giants.

In the ninth inning of Game One, Stengel swatted an inside-the-park home run to beat the Yankees. He hit the ball to deep left center and galloped on bowed legs in a race against Yankee outfielder Bob Meusel's strong arm. As he rounded second, a piece of foam rubber Stengel kept in his shoe for comfort worked its way loose and popped out. Thinking he had thrown a shoe, Stengel began to hobble, like a man with one leg shorter than the other. Waved home from third, Stengel staggered down the line and threw himself across the plate in a tangle of arms and legs.

Stengel was thirty-one years old, so hyperbolic press reports played up the old-man angle of the mad dash. They described Stengel tucking in his long, white beard before hitting the ball, made references to "Gramps" Stengel getting wheeled to the plate, and marveled that his aged varicose veins held out during the run. Funny stuff to readers accustomed to wiseguy baseball scribes. However, the Lawsons of Glendale, California, digested every word as fact, or near fact.

"What do you think of my hero now, Pops?" Edna asked her father as he read the next day's sports pages.

Mr. Lawson slowly lowered his paper and gazed at his daughter with fatherly concern. "I hope," he said, "that he lives until the wedding."

Casey Stengel

◆

In the summer of 1932, as a twenty-two-year-old right-hander fresh out of the minor leagues, Gordon McNaughton pitched six games for the Red Sox. In the summer of 1942, he was thirty-two years old and out of baseball.

On the afternoon of August 6, he was in the Chicago hotel room of Mrs. Dorothy Moose. Three weeks earlier, Mrs. Moose, age twenty-seven, had left her husband—a wealthy racehorse owner—in favor of McNaughton. Soon Mrs. Eleanor Williams, a dice girl in a roadside tavern, showed up at the hotel room, brandishing a pistol. Four years earlier, Mrs. Williams, age twenty-five, had left her husband and child in favor of McNaughton.

Mrs. Williams confronted McNaughton, accused him of "double-crossing" her, and called him a "two-timer, and no good." After further discussion, she raised the pistol and fired twice, one slug striking McNaughton in the chest and killing him. Mrs. Williams waited in the hotel corridor for the Chicago police to arrive and surrendered quietly. "I'm glad I shot him," she said as the police led her away.

◆

In early January 1923, a citizen telephoned a Cincinnati newspaper with a tip for a human interest story. John ("Rube") Benton, the Reds' veteran left-hander, was driving a truck for the Cincinnati Iron and Steel Company. The baseball writer put together a story detailing Rube's industriousness and threw in a line about how Benton had settled down nicely since "marrying and becoming a proud father."

Next day, Benton telephoned the newspaper and told the writer to get his facts straight. Yes, he had settled down and married, but no, he wasn't driving trucks of any sort during the off-season. The writer apologized, and Benton accepted, citing "no harm done."

Shortly thereafter, the writer received another telephone call. Boston Braves right-hander Larry Benton, also a Cincinnati resident, was on the line and told the writer to get his facts straight. Yes, Benton was indeed driving a truck in the winter, but no, he had no wife or child. He was a bachelor, and his girlfriend had read in the morning paper about Rube Benton, big-league pitcher and truck driver, who was married with a family. Not surprisingly, when Larry Benton visited her that afternoon, he was met with "great frigidity." The fine mess was tidied after much explaining by Larry Benton, a telephone call from the baseball writer to the girlfriend, and finally a telephone call from Rube Benton to Larry Benton's girlfriend.

◆

Shortstop Sam ("Red") Crane played seven seasons in the big leagues before settling into a minor-league career after the 1922 season. While playing for Reading of the International League in 1927, Crane was smitten by divorcee Della Lyter. The following spring, Crane was set to take a better deal to play for the Buffalo Internationals. Instead, he tore up his contract and gave up baseball so he could stay with Lyter in Harrisburg, Pennsylvania.

More than a year later, on the Saturday night of August 8, 1929, Crane was at home and drinking heavily. Finally he got his gun and went to Bria's Hotel, where he found Della and brick salesman Jack Oren in a side room. Oren was strumming a ukulele when Crane burst through the door and opened fire. Two shots struck Della in the stomach. When Oren smashed the ukulele over Crane's head, Crane shot him twice. Lyter and Oren died from their wounds.

Sobering up five hours later, Crane turned himself in at the police station. "They say I shot somebody," he said. He was convicted and sentenced to twenty years.

◆

Here is a true story from the winter of 1978–79 when the Red Sox–Yankees rivalry was at its hottest. The names have been changed to protect the not-so-innocent.

Fred was a New Yorker, a Boston-area college student, a lifelong Yankee fan, and a resident of a coveted single dormitory room. Joe was a New Englander, completely uninterested in baseball, and a resident of a double room shared with a pesky roommate. Joe was enamored with Mary, another student at a Boston-area college.

Joe finally landed a date with Mary. He wanted to take her out on the town, then go someplace quiet to chat. It was far too cold for a stroll through the park, but he hated the idea of bringing her back to his room, where they could watch his roommate do homework. Joe entreated Fred to loan his coveted single room for the evening, but Fred refused. Joe appealed to his sense of friendship, but again Fred refused. When Joe offered a case of beer as rent, Fred gave him the key.

After a lovely evening, Joe and Mary returned to the single room for a nightcap. Not wanting to convey the wrong impression—a "borrowed room" would make the whole deal sound terribly predatory—Joe pretended the room was his. On the second light beer, Mary casually inspected the premises. Suddenly she spied the *Yankees, 1978 World Champions* banner strung prominently over the desk. "You like the *Yankees?*" she sputtered. Mary was a lifelong Red Sox fan.

She spent the rest of the evening debating Mickey Rivers versus Bill Lee, Ron Guidry versus Jim Rice, and Bucky Dent's incredible luck. Joe spent the rest of the evening not holding up his end of the conversation.

◆

When he was manager of the Cardinals, Branch Rickey assumed a protective, fatherly role toward his younger players. Early in spring training, Rickey customarily addressed his troops to advise them to avoid all temptation, especially booze and dames. "You're here to train for the Cardinals, not run around with women," Rickey preached.

In spring 1920 outfielder Heinie Mueller was among the impressionable youngsters subjected to Rickey's sermon. Relatives of Mueller lived in the town where the Cardinals trained. One day, he was accompanying his cousin Lulu to an ice cream parlor when he spotted Rickey walking down the sidewalk in their direction. Mueller pushed Lulu into a doorway, told her to stay put, and scampered out of sight. After Rickey passed and turned the corner, Mueller returned to his angry cousin.

"I don't care how mad you get," he said. "That was Mr. Branch Rickey, manager of the Cardinals. And after all, I'm down here to train with the Cardinals, not run around with women."

◆

At dawn on March 10, 1941, Latin dancer Francisco Colladra Carreno burst into a room at the Nacional Hotel in Havana and found his wife with Brooklyn Dodgers pitcher Van Lingle Mungo. In the ensuing scuffle, Carreno suffered a variety of injuries.

Mungo was demoted to Montreal of the International League. Carreno was unable to dance for some time and sued Mungo for twenty thousand dollars in lost income.

◆

In the summer of 1933, the year after he batted .336, Cardinals outfielder Ernie Orsatti hit .298. The following winter, on February 16, 1934, Orsatti was in a Los Angeles courtroom seeking a divorce from his wife, Martha. Orsatti alleged she called him "harsh names," squandered up to seven hundred dollars a month from his salary, and ignored members of his family when they visited their home. Not that she was antisocial. The ballplayer's sister, Mrs. Estelle Jacobson, also testified she had seen Mrs. Orsatti "drinking and sitting on the laps of male guests" at parties at the family home.

Orsatti was granted a divorce. He used it as a great excuse for the thirty-eight-point drop in his batting average. "How did your wife's conduct affect your efficiency in your work?" the judge asked.

"It affected me very much," said Orsatti. "I was very nervous."

Johnny Evers looks as shy as a young boy in the presence of a woman on the field.

◆

American Leaguers were telling this story in the late 1920s:

One evening on the road, several members of the White Sox were invited to dinner by a number of young ladies. After the meal, the ballplayers and their hostesses settled down to play cards.

A young country kid new to the White Sox was particularly enraptured by a striking brunette. Later in the card game, she got up from the table and started toward the kitchen to prepare dessert for the boys. "If you will excuse me," she said with a smile, "I'll go put on the percolator now."

"Aw, shucks," said her ballplayer admirer. "Don't bother to make any changes. You look swell in what you've got on now."

◆

On Friday night, January 11, 1929, firefighters answered a call at 47 Quincy Street in the Boston suburb of Watertown and found the tidy two-story house in flames. They crawled through the smoke and fire to an upstairs bedroom, where they discovered the burned body of a thirty-one-year-old woman, identified as Mrs. Helen Kinder, wife of prominent Back Bay dentist Dr. Edward Kinder. Returning from boxing matches at Boston Garden, Dr. Kinder approached his burning home, was told of his wife's death, and collapsed.

On Saturday, authorities began to investigate the blaze. Mrs. Kinder's burial was scheduled for Sunday in West Roxbury; and the Kinders' nine-year-old daughter, Dorothy, was summoned from her Wellesley boarding school. It was also announced that Yankees star Babe Ruth, an "intimate friend" of Dr. Kinder, would attend the rites.

On Sunday the funeral was postponed, and a scandal hit the newspapers. There was no Mrs. Kinder. The dead woman was Mrs. Helen Ruth, estranged wife of the Babe. Young Dorothy was identified as the Babe's daughter.

On Monday Mrs. Ruth's brothers and mother said they suspected foul play in Helen's death, and they demanded the body be analyzed for traces of drugs or poison. Dr. Kinder arrived at the Watertown police station with his lawyer and admitted he had been living with Mrs. Ruth, but hadn't married her. Police grilled him for three hours, then cleared him of all suspicion.

A tearful Ruth, meanwhile, was holed up at the Hotel Brunswick in Boston, where he received seventy-four letters and thirty-one telegrams of sympathy, including dispatches from Lou Gehrig and Miller

Huggins. Ruth reported he had married the former Helen Woodford, who was then a Boston waitress, on October 18, 1914, and the couple had been separated since 1927. He had learned of his wife's death in New York when a friend showed him a diamond pin, now partially charred, which he had given her.

On Tuesday state and local authorities announced the fire was probably caused by faulty wiring. The medical examiner's autopsy revealed no evidence of criminal activity, and the case was closed.

On Wednesday the Babe visited his wife's coffin at her family's home in South Boston. He broke down in tears and had to be helped to his car. On Thursday Mrs. Babe Ruth was buried at Cavalry Cemetery.

On Quincy Street in Watertown, youngsters ran and played in the street as a cab pulled up at the end of the block. A hulking figure in a huge overcoat emerged from the back seat and walked slowly up the road. The youngsters stopped playing. They instantly recognized the moon-faced man as the great Babe Ruth. Still, none of the starstruck children approached. They knew why he was there. Ruth walked up to the blackened frame of the burned-down house, stood silently in the street, and stared into the ruins. After a moment, he turned away and huddled deep into his overcoat as he plodded quietly back down the road, eased into the waiting cab, and rode away.

MONEY

One afternoon in Detroit circa 1950, the St. Louis Browns emerged from the clubhouse tunnel, clomped into the visitors' dugout, and blinked at the huge crowd packing the decks at Briggs Stadium. Always in the red, the Browns loved when they received cuts of hefty receipts on the road. Lord knew, they weren't drawing crowds at home.

By the first pitch, a light rain had begun to fall. By the third inning with the game a scoreless tie, the rain had quickened. There was a good chance the big gate would wash away. Browns manager Zack Taylor eyed the gray sky, paced the dugout, and barked instructions to his men. "Swing at anything," Taylor told them. "Just get three outs. Just get this game in. We need the money."

In the days when uniforms were baggy and the grass was real, baseball was relatively short on cash. Despite the golden nostalgic hue to the era, crowds were not large in the 1930s. There was no television, so there was no television revenue. Some teams had some money, and some tycoons were willing to squander chunks of the family fortune on their ball club toy. But no team could afford to make players into millionaires. "The ball clubs just didn't have the money," said Tommy Holmes, outfielder with the Boston Braves from 1941 through 1951. "One year, the Braves drew like 287,000 people. They just didn't have it."

Whatever was stacked upstairs in the safe, team moguls were reluctant to pass along significant amounts to the hired help. Players lived middle- or upper-middle class lives, but, compared to modern baseball bucks, they were paupers. Old-time ballplayers tell stories about the skinflint era the way Depression survivors tell their children about stale bread dinners and cold water flats: slightly romanticized and with a touch of pride. "We didn't think about money, money, money, and more, more, more," said Hall-of-Famer Johnny Mize, first baseman for the Cardinals, Giants, and Yankees from 1936 through 1953.

Babe Dahlgren (left) *and Phil Cavarretta*

Old timers were required to beg harder to gain less. Holdouts and contract squabbles are well documented throughout baseball history, but formerly they battled for thousands, not millions. There were no lawyers, no unions, no arbitration hearings, no complex filing deadlines, and no free agent re-entry pools. Bygone haggling seems comparatively quaint, even when adjusted for inflation. "They say the dollar went further in our day," said Babe Dahlgren, first baseman for the Yankees and others from 1935 through 1946. "But I'll take a million anytime, in any era." Old contract talks were less like corporate mergers and more like buying a scarf at a Casablanca bazaar.

"You bartered on your own," said Holmes. "When I hit .352, I bartered. I went to Mr. Perini [owner Lou Perini] and told him I wanted more than he was offering. He told me he'd give me half now and the other half at the end of the season if I hit .350 again."

Contract volleys between owner and player were seldom bitter. Possibly, the reason was that old-time players had almost no clout and couldn't afford to bristle the boss. The team mailed a contract in the winter. If the player didn't like the sum, he mailed the contract back unsigned. If the team preferred not to sweeten the offer, it dispatched the same deal to the player and told him to sign it or sit out the season. Before Marvin Miller's union in the mid 1960s and free agency in the mid 1970s, that was the choice. Not many ballplayers could afford a summer off. Giants outfielder Turkey Mike Donlin actually skipped the 1907 season over a contract dispute, but few wanted to emulate a man nicknamed "Turkey."

There are many stories of players getting together with owners and simply chatting out a square deal man to man. Gooey sentimentalists recall stories of contracts hammered out on hunting trips and pine for the old days. Those were simpler times, when lawyers and agents stayed out of it and paternalistic owners watched over their players as if they were sons. "Papa" owner ruled the boys with a stern, velvet hand but would never let them go hungry. "That's a lot of bullshit," said Dahlgren. "I got screwed. I got screwed, and I still dream about that every night."

History confirms that many players trusted owners and were thoroughly exploited. Hall-of-Famers found their big-league careers over, then headed back to the bush leagues to play past their fortieth birthday just to draw a salary. The body of Cubs slugger Hack Wilson stayed on ice in Baltimore for two days in 1948 until the National League stepped forward to finance his burial. The day he was elected to Cooperstown, pitcher Grover Cleveland Alexander was making a paid appearance at a flea circus in Times Square. Yankees slugger Babe Ruth was considered handsomely paid in his day, but he endlessly haggled with the Yankees, who never paid him more than eighty thousand dollars. Unlike the modern era's relentlessly upward spiral, old-time salaries went down as a player's skills diminished. Ruth's last contract offer from the Yankees was for one dollar, which was their way of telling the most god-like figure in the game's history to get lost.

Athletics manager Tony La Russa likes to tell a story about the talk he had with his slugger, Jose Canseco, after the young Oakland outfielder totaled forty-two home runs with forty stolen bases one season and was awarded a deal worth $1.6 million per year. "How did you do in school?" La Russa asked. "Not too good," said Canseco. "But I learned the new math. Forty home runs plus forty steals equal 1.6 million." Fans heard the statement and became more awed by Canseco's ego and paycheck than his playing skills.

Money has changed the way the masses view their hardball heroes. The archives show few old-timers were judged against their salaries. They were ball-players, as opposed to millionaire ballplayers. Fan resentment was low. Old-timers were easier to root for because they were easier to identify with, and many of them worked off-season jobs to keep the wood stove hot. They had to watch their budget: sidebets with teammates meant something, World Series shares meant a lot. When they misbehaved, fines were enough to slap them back into line. The money stories they tell have the relatively folksy ring of middle-class guys looking for a few dollars more or living beyond their means. "You know what I liked best about opening day?" said Holmes. "Opening day meant the baseball season had started again, and you were going to start getting paid again. You needed that money to eat."

Old-timers seldom intend to paint their present-day counterparts as greedheads. The ancients don't care if above-average outfielders drive cars favored by Arab oil barons. Neither do they care if millionaire ballplayers count the change after a clubhouse boy fetches a hamburger and fries for them. They don't even mind too much when able-bodied young men with rich portfolios charge ten dollars per autograph. But old-timers do mind if modern players act like millionaires on the field.

"There's a certain flatness in many of them today," said Holmes. "When they get the big contract, they flatten out. I hate to say it. We played harder. We had to play harder if we wanted to eat. Whether that was good or bad, it still made you get off your butt and play."

"I don't watch much baseball anymore," said Mize. "I don't find it interesting. They walk down to first on bases on balls. They take a couple of steps, then stop on balls to the outfield. They catch the ball one-handed over their head, which gives the baserunner a couple of extra steps. They play like amateurs. They play like Little Leaguers."

The lament sounds throughout the lore. It is only natural. Survivors of the Depression tell stories about grumbling stomachs. Their fathers told them stories about walking forty miles to school every day. "Too much money is hurting baseball. The present crop of big leaguers does not think enough. The average ballplayer now is more or less satisfied with his salary. He is getting as much as he dreamed he would get. Now he feels that he has arrived. He no longer needs to fight and stay awake planning and thinking. The result is less intelligent baseball on his part and often a bit of laziness," said Tris Speaker. He said it on August 26, 1926!

Nevertheless, the money of the 1990s is unprecedented. Old-timers worry that the modern player will get old and rich, look back, and still regret something. Players from the 1930s and 1940s didn't make millions, but most say they had more frolicking fun than the megabuck boys. Big money brings big pressure, and worrying about deferred payments and decimal points and option years and bonus clauses allows less time for a player to feel the sun on his face. As they age and get soft around the middle, ballplayers tell more stories about warm feelings than cold cash.

"I still dream that I'm playing," said Holmes. "About once a month. I'm in Pittsburgh, and I'm wondering where the hell my uniform is. I miss it. I'd play for nothing if I could play today. I really would. For nothing."

During spring training in 1930, Yankees slugger Babe Ruth and team owner Col. Jacob Ruppert were embroiled in another famous salary dispute. Ruth had just finished a three-year deal at seventy thousand dollars per season, and he wanted a raise to eighty-five thousand dollars. Ruppert offered eighty thousand.

During the stalemate, Ford Frick—then a baseball writer for the New York *Journal,* later the commissioner of baseball—was filing his overnight story in the St. Petersburg Western Union office. Dan Daniels of the New York *World-Telegram* passed by, saw Frick through the window, and stepped in. "Why the midnight oil?" Daniels asked.

"Ruth says he's sore," said Frick. "He won't put on a monkey suit tomorrow if the colonel doesn't meet his price. If he doesn't get his contract by noon, he's going to pack and go back to New York."

Daniels sat down at a typewriter, scrolled in a sheet of paper, and began to bat out a two-thousand-word story about the Ruth ultimatum. Daniels filed and went to bed. First thing the next morning, he received a telegram from his newspaper: Fine Job on Ruth Exclusive.

His heart skipped. Exclusive? Frick had handed him the story. Didn't Frick's paper run it, too? Daniels telephoned his office. "Nope," his editor said. "You got it alone."

Daniels frantically sought out Frick. "Fact is, during the night the Babe changed his mind and telephoned me," Frick said. "He said, 'Ferget that story, kid.' So I killed it by telegraph and went back to sleep."

Tris Speaker

More panicked than before, Daniels desperately hunted down the Babe. "Hey, what about that quitting yarn?" the frenized newsman said. He hoped and prayed the slugger had awoken disgruntled. "Who, me?" said Ruth. "I feel like playing baseball

Babe Ruth (left) *and Jake Ruppert*

today. I'm gonna play against the Braves."

Daniels groaned. His palms were sweating. "You got my pants on a hot spot," he told Ruth. "You gotta quit, like you said. Either that or sign before noon today. If you don't do one or the other, I'm a bum with my boss."

"Nuts," said Ruth. "I ain't gonna sign for a lousy eighty thousand dollars. I want eighty-five thousand dollars."

Daniels groaned again. He explained the situation to Ruth. He begged. He pleaded. He whined. He told Ruth his integrity, his reputation, and his job with the newspaper were at stake. "Okay, okay," Ruth relented. "If it's that bad, go tell the colonel. I'll sign."

Daniels yelped and set out to find Ruppert. He searched the city, street by street, until he found the dapper, stout owner with the walrus moustache strolling along the waterfront. "Colonel," said Daniels, out of breath. "Babe says he's ready to sign. How about it?"

Ruppert stared blankly at the newspaperman. "No hurry," he shrugged.

"It's a matter of life and death!" Daniels shrieked.

Ruppert meandered back to the hotel. Ruth wandered up to the owner's suite and signed his new contract for eighty thousand dollars. It was 11:45. Daniels's reputation was saved, with fifteen minutes to spare.

"Ruth doesn't know," Ruppert chortled years later, "but I would have paid him one hundred thousand dollars if he had insisted hard enough."

◆

Traveling with the team one evening in the summer of 1922, Cardinals first baseman Jacques Fournier ate supper in the train's dining car. At a table across from him, teammates Del Gainor and Lou North were finishing a large meal. When the waiter was busy at the far end of the car, the pair settled the check, hopped out of their seats, and hotfooted through the door.

Fournier called over the waiter and asked what kind of tip Gainor and North had left. The waiter showed him: a nickel and a Canadian dime. "That was a mistake," fumed Fournier, who hated ballplayers who stiffed working folks. "You go back to car X–1 and ask for Del and Lou, and I'm sure they'll fix you up."

The waiter took the advice. He returned shortly with a report: North had grudgingly replaced the Canadian coin with a U.S. dime, but Gainor refused to turn over more than the nickel.

◆

When he was with the Red Sox, pitcher Lefty Grove made an annual off-season visit to the estate of team owner Tom Yawkey in South Carolina to hunt and to hammer out a contract for the following year. At the end of his visit one winter, Grove loaded his car with deer, turkey, preserves, pine saplings, chickens, and eggs. Grove hopped in and started the engine. Yawkey raised his voice above the motor. "Hey, Mose," he shouted. "How about the contract? We forgot—"

"Damn the contract," interrupted Grove, revving the car. "Where is it, anyhow?"

Yawkey rushed into the house and returned with a blank contract. Grove snatched it from his hand, scribbled his signature at the bottom, and handed it back. "But what about the money?" Yawkey asked as Grove shifted the car into gear. "How much?"

"Put in anything," retorted Grove as he roared away.

◆

Milwaukee manager Connie Mack had a stack of enthusiastic reports on pitcher Rube Waddell. A quirky, hard-throwing, hard-living left-hander on the local team in Punxsutawney, Pennsylvania, he was occasionally brilliant with the Pirates before he jumped the club. Mack telephoned Waddell to offer a contract with Milwaukee, which was then a minor-league team.

"Hello, Rube," said Mack when Waddell came to the phone. "This is Connie Mack."

"Who the hell are you?" Waddell wanted to know.

Mack pressed on. He said Milwaukee had a good team and had the chance to be great if it could land a pitcher like Waddell. Rube was unimpressed. "I realized later,"

Jack Fournier

Mack once recalled, "I should have put in my time talking about Milwaukee beer."

"They like me here," Waddell said. "They do everything for me, and I couldn't let them down. There's not enough money in Milwaukee to make me run out on them."

Mack hung up, but he didn't give up. Dispatching a telegram each day for two weeks, he followed up each one with a letter. Finally Mack received a wire in reply: "Come and get me."

Mack journeyed to Punxsutawney, planning to spirit Waddell out of town in secret lest the locals riot over the loss of their star pitcher. After sticking Mack with the check for breakfast, Waddell suggested they go for a walk. "I got a few little odds and ends to square up before taking off," he said.

First stop was the grocery store. Waddell asked the owner how much he owed. The owner took a while but finally produced a grand total. Rube took the bill and handed it to Mack.

Waddell and Mack made thirteen more stops. Mack settled the tab at the men's clothing store, the sporting goods store, the tailor shop, the barber shop, seven saloons, the Adams Express Company, where Waddell was still in arrears for a dog he had received express C.O.D., and the pawn shop, where they retrieved Waddell's watch. Mack was nearly out of cash and wondered if he'd have enough left for the fare back to Milwaukee.

Mack then escorted Waddell to the hotel, where he hid the pitcher until fifteen minutes before their train was scheduled to leave. Mack was nervous. He was certain the fourteen bill-paying ceremonies had tipped the locals about Waddell's defection, and he was certain they would do something to try to stop it.

At the station, Mack purchased two one-way tickets and nervously waited with Waddell on the platform. Suddenly a group of grim-faced men appeared, surveyed the crowd, saw the manager and the pitcher, and marched toward them. "Here comes trouble," said Mack.

One of the grim-faced men walked straight to Mack and stuck out his hand. "My friends and I have come down here to thank you," he said. "You're doing us a great favor. Waddell is a great pitcher. But we feel very strongly that Punxsutawney would be better off without him."

◆

While vacationing in Havana one off-season, Babe Ruth was approached by a group of promoters who sold him on the idea of starring him in a quickie film. Ruth agreed, the film was shot, and the promoters cut him a check for twenty-five thousand dollars.

Ruth was proud of picking up so much money for so little work. For months he carried the check wherever he went. Out on the town, on golf courses, and in taverns, Ruth liked to reach into his vest pocket, slip out the check, and watch his pals marvel at all the zeroes.

Eventually the novelty wore thin, and the Babe brought the beer-stained check to his bank. He pushed it through the teller's window, and after a moment the teller pushed it back out. The check had bounced.

◆

In the spring of 1908, Philadelphia Athletics catcher Ossee Schreckengost visited manager Connie Mack's office and sullenly announced he would not sign his contract for the upcoming season.

"What's the matter, Ossee?" said Mack. "I gave you an increase."

"No, Mr. Mack, it isn't that," said Schreckengost. "It's Waddell."

Rube Waddell, the Athletics' lefty pitcher and notorious hell-raiser, was his roommate. Mack figured old Schreck wanted Waddell's kind of money. "I'm sick and tired of having him come to bed after I'm comfortably settled and get to reading with the light on full blast, eating a bag of crackers," Schreckengost blurted. "I've slept in cracker crumbs for two years now, and I'm not going to sign this contract unless you put a clause in keeping Rube from eating crackers in bed."

◆

When Ben Johnson and friends formed the American League in 1901, Clark Griffith was designated the chief headhunter. As arrogant National Leaguers scoffed, Griffith drew up a list of forty prominent National League players and vowed to induce all of them to jump to the renegade league.

With single-minded determination, Griffith carried his crusade from New England to Georgia to Kansas City. To lure outfielder Fielder Jones from the Dodgers, he trudged three miles through the snow to Jones's upstate New York home. Griffith grabbed catcher Billy Sullivan, pitcher Jimmy Callahan, outfielder Sandow Mertes, third baseman Jimmy Collins, and pitcher Big Bill Dinneen. Before long, he had bagged thirty-nine of the forty names on the list. The lone holdout was Pirates shortstop Honus Wagner. When Griffith marched through the snow after him, Wagner barricaded himself in the upper floor of a Carnegie, Pennsylvania, pool hall and shouted out the window, "Go away, you! If I talk to you, I'll jump the Pirates, sure!"

Happy with a thirty-nine-for-forty season, Griffith was back on the trail the next winter. On one stop, he visited Philadelphia to coax catcher Ed McFarland out of his Phillies' contract. McFarland wouldn't sign without a bonus. "Of course I'll give you a bonus to jump your contract," Griffith agreed.

"Yeah," McFarland grumbled. "You talk big, but where's the cash? I want five hundred dollars to jump, and I want it right now."

Griffith had less than ten dollars in his pocket, and he had no way to contact the American League money men. "Five hundred?" he said without hesitation. "That's easy, with all the money we've got in our league. You stay right here, and I'll bring it to you."

Griffith returned after two hours, reached into his coat pocket, and plunked five hundred dollars in front of McFarland, who immediately signed an American League contract. Where did Griffith get the cash? He borrowed it from the owner of the Phillies.

◆

The maternal grandfather of Red Sox scout and former Twins manager Sabath ("Sam") Mele was named Sabato Cuccinello. Sabato promised his daughter that if she named her first son Sabato, he would bequeath the boy a generous sum of money.

When Mele was born, his mother named him Sabato. Still her father was not satisfied. The baby's name was Sabato Mele, not Sabato Cuccinello. Sorry, but no money, said Gramps. When Mele's uncle had a son, he named the boy Sabato. He was a Cuccinello. Cousin got the money.

"My mother was mad for a long time, just about till the day she died," said Mele. "Imagine that? I got named Sabato first, and the other one got the money. I had to go to City Hall to change my name to Sabath. And the other Sabato who got the money has since changed his name to Louis."

◆

At the conclusion of the 1929 World Series, the Athletics were asked about each man's plans for his winner's share of $5,620.57.

"I am going to give half of it to endow an institute for blind umpires and the other half to a sanitarium for violent autograph seekers," said outfielder Bing Miller.

"I'm going back to Montclair [New Jersey] and paint the town red," said outfielder Mule Haas.

"I'm going to pay off the mortgage on the home I bought for my mother last year. I know it sounds funny, but that is the truth," said outfielder Al Simmons.

"A few dollars of it are going into new bowling balls," said third baseman Jimmy Dykes.

"I'm going to buy myself a new saddle and a set of spurs," said outfielder Walter French.

"What I get I'm going to put in the bank, so I won't have to eat snowballs this winter," said outfielder Bevo LeBourveau.

"What am I going to do with it? I owe it already," said catcher Cy Perkins.

◆

Jim Lonborg was pitching for the Winner, South Dakota, Pheasants in the Basin League in the mid 1960s when big-league scouts started to come around. "There was a lot of college talent in the Basin League," said Lonborg. "Jim Palmer was on our team."

A premed student at Stanford, Lonborg wasn't sure how his baseball plans would unfold. He was certain, however, which major-league team would sign him: the Orioles. "We knew they were interested," said Lonborg. "They sponsored our team."

Back in California at the end of his college career, Lonborg and his father entertained offers. The Orioles delivered a nice proposal. Then there was a call from Red Sox scout Danny Doyle. Lonborg and his father met with Doyle in a hotel room and listened to the Boston sales pitch. When Doyle delivered the Red Sox offer, Lonborg and his father tried hard not to catapult out of their chairs.

"I remember when we were walking out, my father and I looked at each other as if to say, 'Do you believe this?'" Lonborg recalled in the summer of 1990. "We were hicks from central California. We had never seen that kind of money."

Out of courtesy to the Orioles, the Lonborgs related Boston's amazing proposal. "They were flabbergasted the Red Sox had made me that kind of offer," said Lonborg. Overwhelmed by Boston owner Tom Yawkey's moneybags, Lonborg signed with the Red Sox. Boston's boggling offer: eighteen thousand dollars.

◆

When he was with the Pirates, fun-loving shortstop Rabbit Maranville got into a barroom brawl and the ball club fined him five hundred dollars. Pittsburgh owner Barney Dreyfuss gave the Rabbit a chance to redeem himself. "If you're a good boy the rest of the year," Dreyfuss said, "I'll give that five hundred dollars to your little daughter as a present at the end of the season."

Maranville stayed out of trouble. At the end of the season, Dreyfuss called him into his office and, as promised, handed him a $500 check.

"Fine," said Maranville. "But what about the interest on this dough?"

◆

◆

During the 1931 season, Yankees outfielder Babe Ruth wagered pitcher Lefty Gomez $1,500 to $25 that the weak-hitting (.147 lifetime) hurler wouldn't total more than ten hits all season. By late September, Gomez had scratched out eight.

Ruth's money still seemed safe, for Gomez was a horrendous hitter. During an afternoon game at Yankee Stadium, he collected his ninth hit against Athletics pitcher Rube Walberg. Three consecutive New Yorkers had reached base before Gomez stepped to the plate and cracked Walberg's first pitch for a crisp single to the outfield. Walberg gave a startled look at the ball as it whizzed past, then silently walked off the mound toward the dugout, not waiting for manager Connie Mack to remove him. "When that guy can get a hit off me," Walberg said in disgust, "then I know I got no business pitching."

Somehow Gomez rang up one more hit, and, as he stepped in for his last at-bat on the last day of the season, he still had ten. Everyone in both dugouts knew about the bet, and everyone was pulling for the relatively underpaid underdog. Then St. Louis Browns righty Sad Sam Gray lobbed an obligingly fat pitch. Gomez swung hard and trickled a slow roller to shortstop. Red Kress politely took his time getting to the ball and heaved a soft throw. Gomez beat out the hit and beat the Babe out of $1,500.

◆

Throughout the winter of 1916–17, Casey Stengel wrestled with Brooklyn over a new contract. Finally he grudgingly accepted a pay cut of $1,300. On opening day at Ebbets Field, Stengel brought a copy of his contract and a pair of scissors to right field during batting practice. "Did you get your money back, Casey?" one fan yelled. "What kind of contract did you get?" shouted another.

"I didn't get such a big one," Stengel shouted back, theatrically shortening the contract with the scissors.

The Dodgers finished seventh in 1917, and Stengel batted just .257. "We owe for this ballpark, too," Charles Ebbets scolded Stengel afterward. "And you haven't helped pay for it."

"I must have given you a concrete pier when I took that pay cut," said Stengel. He was traded to Pittsburgh.

◆

Pitching for Cincinnati in 1933, hot-tempered Paul Derringer often ran afoul of hot-tempered general manager Larry MacPhail. Once MacPhail fined Derringer $250 and suspended him for three days for failing to slide into a base, even though he was out by fifteen feet. When the suspension was finished, MacPhail called Derringer to his office to harangue the pitcher further.

As the executive ranted, Derringer suddenly reached forward, grabbed a heavy inkwell off the desk, and hurled it at MacPhail's head. It missed by an inch. MacPhail silently reached into his top drawer. Back to his senses, Derringer braced. He was sure MacPhail was going for a gun.

MacPhail slapped a checkbook onto the desk, wrote out a check to Derringer for $750, and handed it across the desk. "Here," MacPhail said. "I'm paying you back the money I fined you."

Derringer glanced at the figure. "But what's the extra dough for?" he asked.

"That's a bonus for missing me, you [expletive]," MacPhail answered.

◆

◆

In its early days, the Pacific Coast League had the same problem confronting the big leagues in the 1990s: how to put bite behind disciplinary fines. Fines mean almost nothing to modern players because they have so much money. Fines meant almost nothing to the old Coast League players because they had *no* money. Teams were failing, and salaries were in arrears.

"That will cost you fifty dollars," umpire Jack Sheridan snapped one day to a complaining player in Oakland.

"Make it a thousand," sneered the player. "I haven't got any money, and neither does the club."

Next day, the same player staged an obscenity-laden tantrum. Sheridan approached him, reached into the player's pocket, snatched his meal ticket, and punched out fifty cents' worth of dinner.

◆

At the start of his twentieth season in the big leagues, Babe Ruth was asked to recall his rookie year in 1914, when he joined the Red Sox in midseason. Did he remember the day?

"Sure," said Ruth. "It was in June 1914, and I got into Boston at noon and Bill Carrigan told me I was to pitch at three o'clock."

Who was his catcher? "I don't remember," said Ruth.

Who pitched against him? "I don't remember that, either," said Ruth.

There was a pause. Ruth was asked what, if anything, he remembered about his 1914 contract.

"Contracts, you mean," said the Babe. "I signed four different contracts for four different salaries that year. I signed with Bal-timore for six hundred dollars and they raised it to twelve hundred dollars and later they raised it eighteen hundred. Then I signed with Boston for twenty-five hundred, and it looked like a million to me."

Ruth's yearly salaries during his big league career:

1914 — Red Sox	....	$ 2,500
1915 — Red Sox	....	$ 3,500
1916 — Red Sox	....	$ 3,500
1917 — Red Sox	....	$ 5,000
1918 — Red Sox	....	$ 7,000
1919 — Red Sox	....	$ 10,000
1920 — Yankees	....	$ 20,000
1921 — Yankees	....	$ 30,000
1922 — Yankees	....	$ 52,000
1923 — Yankees	....	$ 52,000
1924 — Yankees	....	$ 52,000
1925 — Yankees	....	$ 52,000
1926 — Yankees	....	$ 52,000
1927 — Yankees	....	$ 70,000
1928 — Yankees	....	$ 70,000
1929 — Yankees	....	$ 70,000
1930 — Yankees	....	$ 80,000
1931 — Yankees	....	$ 80,000
1932 — Yankees	....	$ 75,000
1933 — Yankees	....	$ 52,000
1934 — Yankees	....	$ 37,500
1935 — Braves	....	$ 25,000
22-year-total	....	$856,000

◆

Before the start of the 1933 season, the San Francisco Seals of the Pacific Coast League were interested in first baseman Jack Fenton of Memphis of the Southern Association. The Seals wired Memphis and asked about purchasing the player outright. Memphis wired back and told San Francisco to make an offer.

Because of the economic conditions of the day, the San Francisco team was short of cash. The Seals wired back a proposal: a case of Santa Clara prunes in exchange for

Paul Derringer

they expect for twenty-three hundred dollars a year?" Tierney snapped.

♦

Some twenty steps from the bratwurst stand not far from the visitors' clubhouse at Milwaukee's County Stadium, a plaque was affixed to the wall. In brass lettering it read: Old Time Ball Players Association of Wisconsin Sand Lot Hall of Fame.

To the average fan from the East, most of the names were just strangers with German ancestry: George Goesch, Oscar Rohr, Larry Kehl, Hilbert Wegner. A few, however, rang familiar: Ken Keltner, Steve Bartkowski, Tony Kubek, Sr.

"That's my dad," said Tony Kubek, Jr., the ex-Yankee shortstop and distinguished baseball broadcaster, on a rainy afternoon in spring 1988. "I had never seen that plaque. He played for the old Milwaukee Brewers, the old Triple–A team, in the 1930s. He hit .350 one year and was offered

Benton. Memphis agreed. The deal was completed on March 25.

♦

During a game in the summer of 1924, Boston Braves third baseman Cotton Tierney robbed Pittsburgh batter Pie Traynor of a hit with a spectacular diving catch. As the teams switched sides, Traynor complimented Tierney, one third baseman to another. "That's what they're paying me ten grand a year for," Cotton said breezily.

In the ninth inning, Tierney botched a routine grounder to lose the game for Boston. Afterward, Traynor asked him what had happened on the play. "What do

Pie Traynor

a professional contract with the St. Louis Browns. But he couldn't afford to take it. Too many kids at home to support. So he stayed home and worked at the tannery. That's the way it was in those days. People complain about free agency. They don't remember when good players like my dad were run out of the game."

◆

During one off-season, Athletics lefty pitcher Rube Waddell visited manager Connie Mack and told him he had received an offer from another club, including a two-thousand-dollar signing bonus, even showing Mack the certified check to prove it. Mack told Waddell the Athletics would offer a better signing bonus if he would return the next day.

When Waddell came back, Mack offered him five hundred dollars in one-dollar bills. Waddell looked at the stack of singles, looked at the two-thousand-dollar certified check, and gleefully opted for the five hundred dollars.

◆

In the winter of 1930–31, Cubs owner Bill Wrigley established an aviary on his Catalina Island estate in California. Designed to attract tourists, the venture proved slightly less successful than the Cubbies, if not unlike running a club that bought and sold players like livestock. "One day my manager told me he had bought a bird for fifteen hundred dollars," said Wrigley. "I expected to get nothing less than a bird the size of an ostrich for that price. When it showed up, it wasn't any bigger than my hand. And in a few days, it died.

"I thought baseball was tough until I got into this. You can't trade a bird to any other aviary, and you can't sell one to any other aviary in the league. Besides, there's nothing quite so dead as a dead bird that cost fifteen hundred dollars."

◆

On a rainy afternoon in the spring of 1988, the ball game at Fenway Park was rained out. New to the ballpark that season was a billboard on the back wall of the right-field bleachers, approximately 650 feet from home plate, that promised a new pair of shoes to any player who hit a ball off the sign. Forget footwear, the players laughed. Any batter who smacked a ball that far should have been admitted to the Hall of Fame and the Smithsonian simultaneously.

In the Red Sox clubhouse, the topic of conversation turned to hit-this-sign-and-win-something billboards in the days when the prizes were important to strapped ballplayers. The most famous was in right field at Brooklyn's Ebbets Field, where Abe Stark's clothing store promised Hit Sign, Win Suit. That target, however, was situated beneath the scoreboard. Hitting it required a 300-foot line drive six inches off the ground, or a right fielder who fell.

"I remember one in Rochester," Red Sox third-base coach Joe Morgan said. "You had to hit a ball through a hole in the fence to win $10,000 or a new car or whatever it was. Except the hole wasn't lined up with home plate. It faced more toward third base. The wind would have had to blow the ball sideways to get it through."

Boston general manager Lou Gorman remembered a huge tire above the outfield fence in Kinston, North Carolina. "If you hit it through the tire, you won $250 from the tire company," said Gorman. "Two guys did it while I was there. Jim Price was one. I think the other was Al Oliver."

Morgan suggested making a telephone call to a guy he knew in his hometown of Walpole, Massachusetts. He was Al Meau, who had pitched for the Class D affiliate of the Boston Braves just after World War II. "I remember him telling a story about hitting a sign once," said Morgan.

The telephone call was placed. "In Blue Field, West Virginia, in 1947 I hit a home run through a truck tire and won $100," said Meau, age sixty-one and working as a security guard. "I was making $135 a month at the time. If you hit the sign on one bounce, it was $25. Hit it on the fly, you won $50. Hit it over the sign, you won $75. Hit it through the tire, you won $100. That money helped us pay the bills after our first baby. We've had thirteen since."

◆

One day at spring training in St. Petersburg, Florida, a stadium guard approached Yankees manager Casey Stengel in the dugout. "Fellow over there behind the wire screen called me over, Casey," the guard said. "He says he knows you, that he's from Kankakee, Illinois, where you played ball. Will I tell him to beat it?"

"No," said Stengel. "I'll go see him."

Stengel hobbled to the fence. An elderly man motion to him. "You probably don't remember me, Casey," the man said through the chicken wire. "I used to run a concession stand near the Kankakee ballpark."

Stengel studied the man for a moment. "Wait a minute," the manager said, perking up. "I sure do. Your name is Schneider, and I remember I bought a meal ticket from you early in the 1910 season for $3.50 and the league folded and I'm still owed $1.50 for meals on that ticket. You still in business?"

◆

On the drizzly, humid afternoon of May 9, 1912, Red Sox right-hander Charley ("Sea Lion") Hall grooved a 2–0 pitch to Ty Cobb. The Detroit outfielder slapped it over the right-field fence at Fenway Park, marking the first ball to clear the right-field barrier at the recently opened ballpark. In honor of his feat, Cobb was awarded a gift certificate good for one hat from the Delano Hat Company of Boston.

More than fifteen years later, on December 13, 1927, Frank Delano of the Delano Hat Company received a letter:

"Sirs: Find enclosed a requisition for one hat issued some time ago and which has been lost and only recently turned up. If this bill holds good, send me one 7¼ hat. Anything you choose will be O.K. Send just Augusta, Georgia. Thanking you, I am, very truly, Ty Cobb."

Delano sent a hat to Cobb, accompanied by a letter:

"Dear Mr. Cobb: I have your letter of December 13 and am sending you a hat for the home run you made in 1912. In those

Ty Cobb

days hats were selling for three dollars so you have really benefited by losing this slip. You might, however, send me a ticket to a baseball game sometime, and we will call it square. [Signed] Frank M. Delano."

◆

Year after year, Red Sox outfielder Todd Benzinger started to chip away at his Christmas list a little late in the season, usually around December 24. In 1988, however, Benzinger decided to knock off much of his holiday shopping incredibly early.

Late in the summer, he made a visit to the sprawling souvenir shop across from Fenway Park. "I spent over an hour in there," said Benzinger. "I got Red Sox hats, Red Sox T-shirts, all kinds of Red Sox souvenirs. I got the bulk of my Christmas shopping out of the way."

On December 13, Benzinger, the man with a closetful of Red Sox paraphernalia as Christmas presents, was traded to the Cincinnati Reds. "Now I've got this box of Red Sox souvenirs, and I don't know what I'm going to do with it," he said on the day of the deal. "I can't believe it; two hundred dollars down the drain."

◆

Here are excerpts from a February 27, 1927, letter written by a ballplayer to a team owner:

You will find enclosed a contract which I am returning unsigned because of the $52,000 salary figure. I think you are entitled to know what terms I honestly expect and therefore the figure is not padded with intentions of accepting less. Nor is it based on the suggestions I have received from thousands of fans nor from newspaper articles that have appeared in any parts of the country, but what I feel I am worth from past performances and prospects.

In fine physical condition today, I hope to play as good a game or better than last season. I have exercised all winter and for the past twelve weeks have been working out of doors. The club has profited from five of the best years of my baseball life. During that period, my earning power to the club has greatly increased, while my salary has remained unchanged. If I were in any other business, I would probably receive a new contract at a higher salary, without request, or rival employers would bid for my services. Baseball law forces me to work for the New York club or remain idle.

Taking all these things into consideration, I sincerely believe I am entitled to $100,000 per season. I have made no threats to quit baseball. Such threats are not necessary, because unless I accept your figure I will be prohibited from playing with any other club, and barred from baseball, regardless of my own desires.

With best personal wishes, I am, yours truly, [signed] Babe Ruth.

◆

In 1930 hard-living outfielder Hack Wilson was at the height of his distinguished big-league career: he batted .356 with fifty-six home runs and 190 runs batted in. That winter, the Cubs signed him for $33,500, among the highest salaries in the National League.

In 1931 Wilson slumped to .261 with thirteen home runs and sixty-one RBIs. That winter the Cubs traded him to the Cardinals, who offered him a contract with a $25,000 pay cut. Wilson refused and was shipped to the Dodgers, who signed him at a $17,000 cut.

The following year, Brooklyn slashed his salary another $6,500. In 1934 Wilson was released by the Dodgers, then picked up and released by the Phillies. After playing in the International League for part of 1935, Wilson was out of the game. No longer able to hit baseballs, Wilson started hitting the bottle harder than ever.

For a while, he worked tending bar in various low-rent New York taverns, where he received little pay but much abuse.

"So you're Hack Wilson," patrons sneered. "You're a bum."

"Sure I'm Hack Wilson," he would say through clenched teeth. "But I'm no bum."

Wilson drifted to Baltimore, where during the war he worked as a tool-checker in an aircraft factory. After the war, he took odd jobs. In the summer of 1948, he walked into Baltimore City Hall and asked "for any kind of work." He was given a job as a laborer, followed by work at a municipal swimming pool.

In October, Wilson suffered head injuries in a fall. In mid-November, needing the money, he got out of his sick bed to appear on the "We the People" radio program in New York. Wilson urged young players not to squander their salaries on fast times. The following week, a friend found Wilson unconscious in his squalid Baltimore flat. He died, at age forty-eight, of complications brought on by pneumonia. Hack Wilson's only belongings were the clothes on his back.

◆

You watched him on ancient, herky-jerky, black-and-white game films, have seen Gary Cooper portray him in the movies, and touched his locker in Cooperstown. But when you spoke to somebody who actually lived and worked with the legendary Lou Gehrig, you had to ask: What was he really like? Was there anything at all antiheroic about the guy?

"He was frugal," said Babe Dahlgren, who replaced the Iron Horse at first base for the Yankees on May 2, 1939. "For instance, he would never, ever buy drinks in the clubhouse. We would all buy soft drinks in a particular town, and the clubhouse man would keep track of who bought what and tally up at the end of the series. Lou never bought any.

"One day I bought a Coke, put it down on my stool in front of my locker, and went to the bathroom. When I came out, my Coke was half gone. I looked around the room, and Lou was the only one there."

◆

When he was in the prime of his Hall-of-Fame career with the Philadelphia Athletics, slugger Jimmie Foxx heard the same story every winter when he visited president-manager Connie Mack for a new contract. "Jimmie, I can't pay you what you're worth," Mack would sigh. "But some day, I'll make it up to you." Good natured and trusting, Foxx signed whatever deal was pushed in front of him. His highest salary with the A's was sixteen thousand dollars. His highest big-league salary was twenty thousand dollars with the Red Sox.

In the summer of 1945, Foxx ended his brilliant big-league career at age thirty-seven. Here are highlights of his financial situation and employment record thereafter:

1945—Sales promotions, Hathaway Bakeries, Inc.
1946—Sports announcer, WEEI radio in Boston
1946–47—Player-manager for St. Petersburg (Class C)
1949—Managed Bridgeport, Connecticut, Bees of the Colonial League
1951—Salesman for Doylestown, Pennsylvania, truck company

After he retired, Jimmie Foxx worked at a sporting goods store in Cleveland, Ohio.

1957—Coached University of Miami baseball (salary: $1,500 a year)

1957—Unemployed; listed assets as $400 and 1932 MVP trophy

1958—Coach for the Red Sox' American Association team in Minneapolis

1959—Greeter at Jimmie Foxx's Restaurant, owned by Joe Donato and Nunzio and Tony Magieri, in Galesburg, Illinois

1960—Applied for thirty-five dollars per week unemployment insurance

1960—Worked in garden nursery, Rocky River, Ohio

1961—Filed for bankruptcy in Lakewood, Ohio

1962—Sporting goods salesman at May Department Store, Cleveland

1967—Retired; choked to death on piece of meat, Miami, Florida

◆

One day in the summer of 1978, the Bristol (Connecticut) Red Sox arrived in Jersey City, New Jersey, to begin a twelve-game road trip. Bristol outfielder Barry Butera felt uncomfortable carrying twelve days' of meal money through the mean streets to Roosevelt Stadium, and, before he left for the ballpark, he stashed his wallet deep under his mattress.

After the game, Butera and roommates Bucky Denton and Steve Schneck stopped by the room before heading out to get a bite to eat. When Butera lifted up the mattress to retrieve some spending money, he found his wallet, and a large wad of crumpled bills that had not been there when he left.

"I would have seen it when I put my wallet there," Butera recalled from his New Orleans home in the summer of 1989. "I started peeling off bills. A hundred dollar bill. Another hundred dollar bill. Another. A fifty. To make a long story short, there was about seven hundred dollars under there."

Butera and his teammates stared at the pile of money. They fidgeted as they tried to figure out where it might have come from. A drug deal? Mob money? Mob money from a drug deal? Misplaced chambermaid tips? They also wondered what they were going to do with it.

"Our minds were racing like crazy," said Butera. "Finally we took it to our manager, Tony Torchia, who told us to put it in the hotel safe. If nobody claimed it, we were going to keep it."

That night in their room, the three ballplayers got to thinking. They were in Jersey City, just a hand grenade toss away from New York City. "Which intimidated us to begin with. You read in the papers about people getting killed for fifty dollars. Here we were with seven hundred dollars. We didn't know who had put it there, but we were sure whoever put it there would be back for it," said Butera. They lay in bed thinking. Whoever put the money there would be back for it. The ballplayers stacked furniture in front of the door.

After the game the next night, Butera and his roommates crept into their room accompanied by a half-dozen other teammates, who helped search in the closets,

under the beds, and in the bathroom for vengeful intruders who might have come back for the cash. "We were seriously concerned," said Butera. "We all slept with one eye open."

After the last game of the series was rained out, Butera and his buddies hot-footed from the ballpark to the hotel, withdrew the money from the hotel safe, and streaked across the river to Manhattan. They treated themselves to a boom box, so they might have music during the long bush-league bus rides, and to an elegant dinner, courtesy of the unknown benefactor.

"We had wine and everything," said Butera. "That night we ate pretty well for a bunch of Double-A guys."

◆

In the summer of 1898, lefty Rube Waddell pitched for the Western League team in Detroit. One Sunday afternoon, Waddell wandered to a sandlot game, where he was instantly recognized and was enlisted to umpire behind home plate. Soon he was caught up in the excitement of the game, ordered the young hurler from the mound, and took over the pitching himself.

For the infraction of league rules, he was fined fifty dollars, a hefty sum for a wild spender such as Waddell, who never had more than seventy cents at a time in his pocket. The very next game, however, Waddell greatly pleased the boss. He held Minneapolis to four singles and struck out eleven. Detroit owner Hoss Van der Beck lifted the fifty-dollar-fine and presented Waddell with a bonus of a dozen red neckties.

Buoyed by his performance, the lifting of the fine, and the gifts, Waddell insisted upon pitching the next day against St. Paul. He was whacked for thirteen hits and lost,

Hank Aaron

12–5. An angry Van der Beck reinstated the fifty-dollar-fine and demanded the return of the neckties. Having already hocked them, Waddell was afraid the owner would order him arrested, so he jumped the team and disappeared into Canada.

Anyone who was at the ballpark or watched the game on television will never forget the moment. Dodgers' lefty Al Downing pitched, Braves batter Hank Aaron swung, and the ball soared to deep left-center field at Atlanta Stadium. Los Angeles left fielder Bill Buckner madly scrambled up the wall to try to catch the ball, but it sailed far out of reach into the Atlanta bullpen and into history. Aaron had hit his 715th career home run, one more than Babe Ruth.

Sixteen years later, Buckner was forty years old and scraping out the two final months of his career on the Red Sox bench. Someone asked him about that night in Atlanta and his frenzied attempt to scale the fence.

"I was climbing the fence to try to stop it from being a home run," said Buckner. "Then I was climbing the fence because I wanted to jump over and get the ball. They were offering $30,000 for it, and I was only making $25,000 a year."

STUNTS, TRICKS, AND PRACTICAL JOKES

Right-handed Red Sox pitcher Greg Harris is ambidextrous. He signs autographs, shoots basketballs, and spirals a football left-handed and right-handed. He also throws a baseball left-handed and right-handed. Ten years into his big-league career, no team had let him pitch left-handed in a game. Why not? Well, switch pitching is just never done, that's all.

"Exactly," said Harris. "If there's any way I'm ever going to get to the Hall of Fame, pitching left-handed is it," he predicted shortly after he joined the Red Sox late in the 1989 season. Harris knew history. Only four big league pitchers ever hurled both ways, none of them after 1896: Tony Mullane, Larry Corcoran, John Roach, and Icebox Chamberlain. Harris could make modern-day baseball history with just one pitch. It would be fun, exciting, and a terrific addition to baseball lore.

"I wouldn't want him to do it," scowled the usually jovial Red Sox general manager Lou Gorman, shortly after Harris joined the team. "I'd frown upon it. Let's put it that way. The big leagues are the big leagues. I think you demean the major leagues that way."

Where have you gone, Bill Veeck? When he owned the St. Louis Browns, Wild Bill sent three-foot, seven-inch midget Eddie Gaedel to bat against the Tigers. For a change of pace, exuberant old-timers liked that sort of stuff. Casey Stengel once took off his hat, and out flew a sparrow, which surprised even Brooklynites. When Braves second baseman Connie Ryan one day thought the rain too heavy to play ball, he wore a yellow slicker and carried an umbrella to home plate.

Somewhere along the way, baseball turned frumpy. By the 1990s some dullards considered the hidden ball trick too clownish. By 2000 the knuckleball might be declared undignified.

Antic-loving manager Frankie Frisch thought baseball began to take itself too seriously sometime in the early 1950s. He blamed television and its powers of distortion. When only folks in the ballpark saw the game, a player was willing to run out a home run on all fours if the mood struck him. In the satellite dish age, whacky stunts acquire instant fame and somehow look sillier on videotape than they do first hand. One goofy stunt might make you famously goofy. Most ballplayers would rather trot around the bases, thank you. Stengel's sparrow became legend, but in the 1990s, it would have been a highlight at six o'clock and eleven o'clock and perhaps in a music video.

By 1990 off-the-field stunts were nearly extinct, but the lore shows old-time players game for just about anything that would draw a crowd. A favorite public experiment was dropping baseballs from high places to see if a ballplayer could catch them and to see what happened to the ballplayer's face if he missed them. Millionaire moderns would never dream of such risky foolishness, not any more than IBM would dream of throwing 53 percent of its stock onto a blackjack table. Catch a ball dropped from an airplane? A ballplayer's agent, his team, and Lloyds of London would object. When the Red Sox clinched the 1986 American League East title, ace pitcher Roger Clemens hopped onto a police horse at Fenway Park, and thousands of scared New Englanders howled about their franchise player taking a harmless joy ride.

Joy was once a large part of the baseball experience. The ancients liked to giggle over a first-rate practical joke. It came to them naturally. The old-timers romped through their early years on delightfully disorganized sandlots where they were taught fun was okay. Modern players were immersed in organized, rigidly regulated ball with nifty uniforms and tightly wrapped adult coaches by the time they were seven years old. They were taught that the game was grim business. Whoopee cushions and hotfoots made sense to guys who played ball essentially to extend their boyhood; childish horseplay makes no sense to men who play to extend their investment portfolio for comfortable retirement at age thirty-five.

The rare latter-day practical jokers are commendable. Baseball isn't the same without a few little rascals. When always unsmiling Jim Rice was replaced by spirited and impish Mike Greenwell in Boston's left field in the late 1980s, tense Fenway Park received a touch of friskiness. Baseball needs more of this. Someone has to keep the play in ballplaying.

All work, no play attitudes sometimes start at the top. Modern-day front offices are marked by much big business and almost no monkey business. By

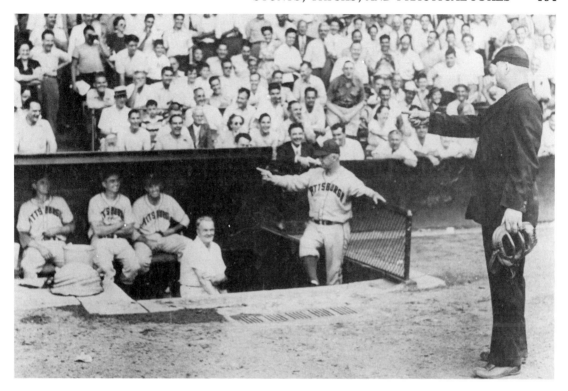

Umpire George Magerkurth ordered Frankie Frisch and the Pirates' bench into the clubhouse after they refused to stop booing him.

1990 baseball teams were honeycombed by management school graduates whose idea of whackiness was using different colored pens. Old-time front offices were filled with baseball guys, many of them rough-and-tumble former pioneers. They got into the baseball business because they liked flannel zipper-front uniforms better than gray flannel suits. The job got done, and sometimes a good time was had by all. Modern-day field managers have swerved into the computer world, with more flow charts and index cards than tobacco juice and crusty anecdotes. Even hard-boiled winners didn't mind occasional daffiness in the past. Giants manager John McGraw was a strict disciplinarian, but he once sneaked a cigar store Indian into the hotel bed of Reds outfielder Dummy Hoy just to hear him scream.

If Stengel were alive, he would ask, "Doesn't anybody here know how to enjoy this game?" In the spring of 1988, a sportswriter mulled the modern state of baseball silliness. What would they do to Stengel about the sparrow? Release him the next day. How about Connie Ryan's rain slickers? Suspend him, fine him, and make him do one thousand hours of community service. Eddie Gaedel? Good question, the reporter thought. What would baseball do if a prankster owner trotted out a three-foot, seven-inch pinch hitter?

A telephone call was put through to Red Sox general manager Lou Gorman, a good man, a true lover of the game, and the owner of a first-rate sense of humor.

"There's no rule against it," Gorman said. *Great,* thought the reporter. *Baseball hasn't outlawed all forms of frolic.* "But the fine for making a mockery of the game could be something like $100,000," Gorman continued.

Good night, Bill Veeck. Lore tells us the merry days were fun while they lasted.

During the winters of 1907–09, Washington Senators manager Joe ("Poppy") Cantillon operated a run-down tavern in Chicago called the Log Cabin Inn. Featuring a leaky roof, crummy decor, and cheap liquor, the bar was frequented by jockeys, prize fighters, prostitutes, wrestlers, actors, politicians, and baseball players.

An American League umpire during the summer, Jack Sheridan worked in the off-season as a Chicago undertaker. After work he frequently drank himself to sleep at the Log Cabin Inn. Late one evening, Tigers second baseman Germany Schaefer wandered into the kitchen at the Log Cabin and discovered Sheridan in a deep sleep. He was propped in a wooden chair, his head resting against a rusty vent pipe.

Schaefer hurried outside, climbed a ladder onto the roof, and found the other end of the vent. "Jaaaack Sheridan," Schaefer howled into the pipe. "Jaaaack Sheridan. Your time has come."

Witnesses said Sheridan shot from the chair and straight to the bar, where he shakily tried to compose himself by consuming several more rounds of drinks.

Convinced it was just a bad dream, Sheridan resumed his position in the chair near the vent pipe and fell back to sleep.

Schaefer again hurried outside and clambered onto the roof.

"Jaaaack Sheridan," he howled into the pipe. "Your time has come."

Sheridan bolted from the chair, crashed through a Japanese screen near the bar, and careened out the door into the night.

The next season, on a hot August afternoon in Detroit, the Tigers were way behind and everybody was anxious to go home. Sheridan was umpiring behind home plate, and Schaefer was at bat with a one-strike count. The pitch was far outside.

"Strike two!" said Sheridan.

Schaefer didn't turn around. "Jaaack Sheridan," he howled, bat still on his shoulder. "Your time has come."

◆

In the summer of 1899, the Phillies' weak lineup suddenly became strong, especially at the home park in Philadelphia. Before long, the rest of the league determined the Phils must be stealing signs. No one could figure out how.

One day with Washington in town, morning rainstorms left the Philadelphia field pocked with puddles, including one in the third-base coach's box. During the game, Washington bench warmer Arlie ("the Freshest Man on Earth") Latham noticed Phillie third base coach Pearce ("What's the Use?") Chiles standing with his left foot ankle-deep in water.

"Why don't you go back and get your rubbers?" Latham shouted to Chiles. "You might catch a chill." Just then, the Philadelphia batter stroked a home run. Latham shot a look at Chiles, who quickly stepped out of the puddle.

Knowing he had stumbled upon a clue in the case of the stolen signs, Latham coached third for Washington in the next inning. He plopped his left foot into the puddle to see if the position somehow provided a prime view of the catcher's signals. It didn't. He looked into the Phillie dugout. No one met his glance. He looked at the Phillies' infielders. All tried hard to appear nonchalant. Latham knew he was onto something.

When the inning ended, Latham told third baseman Bill Coughlin of his suspicions. Coughlin stepped into the puddle, scratched the mud with his spikes, and felt a clunk. Dropping to his knees, he clawed through the mud and water with his bare hands.

About two inches down, he unearthed a wooden block with a buzzer attached. A wire was attached to the buzzer. Coughlin pulled on the wire, which lifted through the turf.

Coughlin pulled and ripped a line through the ground, following the wire through the infield and into center field all the way to the Philadelphia clubhouse, where he found a Phillie substitute with a pair of field glasses. The trick: the man stole signs and relayed them to the third-base coach via the buzzer. The coach relayed the signs to the batter. "Don't be straining your eyes anymore," Coughlin said, holding up the wire.

◆

Long before the gates opened one afternoon, rookie pitcher Ron Blackburn was all alone on the Pirates' bench. Pittsburgh manager Danny Murtaugh had his pigeon right where he wanted him.

"I guess we'll have thirty to thirty-five-thousand fans tonight," Murtaugh said airily, gazing at the empty stadium.

"Thirty to thirty-five thousand? Not a chance," Blackburn replied. Even a rookie could tell it was one of those nights when a crowd of ten thousand would be high.

Dizzy Dean entertained himself and others.

"Whaddya mean, no chance?" shot back Murtaugh. "I was in the front office today. I know what the advance is. I say thirty to thirty-five-thousand paid admissions, and I'll bet a box of cigars on it."

Blackburn took the bet. A Pirate coach sitting nearby eagerly asked the rookie if he could put in for a box, too. Then it dawned on Blackburn: Murtaugh had said "thirty to thirty-five thousand," not "thirty thousand to thirty-five thousand." If thirty-one people showed up, the manager won the bet.

"Pay me as soon as you can," said Murtaugh.

Blackburn knew the nearest place to get a box of cigars. During batting practice, he went into Murtaugh's office and picked up one of the many unopened stogie boxes flung about. Blackburn carried it under his arm to the dugout and handed it to his manager to square the bet.

"Nice kid," said Murtaugh. "Pays off fast."

◆

One day in the turn-of-the-century Atlantic League, boxer James J. Jeffries was enlisted to umpire a game between Paterson, New Jersey, and Lancaster, Pennsylvania. Jeffries, who had just captured the heavyweight title from Bob Fitzsimmons, was a huge attraction. Four thousand people packed the ballpark.

Anxious to give the crowd a good show, league officials called aside Paterson first baseman Sam LaRoque, a mean-looking fellow with a huge mustache, and Lancaster first baseman Piggy Ward, another muscular tough guy, and told them to argue with Jeffries every chance they could.

A few innings into the game, Ward was thrown out on a close play at first. Charging to the umpire's position behind the pitcher, Ward spun Jeffries around. La-Roque rushed over and spun Jeffries the other way. This continued, while Jeffries kept backing up. The crowd loved it: two ballplayers shoving around the heavyweight champion.

His feelings perhaps hurt, Jeffries wanted to quit in the seventh inning, but league president Ed Barrow wouldn't let him go. Jeffries agreed to finish the game if they allowed him to smoke a cigar as he umpired. They said okay, and during the final three innings Jeffries called balls and strikes while puffing a big, black stogie.

◆

On George Washington's birthday, February 22, 1936, former Senators hurler Walter Johnson was in Fredericksburg, Virginia, on the banks of the Rappahannock River, clutching three silver dollars. His task was to duplicate Washington's famous, alleged feat by throwing a dollar across the 272-foot-wide river.

Congressman Sol Bloom of New York had claimed it couldn't be done and offered twenty-to-one odds. The Fredericksburg Chamber of Commerce had taken the wager. Bloom had sent a 1796 silver dollar for Johnson to use in the attempt. Bloom's bet with the Chamber of Commerce was then called off when they couldn't agree on the width of the river. Bloom claimed it was some one thousand feet wider in Washington's day.

Still, on the cold morning of the big toss, wagering was heavy on the banks of the Rappahannock. As time approached for Johnson's throw, the odds rose sharply in the pitcher's favor. Word had spread that Ray Mann, the local high school pitcher, had been throwing rocks across the river all morning.

Johnson had three coins, two for practice throws and a third for the official heave. His first pitch plopped into the icy water, some five feet short. His second practice pitch was good, landing some ten feet up the opposite bank. The official pitch landed some fifty feet up the opposite bank.

Bloom dispatched a telegram: "Congratulations, Walter. Stop over in Washington on your way home, and let's celebrate. I sincerely hope my dollar was the dollar that did the trick."

Johnson explained the fate of the 1796 coin. "Shucks," he said. "I want to keep that thing. I hear it's valuable."

◆

One day in the early 1950s, legendary Boston *Herald* photographer Leslie Jones decided he wanted to capture Ted Williams's backswing on film. In those days, photographers were allowed on the field at Fenway Park, so when Williams stepped up to the plate, Jones lugged his camera out to a spot near the on-deck circle, set it up, and peered down into the viewfinder.

Williams swung mightily and the bat accidentally flew out of his hands. Looking down into the viewfinder, Jones never saw the speeding Louisville Slugger whiz just inches over his head. The crowd shrieked. Even Williams was horrified. Seated in his box seat, *Herald* publisher Robert Choate dispatched a man to get Jones off the field before he was killed.

Jones left the field but didn't give up. Next day, when Williams stepped up to the plate, a murmur rippled through the crowd, followed by giggles. Williams looked over his shoulder, couldn't keep himself from laughing, and had to step out of the batter's box.

Jones had strolled out to the same spot near the on-deck circle, set up his camera, and peered down into the viewfinder. This time, however, he wore a miner's hard hat.

◆

Among the illiterate bumpkins who joined the Pirates in the spring of 1904 was an outfielder with a huge appetite. Not knowing how to read a menu, he sat next to Honus Wagner at every meal, pretended to read the card after Wagner ordered, threw it aside, and said casually, "Give me the same as him."

One evening, Wagner didn't feel much like eating and ordered just two boiled eggs for dinner. The bumpkin glared at

Walter Johnson duplicates George Washington's feat of throwing a coin across the Rappahannock River.

Wagner in disgust, then hurried over to a table where Pirates catcher Harry Smith was reading a menu. Smith ordered a porterhouse steak, and the bumpkin ordered the same. After that, the bumpkin stuck close by Smith for every meal.

Smith then ordered just a glass of milk for dinner two nights in a row, getting his real dinners via room service. The bumpkin was off again in search of a hearty eater.

However, Smith wasn't finished with him. After a close game in Boston, Smith handed him a telegram, saying it had just arrived at the clubhouse door. The bumpkin found Wagner and took him aside.

"My eyes are bad from the sun," he told Honus. "Read this wire, will yer?"

The telegram was not addressed to the bumpkin; it was for another player, informing him his suit was ready at the tailor's shop in New York.

"Sure," said Wagner. "The wire says they've got a warrant for you down in Tennessee."

The bumpkin turned pale. When he got to the shower room, the other Pirates asked him what the telegram was all about.

"It was an offer from Frank Chance for me to go to the Cubs," said the bumpkin.

◆

In the major leagues, Tom Murphy won 68, lost 101, and conspired on some half-dozen all-time great practical jokes. "We did it quite a few times," said Murphy, who hurled for the Red Sox and five other teams in his twelve-year big-league career, which ended in 1979. "I never did it in Boston, because I usually did it after I had pitched well. And I didn't pitch well very often in Boston."

What Murphy did was allow his identical twin brother, Roger, who looked, walked, and even pitched like him, to put on his uniform and impersonate him.

One time, Angels manager Lefty Phillips selected Murphy as his starter for the exhibition season opener against Chicago. "So I called up my brother and said, 'Roger, how would you like to pitch against the Cubs?' Murphy remembered from his San Juan Capistrano, California, home in 1988.

Roger Murphy's first pitch to leadoff man Bill North bounced fifteen feet in front of the plate. His second pitch sailed to the backstop. Knowing enough was enough, Tom Murphy, lurking at the end of the bench, bounded from the dugout. So did manager Phillips.

"Who is this guy?" the manager shrieked, noticing two Tom Murphys on the mound.

"Hey, get this impostor out of here," ordered Roger Murphy, pointing to his brother.

"Poor Lefty," remembered Tom. "He had no idea who was who."

Another time, when his brother was with Milwaukee, Roger Murphy sneaked into County Stadium, put on his uniform, grabbed a beer, and went up to team president Bud Selig's office.

"This was at about noon on a Sunday," recalled Tom, "and there my brother was, with a beer in his hand, demanding to renegotiate a new contract."

And another time, the day after he had beaten the Dodgers, Tom Murphy let his brother into the Cardinal clubhouse to put on his uniform.

"Murphy was out late last night," manager Red Schoendienst, who was in on the joke, told pitching coach Barney Schultz. "Have him do some running in the outfield."

Schultz approached Roger Murphy. "Have a nice night last night, Tom?" he said.

"That's none of your [expletive] business," snapped Roger. "And you know, I've figured out what I've been doing wrong. I've been listening to you too much."

After Roger and Schultz left the clubhouse, Tom, fearing the joke had gone too far, quickly put on his other uniform. "But the other guys held me down," he recalled. "They wouldn't let me end it."

When Roger Murphy stretched out in the outfield to take a nap during batting practice, Schultz rushed back into the clubhouse. "Murphy's on dope or something," he told Schoendienst.

"Well," the manager said gravely, "if you can't control your pitchers, maybe we should start looking around for someone else to do the job."

Schultz stormed away, but was soon let in on the gag. Remembered Tom Murphy, "Later on, Barney said he knew it was a joke all along."

◆

Late in the 1931 season, Eddie Popowski and his bearded, barnstorming House of David teammates passed from New Jersey to New York through the Holland Tunnel. As they emerged on the New Jersey side, about twenty nervous state policemen waited for them.

The problem was that from the back seat of the car, one of the House of David players had been squirting passing motorists with a water gun. One nervous driver reported a car full of bearded guys, one of them with a gun.

"One of the cops told him to stop shooting his water pistol," said Popowski, "before somebody ended up shooting him."

◆

A few hours before game time one afternoon in the summer of 1990, Red Sox left fielder Mike Greenwell displayed an ugly, hairy, fake spider in his hand and smiled devilishly. Greenwell looked for a few good targets. His trick was to sneak up on a victim, carefully place the critter on his shoulder, then let the victim spy the spider and do the jitterbug.

At the clubhouse table, veteran team traveling secretary Jack Rogers was concentrating on a stack of papers. Greenwell pointed to the tall, quiet, white-haired man and crept toward him. "C'mon, man, you're going to give someone a heart attack," said an onlooker, but Greenwell pushed on.

Rogers didn't notice when Greenwell delicately set the horrible creature onto his shoulder. Greenwell skulked away and stood near his locker to watch the outcome. When Rogers shifted in his seat, the ugly, hairy, fake spider tumbled down the front of his shirt into his lap. With total nonchalance, Rogers glanced at the spider and glanced back at his paperwork. Rogers was a navy aviator during World War II, and spiders don't scare men who have landed airplanes on aircraft carriers.

Greenwell's mouth fell open. "The man has got stones," the ballplayer marveled as the quiet, white-haired man shuffled his papers. "He didn't even budge."

◆

At high noon on July 17, 1922, a crowd of fifteen thousand jammed Times Square, stopping trolley cars and backing up traffic for blocks. The attraction was that, as a stunt to promote the movie *In the Name of the Law,* Yankee outfielder Bob Meusel was going to throw a baseball from the roof of the George M. Cohan Theatre. Babe Ruth was going to catch it on the street below.

At 12:30, Ruth emerged from the theatre lobby and was cheered loudly. The crowd pushed forward to surround him. Six policemen forced an opening in the throng to make room for Ruth's catch. Wearing shirt-sleeves in the sticky humidity, the Babe stood in the gutter and signaled to Meusel to fire away.

Meusel sailed the first ball into the crowd. Ruth dropped the second ball, but he caught the third ball, and the crowd went wild. In all, at least six men were trampled, including one knocked down and kicked by a policeman's horse.

◆

In the fall of 1919, Newark challenged the dynastic Baltimore Orioles for the International League pennant. The race came down to the season's final day, when the Bears visited Baltimore, winner take all.

Pitcher Al Schacht was scheduled to start the big game for Newark; Rube Parnham started for the Orioles. On his way to the ballpark, Schacht passed a five-and-dime store, saw a cheap, loosely wrapped baseball on sale in the window, went inside on a whim, and bought it.

Parnham allowed Newark a run in the first inning, then settled down. Schacht held the powerful Orioles scoreless. After the bottom of the eighth, with Newark still ahead, 1–0, Schacht on an impulse went to the clubhouse and stashed the dime-store baseball in his pocket.

In the ninth the Orioles got a baserunner. Then, with two out, lefty slugger Jack Bentley—the "Orioles' Babe Ruth"—stepped to the plate.

Schacht threw the first two pitches for balls. "Bentley was drooling with anticipatory glee," Schacht later recalled.

The crowd taunted and howled. Schacht stepped off the mound, fussed, fidgeted, wiped his brow, and switched balls. "And I pitched as perfect a strike as ever was thrown in that old Baltimore park," Schacht said. "Bentley tied into it and met it as squarely as Ruth hit that called shot off Charlie Root."

Al Schacht (left) *and Nick Altrock*

Bentley went into his home run trot. "But he got the shock of his life," said Schacht, "when the ball suddenly faded and nestled down into the glove of the second baseman."

While Bentley stood bewildered at first base, Baltimore manager Jack Dunn raced from the dugout demanding to inspect the ball. Pretending to celebrate the victory, the Newark second baseman heaved the ball over the grandstand roof.

"You know, I was often tempted to tell Rube about it in later years, but I hesitated," Schacht said after Parnham's death in 1963. "Even then I was afraid he'd belt me."

◆

Toward the end of Cap Anson's career with the old Chicago Nationals, a number of Chicago baseball writers thought Cap was hanging on too long. Even though Anson was over forty, he was hitting over .300. But the writers, thinking it time for a younger replacement, referred to Anson in their daily stories as the "Old Man."

One afternoon at the ballpark, the crowd buzzed as an unfamiliar figure took Anson's position at first base. The man wore a Chicago uniform, and he also wore a long, scraggly Rip Van Winkle-style beard. Wearing the fake beard throughout the game, Cap Anson rapped out three hits, gleefully running the bases as his "old man" whiskers flapped in the breeze.

◆

When Cardinals pitcher Wee Willie Sudhoff learned he would be opposed one afternoon by Athletics ace Rube

Jack Bentley (left) *and John J. McGraw*

Waddell, he decided to weasel an extra edge for himself. Telephoning Waddell at the A's hotel, Sudhoff persuaded the wild Rube to meet him at the ballpark two hours early.

Out at the ballyard, Sudhoff took Waddell to deepest center field and expressed sincere doubt about Waddell's ability to throw the ball from the outfield to home plate. More than happy to show off his powerful arm, Waddell took position near the flagpole and began firing toward home.

"Not bad," Sudhoff would say after a particularly strong and accurate throw. "But I bet you can't do that again." Prodding, daring, and taunting, he managed to keep Waddell throwing for almost an hour.

When Philadelphia manager Connie Mack arrived, he put an immediate stop to the exhibition. "You shouldn't be doing that sort of thing on the day you pitch," said Mack.

"Just a little warmup," said Waddell, massaging his left shoulder as Sudhoff slinked away. Waddell shut out St. Louis, 1–0, striking out fifteen.

◆

Hughie Critz, second baseman for the Reds in the 1920s, loved to tell stories about bush-league ball back home in the South. "If anybody wants to write an impossible movie scenario or a book which will pass for good fiction," the Mississippi native used to drawl, "all they've got to do is go down there and take down straight the things that happen."

Critz offered an example. When he managed Little Rock in the Cotton States League, former Yankee shortstop Kid Elberfeld was stuck with a horrible, virtually all-left-handed pitching staff. When the team started the season badly, "the butter-and-egg men who owned the club were all asking Elberfeld what the matter was," said Critz. "It got the old boy pretty worried."

One day during a team workout, a crew carrying paint cans and ladders trooped into the Little Rock ballpark. A section of the outfield fence had been sold for a billboard advertisement, and the workmen painted a huge, shiny, black-and-white checkerboard on the fence, with Smoke Checker Cigarettes in small letters at the bottom.

Next game, Elberfeld started his worst lefty, who amazed everyone, including himself, with four hitless innings. Later, with the opposing team's right-handed slugger at the plate, Elberfeld summoned another broken-down lefty from the bullpen. "He was a has-been who hadn't struck a man out since Grover Cleveland was elected," said Critz. The has-been struck out the slugger, swinging.

Ignited by the landmark victory, Elberfeld's charges, led by the now heroic lefty hurlers, embarked on a glorious home winning streak, which Critz remembered as "ten, or maybe fifteen, games. Anyway, they couldn't be stopped. His squad of southpaws went around with smiling faces accepting the plaudits of the multitudes."

They also got cocky. With some wealthy Cotton States clubs willing to pay $5,000 to induce any top-flight pitcher to jump teams, Elberfeld's lefties began to grumble about getting raises. Some hinted they might jump the club and peddle their valuable services elsewhere. Elberfeld finally summoned his pitching staff to the ballpark for a little discussion.

"You guys are just as big stiffs as you ever were!" the manager shouted. "You're rotten. All of you! There isn't a man on the club any better than a high-school pitcher. Now one of you dumb eggs stand there at the plate right-handed and another one go out there and pitch to him."

They did and quickly realized the secret

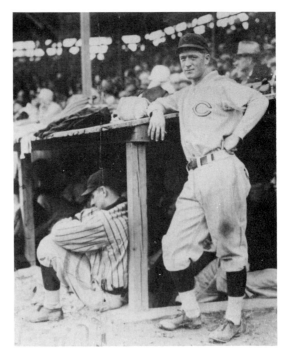

Hughie Critz

of their success: the cigarette sign was set up so the checkerboard was lined up directly behind a left-hander's pitching arm as he released the ball to a righty batter. "That ball sneaked up there like a snake in the grass," said Critz.

The humbled lefties were silent. One meekly inquired, out of curiosity, what exactly was the Checker Cigarette Company, anyway?

"I run the Checker Cigarette Company," snapped Elberfeld. "Haven't started to manufacture them yet. But I thought it would be a good idea to get started with the advertising."

◆

In the waning days of the 1979 season, the Red Sox were in Detroit to play out the season with a meaningless series against the Tigers. The Boston manager was Don Zimmer. And "Zim's a betting man," said Red Sox right fielder Dwight Evans.

Before one of the games, Evans told his manager he wanted to bat left-handed, just for kicks. "No, you're not," growled Zimmer. Evans proposed a little wager, just to liven up batting practice a bit. "Zim," he said. "I'll bet you I get more hits left-handed than you get right-handed."

"You're on," said the manager.

Evans cracked the first pitch into Tiger Stadium's upper deck. Then came a couple more line drives. He launched another shot into the lower deck. "On my first seven swings, I had five hits, three of them homers," said Evans. "Zim was going crazy. I won some money."

What Zim didn't know was that, until he was about thirteen years old, Evans was a switch hitter.

◆

During an off-season tour of Japan, Chicago White Sox pitcher Ted Lyons, New York Giants outfielder Lefty O'Doul, and Red Sox catcher Moe Berg trooped into a tavern to sample a bit of local beer. After taking seats at a table, Berg excused himself for a moment to use the men's room. When he returned, a waitress appeared at the table to take the order. Before the men could say a word, the young woman spoke up.

"Frank O'Doul," she began haltingly, reading from a slip of paper, "ees the ugliest mug I have ever seen. His face would stop a clock. He iss also a loussy beesball player. Some day he will get hit with a fly ball and keeled."

"What's that?" sputtered O'Doul. Lyons laughed so hard he nearly toppled out of his chair. Berg merely looked pained and shocked. The waitress shrugged her shoulders. "No understand," she said.

Of course she didn't. She had merely read a meaningless string of Japanese syllables, strung together by the multilingual scholar Berg to sound like an English language insult of O'Doul.

"You and your languages," said O'Doul. "But I didn't know you knew Japanese."

"I don't," said Berg. "But I'm beginning to get the swing of it."

"Sounds as if you're doing pretty good," said Lyons. "Have you learned the word for *beer* yet? If you have, speak it."

◆

One day in 1908, three members of the Gridiron Club attended a Washington Senators' game. In the course of the engagement, Washington catcher Gabby Street caught an unusually high, foul pop fly. A discussion was started: how high a fly would it be possible for a man to catch?

The topic stayed hot into the evening. Finally the argument centered around whether a man could catch a ball dropped from the top of the Washington Monument. Before the night was over, substantial sums were wagered on the issue.

Next day, a Gridiron Club representative approached Street and asked if he would try it. He refused. The Gridiron man persisted. Street relented, promising to attempt the stunt as soon as he returned from the road trip to New York.

When Street broke a finger in New York and returned to Washington early, the Gridiron man was waiting for him. "I told him I better not attempt it, because I might break some more fingers and be out all summer," said Street. "He seemed so disappointed, however, that I changed my mind again."

Next morning, outfielder Bob Ganley, shortstop George McBride, and Street headed to the Washington Monument. Upon arriving, they found the Gridiron

Frank ("Lefty") O'Doul

him to ditch the trough and just try tossing the balls out. "That carried them clear of the sides of the monument," said Street. "But they went wide and the difficulty was getting under them."

Street moved around to the other side of the monument, out of the sun. Three more balls sailed away, out of his reach. "But the fourth one came down, just right," said Street. "After whirling and teetering around, I braced myself for the catch. I made it. It didn't even jar me at all. It didn't even hurt my hands. I got it squarely in my mitt. I didn't know it until later, but it was the thirteenth ball."

◆

man with a twenty-foot-long trough fashioned from two boards. The plan was to take the trough to the top and roll the baseball out of it.

"It was a bright and dazzling day," said Street. "No kind of day to attempt a thing like that."

The Gridiron man climbed to the top with the trough and thirteen baseballs, and Street put on his mitt. The Gridiron man started rolling balls out for the 555-foot drop.

"The first three or four balls struck the side of the monument and bounded out of reach," Street said. "When they struck the wide cement walk that runs around the shaft, they made a noise like the crack of a rifle and bounced in the air more than fifty feet. I couldn't help but wonder what would happen if I missed one of those and it came up under my chin. Later on, when we examined one of those first balls, we found the side of the hide seared off, as if it had been burned. That was where it had struck the side of the monument."

Finally Street telephoned the Gridiron man at the top of the monument and told

During early batting practice at Tiger Stadium in the spring of 1988, a television cameraman's headset was malfunctioning in the visitors' dugout. It squawked and sputtered on the dugout floor, reminding Red Sox manager John McNamara of a ballpark telecommunication story.

"In the old ballpark in Kansas City, somebody found out you could call the home bullpen from the visiting bullpen," said the Red Sox manager between squirts of tobacco juice. "Lew Krausse was with the A's. He was just a baby then. Moe Drabowsky was in town. He might have been with the Orioles. I'm not sure.

"Drabowsky calls up the A's bullpen and tells them to get Krausse up. So Krausse starts warming up in the second inning. Alvin Dark looks out and asks, 'What's Krausse doing up?' They say, 'You called and told us to.' He says, 'No, I didn't.'

"A couple of innings later, same thing. Dark looks out to the bullpen, and Krausse is warming up again. It happened once more before they figured out what was going on."

◆

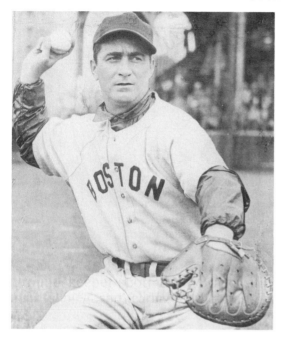

Moe Berg

◆

A sergeant in a gas regiment during World War I, Senators catcher Gabby Street was famous among the troops—and even the locals—as the man who had caught a baseball tossed from the top of the 555-foot high Washington Monument.

"I met a French officer who had been an instructor at a Moroccan university," Street once recalled. "'You have no idea,' he said to me, 'what a talked-of man you were when you caught that ball. Every college and university in the world, I believe, were interested in that thing. Over here we studied and speculated on it from all angles.'"

Street's colonel also had heard of the feat and came up with an even better idea, to catch a ball from the 984-foot Eiffel Tower. "He made all the arrangements," said Street, who was cautious but game to give it a try.

Street, however, got lucky. During the American drive at Saint-Mihiel, he was sprayed by shrapnel, earning him an extended stay in the hospital and canceling the stunt.

◆

In the late 1950s former Red Sox bat boy Donald Davidson worked his way up in the Milwaukee Braves' front office. Davidson, who did public relations and traveling secretary work, was a fun-loving fellow with a fiery temper, and he was a dwarf. The combination of the three made him the target of many practical jokes by the mischievous boys on the Braves.

"We were always playing jokes on him," former Braves slugger Eddie Mathews said from his California home in spring 1989. "We'd check into hotels that would put him on something like the 25th floor. He couldn't reach the buttons for the upper floors in the elevator.

"So we'd be riding up, and he'd ask us to

Charles ("Gabby") Street

push his floor for him. We'd say, 'No way,' and get off and let him ride up and down for a while. It got so he would check the whole team right out of a hotel if they put him on a floor higher than he could reach."

Davidson knew how to retaliate. After pitchers Warren Spahn and Lew Burdette once put his hat in the shower, Davidson nailed their spikes to the clubhouse floor.

"He could outdrink any of us," said Mathews. "Cutty Sark. We used to go outside and put his car wheels up on bricks. He'd sit there spinning his wheels for five minutes before he realized he wasn't moving.

"He also had these stirrups so he could reach the brakes and the clutch. We used to take the stirrup off the brake. We'd watch him drive away and not be able to stop the car. I guess we could be pretty cruel. We all had our fun. Donald's one helluva guy. He's pretty sick now. I still talk to him about once a month. We were all like family in those days."

◆

Sherm Feller, Fenway Park's legendary public address announcer, relaxed at a friend's home one evening in the summer of 1989. The radio was on, and the station was staging a Sherm Feller Sound-alike Contest.

"The prize was two tickets to something or another," Feller later recalled. "My friends said to go ahead and call. So I called."

Feller got through, and said he wanted to enter the Sherm Feller Sound-alike Contest. He got on the air.

"Go ahead and say anything you want," the disc jockey said.

"Ladies and gentlemen, boys and girls, welcome to Fenway Park," Feller intoned with his trademark opening phrase.

"Well, that's not too bad," said the disc

Eddie Mathews

jockey, without enthusiasm. "But why don't you try again next time."

Sherm Feller lost the Sherm Feller Sound-alike Contest. "Can you believe it?" he said.

◆

Week after week, shortstop Rabbit Maranville challenged Braves pitcher Jack Scott to a wrestling match. When other Braves finally goaded Scott into accepting the Rabbit's challenge in a hotel room in New York, Scott threw Maranville heavily to the floor. Maranville lay deathly still. Teammates tried to revive him, but the Rabbit remained motionless and slack-jawed. Scott panicked, fled the room, and headed to the lobby to turn himself in to the police.

Pitcher Art Nehf caught up with Scott and brought him back upstairs, where Maranville had been placed on the bed. His face was ghostly white, and Scott lapsed into near hysteria. Unable to control himself any longer, Maranville—his face coated with talcum powder—erupted in laughter. Scott had to be restrained from murdering Maranville again.

◆

The Giants were training in Los Angeles when the 1933 Southern California earthquake struck, inflicting heavy damage and some loss of life. Most of the ballplayers spent the night of the quake in a park across the street from the hotel. However, three baseball writers assigned to the team—roommates John Drebinger, Garry Schumacher, and Mike Houston—uneasily stayed in their room.

When the other two were safely asleep, Drebinger slipped beneath Houston's bed and at regular intervals gave it a violent shake. With each tremor, Houston would leap up on all fours ready to dash for safety. Then when the "aftershock" subsided, Houston would drop back to sleep and Drebinger would start all over again. By daybreak, Drebinger was tired, but Houston was a wreck.

Throughout the season, Drebinger stifled a laugh whenever Houston related the horrible details of earthquake night in L.A. "Just like a rocking horse," Houston would always end his tale. "That's how my bed shook."

◆

On the morning of August 20, 1938, a crowd of 25,000 gathered in Cleveland's public square to watch several members of the Indians attempt to catch baseballs tossed from the fifty-second floor of the Terminal Tower. Mathematicians estimated the balls would be traveling at 138 mph when they reached the ground.

Cleveland third baseman Ken Keltner was elected to drop the balls. His first few heaves—intended for catcher Rollie Hemsley and coaches Johnny Bassler and Wally Schang—sailed away, landing in shrubs or smacking into the concrete pavement and bouncing six stories high.

Backup catcher Henry Helf was first to make the 708-foot catch, which broke the thirty-year-old record of 555 feet, set when Senators catcher Gabby Street caught a ball thrown from the Washington Monument. "For a second," said Helf, "I didn't know if it was going to hit me in the head or glove."

Frankie Pytlak, another Indians catcher, also made the catch and said, "It stung more than Bob Feller's fastball."

Miraculously, no one was hurt. Almost no one, at least. As Paddy Livingston, age fifty-eight, who caught for the Indians in 1901 and 1912, carried the historic hardballs from the site, he was mobbed and mauled by frenzied souvenir hunters.

◆

When he was a young shortstop for Muskogee in the Western Association, Paul Richards liked to try his hand at pitching. Both hands, actually.

Richards was ambidextrous, and, playing the percentages, he switched hands from batter to batter. Once during a game at Springfield, Illinois, fans were even treated to a matchup of switch pitchers: Richards against Springfield's Paul Creech, also ambidextrous.

By 1989, thanks to the presence of ambidextrous Red Sox pitcher Greg Harris, the American League had ruled a player switch-pitching must declare which hand he's going to use before each batter. There was no such rule in Richards' day.

"The situation became most complicated in the ninth inning," Richards once recalled. "A switch hitter came up as a pinch hitter. I started to pitch right-handed, and he changed. Then I changed. Then he changed. It went on this way for about ten minutes.

"The umpire was going crazy. Finally I threw my glove away and faced him with both arms raised before I began my motion. That fixed him."

◆

In late autumn 1918, after the Armistice ended World War I, a group of American soldiers in France found themselves getting bored. They came up with the great idea to kidnap the exiled Kaiser Wilhelm from his hideaway in neutral Holland and deliver him to the Allies to face a proper trial.

Led by field artillery Col. Luke Lea, who was later a U.S. senator from Tennessee, the seven doughboys piled into two military cars, drove into Belgium, picked up a Dutchman en route to help bridge the language barrier, and motored to the kaiser's castle haven in Amerongen, Holland.

Flashing a set of papers identifying themselves as "American journalists," the men were allowed into the castle and ushered into a receiving room. They could even hear the kaiser's voice in the next room.

Soon an aide to the kaiser appeared, questioned the men about the purpose of their visit, and asked for further credentials. When the Americans couldn't produce any, the aide excused himself and promised to return shortly.

After a while, the Americans heard the sound of Dutch guards in the courtyard, and they decided to retreat. On the way out, one of the Americans snatched an ashtray as a souvenir.

The courtyard was dark, except for searchlights trained on the two cars. The Americans got in, drove slowly toward the gate, and were grateful to see soldiers step aside to let them leave.

When they returned to France, they found the Allies in an uproar. The Dutch government protested the breach of neutrality, and the U.S. state department ordered the eight men placed under arrest. After a time, the case was brought before Gen. John ("Blackjack") Pershing, who ordered the men released and the adventure hushed up.

The man who had grabbed the ashtray was Larry MacPhail, later president of the Cincinnati Reds and the Brooklyn Dodgers, a baseball Hall of Famer, father of one-time American League president Lee MacPhail, and grandfather of the Twins general manager Andy MacPhail.

And the ashtray? "It's brass. It's about eight inches in diameter. It has a wolf's head and it's smoking a pipe," said Lee MacPhail one summer day in 1989 from his New York City residence. "We have it right here in the living room."

◆

In the late summer of 1939, San Francisco Seals catcher Joe Spinz decided to try to emulate Senators catcher Gabby Street and others who had caught balls tossed from buildings and towers. On August 3, as part of the Golden Gate Exposition festivities, Spinz attempted to catch a ball dropped eight hundred feet from a passing blimp.

Sprinz got his glove on the ball all right, but the force of it drove his gloved hand back against his face, fracturing his jaw, badly bruising his nose, and knocking him unconscious. He also dropped the ball.

12

ARGUMENTS AND FISTICUFFS

In the years between the world wars, whenever fines and suspensions were levied after a baseball brawl, former players lamented the mollycoddles who were taking over the pastime. In their day, the old-timers scoffed, a good fight was as common as a postgame shower. In one afternoon scrap alone, the Cubs battled among themselves to leave first baseman Frank Chance with two black eyes, third baseman Heinie Zimmerman unconscious, and outfielder Jimmy Sheckard, who was smashed over the head with an ammonia bottle, in the hospital. No big deal. Just the fellows blowing off a little steam.

"It wasn't a real good day unless there were three fights in the clubhouse after a ball game," ex-Detroit second baseman Charley O'Leary said. He was wistful over his days with noted hotheads Ty Cobb, Claude Rossman, Wild Bill Donovan, and Boss Schmidt, who stayed in fighting condition by using his fists to pound railroad spikes into the clubhouse floor. "The boys didn't enjoy their dinners unless they got that extra exercise."

Arguments and fisticuffs have always been part of the pastime, for many reasons. Baseball is a frustrating, nerve-fraying game. If golf were a team sport, there might be cart-clearing brawls. Baseball is played in hot weather; baseball players endure tiring travel schedules; baseball teammates know contempt bred through nine months and 162 games of familiarity; baseball players can hear what the customers say about them in the grandstand. No wonder lore abounds with stories about players fighting opposing players, players fighting teammates, players fighting managers, players fighting fans, managers fighting fans, and everybody fighting umpires.

Anything can spark hardball hostilities: an off-hand comment, a dirty look, a hard slide into second base, a hard tag at second base, tobacco juice splashed onto somebody's spikes, a collision at the plate, a managerial decision that embarrasses a player, the assassination of an archduke in Sarajevo. The sure-fire way to start a baseball fight has always been to hit a batter with a pitch or come close with one. Beanballs, or even talk of beanballs, have started more fights than cheap whiskey.

"Pitchers dust off hitters. Hitters should start dusting off pitchers in return," a newspaperman told White Sox hurler Sad Sam Jones in a New York hotel room in the summer of 1932.

"How so?" Jones asked suspiciously.

"A batter gets knocked down, he should pick himself up, dust himself off, and on the next pitch accidentally let the bat fly out of his hands," said the newspaperman. "Pitchers accidentally hit batters plenty, don't they? Batters can have accidents, too."

"So that's the idea," said Jones. He got off the bed, reached into a bureau drawer, produced a straight-edge razor, and chased the newshound out of the room.

Umpires are traditionally well-pocked targets, not surprising in a sport that includes "Kill the umpire!" in its lexicon. In the early bush leagues, umpires were often victims of assault. Even in the early big leagues, exuberant players occasionally left umps with bumps.

"If you'd go to bed at night, you [expletive], you could keep your eyes open long enough in the daytime to see when a ball goes over the plate," Red Sox pitcher Babe Ruth shouted to umpire Brick Owens after walking the leadoff batter in a 1917 game.

"Shut up, or I'll throw you out of the game," Owens answered.

"Throw me out, and I'll punch you right on the jaw," Ruth roared.

"You're out of the game right now," said Owens. Ruth punched Owens on the jaw.

Slugging, kicking, and scratching make good lore, but the archives detail plenty of memorable disagreements that did not include physical violence. Hockey has the best fights, but baseball has the best arguments. No other sport grants such generous blocks of time for yelling and screaming at the official. An umpire will let a manager get so close he can smell sunflower seeds on the skipper's breath; he will let a manager holler, harangue, kick dirt, wail till the veins pop from his neck, and hold his breath until he turns blue without penalty, as long as the protest does not include select words or phrases.

"Rene Lachemann once taught me never to use the pronoun *you*," Red Sox manager Joe Morgan said when asked how he avoided ejection when he violently argued pitcher Roger Clemens's banishment from Game Four of the 1990 American League championship series.

After several benchclearing brawls in 1990, some proposed to civilize the game through automatic penalties for players who vacate dugout or bullpen to join a fray. Old-timers worried but should have known better. No matter how hard mollycoddles try, they will never take over the pastime.

When he was a young outfielder in the minor leagues, Casey Stengel's team had strict rules that forbade locker room fisticuffs. One day Stengel was pushed over a steamer trunk by a rambunctious teammate. When Stengel hopped up and hotly pursued his assailant, manager Kid Elberfeld wandered into the room and knocked out Stengel with a single jab to the jaw. "Don't you know?" Elberfeld said over Casey's motionless body. "Fighting isn't allowed in this clubhouse."

Clark Griffith and Joe Cantillon knew each other from way back. They played together for Oakland in the old Pacific Coast League and, after the league broke up, bummed around the Barbary Coast together picking up odd jobs. One of their very odd jobs was to put on a skit three times a night at a San Francisco honky-tonk. Griffith played a bad Indian, Cantillon a noble cowboy. Griffith howled the Indian yells he had learned as a kid, and Cantillon filled him with blank shots. Along with the eggs, tomatoes, and abuse hurled at them each night, they collected enough money to eat.

A decade later, Griffith pitched for the White Sox, and his pal from the scuffling days, Cantillon, umpired in the newborn American League. One day, Orioles third baseman John McGraw singled and on his way to first base muttered a few nasty comments about Griffith.

Griffith was digging at the mound when he heard Cantillon whisper behind him, "Pick McGraw off first."

Griffith looked over and saw McGraw just a foot or two off the bag. "How?" he whispered back.

"Balk him off," Cantillon whispered.

Griffith started his motion toward the plate, stopped, and with a whopping balk move picked McGraw off first by two yards. Cantillon called him out, then threw McGraw out of the game for arguing the call.

As Griffith chuckled, the next Oriole batter reached base. Griffith picked him off, too, but Cantillon waved the runner to second. "That balk move only works on McGraw," he said. An argument ensued, and Cantillon threw his old pal Griffith out of the game.

◆

Leading off the game one day, White Sox outfielder Mike Kreevich was thrown out by umpire Bill McGowan. Chicago manager Jimmy Dykes rushed out to ask why his man was ejected.

"For using bad language offensive to a gentleman," said McGowan.

Dykes wandered back toward the bench, wondering out loud what had happened to the once rough-and-tumble game. McGowan called after him that Dykes, too, was ejected.

"What for?" Dykes demanded.

"For intimidation," McGowan firmly replied.

Dykes narrowed his eyes. "Intimidation? Go away. You don't even know what it means."

"It means delaying the game," McGowan answered. "That's you. Out for intimidation."

◆

During a game in 1913, the Pirates had a comfortable lead, and manager Fred Clarke decided to give a pair of rookies a chance to pinch-hit. The first was a cantankerous outfielder named Roy Wood.

"What's your name, and who are you batting for?" asked the umpire.

"My name's Wood, and I'm batting for myself," the kid snapped. The umpire fumed at the punk's impertinence. He was more angry when Wood slapped the first pitch for a single.

The next rookie pinch hitter stepped to the plate. The umpire still raged quietly. "So what's your name, and who are you batting for?" he said.

"Boo!" answered the kid.

"I'll ask you once more," steamed the umpire. "What's your name?"

"Boo!" said the kid.

The umpire jumped and kicked a clod of dirt. "Get out of the game!" he shouted. "Get out of the park! Get out of my sight before I murder you!"

Clarke rushed from the dugout and persisted for several minutes trying to calm the umpire with an explanation. The kid's name was Everitt Booe.

◆

Umpire Bill McGowan

◆

During a game at Baker Bowl, Phillies infielder Art Fletcher thought the umpiring was tipped slightly in favor of the visiting Giants.

"Why don't you put on a New York uniform?" he screeched at umpire Bill Klem, who heaved Fletcher out of the game.

The banished ballplayer headed to the visiting clubhouse at the end of the Baker Bowl, where the locker room windows looked out on center field. Fletcher dug out some shoe black and a large sheet of wrapping paper and went to work.

A few minutes later, Klem called time

and bounced from behind home plate in a rage. His sharp eyes had spotted the makeshift sign flapping outside one of the clubhouse windows: Catfish Klem. For an unexplained reason, Klem hated to be called Catfish. "Take that sign down, or I'll forfeit the game," he screamed toward the vacant clubhouse windows. Fletcher complied, and after the game the still-outraged Klem convinced the league to fine Fletcher fifty dollars and suspend him for three games.

The suspension and fine helped spread the word around the league. If you want to burn Bill Klem, just call him Catfish. One player came up with the idea of drawing a catfish head in the dirt near second base. Klem saw it, exploded in anger, and tossed the player from the game. Several other infield artists tried the trick and were similarly tossed.

After a while, infielders nervously scratched out even innocent markings in the dust, lest Klem mistake them for a catfish head.

◆

When young Ty Cobb played for Augusta, Georgia, in the Sally League, he roomed with pitcher Nap Rucker. Per custom in the days before locker rooms, the pair dressed for the game in their boarding-house quarters.

One day, Rucker was knocked out of the game early and returned to the boarding house, removed his uniform, and settled into a nice hot bath. It was the first time Rucker had ever beaten roomie Cobb to the tub.

Relaxing in the bath water, Rucker heard Cobb come home, pace the outer room, then crash through the bathroom door.

"Get out of that tub!" Cobb hollered.

"I've got just as much right to a bath as you do," Rucker snapped.

Cobb leaped into the tub and grabbed Rucker by the throat. The pair struggled out of the tub onto the floor and fought bitterly until Rucker pushed away.

"Have you gone crazy?" Rucker gasped.

"Nap, you don't understand," said Cobb, suddenly calm, quiet, and slightly despaired. "I've just got to be first. All the time."

◆

When he was working his way through the bush leagues, umpire Brick Owens delivered a particularly controversial decision in favor of Topeka during a game at Wichita. Owens was beaten, and his clothes were torn before he barely escaped the near-riotous crowd at the ballpark.

In the evening, Owens thought the furor had quieted enough to allow him to venture outdoors. He went to a barber shop, plopped down in a chair, and requested a shave.

"You should have been here this afternoon," the barber said after lathering Owens's face. "You surely missed a great sight. Our baseball team played Topeka, and you never heard such robbery as that [expletive] umpire committed against us."

The barber slapped his straight-edge blade against the razor strap.

"I never saw anything like it in my life," the barber said, slapping the blade harder and faster as he grew angrier with each word. "That dirty thief just stole the game from us. He got a good beating for doing it, but not half enough. The robber should have been killed. And if I had him in that chair where you are right now, I would surely cut his throat. The dirty, rotten, thieving bum."

The barber cooled down a bit and began to shave Owens's face. "Were you in town today?" he asked politely.

"I've just reached the city," Owens shouted.

◆

Around World War I in the southern bush leagues, Texan John King was widely known as the meanest, most ornery ballplayer around. "He always carried that gun with him, and he knew how to use it," Red Sox catcher Bill Moore once recalled. "Why, shucks, he'd just kill you, just like that, if he didn't like you."

"John King. Yeah, I knew him," said Reds second baseman Hughie Critz. "Meanest man I ever knew."

Lured by his .300 average, a number of minor-league teams took a chance on the lefty-hating outfielder, despite his reputation for tantrums punctuated by gunfire. He always lived up to his reputation. After hitless games, King customarily rampaged, often emptying his gun into inanimate objects at the team hotel. Inevitably, employers tired of King's shooting sprees, which left only one problem: no one dared hand John King his release.

"When he signed up," said Moore, a King teammate at Fort Smith, Arkansas, "he told them pointblank that he would never recognize any release until he made up his mind he wanted to move. Said if they ever tried to give him his release, he'd shoot up the place."

When the club was in Paris, Texas, the Fort Smith manager decided King had to go. He sent a man up to King's hotel room to gauge his mood. "The man came back looking a little anxious," recounted Moore. "Said he didn't think it was the right time to broach any unhappy subject to King. It seemed the Texan was cleaning and oiling his gun."

The manager ordered his players to go to their rooms and lock the doors. Then he went to the room above King's and lowered his release paper to him on a string. King screamed, yelled, and smashed furniture but did not resort to gunplay. He was out of ammunition.

Later, his manager in Greenwood, Mississippi, tried a calm, direct approach. "Now, King," he said, "I know a player like you will be wantin' to shift to a better club. So I can give you your release." King produced his revolver and threatened to shoot everyone on the team.

When he played for Fort Smith, King struggled worse than ever with his lifelong slump against left-handed pitchers. In Fort Smith, a grandstand regular customarily brought his pet pig—decorated with bright ribbon—to the ballpark.

One afternoon, King was especially bedeviled by the visiting southpaw. Late in the game, he popped up for the fourth consecutive time. As King cussed his way up the first-base line, the pig with the bright ribbon darted out of the stands onto the field. King retrieved his bat and clubbed the unfortunate porker to death.

◆

At the start of a turn-of-the-century game, Cubs infielder Bad Bill Dahlen approached umpire Hank O'Day.

"Hank," Dahlen said, "if I were to call you a [expletive] along in the second inning, would you put me out of the game?"

"I should say I would," O'Day snapped.

"All right," said Dahlen. "No hard feelings. I'll call you that, and you chase me. I want to get to the racetrack in time for the fourth race."

◆

When he was a Red Sox farmhand for the Double–A team in Bristol, Barry Butera played right field in a game against Jersey City in the twilight at Roosevelt Stadium.

Somebody lifted a high fly ball to right. "I took a couple of steps in, a step back, and just stood there," said Butera in the summer of 1989. "I never saw the ball. The bullpen was right along the right-field line, and nobody in there saw it either. Nobody saw the ball in the air, and nobody saw it come down. The umpires didn't see it. Nobody saw it."

An argument ensued. Then one of the umpires spotted a youngster holding a baseball in the right-field stands.

"He was a little kid, behind the right-field fence," said Butera. "The umpire went over and asked him where he got the ball. The kid said it bounced into the stands. Ground rule double. The umpire sent the batter to second base."

◆

Longtime International League umpire Hugh Rorty umpired a game in Lynn, Massachusetts, one day when thick fog rolled in. Haverhill manager Bill Luby rushed over to Rorty, claimed his outfielders could no longer see fly balls, and implored him to call off the contest. Rorty refused. Luby argued.

Rorty called time, borrowed a glove, and had Luby hit him five fly balls. Rorty caught all five and ordered the game to continue.

◆

During his four years in the big leagues—including the 1932 season with the Braves—first baseman Art ("What a Man") Shires had a reputation for a big ego, a big mouth, and a quick temper. He also was known as "Art the Great," a nickname he gave himself after going four-for-five in his debut with the White Sox.

Over the years, the native of Italy, Texas, played big-league ball, boxed professionally at Boston Garden, appeared in walk-on roles in a pair of movies, ran for the Texas legislature, and beat up countless managers and teammates.

In December 1948, he was forty-two years old and running a shrimp house in Dallas when he was arrested and charged in the murder of Hi Erwin, age fifty-six, a one-time minor-league umpire. Erwin had been hospitalized since he was throttled by Shires in a fight two months earlier.

According to detectives, Shires said he visited Erwin's cleaning shop to give his longtime friend a steak. Erwin said that as he walked in, his pal "hit me across the face with a telephone receiver, and I knocked him down without thinking. I had to rough him up a good deal because he grabbed a knife and started whittling on my legs."

After an autopsy, the court ruled Erwin's death was caused by pneumonia and cirrhosis of the liver, and not by the fight injuries. Shires was fined for simple assault.

◆

When Percy Haughton was named president of a syndicate that purchased the Boston Braves in 1916, he decided to call the ballplayers together to deliver an old-fashioned pep talk. Haughton was a Harvard man, and the Braves were hard-boiled guys. When Haughton spoke, the Braves tried desperately to keep straight faces.

Haughton emphasized the spirit of team play as it had been developed at Harvard. Braves manager George Stallings, his face twitching and the sides of his mouth curling up, said he remembered an important phone call and hurried from the room.

Haughton pressed on. "Now, when one of you fights with an umpire and gets put out of the game," he declared, "you are hurting the team more than yourself. Always remember that. So when you see one of your comrades getting hot with an umpire, go up to him and say, 'The team! The team!' That will remind him of his duty and he will restrain himself."

In the fourth inning the next day, Boston shortstop Rabbit Maranville was called out on strikes. Maranville sputtered at umpire Bill Klem, who blasted back. The argument escalated when suddenly Sherwood Magee and several other Braves shot from the dugout, each shouting, "The team! The team!"

Startled, Klem whirled and saw the group of Braves approaching and shouting, "The team! The team!"

"What in blazes is wrong with you?" he hollered. "Magee, you're out of the game. And you. And you. Get out."

All who had come out of the dugout were ejected. Maranville, who stayed calm and quiet as his mates shouted "The team! The team!" stayed in the game.

As Maranville returned to the dugout, he spotted Haughton in a front-row box seat.

"You certainly had the right idea, Mr. Haughton," Maranville said. "Just see how those fellows kept me in the game."

◆

Umpires always hated to see Pittsburgh owner and chronic complainer Barney Dreyfuss barrel toward them in a ballpark corridor. After a game featuring several close calls, umpire Bill Klem spotted Dreyfuss steaming toward the umpires' dressing room. Klem jumped around in front of him.

"Why, hello there, Mr. Dreyfuss," Klem said. "My, but you look wonderful. Never saw you better. How are you feeling?"

"Fine, fine," said Dreyfuss. "Say, I want to tell you—"

"How's the family? How's the boy?"

"Fine, fine. Say, I want to—"

"Could you fix it for me to play at your golf course tomorrow morning? My golf is going stale."

"Well, goodbye, Bill," Dreyfuss said. "I'm in a hurry."

◆

Bush leaguer John King ran the bases like a wild man. He got wilder when called out on a close play.

"Damn it, man!" he would wail at the umpire. "Old John King refuses to be out!"

Once, when he was with Lubbock in the West Texas League, King was called out trying to steal second. He jumped up bubbling with anger. Spreading his arms wide and throwing his head back in an appeal to the sky, he cried out in a mournful voice, "May God strike me dead if I was out!"

The crowd hushed and waited for the bolt of lightning to hit. Nothing happened. King relaxed, turned to the umpire, and said, "See?"

◆

One day in the final weeks of the 1947 season, Athletics second baseman Pete ("Pecky") Suder learned that his father was ill. Suder desperately wanted to catch the 5:00 P.M. train out of Detroit to be at his father's side.

Burned by many Suder practical jokes in the past, Philadelphia manager Connie Mack refused to let him leave the club. Knowing Suder wasn't kidding this time, his Athletics teammates appealed to umpire Bill Summers. Early in the game, Summers obligingly ejected Suder for an imaginary infraction. Mack called the umpire over to the dugout.

"I've already put him out, Mr. Mack," said Summers.

"William," said Mack, "all I've got to put in for him is a young boy."

"Then trot out the young boy," said Summers.

Mack grudgingly trotted out the young boy: Nellie Fox.

◆

One day during a bush-league game in a small southern town, an angry, umbrella-wielding woman fan chased the umpire off the field. Fifteen years later, the umpire was promoted to the National League. One afternoon he rendered a decision against the Giants and heard his name called loudly from the New York dugout. On the top step, manager John McGraw grinned and threateningly waved an umbrella at him.

◆

Amherst baseball coach in the 1920s, Al Wheeler liked to tell the story of the theological student who played alongside him at Oberlin College.

The theological student was the last of the honest men. One day against a Western Conference rival, Oberlin trailed by two runs with two out in the bottom of the ninth. An Oberlin runner was at first, and the theological student was at bat. He cracked a low, hard liner down the right-field line, then stopped running.

"It was fair," reiterated the umpire.

"It was foul," said the player.

"It was fair," said the umpire.

"Foul," said the player.

As the right fielder chased down the ball, the argument raged. So did the Oberlin coach.

◆

When Bob Turley pitched for the 1954 Orioles, he was young and plagued by control problems. During a game against the White Sox at Comiskey Park,

Turley also was plagued by home-plate umpire Ed Hurley, who refused to grant the twenty-three-year-old righty strikes on borderline pitches.

After several consecutive close ones that were called balls, Orioles catcher Red Murray turned on Hurley in animated anger. Wanting to save Murray from ejection, Baltimore manager Jimmy Dykes sprang from the dugout. By the time he reached home plate, it was too late.

Murray was on his knees, eyes closed and hands pressed together in prayer. "Oh, Lord," he beseeched over and over, "please show this blind [expletive] where the plate is."

◆

When he broke in with the Boston Braves in 1942, outfielder Tommy Holmes played under manager Casey Stengel.

"Casey and Frank Frisch were roommates when they were on the Giants together," Holmes began one winter day in 1990. "When Frisch managed the Pirates, Casey wanted to beat them more than anybody else. After the games, they would go over to the Copley Plaza and get drunk together. So Casey loved to beat Pittsburgh.

"One day at Braves Field, we're down by ten runs in the first inning. It started to rain. Casey said to us in the dugout, 'I want to get out here.' So he took off his shoes and socks and rolled up his pants and came out of the dugout.

"He was splashing around in the puddles and asked the umpire, George Magerkurth, where that last pitch was.

"Magerkurth took one look at him and said, 'Casey, if I've got to stay here in this rain, so do you. I'm not throwing you out of the game.' Casey kept splashing around in the puddles, but Magerkurth refused to throw him out."

Casey Stengel (left) *and John Flaherty*

◆

By the fifth inning of the Detroit–Cleveland game at Navin Field, the battered game ball resembled an overripe orange. Home-plate umpire Jack Sheridan steadfastly refused to call for a new one.

"Do you think the league is made of money?" Sheridan growled when Indians second baseman Nap Lajoie complained. "This here ball is in play and it stays in play."

The dilapidated ball would not go away. At one juncture, Indians third basemen Bill Bradley fouled the ball into the stands. A stadium policeman snatched it from a souvenir-hungry fan and threw it back into play.

By the seventh inning, Tigers pitcher George Mullin squeezed the mushy baseball like a sponge and chuckled whenever Cleveland hitters connected solidly only to hit sluggish grounders.

Lajoie stepped to the plate, took a pitch, and again entreated Sheridan for a new ball.

"Not while this one is in play," snapped the umpire.

"All right," said Lajoie. He swiped the ball from the catcher's hand, wound up, and heaved it over the grandstand roof onto Michigan Avenue.

"There," said Lajoie. "It's no longer in play."

◆

On the Sunday afternoon of July 17, 1932, in the North Meadow of Manhattan's Central Park, the Ascension Parish team from Washington Heights engaged the Parama Cubs team from Harlem.

Ascension led, 10–1, when the Cubs came to bat in the eighth. With a runner at third, Parama attempted a suicide squeeze. The batter missed, the runner dashed home, the catcher blocked home plate, and a mighty collision ensued.

When an exchange of punches followed, the Cubs tumbled out of the dugout, fists flying, and the Ascension outfielders sprinted in, fists flying. Soon a first-class melee was in progress. Umpire Walter Carroll gamely waded into the fray to break it up.

At the sound of police sirens, combatants and spectators scattered and melted into the woods. When they reached the diamond, the authorities found only one fan, Walter Fleming, age twenty, who couldn't flee because of a knife wound to his abdomen, and one waterboy, running away as fast as he could in left field. They also found umpire Carroll near home plate, clutching his left ear, which someone had nearly chewed off.

◆

On April 6, 1935, on a ranch near Co-lolotlan, Mexico, two local amateur teams got together for a friendly game of baseball. At one juncture of the contest, an argument erupted over an umpire's call. Soon both teams were engaged in a full-blown fist fight. Spectators poured out of the wooden bleachers to join the fray, and the battle escalated to use of bats, bottles, and knives.

By the time police arrived to quiet the disturbance, three were dead (bludgeoned to death with baseball bats) and one was seriously injured (conked by a thrown bottle). The game was not finished.

◆

On September 29, 1927, in a game against the Senators, Babe Ruth cracked his fifty-eighth home run of the season, which left him one short of his own all-time record of fifty-nine, set in 1921.

Sitting on a stool in front of his locker after the game, Ruth kicked off his spikes, pulled off his socks, and scratched his belly contentedly. A Washington player clattered into the clubhouse, pen in one hand and a baseball in the other.

"Here, you big picklehead," the Senator said, handing Ruth the ball and pen. "You lucky, ugly tramp. Sign this ball."

The astonished Ruth reflexively scribbled his signature on the ball, then handed it back.

"Thanks, you large hunk of pork," said the player as he clattered out the door.

"Why . . ." sputtered Ruth. "Did you hear that mug? Who is he?"

"Aw, that's Hod Lisenbee, the pitcher you

belted that homer off," said Yankee coach Art Fletcher. "That's the ball you hit, and it's his way of paying a compliment."

"Well," said Ruth with great indignation, "that ain't my idea of polite talk."

◆

At the Cincinnati ballpark around the turn of the century, bleacherites customarily moved to the choicer pavilion seats in the late innings. Their usual pathway to the first-class sections was right across the field as the teams changed sides. The Reds' management did not object to the practice.

On the afternoon of home-plate umpire Bill McFarland's first appearance in Cincinnati, the game had proceeded without controversy. McFarland hadn't delivered a single questionable decision. Still after the Reds finished batting in the eighth, McFarland trembled when he heard a rumble from the outfield bleachers and looked up to see hundreds of fans thunder across the field, apparently right at him.

He saw the hungry, predatory look in the eyes of the onrushing fans—competition for the best pavilion seats was keen—and McFarland was sure they were racing to kill the umpire. He flung his mask in the air, sprinted to the players' gate under the stands, ran through the turnstile onto the street, and hopped on a passing trolley.

◆

On Saturday afternoon, August 23, 1952, the New York Giants engaged the Cardinals at St. Louis. In the seventh inning, Cardinals left-hander Alpha Brazle was shutting down the Giants, 3–0, when Bob Elliott stepped to the plate.

The New York third baseman was already zero-for-two. When home-plate umpire Augie Donatelli called strike two, Elliott's patience gave out. He lambasted the umpire, covered home plate with dirt, and was ejected.

On the bench, New York manager Leo Durocher summoned utility infielder Bobby Hofman to resume Elliott's at-bat. Hofman stepped in and took a pitch, which Donatelli called strike three.

"I remember it like it was yesterday," said Hofman, recalling the moment on August 23, 1988, exactly thirty-six years later, when he was the Yankees' director of player development. "I thought the pitch was a little outside. I drew a line in the dirt with my bat about three inches from the plate to show him where I thought it was. Then I walked away.

"He said, 'Keep walking, Bobby. Because that's it.' He threw me out, too."

It might have been the only three strikes in baseball history to dispatch two batters. "The funniest part about it is that the game was in St. Louis," Hofman added. "I'm from St. Louis. So I had about thirty friends and family in the stands. I had to face those people at dinner that night."

◆

In the summer of 1977, Joe Morgan managed the Pawtucket Red Sox in a game at Columbus. "It was a typical game against Columbus for those days," said the Red Sox third-base coach in the spring of 1988. "In the last inning or two, a close play came up and we got screwed."

Morgan shot out of the dugout to argue the close play with the umpire, Steve Fields. "Believe it or not, he had bought me a steak after a ball game a couple of nights before in Richmond," said Morgan. "He also used to always bring me tomatoes from his garden in the summer, if you can believe it."

At one juncture in his tirade, Morgan uttered the forbidden words (he may or may not have insulted the umpire's tomatoes)

and was ejected. The manager refused to leave the field.

"I'll give you thirty seconds to get out of here," Fields said.

"I don't care if you give me a thousand and thirty seconds," said Morgan. "I'm not going anywhere."

After a brief moment, the umpire decided to summon a higher authority from the stands. "I look up, and this big sheriff wearing a Smokey the Bear hat is coming toward me," said Morgan. "It was raining a little bit, so he had on a raincoat. First thing he did when he got to me was open his raincoat and point to his badge. As if I didn't know he was a damn sheriff."

The peace officer escorted Morgan off the field. When they reached the third-base line, the manager spoke up.

"Come on, sheriff," Morgan said, "come inside with me, and we'll have a couple of beers."

"As long as you're on this field, you're my property," the sheriff replied. "Once you get through that door, you can have all the beers you want."

"The sheriff," remembered Morgan, "didn't have any sense of humor at all."

◆

During his early playing days, Clark Griffith pitched for Missoula in the Montana State League. "Well, you young fellows couldn't believe there was a place like Missoula was," Griffith mused years later when he owned the Washington Senators. "Scandalous. Women, whiskey, wide-open gambling. Everything. But what money!"

Griffith became the idol of the town. Around the saloons and billiard halls, hard-bitten miners pooled as much as seven hundred dollars to wager on games when Griffith pitched.

One day, Missoula catcher Kid Spears let

a Griffith pitch get past him. The ball rolled all the way to the backstop, and an opposing runner advanced one base. Spears retrieved the ball, looked up, and saw a half-dozen burly men pointing six-shooters at his head. "Don't ever let that happen again, son," one of them growled.

◆

On April 22, 1940, the Boston Braves' game against the Dodgers at Ebbets Field was postponed because of wet grounds. It was the Braves' sixth straight rainout. At noon Boston manager Casey Stengel gathered his troops at the ballpark for a workout, and when the Ebbets Field groundskeeper spotted the Braves slipping, sliding, and tearing up the grass, he confronted Stengel.

"We're not playing a game that would bring in several thousand dollars for the simple reason that we don't want to riddle the expensive new turf Mr. MacPhail has spread on our orchard, and now you have the nerve to want to cut it to ribbons for nothing," the groundskeeper nagged. "If we wanted to rip up that expensive grass— it was nursed in a greenhouse—we could play today's game and profit from the damage. Mr. MacPhail spent three cents a foot for that carpet."

"I can see your point," said Stengel, as another of his men slipped and ripped an ugly divot in the turf. "If my eyes don't deceive me, however, I detect spike marks on the dirt section of the infield here which resemble imprints of some of those flat-footed Flatbushers. In other words, and getting right down to brass tacks in MacPhail's luxurious office upholstery, if the Dodgers have worked out on this dirt here, I demand the same privilege. After all, we were hospitable in Boston last week, weren't we? Didn't we allow the Dodgers to win our opener? Such generosity is deserving of some slight reciprocation."

"All right," said the groundskeeper. "Your boys can play catch along the base-paths. But I'll tell Mr. MacPhail on you if I catch them stepping one foot on that grass. And for your information, Mr. MacPhail isn't feeling too jovial today. He's just finished figuring the thousands of dollars he's lost in the last week by having two exhibition games with the Yankees and two regular games with the Giants washed out."

"I don't doubt that one bit," said Stengel. "But I don't feel any too good myself. Here we've been feeding these boys good for a week, and they haven't sweat a drop for us in return."

◆

The 1919 Boston Braves loved to horse around and tease one another, but nobody rode Jim Thorpe. The Olympic champion had a gold-medal temper, with brute strength to back it up. Pitcher Al Demaree, his roommate with the Giants, said Thorpe would "grab a man and shake him like a dog killing a rat."

Once on a road trip, Thorpe burst into a teammate's room, picked up the mattress, wrapped it around the player sleeping in it, hoisted the bundle over his head, and heaved it against the wall across the room.

The rudely awakened Brave emerged from the pile of bedding shaken, mumbling, cursing, and vowing to punch out the prankster, whoever it was. Then he saw Thorpe.

"Oh, hello, Jim," the player said pleasantly. "Is that you?"

◆

Ken Coleman, the long-time radio voice of the Red Sox, tells a story about the Boston baseball radio voice of an earlier generation, Jim Britt:

After some dozen years announcing the

Jim Thorpe

Braves and the Red Sox, Britt moved on to Cleveland to call Indians games, with Coleman as his young sidekick. A stickler for proper pronunciation, Britt began to refer to Indians second baseman Bobby Avila (till then pronounced a-VEEL-ah) as Bobby AH-vee-la. This continued into the season, despite a steady flow of protest mail from listeners accustomed to the old pronunciation. The sponsor of Indians radio games, the Carling Brewing Company, also received mail on the subject. Finally the beer company president, Ian Dowie, arranged a meeting with his broadcast crew.

Coleman sat quietly while Britt and Dowie discussed the issue:

Dowie: "You know, Jim, in view of local usage, and given the fact that they have been calling him a-VEEL-ah for some time now, I think we should stick with that pronunciation."

Britt: "Anything you want, Mr. Doughie."

Dowie: "The name is Dow-ee."

Britt: "And the second baseman's name is AH-vee-la."

◆

For thirty-five years, the agency office of Boston publicity man Al Longo was at the Somerset Hotel, which for a time also quartered Red Sox star Ted Williams.

"He had a suite on the second floor," remembered Longo in the summer of 1988. "The rules were that no phone calls were put through to Ted Williams. The operator would take messages, and she'd give them to the bellman, and the bellman would take them up to the room, but not go in. He'd slip them under the door.

"This particular day, a phone call came in. The message went down to the bellman whose name was Frank Acornley. Soaking wet, he did not weigh 145 pounds. Wiry as could be. And a redhead, with a temper to go with it. He took the message up. The door to the suite was open. So Frank went into the room and handed the message to Williams. Well, Ted got up and read him off like you wouldn't believe, because he wasn't supposed to come into the room. Acornley didn't say anything, but went back downstairs absolutely livid.

"Later, when Williams was leaving to go over to the ballpark, Acornley was waiting for him in the garage behind the hotel where Williams kept his Caddy. Visualize this if you can: Acornley was maybe five feet, two inches and Williams was six feet, four. Lean back and look up at the ceiling and point your finger at the ceiling. That was Acornley letting Williams have it, with his finger almost up his nose. He called Williams everything in the book. Of course, Williams had forgotten what he had done. He stood there, hands on hips, not a word out of his mouth, with a big grin on his face. Acornley ended with, 'Yeah, sure, and you're grinning about it, you SOB!' and with that he stormed away. Williams shrugged and went to his car.

"One week later, a phone call came downstairs: 'Frank Acornley, Ted Williams wants to see you, up in his room—now.' Acornley said, 'Tell him to drop dead.' But they ordered him to go on up there.

"With a chip on each shoulder, he walked into the room, and there was big six-foot, four-inch Williams standing there. He said, 'Here, Frank.' There was a big package on the coffee table, about half the size of Acornley himself. 'I'm sorry,' Ted said. 'I want to apologize. I don't know what the hell I did, but I want to apologize.'"

◆

During a 1913 Giants–Tigers barnstorming stop in Fort Worth, star attraction Ty Cobb arrived for the game at the last minute. Cobb had recently taken up golf and had been roaming the links while five thousand fans at the ballpark waited in vain to see the great Cobb take pregame practice.

Nauseated at the display of arrogance, Giants infielders Art Fletcher and Charlie Herzog peppered Cobb with abuse when he finally showed up. The twin-barreled verbal assault continued into the game. Stunned by the unprecedented heckling—no one had dared razz him like that before—Cobb reached first base and shouted a promise to Fletcher at second and Herzog at short: "I'm coming down."

On the next pitch, Cobb broke for second. Herzog covered to take the throw.

Cobb barreled in with spikes high and flashing. Cobb essentially cut off Herzog's pants.

Fletcher and Herzog surrounded the Peach, exchanged pushes and shoves, and issued a challenge to settle the dispute anytime, anywhere. The pair continued to hound and harass Cobb in Dallas. They also hounded and harassed him in Wichita Falls.

Tired of waiting for a response, they finally went to Cobb's hotel room and pounded on the door.

"I'm first," said Herzog. "Wait here and I'll be right out."

In the hallway, Fletcher heard fists pounding and furniture crashing inside the room. Players rushed from nearby rooms to listen. Giants outfielder Benny Kauff begged to get in next. Fletcher argued he was next. A slightly battered Cobb emerged from the room. Herzog was inside, badly beaten. Cobb saw the other Giants lined up in the hallway for a chance to throttle him and complained to Detroit manager Hughie Jennings, "Those guys are crazy. They're trying to get somebody killed."

Fletcher and Herzog continued to pester and challenge Cobb on the team train. Next morning, Cobb had fled the exhibition tour. He left word with Jennings that he had gone to work out with the Reds. As long as Cobb stayed with Cincinnati, Fletcher and Herzog flooded his mailbox with obscene postcards.

◆

The day he broke into the American League, umpire Billy Evans was quickly tested by diminutive (five feet, five-inches, 134-pounds) but belligerent New York shortstop Kid Elberfeld.

In the first inning, Evans ruled Elberfeld out on a close play at first base.

"Ow!" yelled Elberfeld, leaping and churning his fists in the air. "You big, blind bum!"

Evans said nothing. Elberfeld interpreted the silence as a sign of weakness.

"And you're dumb as well as blind," growled Elberfeld, also known as the Tabasco Kid. "I've got a notion to punch you right on the nose."

Evans stepped up close to him.

"Mr. Elberfeld," he said. "I've heard a lot about you. I've heard you're pretty tough. But just between you and me, I've got my doubts. Now here's my nose. Go ahead and poke at it. Only I'm warning you, my arms are not tied. If you want some real action, just throw one at this bugle of mine."

Elberfeld smiled slightly, looked Evans up and down, and asked how much he weighed. Evans said about 175 pounds.

"Well, you big stiff," said Elberfeld, walking away in disgust. "You've got a lot of nerve picking a fuss with a guy who weighs forty pounds less than you do."

◆

In the bottom of the ninth, York had apparently pushed the game-winning run against Elmira when umpire Bill Stewart summoned the players back onto the field. An interference call at second had negated the run.

York manager Hubie Fitzgerald shot out of the dugout and rushed up to Stewart. "You were right, Stewie," he confided. "But what a town to call that in. They've already sent two umpires to the hospital this season."

After Elmira rallied to win in the fourteenth inning, firecrackers, bottles, a bologna sandwich, and assorted debris rained on Stewart as he sprinted toward his dressing room. Under the stands, he was jumped by five men; four pinned Stew-

Tommy Holmes, Ted Williams, and Max West (left to right)

art's arms behind his back as the fifth kicked the umpire in the groin. More angry fans rushed to the scene, and Stewart was hit by a rock and knocked to the ground. Somebody shouted, "Kill the bum!" One fan punched Stewart in the face, another choked him, and another tried to smash a boulder into his head. Someone called the police.

"They finally dispersed the crowd with tear gas," Stewart recalled years later when he was an esteemed National League umpire. "The cops, by the way, were York fans to the end. They set off the first blast of tear gas right in my face."

13

HURTS

In the Brooklyn dugout one afternoon in the 1920s, Dodgers manager Uncle Wilbert Robinson sat quietly on the bench, his hands tucked under his thighs. A player seated nearby chatted about a chronic injury and how he kept playing despite nagging pain. Robinson picked up a snippet of the conversation, perked up, and leaned over to interrupt. "Think you're tough for playing hurt?" asked Uncle Wilbert. The Dodgers cringed inwardly because they knew what was coming: another story about the rough-and-tumble old Baltimore Orioles.

Robinson was an Oriole alumnus and never passed a chance to tell the boys about the hard-headed, iron-willed men of Baltimore. The Dodgers had been subjected to millions of profiles in courage about the legendary turn-of-the-century ballclub, such as the outfielders who cracked open their skulls against concrete walls but kept playing and the catchers whose fingers were snapped off by foul tips but stayed in the game after disinfecting the stump with a squirt of tobacco juice.

"One time one of our boys hit a grounder to short and beat it out," Uncle Wilbert told his captive Dodgers on the bench that afternoon in the 1920s. "But he tripped over the bag and broke his leg. A bunch of us set the leg on the field, using a bat for a splint. Then they propped the fellow on first base." Robinson paused, leaned forward, and lowered his voice.

"And," he said reverently, "they gave the hit-and-run sign to the next batter."

◆   ◆   ◆

Baseball lore is filled with tales of blood and guts, as well as severe cases of hyperbole. More than any other category of tales, injury stories tend to swell with time. Over the years, scrapes become gashes, bruises become shattered bones, and sprains become amputations. In their extreme form, exaggerated injury lore reads like something from a Monty Python routine: arms and legs severed during a collision at home plate, the chap nevertheless gripped a bat with his tongue and singled home the winning run in the ninth.

"That's nothing," says the other fellow, who knows of a pitcher who lost both eyes and pitched using the catcher's voice as a guide.

"Pshaw," says the other. "I had a teammate at Lancaster. . . ."

Plenty of modern players take the field in physical disarray, but their fore-fathers had more reasons to play hurt. Old-time contracts customarily ran for a year or two. Come negotiation time, taking a few weeks off to coddle an aching tendon could cost several thousand dollars. Old-timers also didn't know any better. Sports medicine meant a shot of bourbon and a good night's sleep. Old-time trainers were really rubdown men at best, or terrible quacks at worst. A Chicago Cubs' trainer in the 1930s used Coca-Cola as liniment. A Cubs' trainer in the late 1930s experimented with a therapeutic oven designed to bake pain out of sore arms. To demonstrate the contraption, the trainer placed a hot dog into the machine, closed the lid, and turned it on. There was a muffled sizzling followed by a loud pop. The hot dog had exploded. "Imagine if that was Lon Warneke's arm," whistled one onlooker as the machine was carted off to the scrap heap.

Modern players eat right, get plenty of rest, hone their bodies with free weights and liberal jogging, and are far superior athletes than old-timers, although not necessarily far superior baseball players. Trainers, team physicians, and orthopedic surgeons perform miracles with conditioning, therapy, and two-inch incisions.

Some things about the injury scene never change. Ballplayers, ancient and modern, aerobicized or beer bellied, share a thread of fear in their work. Not many like to admit it, but nobody relishes the idea of getting conked with a pitched ball. The worst injury in baseball history was to Cleveland shortstop Ray Chapman, who squared to bunt one summer day in 1920 and was whacked on the side of the head by Yankee pitcher Carl May's sidearm delivery. Chapman died the next day.

The second most-feared injury is pitching a ball and getting whacked with a line drive to the mound. The career of Indians hurler Herb Score was prematurely ended when he was hit in the face by Gil McDougald's shot to the mound. Red Sox reliever Rob Murphy watched a baseball highlight show one night and chuckled at the scenes of beanball after beanball. "Then they started showing pitchers getting hit by balls back to the mound," said Murphy. "I had to turn it off. I couldn't watch anymore." All of them learn to conquer their fear or get into broadcasting. Some conquered more completely than others. Ron Hunt, whose specialty was getting hit by pitched balls, liked to fire them back to the pitcher, no matter how much his body was stung by the pitch. "I never wanted to give the SOBs the satisfaction of knowing they hurt me," he said in the summer of 1987. By the summer of 2007, Hunt will tell stories about catching Bob Gibson's fastballs in his teeth and spitting the ball back at him. Or something like that.

"Really, this 'Gashouse Gang' stuff is old stuff with me," said St. Louis executive Branch Rickey one day in 1936 while puffing on a cigar and contemplating his team, which included noted roughnecks Pepper Martin, Joe Medwick, and Frankie Frisch. "Our Cardinals think they are tough, rough fellows. But compared with the fellows who used to play in the games between Dallas and Fort Worth, why, they're just a bunch of sissies."

Over the years, baseball players have run into a variety of dangerous off-field utensils, from hedge-clippers and firearms to fillet knives and hammers. Here are some examples:

In summer 1953 Phillies pitcher Curt Simmons lost part of his left big toe when it was caught in a lawn mower.

In November 1974 Oakland reliever Rollie Fingers fell off his horse, injuring his head and right arm.

In 1942, a year before he joined the Dodgers, outfielder Hal Peck shot off two toes in a hunting accident.

During spring training 1969, Twins righty Dave Boswell sliced tendons in his left hand while cleaning fish.

On November 29, 1979, Houston infielder Roger Metzger sawed off the tips of four fingers on his right hand while building a playhouse.

In 1902, when he was in the minor leagues, White Sox catcher Jimmy Archer was working in a barrel factory when he accidentally scalded his arm in a vat of boiling sap.

On November 12, 1978, Pirates outfielder Willie Stargell was accidentally shot

Wilbert ("Uncle Robby") Robinson

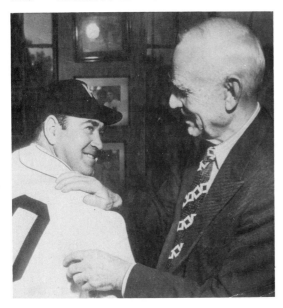

Bobo ("Buck") Newsom

in the left leg during target practice.

In winter 1974, Mets pitcher Jon Matlack smashed a finger with a hammer while helping Tom Seaver repair his porch.

Working during the off-season as a bricklayer in the 1880s, Louisville pitcher Toad Ramsey sliced a tendon in the middle finger of his pitching hand. He couldn't bend the finger thereafter and unwittingly developed a knuckleball.

In April 1979 Mariners infielder Bill Stein crushed a finger on his right hand when it was caught beneath the glass top of a coffee table his young son was tipping over.

◆

On September 13, 1883, Cleveland pitcher Hugh ("One Arm") Daily hurled a no-hitter against Philadelphia. A strapping, curveball-throwing righty, One Arm Daily in fact had two arms. But he did have only one hand.

Eleven years earlier, the fifteen-year-old Daily was working at Baltimore's Front Street Theatre as prop boy and understudy. One day during rehearsal, actors on stage heard a loud explosion from the prop room. When they flung open the door, they found the room thick with gun smoke and young Daily unconscious on the floor. He had been handling an old English flintlock musket—used as a prop, and supposedly not loaded—when the gun exploded and blew off his left hand.

Still, he went on to play baseball. Daily designed an adjustable pad for his handicapped arm, attached the pad over his stump, and used it as a makeshift glove. He handled the sharpest grounders by knocking them down as a hockey goalie knocks down pucks, quickly picking the ball up and throwing runners out. He played six years in the big leagues, won sixty-eight games, once struck out sixteen men in a nine-inning game, and batted .157 lifetime.

"He was good on grounders. And he wasn't that bad a hitter," one-time teammate Dan Brouthers recalled in 1922. "He had one weakness. He was bad on fly balls."

◆

On opening day 1936 Franklin D. Roosevelt threw out the first ball, and Bobo Newsom started for the Senators against the Yankees. In the third inning, New York outfielder Ben Chapman laid down a surprise bunt. Newsom broke toward the ball, then held up to let third baseman Ossie Bluege make the play.

Bluege snapped up the ball and released a quick, blind throw that whacked Newsom in the face some ten feet away. The pitcher hopped in circles in the infield before collecting himself and retaking the mound. He proceeded to win a complete game, 1–0.

Afterward, Newsom's jaw—fractured by Bluege's throw—had to be wired in place. Newsom was asked why he pitched six-plus innings with a broken face.

"The president came to see old Bobo pitch," he said solemnly. "Old Bobo couldn't disappoint him."

◆

In the summer of 1939, Pete Reiser was playing shortstop for Elmira when he heard something pop in his elbow as he rifled a long throw from the hole. A couple of days later, his elbow cracked again. Reiser was dispatched to Johns Hopkins, where bone chips—one wedged against a nerve—were removed.

After several weeks, the cast was removed from Reiser's throwing arm, which was shriveled and weak. Elmira was engaged in a ferocious pennant battle, and Reiser asked manager Clyde Sukeforth for permission to play.

"But you can't throw," said Sukeforth.

"I'll throw left-handed," Reiser replied.

"You can't bat," the manager said.

"I'll do that with one hand."

For several games, he played the outfield and threw left-handed. A switch hitter, he batted lefty only, with his weakened right arm resting lightly on the bat. He consistently shot singles through the infield.

One game, Reiser was presented with a hanging pitch he couldn't resist. He swung hard with both hands and lined a base hit to center. But when he reached first, his right arm was limp at his side, numb from elbow to hand.

He was sent to Brooklyn to see Dodgers team physician D.A. McAleer.

"After your arm was taken out of the cast, how long did you wait before playing?" the doctor asked.

"Oh, a day or two," Reiser replied.

"I should examine your brain," the doctor said. "Not your arm."

◆

◆

Soon after being sold to the Senators in 1935, pitcher Bobo Newsom fast became the toast of Washington. Within a week, he hobnobbed with the vice president, James Garner, congressmen, and senators; got his own radio show; and was hired to write a column for the Washington *Herald.*

Facing Cleveland in his second start for Washington, Newsom was cracked hard on the knee by an Earl Averill line drive in the second inning. Newsom threw out Averill and knelt for a moment, hoping the pain would subside.

"I guess that will make you quit, Mr. Showboat!" shortstop Bill Knickerbocker shouted from the Cleveland bench.

Pete Reiser

Newsom glared at Knickerbocker, rubbed his knee briskly, and waved his manager, Bucky Harris, back to the dugout. He completed the remaining seven innings, striking out Hal Trosky three times, running out three base hits, and covering first base on a bunt.

After the game, Newsom sought out the trainer and said, "My leg's broke."

"You're nuts," said the trainer, who nevertheless examined the pitcher's leg. He felt the knee, looked sharply at Newsom, whistled softly to himself, and called for an ambulance. Newsom had pitched seven innings with a shattered kneecap.

◆

Life was never easy for the St. Louis Browns. "You would need to write a book to tell all the things that went on there," said Al Widmar, Blue Jays coach and former Browns hurler, one of the few old Brownies still active in the big leagues in the summer of 1988. "I think Les Moss, who's coaching in Houston, is the only other one."

In 1947 the Browns lost 95 games. In 1948 they lost 94 games. In 1949, they lost 101 games. So in spring 1950, afraid losing was becoming a permanent Brownie state of mind, management took action. They hired Dr. David F. Tracy to serve as team psychologist.

Of course, in 1950—a generation before psycho-babble—big-league ballplayers weren't keen on letting anybody mess with their heads, besides barbers and fedora salesmen.

"I don't think too many of us went to him," said Widmar. "I think we tried to avoid him, actually. But in those days, we pretty much did what we were told. We were just trying to keep our jobs."

So when Doc Tracy talked, the Browns listened. Sort of.

"His main thing was to try to get us to think positive," remembered Widmar. "He did a lot of talking with the pitching staff. I remember once he told us, trying to emphasize the positive, that it was almost impossible for seven or eight batters to get up and get seven hits in a row on the first pitch. The night he told us that—we were playing the Red Sox, I think—the other team got seven straight hits. Not all on the first pitch, but it was still enough to kind of blow him out of the water."

On May 29, with the Browns in last place, 14½ games out, Dr. Tracy resigned.

◆

One night while the Cubs were in New York, Chicago manager Gabby Hartnett was called to Dizzy Dean's room, where he found the famous righty bleeding from a small gash in his right forearm.

Hartnett called a doctor, then turned to his pitcher. "How did it happen?" he demanded.

Dean spun a lengthy explanation.

"That's out of a book called the *Arabian Nights,*" Hartnett said, shaking his head. "Come again."

"Oh, now I remember," said Dean, launching into a completely different tale.

"Right from Baron Munchhausen," said Hartnett. "Take a deep breath and try again."

Dean tried again. "I like that one better," said Hartnett. "But maybe you can still do better if you keep on swinging."

The doctor arrived and closed Dean's wound with two stitches. Dean continued to offer explanations. Hartnett occasionally interrupted to suggest a good detail or two.

"Maybe you were just scratching your head," Hartnett suggested, "and your arm slipped against one of the corners and you were lucky to save it from being torn off."

Dean was bundled onto a train to Chicago the next day. That afternoon, someone brought a newspaper to Hartnett.

"Here's a new version of what happened," he told Hartnett. "Dean gave it out when the train stopped in Pittsburgh."

"We'll have to wait," said the manager. "The train makes several stops before it gets to Chicago."

That night at the ballpark, newspapermen asked Hartnett what Dean had told him about the cut arm.

Hartnett said he couldn't be sure by Dean's account, but he thought it happened "in a restaurant where a glass fell off the table and just then a taxicab door flew open, causing Ol' Diz to put his arm through the cigar case while the telephone was ringing by his bedside and the Bronx directory jumped up and bit him the length of two stitches. It was pitch dark at the time."

◆

Gordon ("Mickey") Cochrane

Late in the 1930 season, the Philadelphia Athletics were playing an important doubleheader against the Senators. In the first game, Washington was ahead, 6–3, in the ninth when Al Simmons hit a three-run homer. Philadelphia went on to win in the fifteenth inning.

In the opener, Simmons ruptured a blood vessel in his leg. Between games the injury worsened, and manager Connie Mack summoned a doctor.

"Mr. Mack, Simmons is too crippled to play in the second game," the doctor said. "You can use him as a pinch hitter. But he'll have to hit the ball out of the ballpark, because he can't run."

In the second game, the Athletics trailed, 7–3, in the ninth. The bases were loaded. Mack crooked his finger at Simmons on the bench.

"Let's see if the doctor knows what he's talking about, Al," Mack said. "Go up there and hit."

Simmons hit the first pitch for a grand slam.

◆

On the afternoon of May 25, 1937, the Tigers visited the Yankees at Yankee Stadium. In the third inning, Detroit player-manager Mickey Cochrane tied the game with a homer against New York righty Bump Hadley. In the fifth inning, the lefty-batting Cochrane again stepped to the plate.

Cochrane had homered on a high-and-tight fastball, so this time he expected Hadley to pitch him outside. On a 3–1 count, he crouched into the plate. A fast-

Fat Freddie Fitzsimmons

ball sailed high and inside and cracked Cochrane in the right temple. The thud could be heard in the grandstand. Cochrane slowly collapsed into the batter's box.

"His eyes were partially open, and he was making little gutteral sounds," said Hadley, who rushed to Cochrane's side.

"You know, those stars that people are supposed to see when they get socked aren't just things you see in the funny papers," Cochrane said later. "I really saw stars when that pitched ball hit me. They were like fireworks, and I saw all the colors and lights of a skyrocket. I just saw that ball coming at me, then the explosion, and then nothing."

At the hospital, doctors diagnosed a triple skull fracture and gave Cochrane a fifty-fifty shot at survival. Teetering between delirium and unconsciousness,

he told them he had lost sight of the ball three feet from the plate. Cochrane's wife arrived from Detroit at 2:00 A.M. and asked if there was anything he wanted. "Yes," moaned Cochrane, who never played another big-league game. "Get me a new head."

◆

One afternoon in the 1930s during a Giants–Dodgers engagement at the Polo Grounds, New York right-hander Fat Freddie Fitzsimmons was struck squarely in the groin by a screaming line drive back to the mound.

Fitzsimmons managed to pick up the ball and throw out the runner at first to end the inning before dropping to the turf writhing in pain. He was surrounded by worried teammates and the team doctor, who summoned a stretcher. Through clenched teeth, Fitzsimmons said he thought he'd be all right if he could just sit still for a moment. Helped back into the dugout, he pulled himself together, then grabbed a bat—he was leading off the next inning.

Fitzsimmons walked unsteadily to the batter's box as the crowd cheered, then got set to face Brooklyn righty Cy Moore. The first pitch cracked Fitzsimmons in the jaw, knocking him unconscious.

◆

In the spring of 1930, one-time American League president Ben Johnson recalled his playing days, when men were men and often black and blue.

For instance, Johnson told how the catcher's mask was developed by Harvard players in 1877, but "I caught for my college team in 1881, and the only thing I wore to protect myself was a chunk of crude rubber gripped firmly between my teeth. By the finish of the season, I was always black and blue from head to foot, and often times unable to wear a hat because of the bumps and lumps."

Then there was the time a young second baseman was summoned from the minors for a shot at the big leagues. In the second inning, he was spiked by a runner trying to steal second. The youngster continued to play, however, showing no sign of injury.

After the game, the manager noticed the rookie limping toward the clubhouse.

"Reckon I musta picked up a pebble," the second baseman said. In the locker room, he sat on a bench and removed his shoe and stocking.

"Picking up the shoe, he shook it briskly," reported Johnson, "and out fell a toe."

◆

When the hapless 1950 St. Louis Browns had on staff Dr. David Farrell Tracy, the psychologist and expert in the power of positive thinking, one afternoon Tracy called for sore-armed pitchers to come to see him. Lee Stone responded.

Tracy held Stone's right arm, examined it, then began to massage it. "There's nothing wrong with your arm," he chanted. "There's nothing wrong with your arm. It's your imagination. You're Walter Johnson, and he never had a sore arm. It's your imagination." Finally, Tracy gently lowered the arm back to Stone's side.

"There," the doctor said. "How does your arm feel now?"

"It feels fine," said Stone. "Except that's my right arm. I'm a lefty."

◆

On the night of August 18, 1967, at Fenway Park, Jack Hamilton was just another right-handed pitcher with the California Angels. Tony Conigliaro was the twenty-two-year-old swashbuckling slugger with the Red Sox. When Hamilton acci-

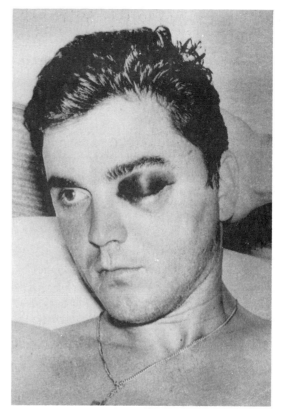

Tony Conigliaro

dentally drilled a fastball into Conigliaro's left eye, everything changed. Tony C. was forever the guy whose fabulous career was derailed by a horrible beaning. Hamilton was forever the guy who beaned him.

"I didn't have that great a career," Hamilton said nearly twenty-three years later from his Branson, Montana, home. "I was only a mediocre ballplayer. But I hate to be remembered for that one thing. It's just something I have to live with.

"It was a fastball that got away," said Hamilton. "I don't think he ever saw the ball. In my opinion, he just froze. I just think he lost sight of it."

"It was awful. Just awful," Bill Rigney, the Angels manager that night, recalled in February 1990. "The sound was just terrible.

A crane begins the wrecking of Ebbets Field on February 23, 1960.

You never forget the sound of something like that."

"I was on deck, and I ran over to him," said Red Sox shortstop Rico Petrocelli, twenty-three years later. "I saw his face. It was blown up like a balloon. No kidding. It was just blown up in that spot, like you would blow up a balloon. The blood was rushing to that area. It looked like someone had cut his eye to allow the blood to get out. Anytime you see something like that, you get some fear. It stays in your mind. No batter alive wants to get hit in the face like that."

The night Tony C. was hit changed everything. For the Red Sox, the "Impossible Dream"—the wild, crazy summer that revived baseball in Boston—had taken a quick, nightmarish turn. "Mostly everybody got angry," said Petrocelli. "All of a sudden, he was out of the lineup and it looked like he would never play again. We were angry at the Angels and everybody else. I remember myself, Yaz, and Jim Lonborg, we got so angry at that moment. We wanted to go out and kill Hamilton."

"I tried to see him in the hospital that night, but the family wasn't allowing any visitors," Hamilton said. "We left town after that, and I never got the chance to talk to him. I knew he was in pretty bad shape. I didn't think there was any point in writing him a letter or anything. I'm sure he didn't think I did it on purpose. I hope he didn't think that."

Conigliaro's cheekbone was fractured, his jaw was dislocated, and his retina was damaged. He did not rejoin the Red Sox until 1969—he had an outstanding season in 1970—but he suffered vision problems that forced him out of baseball. In 1982 Conigliaro suffered a heart attack at age thirty-seven that left him severely incapacitated.

What if he had never been hit? "He had everything ahead of him," said Rigney. "I thought about the night he got hit every time I ran into him."

"I thought about it whenever I got close to somebody with a pitch," said Hamilton, who retired after the 1969 season. "Whenever I see a brushback on TV, it catches my attention. I kind of kept up on what he was doing. I picked up every time I heard his name."

On Saturday night, February 24, 1990, Hamilton was watching late sports and weather on TV when he learned Tony Conigliaro had died at age forty-five. "I wondered if in some way I was responsible for it," said Hamilton. "Maybe I started all the bad things for him. Nobody ever said anything like that. I just kind of thought it. You never know. It's like if you run over a little kid backing your car out of your driveway. It's just something you've got to live with."

FALL CLASSICS

On a gray, chilly day at Fenway Park in early September 1990, the Red Sox secured an important victory in the pennant race. Amid much excitement, Boston ace Roger Clemens had pitched brilliantly and in the clubhouse afterward he said, "That was great. The weather was a little cool, the fans were all bundled up, they were excited. It felt like the World Series out there." A ballplayer can pay no higher compliment to a baseball game.

Some feel the World Series in their bones. The humidity has broken, the pumpkins are frosted, leaves swirl on the wind, and sweaters are out of mothballs. It is football weather, and the baseball season revels in its magnificent denouement.

Some feel it in the pit of their stomach. The World Series is all excitement and anxiety, hardball on a feather edge. One team will reach the top of the ziggurat, the other twenty-five will wait until next year. There is nothing nonchalant about a ballpark blessed with a "fall classic." There are red, white, and blue banners on the box-seat rails, not an inch of standing room, and simmering emotion in the air. There is nothing nonchalant about fans with a team in the World Series. If they cared about their heroes all summer, they care about nothing else come the World Series. William Frawley, who played Fred Mertz on "I Love Lucy," insisted upon a clause in his contract giving him time off whenever his beloved Yankees swaggered into the series. There is nothing nonchalant about ballplayers in the World Series. Getting there was a boyhood dream, and they admit it, no matter how sappy it sounds. Getting there is a badge of honor. Players in the World Series walk out of the clubhouse tunnel directly into baseball lore.

For a ballplayer, winning the series means a fat check, great fame, and a happy soul. The euphoria lasts forever. Money cannot buy a world championship ring. Not even a multimillionaire ballplayer's money. He can't even demand one in

The first pitch of the second game of the 1953 World Series at Yankee Stadium.

his next contract. It is the thing a devoted ballplayer desires most, even more than an endorsement package. After he joined the Red Sox from the world champion Dodgers in 1989, outfielder Danny Heep took delivery of his World Series championship ring at Fenway Park. Boston left fielder Mike Greenwell peeked over from the adjacent locker, scowled like an infant deprived of a pacifier, and squealed, "I *want* one."

Most ballplayers think hard about immortality, and during the World Series timeless fame and infamy strike crisply. Lore is specific about this. The smallest moment in a World Series often becomes the biggest moment in a player's life.

On the Sunday afternoon of October 10, 1920, Cleveland's League Park was filled for Game Five of the Indians–Dodgers World Series. Leading off the Brooklyn fifth, with the Indians ahead, 7–0, Pete Kilduff singled to left. Otto Miller singled to center, sending Kilduff to second. Clarence Mitchell smashed a line drive up the middle. Indians second baseman Bill Wambsganss moved right, caught the ball, stepped on second to double up Kilduff, and hurried down the baseline to tag Miller, who had been running from first. When he died sixty-five years and two months later, the headline over Wambsganss's obituary in the New York *Times* read:

> Bill Wambsganss Dies at 91;
> Made a Triple Play in Series

World Series lore is harsh and powerful. Entire careers are shaded by World Series moments. Some men, such as Ernie Banks, Rod Carew, and Gene Mauch, never got there. Their long careers are partially defined by what they didn't experience. How a player performs if he gets there is a favorite gauge of hardball guts. Yankee catcher Yogi Berra's superb career is judged truly great because he stood up well in fourteen World Series. Ted Williams was the finest hitter who ever lived, but hateful critics love to bring up his .200 batting average in the 1946 series. Reggie Jackson was Mr. October and beloved in New York. He was replaced by the great Dave Winfield, who batted .045 in the 1981 series and never captured the heart of the Big Apple. His owner, George Steinbrenner, went so far as to nickname him Mr. May, the worst epitaph for a ballplayer. Tiny Giants infielder Heinie Groh batted .474 in the 1922 World Series and thereafter ordered license plate number 474 for his automobile.

Entire franchises are haunted by World Series moments. Red Sox history is rich with splendid players and powerful lineups, but as of 1990 they hadn't won a World Series since 1918. They lost seven-game decisions in 1946, 1967, 1975, and 1986, and their name became synonymous with futility. As of 1990, the Cubs hadn't played in a World Series since 1945, leaving their legions downright envious of Red Sox fans. The Mets shed their laughingstock label the moment they chiseled themselves into World Series lore. Nearly three decades into their existence, there is still something dinky about the Angels because they have never reached the series.

Not much World Series lore is passed along by players during quiet hours in a June dugout. Series lore achieves instant, public fame. There is no waiting period for classic "fall classics" moments; they are immediately hammered into the granite. The World Series is every fan's common ground: during the series, every baseball lover in the country watches the same game. All remember the leaves they raked in 1960 when Bill Mazeroski whacked his home run, the classes they cut in 1969 when the Mets flabbergasted the Orioles, the neighbors they awoke in 1975 when Carlton Fisk clanged an after-midnight blast off the foul pole, and the champagne bottle they heaved out the window in 1986 when Bill Buckner let the grounder slither between his legs. The World Series is baseball at its most intense and vivid, for better or for worse. The best anyone can say about a ballgame is it resembled the World Series. The worst anyone can say about a mistake is it was like messing up the World Series.

From 1907 through 1919, Henry ("Heinie") Zimmerman played 1,456 games in the big leagues and batted .295 lifetime. In Game Six of the 1917 World Series, with the White Sox a victory away from the world championship, the Giants' third baseman committed a mental error. The game was scoreless in the top of the fourth. With White Sox on the corners—Eddie Collins at third and

Shoeless Joe Jackson at first—Chicago outfielder Happy Feisch hit a comebacker to pitcher Rube Benton. Collins was caught between third and home. Benton threw to Zimmerman, who blew the rundown. He held the ball and vainly chased Collins all the way to the plate. Chicago scored three times in the inning and proceeded to win the game, 4–3, en route to winning the championship.

After the 1917 series, Zimmerman made more mistakes. Before the 1920 season, he was banned from baseball for conspiring with gamblers. He had acted as a bagman to solicit Giants to fix games. In 1928 Zimmerman's brother-in-law, bootlegger and mobster Joe Noe, was riddled with bullets in front of a New York nightclub. In 1929–30 Zimmerman himself went into partnership with mobster Dutch Schultz to purchase a speakeasy. In 1935 Zimmerman was implicated with Schultz in an income-tax-evasion trial. In the later years of his life, Zimmerman worked as a Bronx steamfitter.

On March 14, 1969, fifty years after his final big-league game, Zimmerman died at the age of eighty-two. The New York *Times* headline the next day read:

Giants Heinie Zimmerman Dies:
Committed 1917 Series "Boner"

The Senators led the Pirates in the 1925 World Series, three games to one. In the early innings of Game Five, Pittsburgh was leading, 1–0. Moon Harris, so nicknamed because of the crescent-shaped scar he brought back from World War I, reached first base for the Senators.

The next batter, Roger Peckinpaugh, cracked a hit to the right-field corner. Washington third base coach Al Schacht held Harris at third, but immediately had second thoughts.

"Kiki Cuyler fielded the ball, then threw it to second," Schacht recalled. "If I had kept Harris in motion, I'm pretty certain I could have scored him. I didn't think much of it at the time because we were still in pretty good position. Men on second and third and one out."

The next batter popped up. The next flied out. "Pittsburgh finally beat us in that game, 6–3," said Schacht. "But if I had scored Harris in that early inning to tie it up, it would have been a different ball game." The Senators went on to blow the series in seven games.

Two weeks later, Schacht lounged on a deck chair aboard the S.S. *Paula,* steaming out of New York for the long, leisurely cruise to California. Tucking a blanket around his legs, he breathed sweet ocean air and daydreamed about how to spend his World Series money, a losing share worth $3,734.60.

Suddenly a pageboy interrupted with a telegram. Schacht ripped it open. It was from Washington owner Clark Griffith. "Good old Griff," Schacht thought to himself. "Probably seeking my advice on something."

The telegram read: "Have a good time. Remember you would have had $5,332.72 to spend instead of $3,734.60 if you had used better judgment with Joe Harris."

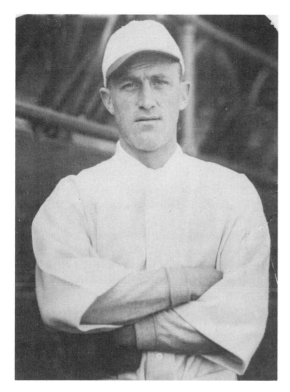

Bill ("Wamby") Wambsganss

◆

The final score of Game Two of the 1913 World Series was: Giants 3, Athletics 0, dead 2. Per custom before radio and television days, fans across the country assembled at newspaper offices, telegraph outposts, and public bulletin boards for play-by-play updates of the games. For excitement, it was almost as good as being there.

Sometimes it was too much like being there. In Philadelphia, fans gathered to monitor the game at an electric scoreboard. In the first inning, A's third baseman Frank Baker, who had slammed a home run in Game One, stepped to the plate. "Give us another homer, Baker!" yelled onlooker John Shorrick. When the

reproduction showed Baker had struck out, Shorrick keeled over on the pavement and died.

Meanwhile, in New York fans watched the game at a Park Row bulletin board. They grew anxious as the contest entered extra innings in a scoreless tie. When news flashed that Christy Mathewson had singled home the go-ahead run in the top of the tenth, an unidentified onlooker, who carried a Bowery Mission membership card, dropped dead onto the sidewalk.

◆

The October 8, 1913, court proceeding in downtown Tunkhannock, Pennsylvania, progressed routinely, until they tried to summon one of the witnesses. A quick check of the courthouse and the grounds determined the elderly man was gone.

Court officers sent to search the town for the missing witness found him quickly. They discovered the old man smiling and clapping as he watched updates of Game Two of the World Series on the local scoreboard.

"I used to play amateur baseball myself, in Chicago," said the man, G. B. Mathewson, father of the Giants' Game Two starter, Christy Mathewson, as officers escorted him back to court. "I've never even dreamed that my boy would achieve the fame as Christy has in the baseball world."

◆

During the 1944 baseball season, St. Louis Browns manager Luke Sewell and St. Louis Cardinals manager Billy Southworth shared a one-bedroom apartment in St. Louis. The arrangement worked out nicely. When the Browns were in town and the Cardinals were on the road, Sewell lived there. While the Car-

Joe ("Moon") Harris

dinals were in town and the Browns were on the road, Southworth lived there.

When the season ended, there was a problem: Sewell and Southworth were scheduled to be in town at the same time. Amazingly, the Browns and Cardinals were in the World Series.

By the time Southworth reached the apartment, Sewell was already there, exercising squatter's rights. Southworth moved to a hotel.

◆

During the 1940 Tigers–Reds World Series, the United Press office in New York received the following message from its London bureau as the British capital was getting pounded by the twenty-sixth consecutive night of German bombing: "Beleaguered exiles would greatly appreciate daily World Series scores and batteries."

◆

During the 1927 Yankees–Pirates World Series, a pitch-by-pitch Play-O-Graph board in Springfield, Massachusetts, drew huge crowds who wanted to keep track of the series as it happened. As an added attraction, the scoreboard operators advertised they would toss a genuine big-league baseball into the crowd after each World Series home run.

During Game Three, Babe Ruth cracked out the first homer of the series. As promised, someone heaved a baseball to the pulsating mob.

The ball sailed high into the air, then plopped neatly into a baby carriage that was occupied by a baby. The crowd surged after the ball, brushing the horrified mother out of the way, and closing around the carriage.

Al Schacht (left) *and Nick Altrock*

Billy Southworth

A quick-thinking Boy Scout reached in and snatched the baby to safety. After the ball was retrieved and the dust cleared, the carriage was found, crushed flat.

◆

On the night of October 4, 1944, a couple of war correspondents attached to a division of American paratroopers on the Holland–German border huddled in a bombed-out building to listen to Game One of the Browns–Cardinals World Series.

In the last half of the third, the Cardinals had the bases loaded against Browns starter Denny Galehouse. Cardinal Whitey Kurowski was at the plate. The correspondents listened anxiously for the next pitch.

Suddenly the night was split by a deafening roar. As the walls shook, the Americans pulled on their helmets and said their prayers. They were in the middle of an artillery barrage.

When the shelling stopped, the night was still again, except for the ball game crackling over the radio. The war correspondents were miffed. It was the fifth inning; the Cardinals had failed to score; and they had no idea how Galehouse had gotten out of the jam.

◆

During the 1925 Pirates–Senators World Series, the Louisville *Courier-Journal and Times* concocted a three-dimensional way to keep the masses up to date on the series. The newspaper hired local ballplayers to assemble at a local field. Each player wore a radio headset tuned into the ballgame. As they listened, the players acted out what was happening at the faraway series.

During Game Two, the batter stood at the plate and listened intently to his headset. He hesitated a moment, then dropped to the ground and writhed in mock pain.

During the 1957 World Series, supporters of Cuban revolutionary leader Fidel Castro threw pamphlets from the stands calling for Americans to help him "fight Batista and Communism." Coach Connie Ryan of the Milwaukee Braves is in the foreground.

His teammates took the cue and gathered around him in mock concern.

At the game in Pittsburgh, Senators third baseman Ossie Bluege had been beaned by a pitch.

◆

On October 2, 1940, Sen. J. W. Elmer Thomas of Oklahoma was on the Senate floor delivering a speech condemning the proposed Truth-in-Fabrics bill. Thomas noticed many members absent and many others gathered around radios in the cloak room.

"I admit that this bill, which will cost every consumer money, cannot compete with anything so important as a baseball game," Thomas said. "At the end of the first inning the score is Detroit 0 and Cincinnati 0."

The House of Representatives avoided the conflict altogether. It knocked off work twenty minutes before the first pitch.

◆

Here are some tidbits from the first World Series, played between Boston and Pittsburgh in 1903:

Going into the series, Pittsburgh righty Sam Leever, 25–7 during the season, was hampered by a sore pitching arm, injured during a trap-shooting contest.

Before Game One, spectators climbed atop rooftops as far as a quarter-mile from the Huntington Avenue Grounds.

During Game One, a fan began to climb over the fence that separated the third-base bleachers from the infield. Police spotted him and, as he straddled the fence, tried to push him back into the stands. The tightly packed crowd, however, tried to push him back onto the field. The man served as a human volleyball for several minutes. Police tossed him into the stands

and fans tossed him back out. Finally, he was escorted out across the field.

Before Game Two, scorecards were on sale for fifteen cents each. One customer deplored this as "squeezing the dear public hard."

Before Game Three at the Huntington Avenue Grounds, fans spilled out of the overflowing bleachers onto the outfield grass, where they stood ten deep near the center-field fence. Soon the crowd swelled to unsafe proportions, and police were called to help rescue women and children threatened by the crush. Boston outfielder Chick Stahl himself helped save patrons by lifting them over the right-field fence.

During Game Three, Cy Young was in the club office, wearing his street clothes and helping count ticket receipts, when he was summoned to put on his uniform and pitch in relief.

In attendance for Game Six in Pittsburgh was Eddie Foy, who expressed admiration for the Boston nine. "They are my choice for the series," he said.

When Game Seven was rained out, a

Cookie Lavagetto celebrates after his game-winning double in the 1947 World Series.

Fans roam on the field at Boston's Huntington Avenue Baseball Grounds in October 1903 during the first World Series. Boston beat Pittsburgh.

newspaperman rushed from the ballpark to the telegraph office. "I just sent a special saying the weather here was bright and warm and sunshiny," he said. "I have to kill it."

In Game Eight, with only one out standing between Boston and the World Series championship, Pittsburgh shortstop Honus Wagner stepped to the plate. Boston lefty Bill Dineen was on the mound. Someone in the crowd yelled, "Strike him out!" The sentiment caught on with the crowd, and the throng hysterically took up the chant. Wagner quickly took two called strikes. Then the crowd roared the demand: "Strike him out!" Wagner swung at strike three, and the crowd poured on the field for the first World Series celebration.

◆

During World War II, American troops were hit with thousands of hardships, including the annual struggle with inadequate World Series updates. In October 1943, as baseball-loving Americans crammed the British Isles preparing for D-Day, interest in the Yankees–Cardinals World Series left Britons puzzled.

"World Series?" asked a bartender as American soldiers implored, begged, and bribed him to turn the radio to the BBC's nightly fifteen-minute series recap. "Sorry, I never heard of it."

British telephone operators manning Red Cross clubs were polite but not helpful when besieged by World Series calls.

"Yankees and Cardinals? Who are they?" one said.

Adding to the confusion was the fact that the Americans were also keenly interested in the Little World Series between Syracuse and Columbus. The British didn't know a World Series, big or small, from a World War.

Meanwhile, in the South Pacific Marines jammed tents and gathered around radios to listen to play-by-play accounts. Before long, they had a new will to fight. Japanese radio operators were jamming broadcasts of the games.

◆

Late in the 1922 season, Yankees manager Miller Huggins awoke in his Boston hotel room with his foot stuck out the window. His team proceeded to wallop the Red Sox that afternoon.

On the eve of the World Series against the Giants, Huggins remembered Boston. That night, he slept with his foot stuck out the window. The Giants swept the Yankees.

◆

During Game Two of the 1923 World Series, the Giants had Ross Youngs at third and Irish Meusel at third with two outs. New York manager John McGraw dispatched Hank Gowdy, the aging World Series hero of the 1914 Braves, to pinch-hit for outfielder Bill Cunningham.

Yankee pitcher Herb Pennock called time and summoned catcher Wally Schang to the mound. Manager Miller Huggins joined the conference. All were perplexed. No one knew how to pitch to Gowdy, who had joined the Giants in midseason.

Finally, Babe Ruth trotted in from right field and solved the problem. "Pitch him what the Athletics didn't in 1914," he told Pennock.

Schang returned behind the plate. Ruth went back to right. Huggins went back to the dugout. Gowdy flied out to left.

◆

On October 15, 1923, the Yankees beat the Giants, 6–4, to win their first World Series. The pinstriped champions included former Red Sox Jumping Joe Dugan, Wally Schang, Everett Scott, Bullet Joe Bush, Herb Pennock, Waite Hoyt, and Babe Ruth.

The next day's Boston *Herald* ran a team photo of the World Series winners with the bitter headline: "Red Sox Alumni Become Champions of the Baseball World."

◆

All things are the same, except you are there. Babe Ruth at the bat, pitch-by-pitch in Game Two of the 1923 World Series at the Polo Grounds:

First inning, with one out and Jumping Joe Dugan at first: Ball one, high. Ball two, low. Strike one, called. Ball three, low. Ball four, two feet outside.

Fourth inning, leading off: Ball one, high and outside. Strike one, swinging. Ball two, low. Fastball down the middle; Ruth crushes it deep into the right-field stands.

Sixth inning, with one out: Foul, strike one. Ball one, low. Foul high into the stands, strike two. Curve high, ball two. Foul into the stands. Fastball high; Ruth lines it into the right-field stands.

Seventh inning, with two out: Ball one, low. Strike one, swinging. Ball two, low. Check swing at a curveball. Home plate umpire Hank O'Day calls ball three; Giants appeal to third base umpire Billy Evans, who rules Ruth did not go around. Ball four, low. Ruth is picked off at first base.

Ninth inning, with two out and Dugan at second: Ball one, three feet over Ruth's head. Strike one, called. Ruth wallops the next pitch to deepest center field, where

The 1943 St. Louis Cardinals: Lou Klein, Harry Walker, Stan Musial, Walker Cooper, Whitey Kurowski, Ray Sanders, Danny Litwhiler, Marty Marion, and manager Billy Southworth (left to right).

it is chased down and caught by Casey Stengel.

◆

In Game Seven of the 1946 World Series, Harry ("The Hat") Walker batted home Enos Slaughter from first base to give the Cardinals a 4–3 decision over the Red Sox. The hit made Walker, in some respects, the granddaddy of Red Sox postseason misery. Bob Gibson, Tony Perez, Bucky Dent, and Mookie Wilson all tacked their portraits next to his.

"That hit comes up all the time," said Walker from his Birmingham, Alabama, home in the fall of 1989. "It will probably come up again during this World Series."

Here is Walker's own description of his eighth-inning run batted in, which to this day conjures controversy, disagreement, varying versions, and, in New England, uncontrollable sobbing:

Bob Klinger threw me a sinker ball low and away. I hit it that way. Slaughter was stealing on the play. I hit the ball solidly; it was almost out to the warning track. To hear Slaughter tell it today, you'd think it was barely past shortstop. Some say it was a dying quail. But if it was such a short hit, why in the world did the ball come back into a relay man? It was a double right from the beginning.

Johnny Pesky did not hold the ball that long. He just turned, looked, then threw. There really wasn't any play at the plate, anyway.

I had the same thing happen to me once in the minors. We were playing in the Little World Series. I hit a home run in Montreal to win it. I fouled off fourteen pitches, then hit one out. They carried me off the field.

Then to have it happen again in the World Series—it was just the most exciting thing I ever had happen to me.

For his World Series heroics—he led St. Louis with a .412 average and six RBIs—Walker got a championship ring and $3,742.34 as a winner's share. He was still miffed about something he didn't get.

"I had a heck of a World Series, led the team in hitting and everything," he said. "After the World Series, Wheaties signed up about ten of us. And I wasn't one of them."

◆

Johnny Mize's 300-foot single off the right field screen in the 1949 World Series.

On October 6, 1948, the Braves and Indians battled in Game One of the 1948 World Series. Johnny Sain started for Boston, Bob Feller for the Indians. With two out in the bottom of the eighth, the game was still a scoreless tie. Braves second baseman Sibby Sisti was at first, and catcher Phil Masi was at second. The 40,135 shivering patrons at Braves Field knew this was the home team's best chance to crack Feller, who had allowed just one hit.

In stepped lefty-hitting Tommy Holmes, who in his previous three at-bats hadn't hit a ball out of the infield. Holmes took a nasty curve outside for ball one. *Oh, no,* Holmes thought to himself. *He's got a great curveball, too.*

Next pitch was an outside fastball, which Holmes fouled off. Next pitch was a fastball high and outside, which Holmes sliced to the left, past third baseman Ken Keltner, into left field. Clutching his cap in his right hand, Masi scored; the Braves beat Feller, 1–0; and Boston rejoiced.

Forty years later, Holmes still rejoiced. "Right now, talking about it, I'm getting goosebumps," he said, remembering the moment exactly forty years later from his Woodbury, New York, home. "I can still see Feller out there on the mound. It was a great thrill. This time of year, I always think of that game."

◆

With his partner Sandy Giampapa, Al Longo ran the Publicity, Inc., business in Boston's Kenmore Square for more than forty years. He tells a story about the time during the Braves–Indians World Series in 1948 when he walked into the lobby of the Somerset Hotel and spied comedian Lou Costello approach Braves owner Lou Perini.

"Costello was with another fellow. Not Abbott," said Longo. "They had come in from California, but didn't have any tickets for the game. Costello went up to Perini and introduced himself.

"He said, 'Gee, Mr. Perini, I don't have any tickets to the game. I'd appreciate it if you could help me out. As a matter of fact, I'll be happy to do the "Who's on First" routine out at the ballpark.'

"Perini's expression didn't change. He said, 'Gee, Lou, I'm sorry. But I just don't have any tickets.' This is the owner of the team talking, now. Costello says, 'But all you have to do is get me in. I'll sit on the roof. I'll do the routine. Just get me in.' Mr. Perini says he's sorry and leaves him standing there.

"Sandy and I got on the elevator. There were already some people in there. Costello and his friend got on with us. In those days, the elevators were manually operated. The operator shut the door, but the elevator didn't move.

"Finally the operator says, 'I'm sorry. But someone will have to get off. There are too many people in the car.' Costello turns to his friend and says, 'I can't believe this. I come all the way from California to see the ball game, but I can't get tickets from the owner of the team. And now I'm in an elevator that won't go up.' Costello and his friend got off, and we went up. I can still see him standing there in the lobby, with this great big cigar in his mouth, without any tickets. I never did find out whether he ever got into the ball game."

◆

In the second game of the 1919 World Series, White Sox first baseman Chick Gandil stepped to the plate to bat against Cincinnati's Slim Sallee. Suddenly play was stopped. A passenger plane was swooping dangerously low over Redland Field.

When the plane droned over the infield, a human figure appeared at the door, then plummeted to the ground, nearly landing on shortstop Larry Kopf.

A policeman stationed at the grandstand railing ran onto the field, approached the scene, and saw the victim was just a dummy. The policeman carried it off the field and used it as a seat, from where he watched the rest of the game.

◆

During Game Five of the 1911 World Series at the Polo Grounds, Athletics right fielder Danny Murphy misplayed a fly ball, allowing Laughing Larry Doyle to score the winning run for New York.

After the game, Murphy climbed into a taxicab immediately outside the clubhouse door. Still distraught over his mistake, he sank into the rear seat of the cab. Suddenly a friend from Connecticut called to Murphy from the sidewalk. The ballplayer leaned through the window to shake hands.

Just then, Athletics outfielder Rube Oldring stepped into the cab and plopped down in Murphy's seat. When Murphy finished greeting his friend, he folded down one of the cab's rear-facing seats and settled in.

As the cab pulled away from the curb, an overly enthusiastic Giants fan rushed the car, wildly running as if he were a bomb-tossing assassin. The fan heaved an armload of smelly garbage through the rear window. The entire mess splattered Oldring, covering him with rotten tomatoes, cabbage, and succotash. Murphy was untouched, although he had an excellent view of what would have hit him if he hadn't lost his seat.

Next day in Philadelphia, the game was tied at 1–1 in the Athletics' fourth inning. Home Run Baker singled. Murphy singled,

The crowd watched St. Louis take batting practice during the 1946 World Series.

sending Baker to third. With the infield playing in, Harry Davis bounced to the second baseman, Doyle. Instead of shooting for Baker at the plate, Doyle tried to tag Murphy in the base line to start a double play. Doyle jabbed the tag twice at Murphy's belly. Murphy jackknifed out of the way twice. Doyle then threw home, but was too late. All runners were safe. The Athletics proceeded to break the game open and won, 13–2.

Doyle's missed tag was the difference. Why did Doyle miss the tag? "He missed me by only that much," said Murphy, placing his thumb and forefinger a half-inch apart. "And he wouldn't have missed me if I had been eating. But on account of that stuff all over Oldring, I couldn't eat supper the night before or breakfast that morning, or even lunch."

◆

On the night of October 25, 1986, at Shea Stadium in New York, the Red Sox engaged the Mets in Game Six of the World Series. Boston was one victory away from winning its first world championship since 1918. The game was tied, 3–3, after nine innings. The tenth inning didn't begin until after midnight, early in the morning of October 26.

In the bottom of the tenth, the Red Sox held a 5–3 lead with two outs. Against Red Sox reliever Calvin Schiraldi, Gary Carter singled, Kevin Mitchell singled, and Ray Knight singled, scoring Carter. Red Sox righty Bob Stanley relieved and threw a wild pitch, Mitchell scoring from third to tie the game. Mookie Wilson slapped a soft, bounding ground ball that scooted between the legs of Boston first baseman Bill Buckner, and the Mets had completed one of the most incredible comebacks in World Series history.

The following is a look at the actual horoscopes, as they appeared in the October 26 Boston *Herald,* for the principal figures of that infamous inning:

Ray Knight and Kevin Mitchell (Capricorn): "Slowly but surely you will come to realize just how fortunate and protected you really are."

Mookie Wilson (Aquarius): "Circumstances beyond your control now force you to . . . make decisions which will alter the pattern of your working life."

Gary Carter (Aries): "All the turmoils, conflicts and uncertainty of the past few years are slowly being swept away."

Calvin Schiraldi (Gemini): "Any truly resolute, ambitious, and astute Gemini could not wish for a better time to throw caution to the winds."

Bob Stanley (Scorpio): "You have given a lot of time and thought to certain plans or projects and probably suffered a great deal in private, and it really would be a pity to miss out on what could be the opportunity of a lifetime."

Bill Buckner (Sagittarius): There may be a scene to end all scenes . . . and one particular relationship may never be the same again. But personally, emotionally and professionally everything must be laid on the line."

◆

During Game Three of the 1933 World Series, a blue pigeon landed on the infield at Washington. Watching from the press box, Babe Ruth immediately recognized the bird. During each Yankee visit that summer, it had accompanied him in right field. Senators' fans considered it something of a good luck charm.

Giants infielders tried to shoo the bird away, but it defied the visitors, hopping ten yards out of anybody's reach. Finally they gave up and played the game with the bird dodging ground balls and pecking at the grass. Washington proceeded to win Game Three.

During Game Four, the pigeon arrived before the first pitch. Washington and New York remained tied at 1–1 through nine innings. When the pigeon disappeared, the Senators lost in eleven innings.

During Game Five, the pigeon was not sighted through the first seven innings. Washington and New York were tied at 3–3,

but the Giants threatened with one out in the eighth. Suddenly the pigeon landed on the infield. On the next pitch, New York shortstop Travis Jackson grounded into a double play.

After the double play, the pigeon disappeared. In the tenth, Mel Ott's home run won the World Series for the Giants.

◆

In the fall of 1929, an editor at a Havana newspaper came up with a terrific idea: a World Series contest that would award winners all-expense-paid trips to the United States to see the "fall classic."

By late September, the Cubs and Athletics had secured pennants. Meanwhile down in Havana, the newspaper announced its twenty-two winners. On the afternoon of September 29, the lucky twenty-two fans boarded the ocean liner *Siboney* and embarked on their journey to the series, scheduled to commence on October 8 at Wrigley Field.

That evening, while the winning Cubans were out to sea and steaming north, officials at the newspaper were overcome with a sickening realization. They had taken care of transportation, rooms, and expenses, but had forgotten to secure tickets to the games.

Frantically, they contacted team officials in Chicago and Philadelphia. Like anybody requesting twenty-two World Series tickets a week before Game One, they were told the awful truth: sorry, all sold out.

◆

Before Dodger Kirk Gibson beat the Athletics in Game One of the 1988 World Series, Dusty Rhodes was the only man in baseball history to grab a bat, pinch-hit in the bottom of the ninth inning or later of a World Series game, and clout a game-winning home run. The day after Gibson's blast against Oakland reliever Dennis Eckersley, Rhodes could tell Gibson what to expect for the rest of his life.

"They will never, ever, let him forget that," said Rhodes, the former Giants outfielder, then age sixty-one and working a tugboat in New York harbor. "Never in a hundred years. Never, ever, ever. No matter how many times he strikes out, all they'll remember is that home run."

Rhodes's unforgettable home run came in Game One of the 1954 World Series. In the eighth inning, Willie Mays had made his astonishing over-the-shoulder catch of Vic Wertz's 460-foot blast to center field. In the bottom of the tenth, New York and Cleveland were still tied, 2–2, with Giants on first and second, and one out.

Rhodes was sitting on the bench, steaming at manager Leo Durocher. "I was still kind of mad at the time," drawled Rhodes, Alabama accent intact despite thirty-five years in New York. "Last game of the season in Philadelphia, Leo said, 'The starting lineup tonight is the starting lineup in the World Series.' I played that night.

"So next day is an off-day, and we're working out at the Polo Grounds. I'm hitting in the cage, with all the newsmen around. They said, 'Starting lineup come over here for pictures.' I said, 'I'll be with you in a minute.' They said, 'Stay where you are, you ain't playing.' Next day during the game, I was still fuming."

In the tenth inning of Game Two, Durocher told him to pinch-hit for Monte Irvin against Indians righty Bob Lemon.

"My intention was to take the first pitch," said Rhodes. "But he hung me a curve. It looked like a balloon up there. So I took a swing and the wind caught it."

It plopped into the short right-field stands at the Polo Grounds and into baseball history. "I can still see Dave Pope jumping for it out there," said Rhodes. "Wertz hit one 460 feet, and Mays caught it. I hit one 250 feet, and I'm a hero for forty years. I turned around and looked at Bob Lemon, and he'd thrown his glove into the stands. It went further than my home run did."

The home run carried Rhodes deep into baseball lore. "I still get three or four letters a week from people looking for me to sign, and they include, 'Congratulations on your home run,'" said Rhodes. "I heard Howard Cosell report once it was the cheapest home run ever. I'll tell you one thing: my home run stayed in the air longer than his television show stayed on the air."

Rhodes proceeded to tilt the series from the bench. In Game Two he tied the game with a pinch single, then stayed in the lineup and homered in his next at-bat. In Game Three he pinch-hit and singled with the bases loaded.

"Once in a while when you're down in the dumps, you think about it and it picks you up," said Rhodes. "I've got a film of that World Series. I showed it just the other day."

To whom did he show it? "To me," he said.

WINTER

On the last day of baseball season, ballplayers take showers, get dressed, stuff cardboard boxes, and linger a little longer in the locker room. They pause, like men just finished with an eight-month assignment. If the season was especially glorious, some stay in uniform to nurse beer and bathe with champagne, hours after the last out, clinging to summer for a few final moments. Addresses and telephone numbers are exchanged, hands are shaken, backs are slapped, and farewells are delivered. No one asks anyone to sign his yearbook, but otherwise they part like students leaving for summer vacation.

Ballplayers scatter to winter vacation, also known as the off-season. It is the baseball man's precious time to unwind for four months without the structure of a team or the encumbrance of a relentless schedule. Even if a ballplayer loves the job, he welcomes the respite from fans, baseball writers, managers, owners, and nasty curveballs with the bases loaded.

The archives show ballplayers have devoted their break to a wide variety of endeavors. Some relaxed, some worked, some picked at shriveled fruit cups on the banquet circuit, and some ate and drank until they were incredible balls of flab. The original concept of spring training came to Chicago manager Cap Anson when he noticed his charges had developed generous beer bellies over the winter.

A common subject of winter lore is hunting. In his off-seasons, Athletics manager Tony La Russa lectures on the college circuit about animal rights. Baseball men more commonly spend their off-seasons shooting at the critters.

To the average ballplayer, outdoorsy off-season fun has always held a natural attraction. In the days before Nautilus workouts, old-timers thought long hikes through the woods were a good way to stay in shape. Many were old country boys; some were city boys such as Babe Ruth. All enjoyed getting away from the hustle of their summer addresses, such as St. Louis, Chicago, or New York, to

Dizzy Dean, Branch Rickey, and Frankie Frisch (left to right)

the quiet woods, where they could crunch through snow and leaves and chew tobacco. Winter editions of the newspapers included photographs of familiar ballplayers in unfamiliar garb, such as huge field coats, toting shotguns or rifles, and posing with jowly hunting hounds. Sometimes they posed with the carcass of a beast unlucky enough to wander into the crosshairs of men with fabulous hand-eye coordination.

The call of the wild endures. Ballplayers can test themselves in the woods and fields with no pressure to perform, unless they hunt for dinner. No sports-writers second-guess them. Squirrels, chipmunks, and other spectators don't boo.

The only plays that make the big city papers are near-death experiences. Much winter lore centers around mishaps in the woods, such as the time Branch Rickey nearly had his head blown off by his grandson's shotgun, or the time a vigilant dog saved baseball when he scared off a poisonous snake about to strike the Babe.

Some ballplayers cleared their cluttered heads without firing a shot or setting foot in the woods. For some the reward was getting home, where the townsfolk didn't ask for autographs and where neighbors still yelled about the windows broken with baseballs thrown long ago.

An often told story, applied to various players of several generations, detailed the time the famous World Series superhero returned to his sleepy small town and bumped into an old man on Main Street. "Say, Joe," said the old man, "haven't seen you around for a while. Been away?"

Most wanted the old neighborhood to treat them with just such a lack of fanfare. When Yankees pitcher Red Ruffing came home one winter, the Nokomis, Illinois, town fathers requested permission to put his name on a banner strung across Main Street, hyping the town as the home of the great Red Ruffing. When Ruffing refused, the town fathers asked why. "I might move," Ruffing shrugged.

In the old days when money was short, ballplayers often hurried straight into other jobs once the season was over. They signed on for any sort of occupation, from fixing cars to selling sporting goods to making absolute fools of themselves in vaudeville shows. Modern players make more money on the memorabilia and card show circuit, where they are required to sign their names but not to sing, dance, and tell bad jokes.

Another popular off-season occupation for ballplayers was baseball. Some played to see the world; off-season tours to far-flung places like Australia, Japan, and France were common. Some played for fun. Many played for a few extra dollars. Sometimes the ancients hooked up with semipro or town teams on a per diem basis. Often they made better money with traveling teams. Two notable barnstormers were Cardinals pitcher Dizzy Dean and the greatest attraction of them all, Babe Ruth.

The famous big leaguers toured the backwoods and played any local nine that cared to take them on. There was no color line on the off-season tour, and many stories from winter lore painfully illustrate the tragedy and shame of baseball's Jim Crow era. Dean was beaten by the Negro Leagues' great Satchel Paige in several classic duels. Yankees slugger Joe DiMaggio batted against Paige one winter and declared him the best pitcher he had ever faced.

Winter ball still thrives in the Caribbean, Mexico, and in South America. Big leaguers use the Latin leagues the way a student uses summer school. Most are fledgling players trying to collect extra experience, learn a new position, or shake old demons. Winter ball means island paradises, a huge language barrier, and occasional political intrigue.

Often players return with tales of the bizarre. When he was a young Red Sox outfielder, Brady Anderson spent a winter season in Mexico and saw a groundskeeper try to dry a rain-soaked diamond by pouring gasoline on it, ending up setting the field on fire.

"A lot of guys would try to leave, but they couldn't get out of the country," said Red Sox manager Joe Morgan, a veteran of Caribbean winter ball from his years managing in the Pirates' system. "They'd just get sick of it. But they couldn't get out because the club owners had all the visas. Some went even as far as to wire home asking someone to send a telegram saying that Mother had died. But the club owners would know it was a fake, because they saw the original request, too. They read everybody's mail."

Each year, from John McGraw to Fred McGriff, when the middle of February arrives, pitchers and catchers pack gear for spring training and can't believe the off-season flew by like a fastball. Like students going back to school, they return to their lockers amazed at how swiftly the break passed. They also return with stories: what I did on my winter vacation.

One afternoon before a game in the summer of 1936, Cubs coach Charley O'Leary was in the dugout telling a few of the boys about the old days of vaudeville, where many ballplayers found winter work. "Well, I'll tell you the worst act ever seen on the stage," O'Leary said. "It was Germany Schaefer and Nick Altrock. They sang like bullfrogs, those fellows. They rehearsed in a wine room in the back of a saloon."

During the act, Detroit second baseman Schaefer and White Sox pitcher Altrock told jokes, or at least what they tried to pass as jokes:

Altrock: "I was down your way last night and your house was all lighted up."

Schaefer: "Why didn't you come in?"

Altrock: "I didn't know where you lived. (Pause.) Say, I saw your brother looking out the window."

Schaefer: "Yes, he looks out for the whole family."

O'Leary shook his head in disgust as he repeated the lines. "When they got on the stage, Germany Schaefer was wearing a bird cage on his head with a canary in it," he said. "Just murder. That's what it was."

Someone asked O'Leary, a former Tigers shortstop, if he ever appeared onstage to make a few dollars in the winter. "Almost," he said.

After the Tigers won the World Series in 1907, O'Leary was set to receive five hundred dollars to join Schaefer and Altrock on the tour. Tigers owner Frank Navin heard about it and summoned O'Leary. Rather than see another of his players wear a bird cage in public, he offered to tack on five hundred dollars to O'Leary's 1908 contract in exchange for a promise to stay out of vaudeville.

◆

In mid-December 1935, up-and-coming Red Sox outfielder Art ("Skinny") Graham stopped by the team's offices at Fenway Park. Boston general manager Eddie Collins delivered a big-league pep talk to Graham, the kind of off-season boost he thought might perk the young player's confidence.

"Skinny, never saw you look so good," Collins said. "You're going to have a fine year this coming season for the Red Sox. You have all the qualifications. You can run as well as anybody on our club. You can

Joe DiMaggio and teammates celebrate his record-setting hitting streak.

field brilliantly. Your throwing arm is strong. And you should be able to hit as well as anybody on the squad.

"I've seen enough of you right here in Boston with the Red Sox to be convinced you have the ability to make the big-league grade. If you have half the ability your minor-league manager, Nemo Leibold, promised you have, you'll be all set as a regular under the big top.

"Yes, sir, Skinny, there's a job awaiting you with the Red Sox next year. You ought to be able to carve yourself a place there. We've got nobody with any more talent than you have. You've got the speed, the power, the patience, and the eye. Now go out there and make good!"

Graham never played another inning in the big leagues.

◆

When he returned home to Kansas City after his first big-league season in 1912, outfielder Casey Stengel was of-

fered fifteen dollars to play in an exhibition game against the Senators' great pitcher, Walter Johnson. Stengel had batted .316 in seventeen games with the Brooklyn Dodgers and was convinced he was one of the greatest hitters in the game. "It isn't the fifteen dollars," Stengel said when he accepted the offer. "I want to hit against Walter Johnson."

Stengel eagerly traveled to Coffeyville, Kansas, where the game was the centerpiece of a gala homecoming bash for Johnson. First time up against the Big Train, Stengel swung at and missed three straight pitches. Next time up, Stengel told himself, "I won't swing so hard at this man, I'll just try to meet the ball." Swinging softly, Stengel again completely missed three straight pitches.

Third time up, Stengel tried to break Johnson's spell with a bunt. He bunted at and completely missed three straight

Nick Altrock

Eddie Collins (left) *and Connie Mack*

pitches. Fourth time up, Stengel hit the first pitch for a long foul to the opposite field. Then he completely missed the next two pitches.

Milling round the festivities after the game, Stengel was approached by several strangers who said, in all sincerity, "So you're that great man they were talking about in 'Casey at the Bat.'"

◆

On January 25, 1926, Washington outfielder Goose Goslin visited his pal, magistrate Edward J. Carney, in Philadelphia. The judge invited the ballplayer to the courthouse and asked if he'd like to sit with him on the bench as he heard the day's cases.

"All right," said Goslin. "But don't ask me to fine anybody. I'm opposed to fines."

"I'll tell you what to do," said Carney. "Just watch for my signals."

The first case was a drunk and disorderly charge. The accused was still slightly

drunk. "What do you say, ump?" the judge asked Goslin.

"He's out," Goslin said. The judge hammered his gavel, and the grateful, drunken man stumbled out of the courtroom.

For the next hour, the accused—charged with offenses that ranged from dice playing to carrying a pocket flask—appeared before Carney and Goslin. One by one, all sixty-four were set free.

"What's the best idea you got from your experience?" the judge asked Goslin when the docket was clear.

"That there is a train back to Washington pretty soon," said Goslin. "This league isn't fast enough for me."

◆

During off-seasons in the early part of the century, big leaguers commonly moonlighted on town teams in America's backwoods. To the locals, the games were as good as big league. More than allegiance rode on the outcome. Townsfolk loved their teams with such intensity they often wagered entire paychecks on them.

"I never saw a region where there was such an intense rivalry between towns except out in Idaho, back around 1906 or 1907," Washington pitcher Walter Johnson once recalled. "If you were indiscreet enough to walk up to a pool table in Emmett and casually drop a word of praise for the Caldwell pitcher, your widow would stand a fair chance of collecting, and the Emmett coroner would probably put it down as suicide."

In his first visit to Caldwell, Johnson pitched for the Weiser, Idaho, team. Throughout the early innings, a Caldwell fan heckled the Weiser first baseman, who heckled back. By the third inning, Caldwell was losing and the verbal war between the first baseman and the fan escalated into violence. The spectator charged down the

Washington's Tom Zachary, Fred ("Firpo") Marberry, Alex Ferguson, and Walter Johnson (left to right)

grandstand, tore through a wire screen that separated the seats from the field, and tackled the Weiser first baseman. Players from both teams converged on the scene, and a battle raged.

When order was restored, the Weiser first baseman and manager were placed under arrest. The Caldwell crowd was delighted, but only for a moment. Soon the fans realized the game could not continue with the Weiser first baseman in custody; there were no bench players. The crowd stirred angrily over the prospect of the game being called off after three innings, with the home team behind.

"But there it was," remembered Johnson. "The men were under arrest and had to be held for a hearing. Then some inspired genius got the idea of rushing off and locating the justice of the peace."

The genius found the town deserted and the courthouse closed. Everybody was at the game, where the justice of the peace was quickly located in the grandstand, hollering with the rest for the game to resume. The situation was explained, and the justice of the peace conducted court on the infield. A hearing was held, bail was set, and a bond was given for the Weiser first baseman and manager to appear in court. "All in less than ten minutes," said Johnson. "After this striking example of Idaho efficiency, the game went on."

◆

During an off-season trip through Japan, Boston Braves shortstop Rabbit Maranville secretly soaped the favorite bat of Philadelphia slugger Al Simmons. In

Goose Goslin

his first trip to the plate, Simmons fouled off a series of pitches, eventually struck out, returned to the bench, and smashed his ex-favorite bat to splinters.

Later in the tour, Maranville couldn't help telling his teammates about his plan to slip into the ranks and march with the Japanese army as it passed on its parade route past the team hotel that afternoon. Simmons, who had been tipped off about the soap prank and its perpetrator, anonymously informed the Japanese authorities, who arrested Maranville moments after he joined the parade.

Freed a few hours later, Maranville went to the ballpark and attempted to teach his trademark vest-pocket basket catch to Jap-

anese players, who then spent the afternoon getting conked on their foreheads with baseballs.

◆

Smoking a fat cigar and lounging in a deep chair in a Cooperstown hotel lobby on the morning of Carl Yastrzemski's induction into the Hall of Fame, former Red Sox coach Eddie Popowski bubbled with memories. One of them was about the time he, Yaz, and Red Sox outfielder Reggie Smith embarked on a pheasant hunting trip on Long Island.

"Opening day of hunting season was on a Holy Day," said Popowski. "The season started that morning, so we decided to go to 7:30 mass, then go hunting. We got to the church, but mass didn't start on time. It was about fifteen minutes late and didn't get finished until almost 8:30.

"On the way out, the priest was greeting everybody at the door. Yaz went up to him and said something about mass being late. He said, 'Father, don't you know it's opening day of hunting season?'

"The priest said, 'I know it's hunting season. I bagged my limit this morning. That's why mass started fifteen minutes late.'"

◆

In late April 1988 the Red Sox slogged through a road trip that encountered rainy, cold weather at each stop. After yet another postponed game in Chicago, the clubhouse conversation turned to bad-weather baseball. Red Sox pitching coach Bill Fischer reported how it was sometimes easier to play a game in Wisconsin in the dead of winter than in Chicago in the middle of spring.

"They play snowshoe softball in Wisconsin," said Fischer. "They play it on a frozen lake with softballs painted red. And everybody wears snowshoes. They get a few thousand people to watch. They park their cars around the lake and sell hot dogs. I never played it, but I watched it. Funnier than hell. Guy hits one deep, the outfielder can't get to it on snowshoes. Guy who hit it can't get to second on snowshoes, either."

◆

During his first two years in professional baseball, Casey Stengel devoted his off-season to studying dentistry at Western Dental College in Kansas City.

"I'll never forget the dissecting class at the dental school," Stengel once recalled. "The work was naturally very serious, but once in a while fellows would fool around with those bodies when nobody was looking, and the first thing you knew you'd find an extra thumb in your pocket."

One time Stengel went straight from school to visit a long-time pal, Harold Lederman, whose father owned a cigar store in Kansas City. Stengel met Lederman at the store, shook hands, and left a severed finger in Lederman's palm.

◆

During an off-season in his hometown of Darrtown, Ohio, Dodgers manager Walter Alston was kidded hard by a hunting buddy about his poor marksmanship. One morning the two men were in the brush when they spotted a hawk perched on a nearby hill. Alston deferred to his pal, who fired. The bird didn't budge.

The shooter glanced in bewilderment at his gun, sighted again, and fired again. Again the bird didn't budge. The man kept blasting and the bird kept staring back impassively. Alston gleefully teased his pal about not even getting a shot close enough to make the critter fly away.

The hunting buddy didn't know that the night before, Alston had wired a dead hawk

in an amazingly lifelike position to a stake on the hill.

◆

In the winter of 1917, Red Sox lefty pitcher Babe Ruth—a twenty-three and twenty-four-game winner the previous two seasons—sought a raise. Tight-fisted and short-monied owner Harry Frazee refused to give him one. One cold afternoon, Ruth discussed the dilemma with sports promoter Steve Mahoney.

Mahoney came up with an idea. "Babe, with your hitting power and footwork, you're a shoo-in for big dough in the ring," he said. "Ten thousand is just prune bits in the boxing game."

Ruth was hesitant. "What if I get blinded?" he asked.

"Never mind, never mind," said Mahoney. "Do as I say."

Mahoney escorted Ruth to a Boston gym, where the Babe tapped the speed bag, shuffled through shadow boxing, and even sparred a few rounds with a few broken-down ring rats. Later that day, Mahoney telephoned Frazee and told him all about Ruth's new wintertime hobby.

"Say," Mahoney suddenly said, as if the idea just hit him. "Your meal ticket is apt to wind up in the psycho ward if some pug belts him on the button."

Frazee grabbed a taxi and hurried to Ruth's quarters at the Putnam Hotel, where he gave the ballplayer a lecture about hazardous off-season pursuits. He also gave him a raise.

◆

During the 1930s in Chester, Pennsylvania, competition among volunteer fire departments was intense. They raced hard to be first at the scene of a fire, and after the blaze was extinguished they customarily turned their hoses on one an-

Danny Murtaugh

other. Among the toughest and proudest volunteer stations was the Franklin Fire Company in the Seventh Ward, whose youngest and most gung-ho volunteer was twenty-one-year-old Danny Murtaugh, who spent his summers playing minor-league baseball.

In the middle of the night one winter, Murtaugh was asleep in his apartment when the Franklin Fire Company alarm sounded. According to the rules, the first man to reach the firehouse got to wear the assistant foreman's coat. Murtaugh leaped from his bed and hurried down the stairs two at a time, chasing visions of the coveted coat.

He burst out a back door, sprinted through a maze of back alleys, clambered over a series of fences, and arrived wheezing at the firehouse. He was first.

Proudly wearing the assistant foreman's coat, Murtaugh jumped on the back of the fire truck as it roared out of the garage. He regained his breath as the truck clanged down the streets of Chester to the fire, which blazed at a house across the street from his apartment.

◆

Besides hockey, snowplowing, and bowling, over the years the favorite off-season pastime for Red Sox manager Joe Morgan was pheasant hunting. "I've done it since about 1945," said Morgan just after Thanksgiving 1988. "But this year I got nothing again. First I went to the World Series. Then I went to Toledo for a wedding. And then I went to Ireland. So I only went out hunting about four times."

With Morgan on the prowl, the pheasants strolled the woods with impunity. "None," he said, when asked how many of the birds he bagged that season. "My son got two. I haven't had too many over the years. I'm one of the worst shots in .12-gauge history."

His most memorable expedition? "This is a true story," he began. "I was out hunting and the pheasant stood up in front of me. So I put the gun up to shoot, and the son of a gun just fell right over. I didn't fire a shot. I went over to look at him, and he was deader than a doornail. He must have had a heart attack. When I cleaned him, there wasn't a pellet mark or a scratch on him at all."

◆

When he faced barnstorming teams of white major leaguers, the Negro Leagues' great pitcher Satchel Paige liked to feign obsequiousness, just to make the payoff a little more enjoyable. For instance, one off-season afternoon Paige engaged the barnstorming Dizzy Dean All-Stars, which included the famous slugging Cardinal outfielder Pepper Martin.

Like any baseball fan in America, Paige knew exactly who Martin was. But as the first batter stepped to the plate, Satchel asked, "Are you Mr. Martin?"

When the second batter stepped up, he asked, "Are you Mr. Martin?"

Martin finally came to bat. "Are you Mr. Martin?" asked Paige. Martin grinned and swung his bat.

"Mr. Pepper Martin?" Paige persisted. Martin smiled wider.

"They tell me you kin hit," said Paige. He paused. "Then hit this."

He struck out Martin on three pitches.

◆

On February 8, 1906, several New York Giants and other ballplayers were scheduled to attend a banquet in upstate Troy, New York. That morning, the ballplayers and several of their cronies boarded a train in New York City bound for Albany.

Trouble started soon after the train pulled out of Poughkeepsie. Many of the players, notably Giants center fielder Turkey Mike Donlin, began to show signs of spirited drinking. Taking virtual control of the compartments, the boys playfully began to hurl baseballs, empty bottles, and luggage around the car. When a conductor arrived on the scene and demanded order, Donlin punched him in the face; when a porter arrived to help his colleague, Donlin drew a pistol and pointed it at him. As several frightened passengers scattered, more level-headed members of the party persuaded Donlin to surrender the gun.

Alerted by the conductor by telegraph, Albany police waited for the train at the next station. Donlin, Southern League pitcher Walter Bennett, and another man were placed under arrest. Giants second baseman Billy Gilbert, third baseman Art

Leroy ("Satchel") Paige and friend.

Devlin, pitcher Hooks Wiltse, and two other minor leaguers were set free.

Not wanting to proceed to the banquet without their incarcerated chums, the ballplayers hunted for bail money. They appealed to members of the New York legislature, who convinced several local sportsmen to bail out the jailed Giants. All made it to the banquet in time for the opening speech.

◆

On October 21, 1924, the White Sox, Giants, and other big leaguers arrived in London on the first stop of their off-season European baseball tour. The British press got its first look at real live American ballplayers.

"I expected a gang of huskies, a bunch of toughs with a Bowery accent and an Apache slouch," one newsman wrote. "Instead, I met eighteen clear-eyed American university graduates, shy as a bevy of schoolgirls. 'Why are you like this?' I asked in disgust. 'You've ruined my report. England expects you to chew gum and talk like O. Henry.' I then learned that financially it is much better to be a first-class pitcher on the White Sox than prime minister of England, and it is a much safer job, too."

Another told his readers, "The umpire wears a mattress and head shield and is thrown at principally by the visiting crowd. The pitcher gets so much money that he could employ Rockefeller to put oil in his car. The duty of the rooter is to tell the other side their shortcomings as public entertainers."

Two days later, the teams staged their first exhibition at the Everton football grounds in Liverpool. Chicago won, 16–11. After the game, Braves first baseman Stuffy McInnis was explaining the finer points of baserunning to a fan when a souvenir hunter snatched his glove. All in all, the Britons complained about the noise, the pace, and the high score of the American pastime. The ballplayers complained about the damp British turf, which they termed "not adaptable at all for sliding."

◆

Hungry for entertainment one winter day, Cubs pitcher Pat Malone went to see the Cubs' vaudeville quartet, consisting of outfielders Kiki Cuyler, Cliff Heathcote, and Hack Wilson and catcher Gabby Hartnett. Malone expected the worst. Years later he recalled, "Well, I knew Heathcote could sing and Cuyler wasn't bad. But Hack and Gabby, all they could do was roar like lions. I went to see just how bad they'd be."

Malone watched the show and was astonished. "They were great," he said. "I couldn't figure it at all. Harmony and everything. Great." Malone went backstage to congratulate the singing ballplayers,

where he discovered the secret of their success: two professional singers hidden under the stage during the performance and lots of lip-synching. "Hack and Gabby were phonies," said Malone. "They just opened their big mouths, and the two guys under the platform did their singing for them. I knew there was a catch."

◆

In the winter of 1926, Cubs catcher Mike Gonzalez and a number of big-league ballplayers toured Mexico. They greatly enjoyed the cultural experience and the off-season baseball experience, but most of all they treasured the generous paychecks.

In the 1927 off-season, Gonzalez and his men returned for more hardball south of the border. One afternoon in November, the American ballplayers lounged around the ball park. Next day was payday. As the boys discussed the various grand plans they had for their first checks, suddenly a troop of Mexican soldiers stormed onto the premises. The soldiers explained to the ballplayers that the team paymaster was suspected of having rebel sympathies. They dragged him out, propped him against a nearby wall, hastily formed a firing squad, and executed him.

For once completely forgetting about their paychecks, the ballplayers left the park. Soon they all bumped into one another at the train station, where they caught the next departure for San Antonio. "No more Mexico," said Gonzalez upon arriving in the States.

◆

Detroit manager Hughie ("Ee-yah") Jennings was a notorious bench jockey, but when they really wanted to shut him up fast, opposing players knew exactly what to say. They merely yelled back, "How tumultuous and controversial season.

"Babe," Walker said as the crowd listened, "a kid just stopped me on the street and asked me for a dime. He wanted to make up a quarter and buy a Babe Ruth cap. Don't you think you owe something to that kid and others like him?"

Close to tears brought on by either emotion or cigar smoke, Ruth made his own speech. "I know as well as anybody else just what mistakes I made last season," he said. "Getting suspended for six weeks, throwing dust at an umpire, climbing into the stands after a fan, and other things. There's no use in me trying to get away from these things. But let me tell you something. I want to tell the New York newspapers and the fans that I've had my last drink until the middle of October."

◆

Besides drinking, chasing women, and riding fire engines, Philadelphia Athletics pitcher Rube Waddell enjoyed acting. One off-season at the height of his stage career, Waddell was the star of a melodramatic vaudeville play entitled *The Stain of Guilt*. In the show he was required to save the girl and slug the villain.

One problem was that Waddell punched his fellow actors with such dazzling realism that the producers had to rotate villains. No one actor could withstand more than three consecutive performances, which meant three consecutive punches, in one day. Before long, the problem solved itself. One night without explanation, Waddell deserted *The Stain of Guilt*. He resurfaced tending bar in Camden, New Jersey.

◆

After the 1913 World Series, many of the world-champion Athletics, the National League-champion Giants, and a

Hughie Jennings

deep was the water?"

The deadly wisecrack referred to an incident years earlier when Jennings brought the Tigers to Cornell University, his alma mater, for an off-season exhibition game. The players dressed in a locker room near the indoor pool, and after the game Jennings thought a swim would be a great idea. He threw on his trunks, raced from the dressing room, bounded onto the spring board, executed a nifty swan dive, and nearly executed himself. There was no water in the pool.

◆

On November 13, 1922, Yankees slugger Babe Ruth attended a banquet in New York and quickly felt he would soon get sent to his room without dessert. Taking his turn addressing the crowd, New York state senator Jimmy Walker, later the New York mayor, scolded Ruth about his

The home run king celebrated another birthday in style.

number of other big leaguers and their families set off for an off-season tour of the Far East. From the start of the journey aboard the steamship *Empress of Japan,* many realized they would have been better off to have stayed home and gone bowling. As the ship eased away from her berth in Victoria, British Columbia, umpire Jack Sheridan hopped atop a lifeboat, waved wildly back to the handkerchief-waving well-wishers on shore, and lost his false teeth overboard.

During one of the many storms the ship encountered on the high seas, Giants pitcher Hooks Wiltse was being tossed around his cabin when his steamer trunk broke loose, sailed across the room, and crushed his pitching hand. Another member of the baseball party, Harry Burchell, was reading in the ship's library when a wave crashed through the window,

knocked him off the couch, and flooded the room with two feet of water.

Seasickness was a major problem. White Sox pitcher Red Faber and Tigers outfielder Wahoo Sam Crawford spent most of the journey in their cabins. Others spent it gripping railings and leaning over the side. Giants manager John McGraw lost twenty pounds.

When weather permitted, which was seldom, players pulled on uniforms and worked out on the promenade deck, which was enclosed by a net. As the pitchers threw, members of the British crew watched. Among the fascinated was Capt. W. Dixon Hopcraft, who had thought curveballs were a myth, a bit of the "usual American bunk," until he saw one with his own eyes.

When the weather was bad, which was often, players devised ways to work out below decks. A top innovator was Giants outfielder Jim Thorpe, who taught the others how to skip rope, wrestle, and box to stay in shape. A favorite workout was "horse" racing in the dining salon. The favorite horses, who had to gallop through the dining area on hands and knees, were Thorpe, Washington second baseman Germany Schaefer, and St. Louis outfielder Steve Evans. The favorite rider was six-year-old Dan Callahan, son of White Sox manager Nixey Callahan.

By the time the ship approached Yokohama, many aboard had already booked their return trip via the trans-Siberia railroad to Paris.

◆

O n the afternoon before the annual Boston Baseball Writers' banquet in January 1989, Red Sox left fielder Mike Greenwell fielded questions at the affair's press conference. Greenwell entertained questions about his off-season workout, his contract, his place in Boston's left-field tradition, and his goals for the upcoming summer. After fifteen minutes of questions and answers, Greenwell prepared to surrender the podium. He asked if there were any other questions.

From the back of the room came an inquiry. "Mike," a bearded man called out, "is there any pitch you can't hit?"

Greenwell peered to the back of the room and smiled when he saw who was asking: Twins ace reliever Jeff Reardon. Always anxious to help opposing pitchers, Greenwell quickly issued a response. "Yeah," he said to Reardon, so the pitcher could file it away for the summer, "that one right down the middle."

◆

With three weeks left in the 1911 season, Athletics pitchers Jack Coombs, Chief Bender, and Cy Morgan had signed to tour with the Pearl Sisters in a vaudeville act called "Learning the Game," which required the players to sing, dance, and wear their uniforms on stage. Morgan was known as the Minstrel of the Diamond, with much off-season theatre experience. Coombs was said to have acting potential. Bender's top theatrical asset was his smile.

In Game Three of the World Series, Coombs out-dueled Giants great Christy Mathewson in an eleven-inning masterpiece. When he returned to his Somerset Hotel room in New York that evening, he found two men waiting for him. Coombs was certain of trouble, but the men made an offer. They were vaudeville agents, and now that Coombs was a big World Series hero they wanted him to sign on with them and break away from the Pearl Sisters.

◆

On February 28, 1932, Ed Morris enjoyed his last day of the off-season before departing for the Red Sox' spring training camp in Savannah, Georgia. A six-foot, two-inch right-handed pitcher, Big Ed

had won nineteen games for the 1928 Red Sox, prompting the Yankees to offer fifty thousand dollars and two ballplayers for him. Tired of peddling their best to New York, Boston declined. A sore arm and a lazy work ethic rendered Morris less successful during the next three years, but on the eve of the 1932 season he was optimistic. He had spent the winter hunting and fishing in the woods near his Flomaton, Alabama, home and was in top physical condition.

The night before he was scheduled to leave, Morris was treated to what had become an annual going-away party. Across the state line in Florida, Morris, seven of his friends, and a never determined number of women gathered near Escambia Creek for a fish fry in the ballplayer's honor. The bashers frolicked into the night with the usual eating, drinking, and carousing.

No one was quite sure how it started, but an argument flared between Morris and his friend Joe White, a Brewton, Alabama, filling station owner. The argument led to shoves, which led to punches. Morris swung wildly at White, missed, tumbled to the ground, and rolled onto his back. White pounced on the pitcher, whipped out a pocket knife, and stabbed him twice in the chest. Two other party-goers were slightly cut when they tried to subdue White. Gravely wounded and losing large amounts of blood, Morris broke away from his friends and dived into a stream in a wild attempt to swim home. Pulled from the water, the guest of honor was transported to a hospital, where he died three days later.

◆

During an off-season barnstorming match one winter, big-league catcher Paul Richards stepped to the plate to bat against the Negro Leagues' legend, Satchel Paige. Richards was curious about the famous Paige and told himself to take the

Josh Gibson

first pitch so he could get a look at the man's stuff.

Paige delivered a sidearm pitch that blurred across the outside edge of the plate. "I never even saw the ball, it went by so fast," Richards recalled years later. As Richards stood in silence, stunned by the velocity of the pitch, catcher Josh Gibson shouted out to Paige. "Satchmo," he admonished. "When I want that change-up pitch, I'll call for it. Now you start pitching and bring that fastball of yours in to me."

◆

In pre-World War II off-seasons, many prominent ballplayers migrated to Hot Springs, Arkansas, to warm up for spring training. Their regimen included lots of golf, nightlife, mountain climbing, and bathing in the therapeutic waters. Some of the boys, however, severely frowned upon one activity: baseball. Legend says a group

of Yankees and Indians once were preparing to depart Hot Springs for their respective training camps when a Cleveland player, digging through his bag, let out a yowl.

"Gosh," he said. "I must have left my spiked shoes at the ballpark."

"What?" the Yankees said in chorus. "Is there a ballpark in this town?"

Yankee pitcher Urban Shocker once brought along a dozen baseballs to Hot Springs. One morning Shocker convinced catcher Wally Schang to play catch with him in a vacant lot along the main drag near the hotel. Driving past in a big car were Yankees slugger Babe Ruth and second baseman Mike McNally, their golf bags in the back seat. Both men were smoking big cigars. "Stop the car!" shouted Ruth when he spotted Shocker and Schang throwing a ball back and forth. Ruth motioned a pedestrian, who was a local resident, over to the car.

"Who are those fellows?" asked the Babe.

"Ballplayers," said the pedestrian.

"What?" bellowed Ruth. "Common ballplayers? This place is going to the dogs. To the country club, James, and make it snappy!"

"As for you, Shocker," McNally shouted as he put the car in gear, "you're suspended from the Whist Bridge Club for conduct unbecoming a gentleman."

During his off-season visits to Hot Springs, Ruth developed his lifelong love of golf. Dressed in several layers of sweaters and wearing his cap backward, the Babe would start just after dawn and customarily hack out fifty-four holes before dinner. Fairways at the Hot Springs course were lined by thick woods, and in the early days Ruth was known to spend hours whacking foliage. His game improved in later years, although his demeanor on the links did not. When he topped a drive, Ruth was known to shout expletives in-

An estimated 500,000 cheering fans turned out to cheer Babe Ruth when he toured Japan in 1934 (Over-exposed spots on the photograph were caused by exploding fireworks).

Wally Schang

stead of "Fore." When he sliced balls off the course, the woods and hills were alive with the sound of Ruthian curses. Witnesses said they could sit on the clubhouse porch and follow Ruth's progress around the course by ear.

◆

Two weeks after the finish of the 1912 World Series, ballplaying on Sunday—illegal at the time—was rampant on the sandlots of New York City. A Harlem police inspector directed his men to crack down on Sabbath hardball. On Sunday, October 28, Gotham's men in blue raided the diamonds.

Arrests were made at Olympic Park and at the Lenox Oval. More than two dozen illicit ballplayers were hauled in front of the magistrate at the Harlem courthouse. Among those arrested were Washington second baseman Germany Schaefer, Giants pitcher Louis Drucke, Giants outfielder Josh Devore, Yankees first baseman Hal Chase, Washington pitcher Nick Altrock, and former Giants outfielder Cy Seymour. The ballplayers claimed ignorance of blue laws banning baseball. They were each fined five dollars, a price they were happy to pay for love of the pastime.

◇ 16 ◇

BALLPLAYERS

Chuck Connors was lucky. In the late 1950s, the square-jawed actor portrayed Lucas McCain in the popular television western "The Rifleman." All grown up, he was getting good money to fire toy guns, ride horses, and chase bad guys, just like a little boy. A red-blooded American could ask for only one fantasy better.

"Just give me a baseball uniform, a set of spikes, a glove, a Triple–A team to play for, and a shot at the majors again," said Connors in the spring of 1987. He was sixty-five years old and thinking of his ballplaying days, which included brief, precious moments with the Brooklyn Dodgers and Chicago Cubs. "You can take the Hollywood fame, the house, everything. Just let me play baseball. That's life to me. That's beautiful. To me, playing baseball is peace."

Even a guy who played cowboys for a living remembered ballplaying as the best years of his life. Fellows lashed to suits, ties, and desks share a greater chunk of the longing. In moments of frustration, usually when a ballplayer scoots past without honoring an autograph request, fans disparage their hardball heroes with a hiss, "If you couldn't play baseball, you'd have to find real work like the rest of us." *Precisely,* smiles back the ballplayer.

"It always makes me feel tired when I hear people in the grandstands say if this or that ballplayer hadn't been lucky enough to hit or pitch a baseball, he might have been a ditch-digger," Babe Ruth once said. "Of course he might. And that goes for fellows in any other line of business. If Luisa Tetrazzini or Mary Garden hadn't had such wonderful voices, they might have been working around the house like any other woman and wanting to be taken out on Saturday night to see what's going on in the world."

Lore shows baseball players fell in love with baseball like the rest of us.

They played catch with their fathers, sneaked into the ballparks, kept bubblegum cards in a shoebox, and mimicked favorite players. Unlike the rest of us, their imitations came to resemble the real thing. When time came for everybody to go inside and get to work, they were allowed to stay out and play.

The average man keeps in touch with childhood through baseball. The ballplayer, if he knows what's good for him, embraces childhood every day he goes to work. If he stays in shape, a ballplayer can keep it up into his forties.

"I'm really looking forward to this year," said first baseman Rick Lancellotti in February 1990, when he readied for his fourteenth minor-league season at age thirty-three. "I may get discouraged, and shot down, and chopped off at the head, but I will *not* under any circumstances allow myself to give up. As long as I've got a uniform, I'm still a kid."

Sometimes professional baseball feels like a job. Players contend with tremendous pressure, contract worries, grueling travel schedules, unforgiving fans, ceaseless autograph requests, and newspaper reporters who tend to make fun of them. Then the ballplayer steps up to bat or trots to the outfield, and the game is as satisfying as it was on the sandlot. At least it should be. There is no excuse for stress after a vigorous session of catch, especially when someone else will chase the balls that get away. "Ulcers," an old-timer said one day in the 1950s, shaking his head when he read about a big leaguer's stomach ailment. "Can you imagine anybody who plays baseball for a living coming down with ulcers?"

Ulcers, and worse. Ballplayers have extraordinary athletic talent but endure the same demons as men with poor reflexes. The archives are filled with stories of ballplayers who were drunks, drug addicts, wife beaters, sex offenders, cheapskates, wild spenders, overeaters, and lousy dressers. The simple pleasure of the game should ease distress, but some souls can't be soothed even by baseball. Occasionally the game drove desperate men into further desperation. Lore is spotted with examples of suicides abetted by the game. Sometimes even childhoods are miserably unhappy.

From the dead-ball era to the days of domed stadia, traits common to ballplayers are the same. They tend to be intensely competitive, moody, superstitious, individualistic, and selfish. However, the players' backgrounds are wildly diverse, even if in the 1990s they all seem to come from California. Some worked hard to master the game. Some were born masters. Some overcame squalid backgrounds to play baseball for a living, which wasn't easy when their tummies told them to get steadier work. Some were born wealthy. Many might have dug ditches if not for baseball, but some might have sung opera.

Baseball history includes ballplayers with magnificent talents outside the pastime. Red Sox legend Ted Williams was a heroic fighter pilot. Yankee infielder

Babe Ruth and entourage.

Bobby Brown became a cardiologist. Red Sox catcher Moe Berg spied on the Nazis during World War II. Ty Cobb was a shrewd businessman. Babe Ruth was a skilled shirtmaker. They stuck with the game for as long as they could because almost nobody likes to pull out of childhood before it's necessary, lest they live to regret it.

"Throwing a baseball is hard on the bow arm," violinist Malcolm Lowe, concertmaster of the Boston Symphony Orchestra, said in the spring of 1987. "The French school calls the bow arm the soul of the violinist. It's extremely sensitive. Throwing a curveball is definitely not good for it. So when I was sixteen, I decided to stop pitching. Sometimes, I tell people I wish I had tried baseball instead. If I weren't so old, I might try it now."

Old age is the ballplayer's relentless demon, and many don't fully appreciate the joy of the game until it's on the way out, or long gone. As a sportswriter observed in the 1930s, some don't say hello until it's time to say goodbye. On

Old-Timer's Day at the ballpark, ex-players return gray-headed, soft-bellied, and smiling because for a moment they're back in uniform. They tell stories of their playing days the way other men tell stories of childhood. All around them, lean, young big leaguers scowl because all those old guys clog up their clubhouse or because the lettuce was limp in the pregame salad. If they only knew.

For a ballplayer, the end comes hard. His baseball days stop some twenty years after they end for most men. Like tonsillectomies, the cutoff of innocence gets trickier as a person gets older. Sometimes ballplayers are dumped with adolescence and midlife crisis in one bundle. Not many professions begin at age seven and stop at forty. Ballplayers feel young longer, then, once they stop playing, feel older than anybody else their own age. Babe Ruth was forty when he retired from the game in June 1935, and on his way to his hotel residence from Braves Field, he cried in the car. Playing the pastime provides a grip on youth, vigor, and simple pleasure and it isn't easy to say goodbye. Few leave before the game asks them to. No one could blame a ballplayer for hanging on to the best years of his life. Why did a man like Satchel Paige play baseball until he was fifty-nine years old? Because he could. Ballplaying is even better than playing cowboy.

"I just got back from spending two weeks in Vero Beach with the Dodgers," Chuck Connors, the former television cowboy and former big leaguer, was saying in the spring of 1987 from his home in the Hollywood hills. "The tug is still there. I spent hours every day wishing I was twenty-two again with the chance to play ball."

As a lad growing up in Carnegie, Pennsylvania, in the late 1800s, Honus Wagner was expected to learn a trade and earn a living, despite his hankering for hardball. In his early teens he became an apprentice at his brother's barber shop.

His job was primarily to keep the shop tidy, dust off customers, run errands, and now and then on Saturday afternoons, perform spare shaving work. Wagner, however, also signed on as a pitcher with the town team. Often on Saturday afternoons, teammates dropped by the shop to tell him of a game that afternoon. Young Honus would slip away, play ball, then return to the shop at night to complete his chores.

One Saturday an old miner visited the shop, and Wagner was assigned to shave him. "He had a beard like a shoebrush," Wagner recalled years later. "He didn't care who shaved him."

Wagner lathered the miner's face and had shaved one side of the man's chin when he heard a whistle outside signifying his teammates were there. The miner had dozed off. Wagner stepped out.

"You got to pitch a great game today," one of the boys told him. "If we win, we're all going to get new uniforms, with letters on 'em."

Wagner excitedly hurried off to play baseball, leaving the miner half-shaved and asleep back in the barber shop. That night at home, Wagner's brother fired him.

Honus Wagner appeared in the dugout with Pittsburgh Pirates during Booster Day in 1929.

"You're finished as a barber," he said.

Recalled Wagner years later, "I was tickled."

◆

Bob Cremins pitched four games for the Red Sox in 1927. In the six decades after his brief major-league career, he coached high-school football, worked in town and county politics, commanded an attack boat during World War II, pitched batting practice for the Giants at the Polo Grounds and the Dodgers at Ebbets Field, designed boxing-ring canvasses, drew cartoons for the Philadelphia *Bulletin,* and painted portraits, which at age eighty-two he had not yet given up. "It keeps me out of trouble," he said in the fall of 1988.

Some of his best memories are of the summer of 1927 in Boston.

"I used to live on Hemenway Street and walk to the ballpark," said Cremins, a five-foot, eleven-inch, 160-pound lefty in his hurling days. "You walked everywhere then. I remember I used to come out after the game and the kids would walk with me, asking me for autographs. I would say, 'You don't want my autograph. I'm a nobody.' They'd say, 'Oh, please.' Finally they'd pester me into signing. Then they'd look at it and say, 'Who the hell is this guy?' I never got a chance to get a swelled head, thank God."

There was one thing he liked to brag about, though. "I got Babe Ruth out once, you know," he said. In 1927 Ruth was slamming sixty home runs and capturing America's imagination. On September 5, the Babe and the Yankees were clubbing the Red Sox at Fenway Park. Exasperated Boston manager Bill Carrigan looked down his bench and asked if anyone wanted to pitch. Cremins raised his hand.

The first man he faced was Ruth. Catcher Grover Hartley signaled for a fastball. A terrified Cremins heaved a pitch that barely reached the plate. Ruth swung so hard he nearly knocked himself down. The next pitch was equally weak; Ruth unleashed a mighty swing but hammered it on the ground to first baseman Phil Todt, who stepped on the bag for the out.

Back on the bench, veteran hurler Slim Harriss asked Cremins how he felt out there. "I'm still scared," Cremins said.

"Let me tell you," said Harriss, squirting tobacco juice. "The first time I pitched against the guy, I was scared, too."

Now and then he is reminded of his summer in Boston in 1927, but still doesn't get a swelled head.

"My grandson came to me the other day with a sports memorabilia book, with prices in it," Cremins said. "He said, 'Grandpa, you're in the book.' I said, 'Oh, yeah?' He said, 'Yeah. It's right here. You want to know how much your autograph is worth? Fifteen cents.' Can you imagine that?"

◆

In the mid 1950s in Mobile, Alabama, outfielder Hank Aaron would return

Joe DiMaggio, age 20, during his last year with the San Francisco Seals (1935).

from his summer work with the Milwaukee Braves and head over to the ballpark in the Toulminville section of town to reacquaint himself with old friends.

"A lot of players would be at that ballpark," Aaron said in the summer of 1987. "A lot of guys who would be away playing ball would get together there. My younger brother, Tommie, who's passed away, used to talk about those days all the time."

Aaron especially remembered two young players from the Toulminville ballpark. One was a tall, skinny first baseman named Willie McCovey. The other was a quiet, hard-hitting outfielder named Billy Williams. "I can close my eyes and see McCovey and Billy Williams playing in that ballpark," said Aaron. "The infield wasn't too smooth. In the outfield you thought you were picking up a baseball and you'd pick up cow manure. I can still see them."

Four years older than the other two and already in the big leagues, Aaron was the guy McCovey and Williams looked up to. "I think they looked up to me," said Aaron. "I think there was a friendly competition to keep up with the standards I set. More than any of us, I think Billy benefited from that competition the most. As gifted a natural ballplayer as Billy was, he taught himself a lot of things and made himself better."

The three had a lot in common. "All of us came from the same background," said Aaron. "We didn't have coaches. We didn't have baseballs. I didn't have a baseball when I was a kid. If Billy did, he didn't have many. I didn't have a baseball bat. I'm sure Willie didn't either. You're talking about growing up from nothing."

By July 1987 the three had something else in common: they were in the Hall of Fame. "I used to dream of all three of us playing on the same team," said Aaron. "But I didn't think about all three of us in the Hall of Fame. I never really thought about the Hall of Fame until Satchel Paige, who's also from Mobile, was inducted in 1971. Four Hall of Famers. I guess we've represented Mobile pretty well."

◆

On a summer evening in 1989, the two elderly men sat on the hotel veranda and gazed at the postcardlike panorama of Lake Otesaga in upstate New York. Like millions of American fathers, each had raised his son on baseball. They helped, taught, encouraged, and just plain played ball with their boys from Little League on up. The next day, the men on the porch each had a son entering baseball's Hall of Fame.

"I coached him in Little League," said Ted Bench, father of inductee Johnny. "Started him when he was seven years old. He could catch the ball and throw the ball. Not too many Little Leaguers can do that. So I put him behind the plate. I tried to show him the things I knew."

"I played with him. I played alongside

him," Carl Yastrzemski, Sr., said of his son the inductee. "When he was sixteen, we played on the same team in Bridgehampton [New York]."

In quiet moments on the eve of the induction, Ted Bench and Carl, Sr., couldn't help but remember the early days when it was just father with his son, a baseball, and a couple of gloves.

"You remember a lot of things," Yastrzemski, Sr., said of the long-ago times in Bridgehampton. "It kind of all comes to me now."

"Those days," Ted Bench said of the old days in Oklahoma, "are going through my mind a lot."

◆

As a youngster, Germany Schaefer, the one-time second baseman for the Tigers, Senators, and others, longed to join the circus. One day when the big show came to Chicago, Schaefer sought out the circus manager, begged him for a chance and secured a tryout as an acrobat.

Schaefer reported that night and was issued a costume with silk and satin tights. He was told the outfit belonged to a leaper who had been killed in a fall two nights

Oscar ("Ossie") Vitt (left) *and Bob Feller*

Heinie Groh

on the animal's neck. He jumped to the second elephant and landed hard on the animal's forehead. He jumped to the third elephant and slid off the animal's rear end. He made a running jump at the first camel and slammed into the animal broadside. Schaefer rolled on the ground; the camel stepped on him.

The audience roared as Schaefer staggered and limped to the dressing room. Draping himself across a steamer trunk, he gasped and called for liniment. The crowd continued to clap and roar. The circus manager rushed in.

"Son, that was the best I ever saw," he shouted. "Not a clown in my whole outfit could do that. They want you out there again. Come on back and do it all over again."

"I handed in my resignation right then and there," Schaefer recalled. "I figured I was more suited for baseball."

◆

earlier. "Fine stuff for a beginner," he recalled later.

The music started as the acrobats paraded to the packed bigtop. Last in line, Schaefer surveyed the scene. Beyond a giant springboard, three elephants and three camels were lined up. The acrobats were supposed to tumble along the backs of the beasts and land lightly on their feet in the sawdust beyond.

One by one, the acrobats catapulted high off the end of the board and bounded gracefully along the elephants and camels. The crowd roared and clapped loudly with each jump. Schaefer, too, was taken by the show. "Before I realized it, I was all alone," he said. "Plainly, I must go. And I went."

Schaefer vaulted high and overshot the first elephant's back, instead landing hard

In August 1988 the 1948 Braves held a Boston reunion and Francis Lundberg, age eighty-six, of Newtonville, Massachusetts, found himself reminiscing hard. "I worked at Braves Field when I was thirteen or fourteen, moving the seats back, picking up pieces of paper and cigarette butts," he said. "I got the job by hanging around the ballpark. I always carried my glove with me, wherever I went. In those days, they used to let us come onto the field and shag flies. An hour and a half before the game, I would be out there with Hank Gowdy and Rabbit Maranville and Dick Rudolph.

"I used to love to shag flies. You ought to hear the applause when I caught some of those balls. I was a pretty good ballplayer in those days. I'll never forget the applause I got, shagging those flies out there."

◆

On a Friday afternoon in May 1932, Harvard engaged Georgetown on the diamond at Soldiers Field in Brighton, Massachusetts. In the stands were the usual collegians and an unusual number of older men. The graying fellows were there to watch the Georgetown center fielder, Johnny Evers, Jr., son of the old Cubs and Braves second baseman.

The old-timers watched young Evers's every move. He was a little bigger than his father, but he trotted in from the outfield with the same funny lope. Unlike his father, young Evers couldn't hit. He choked up on the bat and spanked the ball, but not with authority. "I'm afraid I shall never be able to hit well enough to get far," young Evers said. "I'm studying law and probably will stick to that."

Evers said his father gave him many technical tips about baseball but didn't see him play much "because he was always traveling." Evers, Sr., was said to be most proud of his son's college baseball letter, something he never got the chance to earn.

Evers, Jr., was asked if he remembered the first time he saw his father play in the big leagues. "Yes," he said. "It was the World Series of 1914 between the Braves and the Athletics. My mother took me to one of the games. I cried all through it because she didn't take me to see Charlie Chaplin."

◆

Pawtucket Red Sox manager Ed Nottle grew up in Philadelphia in a neighborhood that would make Slip Mahoney, Satch, Whitey, and the other Dead End kids proud. "They tell me there are nice sections of Philadelphia," said Nottle. "I guess there are. But I never saw any."

The urban jungle notwithstanding, Nottle and his pals still managed to play baseball, sort of. "We'd play stickball on the rooftops," said Nottle. "Halfball. Halfies, we'd call it. Hoseball."

Hoseball? "We used to steal hoses from the people who could afford them," he said. "We thought people who could afford hoses were rich. You cut the hose into little sections and throw them. If you hit them just right, you could make them fly. We used to hit them over the Reading Railroad terminal."

Trying to hit whistling hose sections must have made trying to hit major-league curveballs easy. "Not for me. I never could hit curveballs," said Nottle. "Maybe that was my trouble. Too much hoseball. When I got into pro ball, everybody was throwing me baseballs."

One more question: How in the world do you play stickball on a rooftop? "Very carefully," said Nottle. "Every time you hit a patch of pigeon [expletive], you slide."

◆

The middle-aged fellow walked down Main Street in Cooperstown, New York, on the Friday afternoon before the 1989 Hall-of-Fame induction of Johnny Bench and Carl Yastrzemski. He wore a Red Sox cap, cut-off jeans, sneakers, and a white T-shirt with black letters proclaiming "I Played Against Yaz in HS."

"For two years," said Hugh King, age forty-seven, a Long Island schoolteacher. "I was at East Hampton High School when Yaz was at Bridgehampton. I remember standing in the potato field in right field out in Bridgehampton. And he still used to hit the ball over my head." King also once faced Yaz, the high-school hurler. "Struck me out," he said. "On three pitches."

With those kinds of high-school memories, King just had to journey upstate to see Yastrzemski get inducted into the Hall of Fame, and he just had to print up and wear a T-shirt that advertised his link with immortality.

"It's neat," King said of having played against a future Hall of Famer. "I don't think he'd remember me, though. That would make it even neater. But he only got to see my back while I was out there chasing those balls he hit."

◆

Readying for his start against the Browns, Athletics ace Rube Waddell tossed his last warmup pitch. The St. Louis first-base coach began his game chatter. "Get out of here, you big bum," the coach hollered. "You can't pitch."

Waddell glanced over with a wounded expression, dropped his glove on the mound, walked to the outfield, and climbed into the bleachers, where he took a seat among the shirtsleeved crowd. Despite arguments and pleas from his manager and teammates, he stayed there all afternoon.

◆

In spring 1932, right-handed hurler Charlie Devens, twenty-two years old and a member of one of Boston's oldest families, graduated from Harvard and reported to the New York Yankees. "It was pretty scary," Devens, age seventy-nine, recalled from his Milton, Massachusetts, home in the summer of 1989. "I hadn't pitched in the minor leagues or anything like that. But everybody was very nice. They kidded the life out of me, of course. They said I must have millions of dollars and butlers at home."

Among those dressing in the Yankee clubhouse those days was Babe Ruth. "He was quite a guy," said Devens. "Quite a personality. He didn't have any idea who I was,

of course. Except for those who had been there for ten years or so, it was 'Hiya, kid,' to everybody."

Devens posted a 1–0 record that summer. Then, some five months after getting his Harvard degree, he found himself in the New York bullpen as the Yankees engaged the Cubs in the World Series. "I didn't get into the series," he said. "I warmed up once, though. I was scared to death. They put in [Herb] Pennock instead. I remember nobody expected them to call him in because he had pitched the day before. I don't think he expected to be called in either, because he had a pretty good time with some friends the night before. But he went in and got the job done."

Devens was 3–3 in 1933 and 1–0 in 1934. That winter he announced he was through with baseball, got married, and entered the banking business. "I told them when I started I'd play three years," said Devens, who fashioned a distinguished career in banking and investments, besides serving on the aircraft carrier *Intrepid* during World War II. "I was sick the winter before the year I quit. I was going to get married, and I didn't think it was much of a life for a girl to be messing around with. All in all, I decided it was time to get to work."

◆

On October 11, 1903, Ed Doheny planned to attend the World Series game the next day in Boston, where Pittsburgh was scheduled to engage the Pilgrims, forefathers of the Red Sox, at the Huntington Avenue Grounds. Friends hoped a trip to the ballpark to see the decisive Game Eight of the first World Series might lift Doheny's spirits.

Earlier that season, the nine-year big-league veteran was pitching for Pittsburgh when he hallucinated that he was being pursued by detectives and abruptly left the team in Cleveland. Soon he resurfaced at his Andover home, saying all he needed was a rest.

After a few weeks, he rejoined the Pittsburgh club during a trip through Boston. But soon Doheny, apparently crumbling under the pressure of pitching in the big leagues, was back home under medical supervision.

His condition worsened steadily. On October 10, Dr. E. C. Conroy arrived at Doheny's home for their regular session. The five-foot, eleven-inch, 165-pound lefty told Conroy he didn't want the doctor's services anymore, verbally abused him, then heaved him headfirst out of the house. Police were summoned, and after discussing the situation agreed to let "faith-cure doctor and nurse" Oberlin Howorth handle the troubled pitcher.

Next morning at seven, while Howorth's back was turned, Doheny leaped from his bed, grabbed a cast-iron stove leg, and cracked Howorth over the head. While Mrs. Doheny ran to the street screaming for help, Doheny continued to beat Howorth, who was unconscious on the floor. When police arrived, Doheny briefly held them off with the stove leg. Soon they overpowered him, handcuffed him, and carted him to the state hospital in Danvers, where he was declared insane. Next day at the Huntington Avenue Grounds, Game Eight was rained out.

◆

On Friday, August 2, 1940, the Cincinnati Reds played a double-header against the Boston Braves at Braves Field. In the second game, Reds backup catcher Willard Hershberger, age twenty-nine, seemed distracted, went zero-for-five, and failed to field a bunt in front of the plate. Manager Bill McKechnie knew something was wrong and arranged to meet his

Willard Hershberger

catcher in McKechnie's suite at the Copley Plaza.

His teammates knew that Hershberger, who was hitting .309 behind Ernie Lombardi, was prone to extreme mood swings. They suspected he was upset about the team's three-game losing streak, especially the Wednesday night game at the Polo Grounds. On pitches called by Hershberger, the Giants had beaten Bucky Walters on two ninth-inning home runs.

After a two-hour meeting, McKechnie thought he had adequately calmed the distraught, crying Hershberger. He treated the catcher to a roast beef dinner and called it a night. Hershberger spent time in the lobby with some teammates; went for a walk with his roommate, catcher Bill Backer; then went to bed at 11:00 P.M.

The next morning, with a Ladies' Day double-header scheduled for that afternoon, Hershberger breakfasted on eggs and melon. Later, as the Reds trickled through the lobby on their way to the ballpark, they passed Hershberger, who said he'd follow a little later and promised to get four hits that day. Just before the start of the first game, with Hershberger still not at the ballpark, traveling secretary Gabe Paul telephoned him in his room. The catcher said he was ill and couldn't play that day.

Around the seventh inning of the first game, Hershberger was in the bathroom of his hotel, shaving with his electric razor when he took the blade from his roommate's razor, leaned into the bathtub, and slashed his throat. He was found dead by a hotel maid and Cincinnati businessman Dan Cohen, a friend who had returned to the hotel to check on him.

◆

As a lad growing up in New Jersey, Red Sox reliever Bob Stanley was serious about a game besides baseball. "I bowled 167 once when I was six years old," he said one day in 1989, when the pregame dugout chatter turned to the relative merits of candlepin versus ten-pin bowling.

Stanley then recalled the final frame of a hard-fought match, when he was about eleven. Needing a strike to win, he stepped up, rolled the ball, watched the pins scatter, and saw one wobble, but refuse to go down.

"I got mad," Stanley said. Therefore he pulled off the bowling equivalent of charging the mound. He raced down the lane, belly-flopped, slid headfirst, and batted aside the final pin.

Stanley managed to scramble out of the way of the descending pin-setter, but he couldn't avoid the proprietor. "The guy threw me out of the place," said Stanley. "I was banned from that bowling alley."

◆

When Carl Yastrzemski was elected to the Hall of Fame in January 1989, Chuck Schilling planned a little vacation. "I had in mind that when he is inducted, I'd like to take a trip up there to see it," said Schilling. "Years ago, we were very close."

In the minors and in the summer of 1961, the year they broke into the big leagues together with the Red Sox, Schilling and Yastrzemski were roommates. "He was always in front of the mirror in the bedroom, changing his stance, moving his hands around," remembered Schilling, age fifty-one and a junior-high-school math teacher in Selden, New York, on Long Island. "He'd stay after games, after double-headers, to take extra batting practice. A lot of the times, I was the one out there with him. I like to kid people and tell them I taught Yastrzemski everything he knows. I know I was the one who kept the room in some semblance of order. He had clothes scattered all over the place. He'd let them pile up high, then send them out all at once."

For a while in 1961, Schilling looked like the hotter prospect, as well as the better housekeeper. A couple of months into the season, he was batting some seventy points better than Yaz and was playing a solid second base. But Yaz had an excuse: he was the one who had to wrestle with the ghost of Ted Williams.

"The pressure was on him," said Schilling. "You could tell it was getting to him at times. He used to look for people to talk to, to take his mind off it. He was chain-smoking for a while there."

Still, they had some fun. "We used to call him 'Gandhi the Goose,' because he used to walk a little bit funny, like a duck," said Schilling, who lasted five years with the

Ted Williams, Cy Young, and Ray Scarborough (left to right)

Red Sox. "Carl did his share of practical jokes, too. Everybody was a target of his hotfoots. Bill Monbouquette was a prime target."

Over the years, Yastrzemski and his old roomie lost touch. Now and then, however, the early years still touched Schilling. "Some of my kids in class are baseball-card enthusiasts, and they bring some of my old cards in from time to time," he said. "There was one after our rookie season, with me and Yaz on it. It says 'Sox Sockers.' I'm kind of proud of that, being on the same bubblegum card as Yastrzemski."

◆

Early in the summer of 1915, Brooklyn pitcher Charlie Schmutz had a tip for scout Larry Sutton: back home in California, a pretty good righty named Wheezer Dell was pitching for a bush-league team. Sutton promised to take a look next time he was out West.

Each time Schmutz ran into Sutton, he asked the scout if he had checked into Dell. Sutton finally surrendered and scheduled a trip to California to scout Dell, who turned out to be pretty good. Sutton signed him and shipped him back to Brooklyn. In order to make room for Dell, the Dodgers sent Schmutz to the minors.

◆

On April 30, 1952, Red Sox outfielder Ted Williams homered in his final at-bat, then left the ballclub to answer a recall by the Marines. By the following winter, he was piloting fighter jets in the Korean War. Williams never expected to see Fenway Park again. "I expect to be killed, of course," Ted had calmly told friends before shipping overseas.

He was nearly right. After tagging along on two missions to observe terrain and tactics, Captain Williams embarked on his first full-fledged combat mission on the morning of February 16, 1953. The Splendid Splinter, who had not seen combat as a Marine pilot during World War II, flew a Panther jet as part of a two-hundred-plane sortie. The mission was to strike a North Korean troop and supply center south of Pyongyang.

After hitting the target area, Williams pulled away smoothly. "It didn't feel as if a thing had hit me," he said later, but something had. Damaged by enemy flak, Williams's jet spewed flames. His instrument panel lit up, his radio was dead, and his control stick began to vibrate. Williams climbed to gain altitude and headed for the nearest friendly airfield.

Soon, at the Air Force landing strip at Suwon, ground personnel ran outside to see a jet, engulfed in flames, approach the field. "That plane was a ball of fire, burning from nose to tail," a witness wrote later. "Any average pilot would have bailed out." Crash crews raced from their hangars as the aircraft—its wheels jammed in the up position—circled the field, then lined up for the landing.

Using both hands on his control stick as he descended, Williams knew he was coming in too fast but couldn't slow the plane; the wing flaps weren't working. Williams bellied in. "I hit pretty hard and went chugging down the runway," said Williams. "I thought I would never stop."

After the plane skidded to a halt, Williams popped the cockpit canopy and plopped out onto the tarmac as emergency crews extinguished the flames. Anx-

ious observers on the ground burst into cheers. Williams picked himself up, walked into the radio shack to notify marine headquarters, and ate lunch.

In June, with thirty-eight missions to his credit, Williams was shipped home. On August 6, 1953, in a game against the Browns, he returned to the Red Sox lineup, pinch-hit for Tom Umphlett, and popped out.

In the summer of 1926, Carl Hubbell was a twenty-three-year-old farmhand in the New York Giants' system. After his season ended with Toronto of the International League, the lefty hurler passed through St. Louis on his way home to Texas. He decided to stop over and catch a game of the World Series between the Yankees and the Cardinals.

In order to secure a bleacher seat, Hubbell was required to stand in line for more than an hour outside the ticket window at Sportman's Park. Seven years later, when Hubbell himself was a World Series hero, he told the story of his hour-long stand in line to get into the 1926 World Series. Someone asked if it had been worth the wait.

"It was worth it," Hubbell said without hesitation. "I saw Babe Ruth."

When the United States entered the Great War, Boston Braves catcher Hank Gowdy was the first major leaguer to enlist. During Christmas week 1917, Sergeant Gowdy of the Rainbow Division's 166th Infantry found himself straining under a heavy pack, shivering against bitter cold, and slogging across the battle-scarred terrain of France.

Gowdy was his unit's noncommissioned officer in charge of poison gas. His job was he once remembered. So they settled into a ditch near the infantry positions. After the fierce battle had waned, Gowdy returned to the pup tent, found the tent gone, and the ground around it pocked with fifteen-foot-deep bomb craters.

After the war, Gowdy could remember just one other time in his life that came close to combat tension. "I was almost as nervous beginning that World Series in Boston," he said of the 1914 World Series when he batted .545 for the Miracle Braves. "And I came out just as lucky."

◆

Someone who once dined with Babe Ruth recalled the Babe consuming a double appetizer of shrimp, two bowls of mulligatawny, extra vegetables, a huge sirloin steak, a double-serving of chiffon pie, and a full pot of coffee. When finished, Ruth pulled out a huge Corona cigar and prepared to stick it in his mouth.

"Oh, wait," he said. "I forgot."

Ruth produced a bottle filled with a white, pasty liquid. It was stomach medicine. The label prescribed, "One teaspoonful in water after meals." Ruth unscrewed the cap, tilted the bottle back, drained it completely in big gulps, and slammed the empty bottle on the table.

"Nothing like taking care of your health," he said.

◆

In spring 1928 a haggard, dirty, travel-weary young man shuffled to the front desk at the Cardinals' spring training hotel in Avon Park, Florida. His hair was greasy and disheveled, his face was smeared with dirt, and his clothes were tattered. He looked like a bum. He should have; he had hopped freight trains from Oklahoma City to Florida.

Hank Gowdy

to skitter along the front lines after a gas attack, sniffing occasionally to determine if the danger had passed. Besides that unenviable duty, Gowdy was entrusted with showing the men how to use their gas masks. During maneuvers months before, when many complained they couldn't see out of their gas masks, Gowdy had told the regiment baseball team to play an inning while wearing them. The troops were suitably impressed when his center fielder, mask in place, made a running catch. They stopped complaining about the masks.

Gowdy's diciest combat moment came on the front in Champagne. Waiting for battle to start, he and a comrade were holed up in a pup tent near the supply company. For no particular reason, the notion hit Gowdy that they should move. "Something seemed to tell me to find a different place,"

"Tell Bill McKechnie," the young man told the desk clerk, "that his new center fielder has arrived."

Sunk deep in a nearby easy chair, St. Louis manager McKechnie looked up from his newspaper at the mention of his name. The desk clerk caught his eye. McKechnie eyed the messy young man and shook his head from side to side.

"He's not here now," the desk clerk said. "But I'll fix you up with a room."

For days, McKechnie avoided the young man, who looked considerably better after a shave and a bath. But during workouts McKechnie couldn't help noticing him. In the field, the young man easily ran down deep fly balls. At bat, he swatted hits out of the ballpark.

Finally McKechnie gave in. He found out the young man's name and summoned him to his office. "I'm McKechnie," the manager said, extending his hand. "You're Pepper Martin, our new center fielder."

◆

After a 1989 game at Fenway Park, conversation turned to theories of hitting. Boston scouting director Eddie Kasko opined that hitters often think too much these days and told a story to illustrate:

One day, Kasko—at the time an infielder with the Reds—was standing around the batting cage before a game against the Milwaukee Braves. Kasko, Frank Robinson, and others talked hitting philosophy. They discussed how standing close to the plate requires fast reflexes to get around on an inside pitch. They discussed how standing away from the plate requires diving to hit outside pitches. "Just then, Henry Aaron walked by the cage," said Kasko.

Robinson summoned Aaron, told him what they were talking about, and asked his philosophy about where to stand in the batter's box.

Aaron thought a long while. "Gee," he finally said, "I never really gave it much thought. I just wait to see the ball out there." He stuck his hand out just below the letters. "Then I hit it."

◆

Former Red Sox farmhand Barry Butera likes to tell this story:

In the late 1970s, the Red Sox had a hot prospect named Otis Foster playing in Triple-A Pawtucket. Foster had big trouble with his weight. When his heft began to slow his bat speed and hamper his ability to hit the inside pitch, Foster was dispatched to the Double-A team in Bristol to shed some pounds.

"I was down there trying to convert to third base," said Butera. "Every morning Otis would come to the ballpark, weigh in, put on one of those plastic suits, then run around the lake they've got down there. Then he'd come back in and get weighed again."

Despite all the sweating and running, Foster wasn't losing weight. One day as he was driving to the ballpark, Butera discovered why. "He had a girlfriend who used to bake him cookies and cakes and pies," he said. "She brought a picnic basket to the other side of the lake every day and met him out there. He'd run halfway around the lake, then stop and have a picnic. I was driving by one day, and there he was sitting on the grass eating chocolate chip cookies and fudge. He gained weight while he was down there."

◆

Former Minnesota Twins manager and Red Sox player and scout Sam Mele grew up in Astoria, Queens, "about two miles from here, off the Grand Central

Parkway on 33rd," said Mele, one rainy autumn night at Shea Stadium in 1988.

In those Depression-era days there was no Shea Stadium, just a field of tall reeds, but there was most definitely ballplaying in Queens. "We used to play a lot of stick-ball," said Mele. "The streets weren't even paved. You know, I think that's why I turned out to be a pretty good breaking-ball hitter, from hitting those balls bouncing off the ruts and rocks, hitting them with those sticks."

Believe it or not, given the pastime's prevalence among current New York City youths, local police often conducted stick-ball crackdowns. "We used to have a kid stand on one end of the block and a kid stand on the other end of the block to see if any cops were coming," said Mele. "If they caught you playing stickball, they'd take the sticks away from you and break 'em. They didn't want you playing because of broken windows."

◆

In summer 1947 Ty Cobb played in an Old-Timers' Day game at Yankee Sta-dium. As he stepped to the plate, the bald, flabby Georgia Peach received a loud ova-tion. Cobb, age sixty, turned to catcher Wally Schang.

"Wally," he said in a warm, friendly tone, "it's so long since I had a bat in my hands that I'm afraid I might accidentally strike you when I pull back to swing. Would you mind backing up and giving me a lot more room than you used to do in the old days?"

Schang, the fifty-seven-year-old one-time backstop for the Athletics, Red Sox, and Yankees, among others, obligingly moved back several yards. With the catcher nicely out of position, Cobb dropped a bunt in front of the plate.

Guy Bush

◆

In spring 1935, Pirates right-handed hurler Guy Bush was happy to see aging, broken-down Babe Ruth lurching through the National League with the Boston Braves. "I had been with the Chi-cago Cubs for a dozen years and had pitched to Babe only once before in the World Series," said Bush. "I was still so strong I didn't believe anyone could hit anything off me."

One May afternoon in the sixth inning at Forbes Field in Pittsburgh, Bush was sum-moned to relieve and pitch to Ruth.

He surrendered a home run. "I got tagged on a high inside fastball," said Bush. "He just pulled it down the right-field line. No further than one of our .200 hitters would have popped it."

Over the next two innings, the Babe's cheap homer nagged at Bush. The more he thought about it, the angrier he got. "Coming out of the dugout in the ninth, I told our catcher, Tommy Padden, 'Tommy, this great Babe Ruth is coming up again and I'm going to throw a fastball right by that jackass,'" Bush said. "I meant to throw three fastballs by him and watch the crowd laugh as he swung."

Bush's first fastball was slightly outside. "He looked it over like it was a softball," said Bush. "He looked me right in the eye. And I nodded to him and threw another in the same spot."

Ruth smacked it over the third deck. "I never saw a ball hit so far," said Bush. The Babe slowly circled the bases for the 714th and last time. "He just smiled nicely to me as he rounded third," said Bush. "I tipped my hat."

◆

Former Red Sox pitcher Boo Ferriss, age sixty-seven and retired in Cleveland, Mississippi, was saddened to hear about the heart-attack death of baseball commissioner A. Bartlett Giamatti in the late summer of 1989.

"A real shame," said Ferriss. "I think he was on his way to becoming a real great commissioner. He had such a grasp of it all. A brilliant man. And he was a great Red Sox follower."

Boo said he read stories about how eight-year-old Giamatti saw his first Fenway Park game in 1946 and how the commissioner always recalled Ferriss was pitching that day. How did that make Boo feel, to know the late commissioner never forgot watching him pitch as a young boy? "I don't know," he sighed. "Old, I guess."

◆

At the start of the 1909 season, St. Louis Browns righty Bill Dinneen thought his arm was worn out and mulled retirement at age thirty-three. His manager, Jimmy McAleer, insisted Big Bill give the pastime one more try.

Usually a fast starter, in April and May Dinneen couldn't finish a game. McAleer

suggested he take a month off, then try again. Dinneen agreed but insisted he would retire this time if he failed.

During the next month, Dinneen submitted his arm to various treatments and therapies, and rested. Finally he informed McAleer he was ready for the big test. The Browns arranged for him to try his arm during an exhibition game against Springfield, Illinois, of the Three–I League.

Dinneen worked a full nine innings against Springfield. Hammered for dozens of long hits, he dropped a 25–4 decision. Dinneen submitted his resignation that night.

"There was only one pleasant thing about that game," Dinneen once recalled. "There were two veterans on the Springfield club who were to be released that evening. One of them made five hits off my delivery, the other four, each getting a home run among their hits. That barrage finished me. But the liberties those two vets took with my stuff enabled them to hang on for the rest of the season."

Sibby Sisti was the Boston Braves' infielder from 1939 through 1952. In 1978, for the first time since he moved with the team to Milwaukee in 1953, he went back to the corner of Commonwealth Avenue and Gaffney Street in Boston to take a look around Boston University's Nickerson Field, where Braves Field used to stand.

"I was up in Cape Cod, and my wife and I decided to visit friends in Boston and take a look at Braves Field and reminisce," said Sisti in 1988 when he was sixty-eight and a retired truck driver living in Buffalo. "I didn't know what I was going to see when I walked in. It was quite a sight.

"I was looking for the third-base stands, and they weren't there. My wife said, 'It's hard to visualize. Where was home plate?' I said, 'Where those three high-rise dorms are now.' Except for the main entrance, where the offices used to be, most of it was gone."

How does a ballplayer feel when he returns to his old home ballpark and finds it as long gone as a Bob Elliott home run? Sibby Sisti laughed. "Over the hill," he said.

◆

By June 1935 Babe Ruth realized Braves owner Judge Emil Fuchs had signed him purely for publicity and had no intention of ever giving the Babe the manager's job he desperately wanted. Without saying a word to club officials, Ruth summoned newspapermen to the clubhouse before a game and made the announcement.

"I'm getting the hell out of this dump," he declared.

The newsmen left. The Braves stopped pulling on their uniforms, and suddenly the locker room was uncomfortably silent. Finally, a player reached into his locker, pulled out a baseball, and brought it over to Ruth. "Sign this for me, will you, Babe?" he said. "I want to take it home and keep it."

One by one, each Brave carried a baseball to the Babe and asked for his autograph. They wanted something to prove they once played on the same team with the great Ruth.

◆

At three o'clock on the afternoon of April 14, 1936, the hulking figure made his way through the opening day crowd at the Polo Grounds. As he passed, people cheered. It was Babe Ruth, who had retired from the Braves and baseball the previous summer.

Finally reaching Box Twenty-seven, Ruth was surrounded by autograph-seeking fans and cameramen. The Giants were sched-uled to engage the Dodgers in fifteen minutes. "The Star Spangled Banner" was about to be sung. For the first time in twenty-two years, the baseball season was about to begin without the Babe.

"Feels funny," mumbled Ruth. "Funny."

◆

During a Sunday afternoon game in Cleveland in the summer of 1927, umpire Billy Evans called a Yankee baserunner safe at home. The Indians' partisans on hand howled in derision and tossed their scorecards in disgust.

One particularly frantic fan in a mezzanine box turned to the pair of elderly men nearby and asked, "Can you believe that call?"

The older of the two men smiled and shook his head. "The umps was right. Myatt didn't tag him."

"Oh, you old fossil," the fan snarled. "You're nothing but a hick from the country. What do you know about baseball?"

The "old fossil," Cy Young, did not reply.

◆

One afternoon in the summer of 1932, two Pittsburgh baseball writers, one a seasoned veteran, the other a young cub, wandered out to catch a sandlot game. Finding one at a rough baseball diamond in the city's industrial district, they settled into the wooden bleachers and watched.

A strongly built although obviously old man picked up a bat and sauntered, slightly hunched over, to home plate. The man's face was deeply creased and wrinkled. Except for tufts of gray hair around the ears, he was bald. The cub reporter smirked and elbowed his companion. "Look at that old geezer," he said. "That must be old Grandfather Time himself. Look at his—"

Cy Young (left) *and Tris Speaker.*

With a fluid swipe of the bat, the geezer lined a shot to deepest center field. Soon he was standing on second base. "Gee," said the cub. "The old boy can sock, can't he?"

In five trips to the plate, the geezer recorded four hits: a single, two doubles, and a triple against the left-field fence. The out was recorded on a long fly to center field. "Say, that old boy can play ball," the cub conceded after the game. "Did you watch his swing? If he was twenty years younger, I bet he'd be right up in the big leagues. I wonder if he ever played much."

After a long silence, the veteran baseball writer finally spoke. "Yes, I think he played a considerable amount," he said. "His name is Honus Wagner."

◆

In the summer of 1934 a group of boys aged twelve to fifteen organized a baseball league in Peoli, Ohio. All they needed was one more pitcher. To find one, they ventured far outside their age group and enlisted Cy Young, the sixty-seven-year-old former ace of the Red Sox and Indians and a Peoli resident.

Young gamely dug out his old spikes and mitt and pitched regularly for the boys. "Those kids we played took a hefty cut at everything I tossed to them," Cy said. "But the old arm had plenty of stuff in it and I won a couple of games."

Then one afternoon, in the fourth inning of a close game, a youngster batting against Young took a check swing and dribbled the ball in front of the mound. Young ambled in to field it. But he couldn't bend over to pick the ball up: his belly was too big. The runner was safe at first.

The kids caught on quickly. Batter after batter laid down bunts in front of the mound. Young was helpless to pick them up. The game was broken open. Finally, the Peoli manager, a fourteen-year-old boy with a faceful of freckles, walked out to the mound and removed Cy Young from the ball game.

"He sent me to the showers," said Young. "I never felt so washed up in my life."

BIBLIOGRAPHY

American Magazine, articles, 1923–1956.
American Mercury, articles, 1924–1963.
Boston *American,* articles, 1951–1960.
Boston *Herald,* articles, 1881–1990.
Boston *Record,* articles, 1953–1972.
Boston *Sunday Advertiser,* articles, 1951–1972.
Boston *Traveler,* articles, 1953–1967.
Collier's, articles, 1907–1952.
Harper's Monthly, articles, 1900–1939.
Literary Digest, articles, 1911–1938.
New York Times, articles, 1900–1963.
Saturday Evening Post, articles, 1919–1962.

INDEX

References in **boldface** refer to illustrations.